Online Assessment, Measurement, and Evaluation:
Emerging Practices

David D. Williams
Brigham Young University, USA

Scott L. Howell
Brigham Young University, USA

Mary Hricko
Kent State University, USA

 Information Science Publishing
Hershey • London • Melbourne • Singapore

Acquisitions Editor:	Renée Davies
Development Editor:	Kristin Roth
Senior Managing Editor:	Amanda Appicello
Managing Editor:	Jennifer Neidig
Copy Editor:	Maria Boyer
Typesetter:	Cindy Consonery
Cover Design:	Lisa Tosheff
Printed at:	Yurchak Printing Inc.

Published in the United States of America by
 Information Science Publishing (an imprint of Idea Group Inc.)
 701 E. Chocolate Avenue, Suite 200
 Hershey PA 17033
 Tel: 717-533-8845
 Fax: 717-533-8661
 E-mail: cust@idea-group.com
 Web site: http://www.idea-group.com

and in the United Kingdom by
 Information Science Publishing (an imprint of Idea Group Inc.)
 3 Henrietta Street
 Covent Garden
 London WC2E 8LU
 Tel: 44 20 7240 0856
 Fax: 44 20 7379 3313
 Web site: http://www.eurospan.co.uk

Library of Congress Cataloging-in-Publication Data

Online assessment, measurement, and evaluation : emerging practices / David D. Williams, Mary Hricko, and Scott L. Howell, editors.
 p. cm.
 Summary: "This book provides a view of the possibilities and challenges facing online educators and evaluators in the 21st century"--Provided by publisher.
 Includes bibliographical references and index.
 ISBN 1-59140-747-8 (hc) -- ISBN 1-59140-748-6 (sc) -- ISBN 1-59140-749-4 (ebook)
 1. Computer-assisted instruction--Evaluation. 2. Educational tests and measurements--Data processing. 3. Distance education--Evaluation. I. Williams, David D., 1952- II. Hricko, Mary. III. Howell, Scott L.
 LB1028.3.O552 2006
 371.26'0285--dc22
                                                                    2005013814

British Cataloguing in Publication Data
A Cataloguing in Publication record for this book is available from the British Library.

Online Assessment, Measurement, and Evaluation:

Emerging Practices

Table of Contents

Section V. Combinations

Preface

Although most of the 19 chapters in this volume were written in terms of measurement or assessment problems and issues, with little or no reference to evaluation as the larger context in which their meaning might be interpreted, each chapter will be briefly introduced in terms of an evaluation framework, which is developed further in Chapter I. In particular, the chapters after an introductory first chapter are grouped around approaches the authors took to collect evaluation data (Web surveys, student feedback, tests, and combinations), while other evaluation framework elements, such as stakeholders, evaluand (thing or person being evaluated), and criteria that are most relevant, are highlighted in each description.

Introduction to Measurement and Assessment in Evaluation

In "Measurement and Assessment Supporting Evaluation in Online Settings," David D. Williams of Brigham Young University outlines a framework for thinking about measurement and assessment in a more comprehensive evaluation context to help readers consider the other chapters in terms of an evaluation framework in hopes that they will see the common and unique contributions each chapter offers to their own evaluation (and related measurement and assessment) work. Reviewing key evaluation theorists, he notes that to be successful, evaluations must consider context, stakeholders, evaluand definitions, issues and concerns, values and criteria, questions, data collection and analysis, and reporting results, conclusions, and recommendations. He places measurement and assessment in this larger context to suggest a useful way of thinking about the rest of the chapters about online measurement and assessment.

Web Surveys

In "The Context and Culture of the Web as a Research Environment," Paula B. Doherty examines problems and how to resolve them when using self-administered surveys on the Web. Though she does not explicitly address the kinds of evaluation these surveys might be best used for, she discusses applied social research as a form of evaluation and identifies criteria for making surveys work via the Web. She notes the openness of the Web culture, couched in a helpful historical review of the Web, with implications for conducting surveys on the Web. Stakeholders are those the survey might relate to, and the evaluand is anything the survey might focus on, although she also examines the concept of a Web survey as an evaluand.

In "Computer-Adaptive Online Exit Surveys: Conceptual and Methodological Issues," Najmuddin Shaik proposes the creation and administration of adaptive surveys of drop-outs from various higher education programs via online computers. In response to several stakeholders, such as administrators of universities, faculty, students, and particularly dropouts, Shaik explores the contexts of adaptive surveys and theories of dropouts in preparation for a survey approach. The chapter focuses on outlining the ideal characteristics of an instrument to help institutions identify dropout concerns as part of a formative evaluation process.

In "Quality Standards for Web-Based Learning: The Demand-Driven Learning Model," Krista Breithaupt and Colla J. MacDonald identify e-learning programs as generic evaluands and the Demand-Driven Learning Model (DDLM) as a clarification of criteria against which such learning should be evaluated for adult learner stakeholders. They develop a survey to evaluate how well e-learning programs meet the DDLM model and associated standards, and discuss data from three pilot studies.

In "Online Course-Ratings and the Personnel Evaluation Standards," Susan J. Clark, Christian M. Reiner, and Trav D. Johnson examine the use of online university course and faculty evaluations by students via Web surveys. The evaluand is the online formative and summative evaluation process. They use published personnel evaluation standards to meta-evaluate the assessment process, compare it to the traditional paper-based process, and recommend ways to improve it to the stakeholders: university faculty and administrators.

In "Case Study: Developing a University-Wide Distance Education Evaluation Program at the University of Florida," Christopher D. Sessums, Tracy A. Irani, Ricky Telg, and T. Grady Roberts explore the use of Web-based surveys to gather student evaluations. The stakeholders are faculty and administrators seeking summative and formative student feedback to improve distance courses. The chapter reviews the development of an instrument to be used throughout the university, with an emphasis on establishing validity and reliability based on concerns raised by 400 students through a qualitative Web survey, concerns from other institutions, accrediting bodies, faculty, and administrators.

In "Online Program Assessment: A Case Study of the University of Illinois at Urbana-Champaign Experience," Faye L. Lesht, Rae-Anne Montague, Vaughn J. Page, Najmuddin Shaik, and Linda C. Smith report on a university-wide initiative to evaluate off-campus graduate programs using online surveys in comparison with postal surveys. Combining online surveys to students and faculty with in-person interviews of administrators, the focus of the chapter is on formative program evaluation, with summative evaluation resulting as well. They report that better and more immediate communication with stakeholders and more economical use of resources resulted. Off-campus graduate students, university administrators, and faculty were the stakeholders represented by an independent committee established to evaluate off-campus programs.

Student Feedback

In "Cybercoaching: An Emerging Model of Personalized Online Assessment," Ni Chang and Naomi Jeffery Petersen explore the use of online e-mail and word processing to share teacher critique and coaching with university students regarding their writing. They conclude that the focus on formative development process and feedback to the students through coaching as teaching adheres to Vygotsky's social constructivism and is more efficient than many other forms of providing feedback. The main evaluands are students' learning and the quality of the student-teacher instructional experiences, as well as the Cybercoaching model. The authors illustrate use of this teaching-evaluation model from their own instructional experiences.

In "Testing the Validity of the Post and Vote Model of Web-Based Peer Assessment," Bruce L. Mann describes an approach he has developed to encourage university students to summatively evaluate other students' work using a Web-based peer assessment process. He presents validation data using instructor assessments as the standard. Students and faculty are the stakeholders most interested in the value of this model and the resulting performance evaluations. The chapter reviews the theoretical bases for the model and shares results of the validation process.

In "Online Assessment in a Teacher Education Program," Charles W. Peters and Patricia Ann Kenney describe and illustrate an online discussion and feedback process they use to give students formative and summative evaluative feedback via e-mail, "Track Changes" in Microsoft Word, and e-portfolios. As instructors, the authors analyze online discussion among their students, respond to and make online comments, and evaluate the quality of students' portfolios while adhering to theories of social constructivism and collaborative learning. Stakeholders and evaluators are student teachers and teacher educators who employ self-evaluation to study their contribution to the main evaluand: student teaching performance. They conclude that instruction based on a constructivist view of learning is easier using technology.

Tests

In "Variations in Adaptive Testing and Their Online Leverage Points," Roy Levy, John T. Behrens, and Robert J. Mislevy propose a taxonomy that differentiates assessments along three dimensions: (1) observation status, (2) claim status, and (3) locus of control. In detailing the taxonomy, they point out ways in which online assessment enables or enhances these features and highlight the inferential roles that adaptivity can play in assessment. They offer a principled perspective for examining advantageous features of various adaptive testing models, such as reduced time and increased precision in adaptive observation assessments and diagnostic capability in examinee-controlled assessments. Their views apply to a wide variety of stakeholders, evaluands, and kinds of evaluation that use adaptive tests.

In "Using Messick's Framework to Validate Assessment Tasks in Online Environments: A Course in Writing Effectively for UNHCR," Valerie Ruhe and Bruno D. Zumbo argue that various forms of technology (e.g., computerized testing) make old views of validity and assessment outmoded. They claim that Messick's framework brings psychometrics up to speed with these technologies. They illustrate their point with a study that employed surveys and interviews along with online feedback to students and tutors to evaluate a distance writing course for adults and the assessment task itself. They conclude that validation involves values and consequences, not just psychometric qualities of assessments. The online assessment tasks overlap with the value of the course components, and for this reason, online assessment tasks need to be validated in the broader context of the course as a system.

In "Online Assessment and Instruction Using Learning Maps: A Glimpse into the Future," Jim Lee, Sylvia Tidwell-Scheuring, and Karen Barton speculate about using online assessment to accelerate learning via effective links to instruction through quick assessment feedback and instruction generated by computers in response to scores. They examine notions of item adaptive testing, learning maps for instruction prescription, and validation of tests to enhance formative and summative evaluation of student understanding and associated instruction designed to help them through technology. Student (K-12) learning is the main evaluand. Instruction to help them is secondary. Teachers, students, parents, and administrators who are trying to help students learn are the main stakeholders, through tailoring of instruction based on review of learning maps and adaptive test results.

In "Authentic Assessment Online: A Practical and Theoretical Challenge in Higher Education," Smita Mathur and Terry Murray explore the use of online authentic assessment using electronic portfolios and journals, assessment embedded in online discussions, and associated rubrics to encourage continuous improvement of learning in an online environment. They build their approach around assumptions of social constructivism, and examine challenges and strategies to involve students and faculty in higher education as stakeholders evaluating learning in online classrooms.

In "Performance Testing: Validity Issues and Design Considerations for Online Testing," James B. Olsen reviews theoretical literature and builds on the premise that validation of tests should enhance evaluation of learning progress systems and students' learning. He argues for validation as evaluation through both performance and knowledge tests. Criteria for judging the quality of tests are dictated by the validity theory being used, and Olsen reviews two theories by Mislevy and Bunderson. These ideas apply to any situation involving performance assessment at any level and are relevant to stakeholders using tests as part of their evaluation process. Tests are the primary evaluands, and when they are evaluated positively, they can be used to evaluate student learning.

In "Assessment and College Progress: Capacity Building Through Formative and Summative Program Evaluation," Jennifer K. Holtz and Barbara Radner examine performance-based assessment in online courses at all levels, but particularly higher education. They define assessment as determining the relative value of something, in general, or an estimate of how close a student is to the knowledge and ability required, in particular. This assessment is used in formative and summative evaluation of students and courses. They argue that valid assessment is even more critical and challenging in online courses, the biggest challenge being accountability (Is the person doing the work the person getting the grade?). For the authors, the main stakeholders are teachers, students, and administrators, but this process should also enhance accreditation of institutions. They emphasize the linking of instruction, assessment, and integrated evaluation and using the online environment as a reason to enhance assessment. The chapter provides and illustrates tools for assessment in online courses, based on principles that apply to any educational program.

In "Evaluating Content-Management Systems for Online Learning Programs," Deborah L. Schnipke, Kirk Becker, and Jim S. Masters organized this chapter around summative evaluation questions test users and creators and organizations that develop, evaluate, and distribute tests should ask about online test item repositories or content management systems. The evaluands of interest are these Internet-based content-management systems, which can be used collaboratively by many participants to create tests. They discuss characteristics a content management system should provide for building tests relevant to any age group. Stakeholders are test and content management system users.

Combinations

In "Learning by Doing: Four Years of Online Assessment in Engineering Education Research," John C. Wise, Sang Ha Lee, and Sarah E. Rzasa present and reflect upon lessons learned through four study examples they engaged in at Penn State using different online tools. Using online surveys and tests, along with supporting qualitative measures, the authors explored the measurement of intellectual development, the evaluation of a minor within their college, the measurement of effects of an instructional method, and the establishment of validity and reliability using online data collection. Thus, evaluands included measurement instruments, intellectual development, educational programs, and instructional methods of both formative and summative interest to the students and faculty in their engineering college.

In "The Role of Assessment and Evaluation in Context: Pedagogical Alignment, Constraints, and Affordances in Online Courses," Julia M. Matuga distinguishes evaluation as making value judgments based on the assessments gathered in terms of the values of instructors, students, administrators, and other stakeholders. She explores the evaluation of higher education distance courses through the use of formative and summative quantitative measures of all kinds, along with qualitative feedback. Three experiences or cases are presented as context for a discussion of the unique challenges of using assessments to conduct evaluation in online settings.

Conclusion

Taken together with the chapters in the previous two volumes of this series on online measurement, assessment, and evaluation, the 19 chapters that follow provide a tantalizing view of the possibilities and challenges facing online educators and evaluators in the 21st century. As technology evolves and online measurement and assessment follow, the invitation of this volume is to use tried and tested evaluation principles to:

- employ these tools in evaluation systems that support stakeholders;
- clarify stakeholder's values and definitions of the evaluands they want to examine;
- help them think about the questions they most deeply want answered;
- keep the contexts and backgrounds in mind;
- seek to adhere to evaluation standards of feasibility, propriety, utility, and accuracy; and
- help participants realize that technical issues and methods are only of worth when they are in the service of helping people make thoughtful evaluation choices.

David D. Williams
January 2005

Acknowledgments

As senior editor for this volume, I thank and acknowledge my coeditors, Scott Howell and Mary Hricko, who invited me to join them on this third volume. Working with the 42 authors and 52 reviewers of the chapters included in this volume has been an educational and gratifying experience.

All the authors join me in acknowledging each of the 52 reviewers whose expertise, insights, and suggestions have added so much to the quality and value of the chapters in this volume. I have listed alphabetically by last name all reviewers who generously contributed to this volume: Stephanie Allen, Linda Barclay, Jane Birch, Rob Boody, Bruce Brown, Jeremy Browne, Holli Burgon, Olin Campbell, Suzy Cox, Richard Culatta, Joseph Curtin, Randy Davies, Yohan Delton, Dan Eastmond, Nick Eastmond, Deb Gearhart, Andy Gibbons, Abigail Gonzalez, Charles Graham, Mark Hawkes, Richard Helps, Scott Howell, Trav Johnson, Mike Johnson, Kristoffer Kristensen, Barbara Lawrence, Joseph Martineau, Paul Merrill, Deanna Molinari, David Nielson, Danny Olsen, David Pater, Courtney Peck, Tim Pelton, Ana Preto-Bay, Brian Radford, Duane Roberts, Larry Seawright, Sandip Sinharay, Joseph South, Steve Spencer, Todd Stubbs, Richard Sudweeks, Spencer Weiler, Rick West, Wendi Wilcken, Peter Williams, David Williamson, Todd Wilson, Steve Wygant, Stephen Yanchar, and Beverly Zimmerman.

Special appreciation is also due to Holly Baker, Laurel Lee Bingham, Chellae Brooks, Brianne Gillespie, Elisabeth Guyon, and Logan Molyenux of Brigham Young University, Division of Continuing Education, for the numerous and invaluable editing contributions they and their staff have provided to the chapter authors and volume editors. Special thanks also go to Jan Travers, managing editor for the publisher, and her team at Idea Group for their professional support and personal encouragement. I also appreciate my colleagues and family for supporting me in this endeavor.

David D. Williams, PhD
Brigham Young University
Provo, Utah, USA

Section I

Introduction to Measurement and Assessment in Evaluation

Chapter I

Measurement and Assessment Supporting Evaluation in Online Settings

David D. Williams, Brigham Young University, USA

Abstract

This chapter introduces an evaluation framework for interpreting online measurement and assessment as components of evaluation as an introduction to the other chapters in this volume. The evaluation framework includes attention to the evaluation context, stakeholders, evaluand (thing or person being evaluated), issues and concerns, values and criteria, questions, data collection and analysis, and reporting results, conclusions, and recommendations. This framework incorporates online measurement and assessment issues as important elements in evaluations of programs, personnel, and students.

Introduction

The following 18 chapters of this volume explore emerging practices in the use of online assessment and measurement to conduct evaluations of student learning (including tests, surveys, portfolios, and other assessments), educational programs, and personnel. Standards for judging the quality of evaluations in terms of utility, feasibility, propriety, and accuracy have been developed over the last 30 years by the Joint

Committee on Standards for Educational Evaluation (1984, 1988, 2003). Those who created these standards and many other independent scholars (e.g., Carey, 2001; Kubiszyn & Borich, 2003; Popham, 2000; Tanner, 2001; Thorkildsen, 2005; Ward & Murray-Ward, 1999) often use the words *assessment, measurement,* and *evaluation* as synonyms.

But when they describe the use of these three concepts, most authors appear to assume measurement is a means to assessment, and assessment is one important component of a much more complicated process called evaluation. Therefore, in this volume we differentiate among these terms to help readers appreciate the importance of all three concepts and how they can be used to improve measurement, assessment, evaluation, and the online learning and testing the volumes in this series are exploring.

Evaluation involves describing what is and what should be, and comparing the two. To gather information about what is, as well as what should be, assessment is an essential tool. And most assessments involve some kind of measurement process built upon theories of measurement. Scriven (1991), a noted evaluation theorist, summarizes each of these terms:

> *Measurement [is] a determination of the magnitude of a quantity, typically on a criterion-referenced test scale or on a continuous numerical scale. Whatever is used to do the measurement is called the measurement instrument. It may be a questionnaire or a test or an eye or a piece of apparatus. In certain contexts, we treat the observer as the instrument needing calibration or validation. Measurement is a common and sometimes large component of standardized evaluations, but a very small part of its logic, that is, of the justification for the evaluative conclusions. (p. 266)*

> *Assessment [is] often used as a synonym for evaluation in which the judgment [usually associated with evaluation] is built into the context of the numerical results. Raw scores on a test of no known content or construct validity would not be assessment; it is only when the test is—for example— of basic mathematical competence that reporting the results constitutes assessment in the appropriate sense, and of course the judgment of validity is the key evaluative component in this. Another part of the assessment movement, strongly supported in schools as well as colleges, is the move away from paper-and-pencil testing toward something more judgmental and global. (p. 60)*

> *The key sense of the term 'evaluation' refers to the process of determining the merit, worth, or value of something, or the product of that process. Terms used to refer to this process or part of it include: appraise, analyze, assess, critique, examine, grade, inspect, judge, rate, rank, review, study, test, measure. The evaluation process normally involves some identification of relevant standards of merit, worth, or value; some investigation of the performance of evaluands on these standards; and some integration or synthesis of the results to achieve an overall evaluation. It contrasts with the measurement process, which also involves the comparison of observations*

against standards, in that i) measurement is characteristically not concerned with merit, only with 'purely descriptive' properties, and ii) those properties are characteristically unidimensional, which avoids the need for the integrating step. The integration process is sometimes judgmental, sometimes the result of complex calculation, very commonly a hybrid of the two. In short [evaluation] is the sine qua non of intelligent thought and action, and in particular of professional practice. (pp. 139-140)

More recently, these terms were defined by three different authors in the *Encyclopedia of Evaluation* (Mathison, 2005) as follows:

Measurement *may be defined as the set of rules for transforming behaviors into categories or numbers. Constructing an instrument to measure a social science variable involves several steps, including conceptualizing the behaviors that operationally define the variable, drafting items that indicate the behaviors, administering draft items to try out samples, refining the instrument based on item analysis, and performing reliability and validity studies. These studies are necessary to ensure that scores on the instrument are consistent and have evidence of adequately representing a construct. Two theoretical approaches dominate the field of measurement: classical test theory and item response theory.* (Petrosko, 2005, p. 47)

From the Greek, 'to sit with', assessment means an evaluative determination. Roughly synonymous with testing and evaluation in lay terms, assessment has become the term of choice in education for determining the quality of student work for purposes of identifying the student's level of achievement. A more important distinction is between the terms assessment and measurement because educational constructs such as achievement, like most social phenomena, cannot be directly measured but can be assessed. (Mabry, 2005, p. 22)

Evaluation *is an applied inquiry process for collecting and synthesizing evidence that culminates in conclusions about the state of affairs, value, merit, worth, significance, or quality of a program, product, person, policy, proposal, or plan. Conclusions made in evaluations encompass both an empirical aspect (that something is the case) and a normative aspect (judgment about the value of something). It is the value feature that distinguishes evaluation from other types of inquiry, such as basic science research, clinical epidemiology, investigative journalism, or public polling.* (Fournier, 2005, pp. 139-140)

Synthesizing these views, although the terms are often used interchangeably, evaluation most often utilizes measurement and assessment to generate value judgments in a wide variety of situations. Assessment usually refers to evaluation of student learning, but it can be used to refer to evaluation in other settings as well. And measurement is usually viewed in support of assessment and/or evaluation.

Taking the view that evaluation incorporates measurement and assessment into a more comprehensive set of activities and perspectives, what else does evaluation involve beyond assessment using measurement? A review of several sources (Alkin, 2004; Fetterman, 2001; Guba & Lincoln, 1989; Patton, 2002; Stake, 2003; Stufflebeam, 2001; Weiss, 1983, 1998; Worthen, Sanders, & Fitzpatrick, 1997) on evaluation theory and practice identifies several key attributes of an evaluation around which the chapters of this volume are organized: context, stakeholders, evaluand, issues and concerns, values and criteria, questions, data collection and analysis, and reporting results, conclusions, and recommendations.

Context

The background, context, and relevant literature associated with an evaluation are essential for understanding if an evaluation is appropriate at a particular time and with particular participants. Some questions the potential evaluator should ask include: What does the literature associated with the evaluand say are the key issues? How did this evaluand come to be of interest to you? What is your background that is relevant to this evaluation? What evaluation has been done on this evaluand already? Is the evaluand evaluable at present? Why is an evaluation appropriate now? In several chapters in this volume the context is online learning, measurement development to facilitate evaluation of online instruction, and other distance education concerns.

Stakeholders

The audiences, stakeholders, and information users who care about the evaluand and its evaluation need to be identified early because they shape the evaluation in terms of their values, expectations, concerns, criteria, and standards. Some questions the potential evaluator should ask include: Who asked for the evaluation and why? Why do these people care? Who stands to benefit from the evaluation and how? Who is served by the evaluand or should be? Who is likely to use the evaluation results to do something helpful? Who does not usually have a voice in matters associated with the evaluand but has a stake in it? Many authors of chapters in this volume assume that the key stakeholders are faculty, administrators, and students associated with online instructional programs without necessarily identifying them explicitly.

Evaluand

The object of evaluation is the evaluand. This could be a person (as in personnel evaluation), a program (as in program evaluation), a product (as in curriculum or test evaluation), learning (as in student assessment), or anything people value. Some questions the potential evaluator should ask include: What do you already know about the evaluand (what it is, what its objectives are, how it works)? What more do you need to learn to refine the description and definition of the evaluand so you can focus your evaluation on it? Many of the chapters in this volume identify student learning in online environments as the evaluand of most interest. Because assessment is the common term used in evaluating student learning, these authors refer to online assessment without necessarily addressing all the other evaluation issues mentioned in other sections of this review.

Issues and Concerns

Stakeholders may know what their concerns are or they may need help clarifying them. Some questions the potential evaluator should explore with stakeholders include: Do they want summative, formative, or both kinds of information? Do they want to focus on accountability of someone for the evaluand? What concerns do they have about the evaluand? What are they saying they want to know? What is unsettled among them about the evaluand? What information are they asking you to gather? Authors in this volume focus more on formative than summative evaluation, but raise many issues and concerns that could be considered in evaluations of either type.

Values and Criteria

This is the crux of an evaluation, understanding the ideal against which the evaluand is to be judged. Using answers obtained to questions raised in earlier sections, the potential evaluator should work with stakeholders to clarify what their values are regarding the evaluand or aspects of the evaluand they care most about. Based on those values, criteria the evaluand should meet will be identified and standards or levels of achievement on those criteria clarified. Some questions to be addressed are: What values do the stakeholders manifest regarding the evaluand? What do they think the evaluand should be accomplishing (criteria for success)? What standards do they have or how completely do they hope the evaluand will meet the criteria? How will they know when the evaluand is successful to their satisfaction? Authors of the chapters in this volume used learning and measurement theories, concerns of educators and administrators, student values, and many other sources as the basis for establishing evaluation criteria.

Questions

Based on answers the evaluator obtains to the previous groups of questions, they formulate the evaluation questions that will guide the rest of the study. These questions may be descriptive (What is the evaluand doing or how is it currently functioning?) and evaluative (How well is the evaluand doing compared to the ideal?). They may address needs an evaluand might meet, comparison of alternative evaluands that might meet a need, how well an evaluand is being implemented, or what outcomes can be associated with an evaluand. Most of these chapters focus on implementation and outcome-oriented questions, but also attend closely to questions about how measurement can enhance evaluation in online situations.

Data Collection and Analysis

Based on the evaluation questions agreed to as most important by the stakeholders and the evaluator, a plan to answer those questions should be developed. In addition to qualitative data collection, this is the point at which quantitative and technology-based measurement instruments and processes that stakeholders agree are dependable for gathering data must be selected, developed, refined, and used to gather information and interpret it through analysis and synthesis. Many of the chapters in this volume concentrate on this aspect of the evaluation process because data collection using technology is particularly valuable in online educational settings.

Reporting Results, Conclusions, and Recommendations

Based on all previous steps, the evaluator obtains results and summarizes the conclusions and recommendations for concerned stakeholders and interested audiences. Doing so involves addressing the following kinds of questions: What interim and final reports will be given to whom and when? How will the reports be organized, around what points? Will there be oral reports? Written reports? Other formats? What are the results or answers to the evaluation questions? How will results be organized? What displays of results do you anticipate using and why? What recommendations does this study yield? Where will recommendations come from? Authors in this volume report some results of their own studies and explore alternative ways of sharing results as well.

Implications

What difference does it make to think about online assessment and measurement as means to doing online evaluation? The major point to thinking this way is clarification of context. Measurements are only valuable if they are built and used to produce information that people can use appropriately. What is considered appropriate? Only by knowing the context for the measurement can this question be answered satisfactorily. If the measurement is being used in an assessment program or an evaluation study, information about the assessment program and the evaluation study clarifies the context for the measurement being done. Measurements rarely stand alone in practice.

As suggested earlier, assessment is often used synonymously with evaluation. However, many of the concerns to consider for an evaluation described earlier may be overlooked if someone is concentrating on conducting an assessment or testing program about which others have already made assumptions about background, stakeholders, defining the evaluand, clarifying criteria, and so on. By considering the evaluation context in which the assessment is taking place, the assessment can be much richer, helpful, and use the measurement involved in the assessment program more appropriately.

Considering all these issues in an online or distance education context makes these distinctions even more important to explore. People doing measurement, assessment, and evaluation, who think about the questions raised earlier for evaluations, will examine the unique background associated with doing their work online with evaluands that are online. They will ask how stakeholders are different and what additional stakeholders to involve because their experience is online. Evaluators of online evaluands will want to understand how the evaluands are different because they are online and will address those differences in their studies. They will search for criteria, concerns, questions, and standards that are unique to the stakeholders involved because they are working online. As the chapters in this volume illustrate, online evaluators will collect data using online resources and techniques in addition to more traditional data gathering procedures. And analyses, results, conclusions, and recommendations will have implications for online practices and future evaluations.

References

Alkin, M. (Ed.). (2004). *Evaluation roots: Tracing theorists' views and influences.* Thousand Oaks, CA: Sage.

Carey, L.M. (2001). *Measuring and evaluating school learning* (3rd ed.). Boston: Allyn and Bacon.

Fetterman, D.M. (2001). *Foundations of empowerment evaluation.* Thousand Oaks, CA: Sage.

Fournier, D.M. (2005). Evaluation. In S. Mathison (Ed.), *Encyclopedia of evaluation.* Thousand Oaks, CA: Sage.

Guba, E.G., & Lincoln, Y.S. (1989). *Fourth generation evaluation.* Newbury Park, CA: Sage.

Joint Committee on Standards for Educational Evaluation. (1988). *The personnel evaluation standards: How to assess systems for evaluating educators.* Newbury Park, CA: Sage.

Joint Committee on Standards for Educational Evaluation. (1994). *The program evaluation standards: How to assess evaluations of educational programs* (2nd ed.). Thousand Oaks, CA: Sage.

Joint Committee on Standards for Educational Evaluation. (2003). *The student evaluation standards: How to improve evaluations of students.* Thousand Oaks, CA: Corwin Press.

Kubiszyn, T., & Borich, G. (2003). *Educational testing and measurement: Classroom application and practice* (7th ed.). New York: John Wiley & Sons.

Mabry, L. (2005). Assessment. In S. Mathison (Ed.), *Encyclopedia of evaluation.* Thousand Oaks, CA: Sage.

Mathison, S. (2005). *Encyclopedia of evaluation.* Thousand Oaks, CA: Sage.

Patton, M.Q. (2002). *Qualitative research and evaluation methods* (3rd ed.). Thousand Oaks, CA: Sage.

Petrosko, J.M. (2005). Measurement. In S. Mathison (Ed.), *Encyclopedia of evaluation.* Thousand Oaks, CA: Sage.

Popham, W.J. (2000). *Modern educational measurement: Practical guidelines for educational leaders* (3rd ed.). Boston: Allyn and Bacon.

Scriven, M. (1991). *Evaluation thesaurus* (4th ed.). Newbury Park, CA: Sage.

Stake, R.E. (2003). *Standards-based and responsive evaluation.* Thousand Oaks, CA: Sage.

Stufflebeam, D.L. (2001, Spring). Evaluation models. *New Directions for Evaluation, 89,* 7-99.

Tanner, D.E. (2001). *Assessing academic achievement.* Boston: Allyn and Bacon.

Thorkildsen, T.A. (2005). *Fundamentals of measurement in applied research.* Boston: Pearson Education.

Ward, A.W., & Murray-Ward, M. (1999). *Assessment in the classroom.* Belmont, CA: Wadsworth Publishing Company.

Weiss, C. (1983). The stakeholder approach to evaluation: Origins and promise. *New Directions in Program Evaluation, 17,* 3-14.

Weiss, C. (1998). *Evaluation* (2nd ed.). Upper Saddle River, NJ: Prentice-Hall.

Worthen, B.R., Sanders, J.R., & Fitzpatrick, J.L. (1997). *Program evaluation: Alternative approaches and practical guidelines* (2nd ed.). New York: Longman.

Section II

Web Surveys

Chapter II

The Context and Culture of the Web as a Research Environment

Paula B. Doherty, Peninsula College, USA

Abstract

The World Wide Web provides a unique and idiosyncratic environment for applied social research. Examining the context and culture of this environment can better inform research design. This chapter explores attributes of the Web that influence the administration and outcomes of survey research, examines the dual phenomena of self-selection and nonresponse that frequently encumber the implementation of self-administered surveys on the Web, reviews sample loss as it occurs during the multiple stages of survey response, and identifies elements of the research design that can mitigate the effect of this medium—its context and culture—on survey outcomes.

Introduction

The World Wide Web has been a remarkable phenomenon. It is a universe of networked systems, information, and people—merging the technologies of personal computers, computer networks, and hypertext into a powerful, accessible, and global environment. It is interactive and ubiquitous. It is also transitory and potentially invasive. It is increasingly intuitive and commercial.

Launched in 1989, its reach as a communication medium and a research environment is unparalleled. It is projected that well over one billion of the Earth's population will be Web users by the year 2006 (ClickZ Stats, 2004). The impact of the Web has been immediate and "to some extent, has caught survey methodologists unprepared" (Dillman & Bowker, 2001). The survey literature as late as the mid-1990s could not anticipate the eventual influence of the Web on the practice of surveying (Schonlau, Fricker, & Elliott, 2002). According to Schonlau et al., some experts predict that Web-based surveys will eventually replace other survey modes altogether.

The Web provides a unique and idiosyncratic research environment for applied social research. While the growing accessibility of the Web enhances its value as a research environment, its other attributes—some delimited by technology and others by societal circumstances—are qualities that directly influence survey research. It is those attributes, specifically those that are derived from the context and culture of the Web itself, that affect external validity and reliability.

The Web as Context

The word *context* is derived from the Latin words *contextus* (connection of words) and *contexere* (to weave together). The World Wide Web (WWW) is a plurality of connections, a rich texture of networked resources and constructed meaning. Its primary medium is hypertext—a means of connecting content and meaning in non-sequential patterns. This *intertextuality* of the Web has been called an "open fabric of heterogeneous traces and associations…forever shifting and always mobile" (Taylor & Saarinen, 1994, p. 6).

The man who sired this phenomenon, Tim Berners-Lee, envisioned "an organic expanse of collaboration" (Wright, 1997, p. 67). He imagined it to be a social place—a place for dynamic, purposeful interaction, accessible to all—a global village (Daly, 1996).

In 1980, while serving as a consulting software engineer for CERN, the European particle physics laboratory in Geneva, Berners-Lee created a software program for his own purposes, "to keep track of the complex web of relationships between people, programs, machines, and ideas" (Berners-Lee, 1997b, p. 1). It was inspired by his research on how brains use random associations to link thoughts (Jacobs, 1995). This program, which he called *Enquire*, became the seminal idea for the Web, using random associations to access information at distributed locations.

When Berners-Lee returned to the CERN on a fellowship, he wrote a proposal to link CERN's resources by hypertext. He conceptualized a web of relationships, at once complex and simple, diffuse but precise—achieving a natural balance amongst disparate elements. He proceeded to develop the first World Wide Web server and first client, a hypertext browser/editor (Vandendorpe, 1996). In December 1989, Berners-Lee introduced the World Wide Web.

Why the *Web*? It depicts a "decentralized nonhierarchical topology" (Lange, 1995b, p. 34). *World Wide* describes its scope. Berners-Lee describes the Web as an abstract space with which people interact, populated by interlinked pages of text, images and animations, sounds, three-dimensional worlds, and video (Berners-Lee, 1996b)—*contextus* and *contextere*.

It is difficult to overstate the impact of the global system he created. Berners-Lee took a powerful communications system that only the elite could use and turned it into a mass medium (Quittner, 1999). He pioneered the Web's three enabling standards—HTML (the language for encoding documents), HTTP (the system for linking documents), and URL (the system for addressing documents) (Metcalfe, 1995; Wright, 1997). He grounded them on fundamental principles that optimized flexibility. Minimal constraint was the guiding principle. Berners-Lee parlayed the power of hypertext into a common, interoperable, open-standards medium.

The growth of the World Wide Web has been explosive. Data traffic increased from 5% of all telecommunications traffic in 1989 to nearly 50% in 1999, doubling every 100 days, (Young, 1999). "If we can make something decentralized, out of control, and of great simplicity, we must be prepared to be astonished at whatever might grow out of that new medium" (Berners-Lee, 1997b, p. 6).

Berners-Lee's vision was a populist vision. "We have to ensure that the Web exists for people and cannot be exploited...We have to think as hard about the constitution of cyberspace as about any other constitution" (Cavender, 1995, p. D1). In 1994, he formed the WWW Consortium (W3C)—a neutral, open forum where over 250 government, educational, and corporate entities can agree to agree (Berners-Lee, 1998). Its purpose is to ensure interoperability while technologies and protocols evolve (Cavender, 1995).

When asked why he thinks the Web has resonated so strongly with so many, Berners-Lee responds that "the openness of the Web is a powerful attraction. Everyone can not only read what's on the Web but contribute to it, and everybody is in a sense equal. There's a sense of boundless opportunity" (Brody, 1996, p. 39).

The World Wide Web has evolved from a tool to a cultural phenomenon. It has become what its author envisioned: a social space in which we communicate, learn, compute, and do business (Lange, 1995a).

What is the state of the Web today? Web statistics evoke awe:

- Over 945 million Web users in 2004
- Over 51.5 million server sites
- Over 14 million domains
- Over 73 million DSL connections
- Nearly 1.5 billion Web users projected for 2007 (ClickZ Stats, 2004)

Where is the World Wide Web going? Berners-Lee's forecast of nearly 10 years ago may be equally germane today: the evolution of the Web may yet be at the bottom of the 'S' curve, with no view of the top (Berners-Lee, 1996a).

The Web as Culture

The notion of *culture* is common to our contemporary lexicon, yet how we think of culture and how culture is defined can vary widely. What do we mean when we speak of the Web as *culture*?

Some think of culture as "the glass through which we view the world" (Intercultural, 2004). Others think of it as "the medium we live in, like the air we breathe" (Hall, 1977). An anthropologist defines it as: "the acquired knowledge people use to interpret experience and generate behavior" (Beer, 2003). A noted psychologist defines it as a "construction of experience" (Kalekin-Fishman, 2004). *Culture* may be one of the most complex and multi-faceted words in the English language (Williams, 1985), and one of the most fluid concepts (Kalekin-Fishman). "It has now come to be used for important concepts in several distinct intellectual systems and in several distinct and incompatible systems of thought" (Williams, p. 87).

The word *culture* is derived from the Latin root *colere*, "to construct," or "to cultivate," as opposed to that which occurs naturally (Dahl, 1998, 2003). The first anthropological definition of culture was advanced in 1871 by a British anthropologist, Edward Tylor. He defined culture as socially patterned human thought and behavior. By 1938, anthropologists had identified 79 major cultural categories and 637 subcategories. In 1952, two American anthropologists, Alfred Kroeber and Clyde Kluckhohn, published a list of 160 distinct definitions of culture (Bodley, 1999).

While it is not the purpose of this discussion to conduct a comprehensive review of these definitions, it is important to recognize the multiple dimensions of culture and how those characteristics shape the culture of the Web. In the context of the Web, any of the following definitions are germane.

- a system of shared meaning (Smith & Bond, 1998, as cited in Johnson, O'Rourke, & Owens, 2002);

- explicit and implicit patterns of behavior acquired and transmitted by symbols (Kroeber & Kluckhohn, 1952, as cited in Dahl, 2003);

- a set of techniques for adjusting both to the external environment and to others (Kluckhon, 1949, as cited in Miraglia, Law, & Collins, 1999);

- a behavioral map, sieve, or matrix (Kluckhohn, 1949, as cited in Miraglia et al., 1999);

- the collective programming of the mind which distinguishes the members of one group from another (Hofstede, 1994, as cited in Dahl, 2003);

- a web of significance (Geertz, 1973).

Perhaps most relevant is Clifford Geertz's emphasis on webs of significance:

> *Believing, with Max Weber, that man is an animal suspended in webs of significance he himself has spun, I take culture to be those webs, and the analysis of it to be therefore not an experimental science in search of law but an interpretative one in search of meaning.* (Geertz, 1973, p. 5)

Geertz believed that culture is "the fabric of meaning in terms of which human beings interpret their experience and guide their actions" (Park, 2002).

Contemporary anthropologists appear to view culture as descriptive, inclusive, and relativistic (Bodley, 1999). Many reject the notion of culture as "bounded." Instead, they see culture as a "complex web of shifting patterns that link people in different locales, and link social formations of different scales" (Wikipedia, 2004). "It is shared behavior, which is important because it systematizes the way people do things..." (Fisher, 1988, as cited in Dahl, 1998, p. 8). The shared aspect of culture means that it is a social phenomenon. It is manifest through time, context, and space (Trillo, 1996).

"Time is one of the fundamental bases on which all cultures rest and around which all activities revolve. Understanding the difference between monochronic time and polychronic time is essential..." (Hall, 1990, p. 179). Monochronic time is characterized as linear, tangible, and divisible. By contrast, polychronic time can be characterized as the simultaneous occurrence of multiple events (Trillo, 1996).

Context refers to that part of an interaction that imbues it with meaning. Anthropologist Edward T. Hall's concept of *context* relates to the framework, background, and surrounding circumstances in which communication or an event takes place (High-context, n.d.). This can vary from a high context culture in which contextual information is implicit, to a low context culture, in which information must be made explicit (Trillo, 1996). A high-context culture is said to be relational, collectivist, intuitive, and contemplative, while a low context culture tends to be logical, linear, individualistic, and action-oriented (High-context..., n.d.). According to Hall, a high-context culture seeks harmony and consensus. Content is less important than context, and reason is subsumed to intuition. On the other hand, a low-context culture seeks clarity and precision. Content leads to decisions, which lead to actions (High-context, n.d.). It can be argued that the Web is a low-context culture since meaning is derived directly from its content. There is little opportunity to convey contextual information in a WYSWYG (what you see is what you get) environment.

Space refers to the invisible boundary around an individual that is considered "personal" (Trillo, 1996). This sense of personal space can be virtual as well as real. In the world of the Web, the concept of personal space is continuously redefined as push technologies become more invasive and the results of unsolicited e-mail impact personal as well as physical space.

Cultures vary in the level of emphasis placed on personal versus group interests, or individualism versus collectivism. Personal needs and a predilection for autonomy guide behavior in individualist cultures, whereas external expectations guide behavior in collectivist cultures. In general, cultures that are more complex and heterogeneous tend to be individualist (Triandis, 1994, as cited in Johnson et al., 2002). The Web is an individualist culture, and it has been argued that individualistic cultures rely primarily on low-context communication styles (Gudykunst, 1998, as cited in Johnson et al., 2002).

Another cultural dimension is power distance. Power distance is concerned with the degree to which individuals hold power over one another. Individuals will normally strive to reduce the power distance between themselves and a superior (Mulder, 2004). The Web is an equalizer; it is a "low power distance" culture. Persons in low power distance cultures do not accept authority uncritically. This dimension is strongly correlated with individualism.

A further dimension of culture that characterizes social relationships can be described as vertical (hierarchical) versus horizontal (egalitarian). The Web is a cross-sectional, horizontal culture, a "decentralized, nonhierarchical topology" (Lange, 1995b, p. 35). Horizontal cultures tend to place less value on rank or authority; this too is highly correlated with individualism and low power distance.

Nonverbal communication is the "hidden dimension" of culture (Hall, 1996, as cited in Johnson et al., 2002), and it is markedly present on every Web page. Page design and format, color, graphics, and usability all contribute to the efficacy of communication on the Web.

Self-disclosure is a communication trait that is highly influenced by cultural as well as contextual attributes. The Web is both a culture and a context that influences the voluntary disclosure of personal information. Although self-disclosure is most frequently associated with the types of direct, low-context communication patterns observed in individualistic social systems (Gudykunst, 1998, as cited in Johnson et al., 2002), issues of privacy and systems security are factors that directly influence self-disclosure in a cyber-environment.

The Web is a social matrix. What, then, can we suggest are those attributes that influence those who engage in this system of shared meaning, construct experience, and together weave a web of significance? Each of the following is derived from the theoretical traditions noted above:

- polychronic time

- low-context interactions

- personal space

- individualism

- low power distance

- horizontal social relationships

- nonverbal communication

- resistance to self-disclosure

Recognizing cultural orientations, the extent to which Web users operate on polychronic time, rely on low-context communication, guard personal space, exercise individualism, discount power distance, engage in horizontal relationships, value nonverbal communication, and resist self-disclosure can help us better understand the dual phenomena of self-selection and nonresponse to Web-administered assessment instruments.

The Web as a Research Environment

The scope of the World Wide Web provides a unique context for survey research. Surveys are one of the most common, versatile, and important areas of measurement in applied social research (Trochim, 2004). "It is this capacity for wide application and broad coverage which gives the survey technique its great usefulness…" (Angus & Katona, 1953, p. 16, as cited in Colorado State University Writing Center, 2004a).

The primary goal of survey research is to produce a valid profile of the population of interest. The population of interest is frequently represented by a *sample*, or a subset of the whole. A probability sample is derived from some form of *random selection* which ensures that each member of the survey population has an equal probability of being selected. This property of probability sampling enables the researcher to use statistical theory to make inferences from the sample to the survey population. Simple, stratified, systematic, and cluster samples are common variations of random sampling strategies.

In many research designs it is either unfeasible or unnecessary to obtain a probability sample. In these situations, a non-probability sample is used. A non-probability sample can be situational (i.e., convenience sample), purposive (e.g., a sample of experts), or proportional (i.e., quota sample). The results, therefore, are simply the results of those who respond, at a given time, under given circumstances, which may or may not be representative of the whole. Nonetheless, a non-probability sample is not necessarily unrepresentative of the population. It simply cannot rely upon probability theory for explaining representativeness (Trochim, 2004).

Surveys have a wide variety of purposes, can be structured in a variety of ways, and can assume a variety of formats. A Web-based survey enables potential respondents to access and answer a set of questions asynchronously, and to submit their responses electronically by means of the Internet. Some predict that Web surveys will eventually replace other survey modes altogether (Schonlau et al., 2002).

Among the many advantages of Web-based surveys are the ease of administration, rapid return of data, reduced effort in data handling, and potentially lower study costs (Web-Based Surveys, 2004). The Web can be an excellent medium for survey research when the population of interest is *known*, as is normally found in an educational environment. However, there are challenges in achieving response rates that are representative of the population, even when all potential respondents are known.

One of the most vexing concerns about Web surveys is the potential nonrandom nature of the respondent group (Mertler, 2003). Web surveys are self-administered and Web culture is self-directed. While voluntary participation in any survey is subject to a nonresponse effect and a differential probability of selection, this phenomenon is especially problematic with Web surveys, an occurrence that is inexorably associated with the context and culture of the Web. The potentially deleterious effects of voluntary response need to be anticipated (Doherty, 2000; Sills & Song, 2002). Systemic self-selection and nonresponse result in systematic variance, producing sample bias—a matter of considerable concern for survey researchers.

Recognizing the complexity and pervasiveness of culture, and the processes through which it influences human cognition and behavior, it is reasonable to assert that the culture of the Web influences both respondent accessibility and participation. The cultural attributes that may have the most pervasive impact are: polychronic time, individualism, and resistance to self-disclosure.

Self-Selection

The results of any survey are only as representative as the subjects who respond.

Response to a self-administered survey is a matter of choice. "There is very little researchers can do to persuade someone to participate if he/she simply prefers not to participate" (Andrews, Nonnecke, & Preece, 2003 p. 12). Sample bias occurs when nonrespondents differ from respondents in characteristics that cannot be known by the researchers.

Winship and Mare (1992) point out that "nonrandom selection is both a source of bias in empirical research and a fundamental aspect of many social processes" (as cited in Koch & Emrey, 2001, p. 327). Nonetheless, and in spite of this dilemma, most social scientists would prefer to conduct research within acknowledged constraints rather than to dismiss those research opportunities altogether due to methodological difficulties (Koch & Emrey, 2001). Andrews et al. (2003) concur by emphasizing the comparative value in building knowledge based on studies that provide "indicative data" (p. 11). "There is no perfect method for acquiring information. All data collection efforts are attempts to approximate the truth" (Rousseau & Sanders, 2003, p. 2)

Nonresponse

[T]echnology continues to improve all aspects of doing Web surveys: standardized software, user-friendly interfaces, attractive multimedia, merger of technologies (Web, TV, phone, VCR), high-speed transmission, and low access costs. During the next years, increased Internet penetration, massive Web usage, and technological improvements will further expand the application of Web surveys. However, nonresponse to such surveys is a serious problem. (Vehovar, Betagelj, Manfreda, & Zaletel, 2002, p. 229)

Nonresponse occurs when a potential respondent cannot be contacted or does not respond to a request to be surveyed, or when a respondent fails to answer specific questions. The first type of nonresponse (unit nonresponse) results in sample loss. The second type of nonresponse (item nonresponse) affects the quality of the data. Since this latter type of nonresponse is often a function of the psychometric properties of the survey itself, it will not be the subject of this discussion. The focus of this chapter is on the survey mode—the effect that the context and culture of the Web may have on unit nonresponse.

All surveys are subject to some degree of nonresponse. This becomes a matter of concern when those who decline to respond to a survey significantly differ from those who do. "Moreover, the direction of the nonresponder's beliefs, opinions, or attitudes—favorable or unfavorable—cannot be determined. Thus, the results of surveys are biased in unknown directions" (Rousseau & Sanders, 2003, p. 7).

While nonresponse is not unique to the Web as a research environment, it is potentially more problematic given the voluntary nature of Web-administered surveys. A decentralized nonhierarchical topology, and an operational culture that fosters individualism and a horizontal orientation to authority, may be especially conducive to a nonresponse effect. Conventional controls that can accompany paper-and-pencil surveys, especially within educational environments, cannot be implemented on the Web.

The potential for nonresponse bias is endemic to unrestricted Web-based surveys—surveys that can be accessed by any Web browsing person. Web surveys administered to known populations are the subject of this discussion. There are two forms of nonresponse when the sample population is known. The first applies to those instances in which a person is inadvertently omitted from the sample due to a change of e-mail address or any other condition that precludes him/her from accessing the survey. The second occurs when a person declines to participate in the research.

If we assume that the operational environment for this discussion is an organization in which all affiliated members are known (e.g., an institution of higher education), then the true population can be identified. If we also assume, since all affiliated members are known, that each member of the sample population has a known and functional e-mail address, frequently within the organization's domain, then we can begin this discussion at the point at which potential respondents receive an e-mail invitation to participate in a survey. The sample population may be either a probability or non-probability sample.

Vehovar et al. (2002) have identified a number of discrete stages associated with reaching a target population. Since this discussion assumes the target population is known, Figure 1 is an adaptation of the Vehovar et al. (2002) model of progressive response to a survey request. Sample loss can occur at each of these stages, compounding the risk of nonresponse.

> *We can conclude that the stages of the nonresponse process in Web surveys are relatively complex. The corresponding indicators are undeveloped and are lacking standardization...As a consequence, the available research exhibits low values and extreme variation in response rates....* (Vehovar et al., p. 231)

Figure 1. Progressive stages of response to a Web survey administered to a known population (adapted from Vehovar et al., 2002)

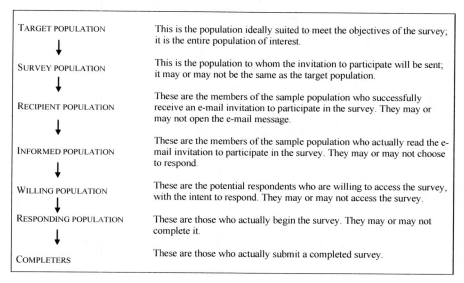

TARGET POPULATION	This is the population ideally suited to meet the objectives of the survey; it is the entire population of interest.
SURVEY POPULATION	This is the population to whom the invitation to participate will be sent; it may or may not be the same as the target population.
RECIPIENT POPULATION	These are the members of the sample population who successfully receive an e-mail invitation to participate in the survey. They may or may not open the e-mail message.
INFORMED POPULATION	These are the members of the sample population who actually read the e-mail invitation to participate in the survey. They may or may not choose to respond.
WILLING POPULATION	These are the potential respondents who are willing to access the survey, with the intent to respond. They may or may not access the survey.
RESPONDING POPULATION	These are those who actually begin the survey. They may or may not complete it.
COMPLETERS	These are those who actually submit a completed survey.

Exogenous Factors Influencing Participation

There are numerous explanations for nonresponse to Web-administered surveys. Among them are the demographic characteristics of the sample population, their social/technical environments, and their attitudes toward both surveys in general and toward the topic of the survey. While these factors are outside the control of the researcher, it is important to be mindful of them as we plan our research design.

Demographic Characteristics. Response rates to surveys frequently vary across demographic characteristics. It is reasonable to expect that this will occur with Web-based surveys as well. Moreover, Web usage varies across demographic characteristics. Active users of the Web will be more likely to participate in Web-based surveys than infrequent users, contributing to a sample bias that results from both self-selection and nonresponse.

Social/Technical Environments. The inclination of Web users to actually respond to a survey will be influenced by the adequacy of their desktop computer (i.e., horsepower), hardware configuration, browser settings, connection speed, and access (e.g., in households in which multiple family members compete for online time). Telecommunications can be a deal-breaker for those who live in bandwidth-deficient locations or those who choose not to afford (or cannot afford) a reasonably high-speed connection.

Attitudes. A positive attitude toward survey participation in general increases the chances for completing a Web survey (Gonier, 1999, as cited in Vehovar et al., 2002). Alternatively, as questionnaires increase in number and frequency, there is increasing evidence of an over-surveyed syndrome. The willingness to participate in any survey is declining as society becomes satiated with survey requests. This phenomenon is likely to have the most significant impact on self-administered surveys, as voluntary subjects will self-select.

The purpose of the survey may be even more important. "In general, survey participation depends strongly on the survey topic, its salience, and the respondent's involvement" (Vehovar et al., 2002, p. 235). This is often the sole motivator within the educational domain, when students are asked to provide feedback about a class or a learning experience. When students view their participation in a survey as either an "investment" in improved education or a chance to have an "equal" voice, they become more willing to bear the opportunity cost of that effort.

All of these factors are fundamentally outside the control of the researcher. They inform our understanding of nonresponse in a Web research environment, but they fail to provide us with guidance as to how we can positively influence response rates when the inhibiting factors are respondent-centered.

Endogenous Factors Influencing Participation

To minimize nonresponse, Cooper and Groves (1996) suggest that researchers manipulate the factors that they can control, that are endogenous to the research design (as cited in Colorado State University Writing Center, 2004b). The following are elements of the research design that the researcher should pay close attention to:

Invitation. The invitation is the hook by which the recipient population is persuaded to become willing respondents. "Potential respondents must feel that their opinion is important and valuable—that their time and effort will be a contribution to a worthy cause. The [invitation] is the key to establishing the value of the research and the importance of each response" (Rousseau & Sanders, 2003, p. 4). It should avoid spam, address the purpose of the survey, identify the source of the survey (i.e., sponsor) and the lead researcher, anticipate concerns, and meet issues of confidentiality.

1.   *Avoid spam.* The marketing research community has issued standards designed to prevent the use of unsolicited e-mail to recruit respondents for surveys (Hogg, 2002). Both the World Association of Opinion and Market Research (ESOMAR) and the Council of American Survey Research Organizations (CASRO) require their members to verify that a substantive pre-existing relationship exists between the individuals contacted and the research sponsor (Hogg, 2002). All researchers should heed these standards.

2.   *Identify the survey sponsor.* Clearly identifying the sponsor in the *<From>* line and using an official banner or letterhead and an influential signature can communicate legitimacy and authority. For example, generating the invitation from the *Office of the President* versus a staff member who is unlikely to be known by the majority of recipients will have a differential impact on the outcome. "Sample persons'

knowledge and attitudes concerning the sponsor can affect whether they complete a self-administered survey" (Dillman, Eltinge, Groves, & Little, 2002, p. 11).

3.   *Personalize the subject line.* Strong norms operate on the Web, shaping a culture that militates against unsolicited contact (Cooper, 2000; Sills & Song, 2002). It is for this reason that the <*Subject*> line must be crafted in such a way that it connotes credibility and establishes immediate relevance for the recipient. It should announce the purpose of the message (e.g., *NSU needs your feedback*). Additionally, if the recipient sees his/her name in the first line of text within the message, s/he may be more likely to consider the salience of the request.

4.   *Understand the cost-benefit ratio.* Why should anyone respond to a voluntary survey? What are the "benefits," and do they outweigh the "costs"? The costs to respondents for participating in a survey include their time, mental effort, and the risk of revealing personal information that may compromise their privacy and, perhaps, their standing with the sponsoring entity (Rousseau & Sanders, 2003). It is the survey researcher's challenge to present persuasive reasons why the benefits of responding exceed the costs. For example, reviewing the social benefits of the survey can communicate the survey's contribution to the common good (Dillman et al., 2002). In other words, how will the intended outcomes of the survey contribute to improved quality or better service or whatever the ultimate goal may be?

5.   *Acknowledge privacy concerns.* The issues of "personal space," privacy and confidentiality are volatile factors in a cyber-research environment. Abuse of privacy norms on the Web undermine the credibility of online researchers, the purposes of their research, and the weight of the anonymity and confidentiality guarantees they offer (Cho & LaRose, 1999). If there is a lingering feeling that any electronic response can be traced to the individual, nonresponse is likely to occur (McMillan, 2004). Try to address these concerns. Emphasize the privacy and confidentiality protections that you have deployed. Attempt to assure your sample population that there is no personally identifiable information associated with their responses, nor a record of whether they have responded or not. If this is not the case, then you should explain why you will be asking (or capturing) individually identifiable information, and how you will use it and protect it.

6.   *Provide full disclosure.* Identify yourself, the purpose, and the significance of your research. Establish your credibility as a researcher. Explain how the resulting data will be used, published, and/or posted to a Web site.

7.   *Reciprocate.* Explain how respondents will be informed of the outcomes. Reciprocity is an essential ingredient to every communication. If we ask a sample population to take the time necessary to respond to a survey, then we should be conscientious about sharing the outcomes with them.

8.   *Be concise, scannable, and objective.* The first screen of your message is the most critical; start with your purpose and how that purpose is relevant to your respondent pool. Be **succinct.** People do not read on the Web, they scan (Wolter, 2003). Write no more than 50% of the text you would use in a hardcopy communication;

and write for "scannability" (Nielsen, 1997). "Chunk" up the discrete sub-topics within your message so they can be quickly spotted and highlight key words. If your recipient population cannot be persuaded by quickly scanning the text of your message, you are likely to lose them.

9.   *Be clear and be credible.* Be clear about the purpose of your research, the timing, the process, the anticipated outcomes, and when respondents can expect a subsequent message reporting the results of your study. Credibility is key to research on the Web. Achieving acceptable response rates largely depends upon how subjects are asked to participate (Andrews et al., 2003).

Survey design. Survey design is strongly related to partial nonresponse, item nonresponse, and data quality (Dillman & Bowker, 2001; Vehovar et al., 2002). The following design features are especially important to the efficacy of a Web-based survey.

1.   *Brief.* "One area of agreement among online researchers is that shorter survey lengths reduce the percentage of respondents who drop out before completing the survey" (Hogg, 2002, p. 2). The applicable mantra here is "the shorter the better." Err on the side of a concise, lean instrument. Be sure you only ask what you need to know and that what you ask produces that information. It is reasonable to assume that busy people, who are already multi-tasking, are likely to be less patient with a long survey than a short one. Twelve questions is a reasonable ceiling.

2.   *Single screen.* A single page design requires only one bandwidth-draw and enables the respondent to quickly evaluate the length of the survey and the time commitment the survey will require. Time-to-complete is one of the most frequent indicators of survey nonresponse (Mertler, 2003). Studies reveal that multi-page surveys take significantly longer to complete than single-page surveys (Timmerman, 2002). A multiple page Web survey can escalate sample attrition for a variety of reasons:

   - "I hate waiting for the next page to load."
   - "I'm a scroller because I like to have everything on one page, and it is easy to move up and down with the scroll. I like to click when the subject is different."
   - "In case I need to reread a little above, it's still on the screen. I can take it at my own speed, and it's easier to keep my place" (Rich, 1999).

3.   *Straightforward.* While it can be difficult to resist using some of the high-end graphical attributes of Web technology, it is important to remain focused on the essential attributes of any survey, which include visual clarity, readability, and completion time. Prior research supports a simple, clean survey design that is quick and easy to complete (Dillman, Tortura, Conradt, & Bowker, 1998; Andrews et al, 2003).

4. *Tested.* Poorly designed questions and response alternatives can create bias. Oppenheim (1992) asserts that every question, every question sequence, and every scale (i.e., answer categories) used in the survey must be tested and re-tested (as cited in Andrews et al., 2003). There are three different classes of problems: (1) comprehension—the way different respondents interpret key concepts and the way they grasp the overall meanings of questions, (2) perspectives—the way different respondents approach answers to the same question, and (3) accuracy— the way different respondents recall information or select appropriate response categories (Foddy, 1996). Beta test your survey with persons similar to your respondent pool. Interview them afterwards; ask them what was clear and unclear, what they thought each question was really asking, and what they did not like about the instrument. Do not risk poor results due to poor design.

Follow-up. Survey researchers frequently recommend some kind of follow-up. Evidence exists that e-mail reminders contribute up to one-third of the final sample size (Vehovar et al., 2002). In addition, follow-ups are likely to contribute to a more representative sample since late respondents often differ from early respondents (Vehovar et al., 2002). However, this can be a tricky undertaking. If survey responses are truly anonymous, the researcher will not know who among the eligible respondents has failed to respond, and a generic reminder to the entire sample population is tantamount to spamming. There are mixed opinions about the efficacy of follow-ups to Web-based surveys.

Conclusion

The World Wide Web is an unfederated, plurality of connections—a universe of networked resources, virtual relationships, and constructed meaning. Its most prominent characteristics are its scope (*global*), association (*voluntary*), convention (*asynchronous*), and consequence (*boundless*). It is both a context and a culture—a "web of significance" that exhibits certain cultural attributes: (a) polychronic time, (b) low-context interactions, (c) personal space, (d) individualism, (e) low power distance, (f) horizontal social relationships,(g) nonverbal communications, and (h) resistance to self-disclosure.

It is this context and culture that provide a unique and idiosyncratic environment for survey research. The growing accessibility of the Web enhances its value as a research environment, yet its other attributes—some delimited by evolving technologies and others by societal circumstances—are qualities that directly influence the validity and reliability of Web-based research.

While there are numerous advantages to this research environment, including the ease of administration, rapid return of data, reduced effort in data handling, and potentially lower study costs, Web-based surveys are encumbered by the potential nonrandom nature of the respondent group. Self-selection and nonresponse can result in systematic variance, invalidating research results.

Sample loss can occur at any one of several stages, a phenomenon that is influenced by multiple factors. Some are outside the control of the researcher—such as demographic characteristics, social/technical environments, and attitudes. Factors that can be influenced by the researcher merit rigorous attention. These include the population frame, the manner in which the invitation to participate is crafted, and the survey design. Researchers must strive to account for self-selection during each stage of their research design and implementation. The Web is a valid survey mode; the threat to validity arises from self-selection and nonresponse.

References

Andrews, D., Nonnecke, B., & Preece, J. (2003). Electronic survey methodology: A case study in reaching hard to involve Internet users. *International Journal of Human-Computer Interaction, 16*(2), 185-210.

Beer, J.E. (2003). What is "culture?" Retrieved June 23, 2004, from *http://www.culture-at-work.com/concept1.html*

Berners-Lee, T. (1996a, July 17). The World Wide Web—past, present and future. *Proceedings of the Meeting of the British Computer Society,* London. Retrieved August 5, 2004, from *http://jodi.ecs.soton.ac.uk/Articles/v01/i01/BernersLee/*

Berners-Lee, T. (1996b, August). *The World Wide Web: Past, present and future.* Draft response to an invitation to publish in *IEEE Computer* special issue, October. Retrieved August 5, 2004, from *http://www.w3.org./People/Berners-Lee/1996/ppf.html*

Berners-Lee, T. (1997b, December 3). Realising the full potential of the Web. Based on a presentation delivered to the W3C, London. Retrieved August 5, 2004, from *http://www.w3.org/1998/02/Potential.html*

Berners-Lee, T. (1998, May 7). The World Wide Web: A very short personal history. Retrieved August 5, 2004, from *http://www.w3.org/People/Berners-Lee/ShortHistory.html*

Bodley, J.H. (1999, May 26). An anthropological perspective. Retrieved July 10, 2004, from *http://www.wsu.edu:8001/vcwsu/commons/topics/culture/culture-definitions/bodley-text.html#top*

Brody, H. (1996). The Web maestro: An interview with Tim Bernes-Lee. *Technology Review, 99*(5), 32-40.

Cavender, S. (1995). World Wide Web's whiz: Talking information with network's inventor. *The Los Angeles Times*, (May 31), D1.

Cho, H., & LaRose, R. (1999). Privacy issues in Internet surveys. *Social Science Computer Review, 17*(4), 421-434.

ClickZ Stats. (2004, May 10). Population explosion! Retrieved July 21, 2004, from *http://www.clickz.com/stats/big_picture/geographics/article.php/151151*

Colorado State University Writing Center. (2004a). Introduction. Retrieved July 10, 2004, from *http://writing.colostate.edu/references/research/survey/pop2a.cfm*

Colorado State University Writing Center. (2004b). Nonresponse issues. (2004b). Retrieved July 10, 2004) from *http://writing.colostate.edu/references/research/survey/com2d4a.cfm*

Cooper, M.P. (2000). Web surveys. *Public Opinion Quarterly, 64*(4), 464-494.

Dahl, S. (1998). Communications and culture transformation: Cultural diversity, globalization and cultural convergence. Retrieved July 11, 2004, from *http://www.stephweb.com/capstone/index.htm*

Dahl, S. (2003, February). An overview of intercultural research. Retrieved July 11, 2004, from *http://stephan.dahl.at/intercultural/about_culture.html*

Daly, J. (1996, April 8). ASAP legends: Tim Berners-Lee. *Forbes ASAP Supplement, 157*(7), 64.

Dillman, D., Eltinge, J.L., Groves, R.M., & Little, R.J.A. (2002). Survey nonresponse in design, data collection, and analysis. In R.M. Groves, D.A. Dillman, J.L. Eltinge, & R.J.A. Little (Eds.), *Survey nonresponse* (pp. 3-26). New York: John Wiley & Sons.

Dillman, D.A., & Bowker, D.K. (2001). The Web questionnaire challenge to survey methodologists. Retrieved July 10, 2004, from *http://survey.sesrc.wsu.edu/dillman/zuma_paper_dillman_bowker.pdf*

Dillman, D.A., Tortura, R.D., Conradt, J., & Bowker, D. (1998, August). Influence of plain vs. fancy design on response rates for Web surveys. *Proceedings of the Joint Statistical Meeting,* Dallas, Texas. Retrieved July 10, 2004, from *http://survey.sesrc.wsu.edu/dillman/papers/asa98ppr.pdf*

Doherty, P. (2000). *Success factors among community college students in an online learning environment.* Doctoral Dissertation, Nova Southeastern University, Canada.

Foddy, W. (1996). The in-depth testing of survey questions: A critical appraisal of methods. *Quality & Quantity, 30,* 361-370.

Geertz, C. (1973). *The interpretation of cultures: Selected essays.* New York: Basic Books.

Hall, E.T. (1977). *Beyond culture.* Garden City, NY: Anchor Press/Doubleday.

Hall, E.T. (1990). *Understanding cultural differences.* Yarmouth, ME: Intercultural Press.

High-context and low-context culture styles. (n.d.) Retrieved December 10, 2004, from *http://www.marin.cc.ca.us/buscom/index_page0009.htm*

Hogg, A. (2002). Conducting online research. *Burke White Paper Series, 3*(2). Retrieved July 16, 2004, from *http://www.burke.com/whitepapers/PDF/B.WhitePaperVol3-2002-Iss2.pdf*

Intercultural communication: What is culture? (2004). *Seattle Times,* (January 23).

Jacobs, P. (1995). Tim Berners-Lee spins a complex, yet simple, Web. *Network World, 12*(7), 59-61.

Johnson, P., O'Rourke, J.B., & Owens, L. (2002) Culture and survey nonresponse. In R.M. Groves, D.A. Dillman, J.L. Eltinge, & R.J.A. Little (Eds.), *Survey nonresponse* (pp. 55-70). New York: John Wiley & Sons.

Kalekin-Fishman, D. (2004, February 15). Culture. *The Internet encyclopedia of personal construct psychology.* Retrieved July 11, 2004, from *http://www.pcp-net.org/encyclopaedia/culture.html*

Koch, N.S., & Emrey, J.A. (2001). The Internet and opinion measurement: Surveying marginalized populations. *Social Science Quarterly, 82*(1), 131-138.

Lange, L. (1995a, June 19). Untangling the World Wide Web. *Electronic Engineering Times,* (853), 108.

Lange, L. (1995b). Where's it all going? *Information Week* (536), 30-34.

McMillan, J.H. (2004). *Educational research: Fundamentals for the consumer* (4th ed.). Boston: Allyn & Bacon.

Mertler, C.A. (2003.) Patterns of response and nonresponse from teachers to traditional and Web surveys. *Practical Assessment, Research & Evaluation, 8*(22). Retrieved December 8, 2003, from *http://pareonline.net/getvn.asp?v=8&n=22*

Metcalfe, R.M. (1995). The Iway peace prize. *InfoWorld, 17*(12), 58.

Miraglia, E., Law, R., & Collins, P. (1999, May 26). Clifford Geertz, emphasizing interpretation from The Interpretation of Cultures, 1973. Retrieved July 10, 2004, from *http://www.wsu.edu:8001/vcwsu/commons/topics/culture/culture-definitions/geertz-text.html*

Mulder, G.J. (2004, March 26). Introduction to culture. *Proceedings of the Punta del Este Conference,* Uruguay. Retrieved July 23, 2004, from *http://www.dbacorporatefinance.com/presentations/Presentation%20GJM%20CULTURE.ppt*

Nielsen, J. (1997, March 15). Be succinct! Writing for the Web. Retrieved July 10, 2004, from *http://www.useit.com/alertbox/9703b.html*

Park, J. (2002). Lecture on interpretive anthropology and veiled sentiments (part one). Retrieved July 10, 2004, from *http://www.arts.auckland.ac.nz/ant/203/lectureweb141516.htm*

Quittner, J. (1999, March 29). Tim Berners-Lee. *Time 100: Scientists and thinkers.* Retrieved July 22, 2004, from *http://www.time.com/time/time100/scientist/profile/bernerslee.html*

Rich, C. (1999). Newswriting for the Web: User studies. Retrieved July 10, 2004, from *http://members.aol.com/crich13/poynter5.html*

Rousseau, E., & Sanders, A.B. (2003, June 1). Survey research methodology. Retrieved July 16, 2004, from *http://www.saem.org/meetings/03handouts/sanders.pdf*

Schonlau, M., Fricker, R.D. Jr., & Elliott, M.N. (2002). *Conducting research surveys via e-mail and the Web.* Santa Monica, CA: Rand.

Sills, S.J., & Song, C. (2002). Innovations in survey research: An application of Web-based surveys. *Social Science Computer Review, 20*(1), 22-30.

Taylor, M.C., & Saarinen, E. (1994). *Imagologies: Media philosophy.* London: Routledge.

Timmerman, A. (2002). *Introduction to the application of Web-based surveys.* (ERIC Document Reproduction Service No. ED 474 097).

Trillo, N.G. (1996). Intercultural communication: Edward T. Hall. Retrieved July 10, 2004, from *http://www2.soc.hawaii.edu/css/dept/com/resources/intercultural/Hall.html*

Trochim, W.M.K. (2004). Survey research. Retrieved July 16, 2004, from *http://www.socialresearchmethods.net/kb/survey.htm*

Vandendorpe, L. (1996). Scientist of the year weaves Web over the world. *R&D, 38*(12), 14-17.

Vehovar, V., Betagelj, Z., Manfreda, K.L., & Zaletel, M. (2002). Nonresponse in Web surveys. In R.M. Groves, D.A. Dillman, J.L. Eltinge, & R.J.A. Little (Eds.), *Survey nonresponse* (pp. 229-242). New York: John Wiley & Sons.

Web-based surveys. (2004). Responsive management. Retrieved July 10, 2004, from *http://www.responsivemanagement.com/websurveys.html*

Wikipedia. (2004, June 26). Culture. Retrieved June 25, 2004, from *http://en.wikipedia.org/wiki/Culture*

Williams, R. (1985). *Keywords: A vocabulary of culture and society*. New York : Oxford University Press.

Wolter, M. (2003, September 5). Web words: Site earns five stars when text is a treat for visitors. *Houston Business Journal*. Retrieved July 17, 2004 from *http://houston.bizjournals.com/houston/stories/2003/09/08/focus8.html*

Wright, R. (1997). The man who invented the Web: Tim Berners-Lee started a revolution, but it didn't go exactly as planned. *Time, 149*(20), 64-67.

Young, J.S. (1999, April). The next Net. Retrieved March 23, 1999, from *http://www.wired.com/wired/archive/7.04/cisco.html*

Chapter III

Computer-Adaptive Online Exit Surveys:
Conceptual and Methodological Issues

Najmuddin Shaik, University of Illinois at Urbana-Champaign, USA

Abstract

Theories of student attrition based on Tinto's Student Integration Model are limited in their ability to provide a comprehensive framework to design a computer-adaptive online exit survey. An alternative framework encompassing the overall impressions and experiences of the dropout students during their stay at the institution is used to design the exit survey. This chapter outlines the conceptual and methodological issues surrounding computer-adaptive online exit surveys, and discusses the design, development, and administration of the survey questionnaire.

Introduction

The high rate of student attrition is of concern to academic institutions because it is a significant source of revenue loss. Tinto's Student Integration Model (Tinto, 1975, 1993) emphasizes the lack of fit between the student and the institution as the key factor in student attrition. However, this model is limited in its ability to provide a framework to design a comprehensive exit survey. An alternate framework (Shaik, 2003) that attributes student attrition to divergent origins ranging from technological failure to organizational weakness forms the basis for developing a more comprehensive exit survey proposed in this chapter. The item response theory (IRT) framework is applied to customize this exit survey in order to minimize students' boredom and fatigue. The online format of the exit survey offers students the opportunity to complete the questionnaire at their convenience, while also enabling the institution to collect and analyze data in real time. This chapter discusses: (a) the significance of student attrition to the institution; (b) the nature and limitation of currently available exit surveys; (c) the need for a comprehensive computer-adaptive exit survey; (d) the conceptual and methodological issues surrounding the computer-adaptive online exit survey; and (e) the design, development, and administration of the survey questionnaire.

Student Attrition

Between 1880 and 1980, the attrition rate of all higher education students in the U.S. was around 45% (Tinto, 1982), marginally lower than the rate in other countries for the same period. The Consortium for Student Retention Data Exchange (CSRDE, 2001) study found the attrition rate to be 20% for all member institutions, 13% for selective institutions (SAT scores above 1,100), and 31% for less-selective institutions (SAT scores below 990). The attrition rates for distance learning programs are even higher than those for the traditional on-campus programs and courses (Rovai, 2002).

Student attrition results in significant direct and indirect costs to the institution. A marginal increase in student retention would result in a significant gain in revenue to the institution. For example, a public institution in the U.S. with a freshman enrollment of 2,000 and a dropout rate of 30% can save $1 million for a 10% increase in retention (Noel-Levitz, 2004). Low retention rates may lead potential students and donors to question the quality and credibility of the institution and, if not addressed, can have serious consequences for the long-term success of the institution (McLaughlin, Brozovsky, & McLaughlin, 1998). According to Filkins, Kehoe, and McLaughlin (2001):

> That retention is an important issue seems beyond debate, given that a variety of federal, state, and private consortia request the reporting of these data. Also retention data are being used as indicators of academic quality in the computation of institutional scores for the U.S. News and World Report annual college rankings. (p. 3)

Assessment Instruments

Surveys are an integral part of university assessment and evaluation activities. Instructor and course evaluation questionnaires administered at the end of each course, program evaluation questionnaires administered to seniors prior to graduation, and alumni surveys are the primary sources of student assessment data. For example, at the University of Illinois at Urbana-Champaign (2004), the format of the instructor and course evaluation questionnaire includes a core set of items on "Instructor Effectiveness," "Student Learning," "Instructional Design," "Technology and Technical Support," and "Assessment (exams, quizzes)," with the option to add items to meet the specific needs of the course and the instructor. Data from the questionnaire are compiled to develop a longitudinal profile of the instructor for possible use in the tenure and promotion process. The program evaluation questionnaire addresses a variety of topics, ranging from program quality to post-graduation employment plans. Data from this questionnaire are compiled to produce summary reports for the administrative units to draw conclusions about the efficacy of the program. Alumni surveys are administered to collect program-specific information by individual departments. These assessment questionnaires are not specifically designed to address the issues of student attrition at the course or program level, even though the data are sometimes used to make inferences about student attrition. There are customized surveys relating to specific issues, such as advising and related services (Nelson & Johnson, 1997), government support services (Anderson, Halter, & Schuldt, 2001), library space (Silver & Nickel, 2002), assessing doctoral program supervisors (Benkin, Beazley, & Jordan, 2000), and restructuring teacher education programs (Whitehead, Hutchinson, Munby, Lock, & Martin, 1999).

There are a few cases where exit surveys were designed to collect data on retention, such as health care service to the elderly (Native Elder Health Care Resource Center, 2004), army services (Department of Army, 2004), teachers (Van Ry, 2002), and students (Kielty, 2004; Eastfield College, 2004). The Eastfield College (2004) questionnaire includes a checklist of 12 items. Kielty (2004) focused on feedback and retention in online classes based on a 10-item questionnaire. The Eastfield College (2004) and Kielty (2004) questionnaires are representative of the exit questionnaires administered at academic institutions and are limited in scope. They are either not developed with proper psychometric analysis or the institutions do not report the psychometric analysis of the instrument.

Regardless of the circumstances of a student's decision to drop out, learning about their perspectives and insights demonstrates the institution's respect for and acceptance of the students' decision. Exit surveys provide both diagnostic and strategic information to the institution. Students who drop out are affected by the sum total of all the experiences acquired over their stay at the institution on a variety of processes, policies, and procedures. If the process of studying the reasons for students' dropout is designed to be blame-free, then it gives students an opportunity to honestly share their perspectives on the causes of the problem and sets the stage for a continued, positive relationship with the institution. The institutions can use students' feedback to design interventions to minimize student attrition. In terms of value, the cost of an exit survey is a marginal fraction of the expense of enrolling a new student in the program (Noel-Levitz, Inc., 2004).

Computer-Adaptive Online Exit Survey

Theoretical Bases for the Computer-Adaptive Online Exit Survey

Tinto's Student Integration Model (Tinto, 1975, 1993) and Bean's Student Attrition Model (Bean, 1980, 1990) have emerged as the leading models to explain and predict dropout phenomena. Tinto's model emphasizes the lack of fit between the student and the institution as the key factor in student attrition. Bean's model emphasizes that students' beliefs about their experiences at the institution influence their decision to dropout. Based on the synthesis of the research on student attrition, Filkins et al. (2001) identified factors influencing student attrition, including academic aptitude, student-faculty interactions, student services, financial factors, and learning communities. Interactions among these factors are also identified as influencing student attrition (Rovai, 2003). The issue of student attrition has also been researched using different strata within the student population, including minority students, commuter students, graduate students, two-year college students, transfer students, and non-traditional students (Filkins et al., 2001). Processes at different levels in the organizational hierarchy, including recruitment and admissions, orientation (Robinson, Burns, & Gaw, 1996), advising (Cuseo, 2003), student services (Turner & Berry, 2000), and the teaching and the learning environment (Tinto, 1997), have a significant influence on student retention (see "Appendix A: Student Retention Components"). From a theoretical perspective, there is a need for a holistic approach to student retention. Shaik (2003) integrated all these factors into a theoretical framework that is used as a basis for developing the exit questionnaire discussed in this chapter.

An important shortcoming of applied research on student retention has been the absence of a standardized psychometrically sound questionnaire with validated constructs and a transparent research methodology (Draper, 2003). In the absence of such a questionnaire, researchers often resort to customized instruments, which make it difficult to evaluate competing theories and validate empirical research. From a broader research perspective, a standardized exit questionnaire would enable researchers to move beyond the "what" question to "why" questions. Besides having a significant diagnostic potential, a standardized instrument also allows researchers to test the theoretical constructs and contribute toward bridging the gap between theory and practice, and provides administrators information to guide interventions aimed at increasing student retention. A definition of dropout that can be uniformly applied across institutions is essential for determining the target group to whom the exit survey should be administered.

Definition of Dropout

For applied research on student attrition to be useful, there needs to be a consensus on the definition of dropout. The terms *attrition, departure,* and *withdrawal* have been used interchangeably in the literature (Leys, 1999). Seidman (1996) reflectively asks:

Are we defining retention/attrition meaningfully to give us an opportunity to measure our results accurately? I do not think so. There is no standard definition of retention and until we develop one and apply it nationally, we will continue to get conflicting and inaccurate results [regarding] our interventions. (p. 19)

Failing to complete one full year of a freshman program of study (CSRDE, 2001) has been used as an indicator of student attrition. In the absence of such data, graduation rates (Lajubutu & Yang, 1998) have been used as a proxy for drawing inferences about student attrition. Unlike the traditional students whose primary goal is to graduate with a degree, many non-traditional students may already have a degree and may be enrolling to acquire a skill or earn transfer credits (Karp & Parker, 2001). It is also common for students to have had multiple transfers between institutions (Kearney, Townsend, & Kearney, 1995), enroll part time, or temporarily stop-out. As a result, a definition based on graduation or completion of freshman year presents an inaccurate view of retention (Porter, 1999; Karp & Parker, 2001).

An alternative is to define retention at the course level. If the student continues in the course beyond the course drop deadline, then it is an indicator of the student's intention to complete the course. This definition accounts for both the traditional and non-traditional students with course-specific goals that may include learning a specific skill, earning transfer credits, and successfully completing the course.

Goal of the Computer-Adaptive Online Exit Survey

The goal of the computer-adaptive student exit survey is to gather meaningful data on institutional policies, procedures, and processes that affect student attrition. The survey should encompass the overall impressions and experiences of the dropout students during their stay at the institution regarding recruitment, admissions, orientation, advising, student services, faculty services, and the teaching and learning environment.

Adaptive Questionnaires

Typical online versions of instructor and course evaluation questionnaires, graduating senior exit surveys, and alumni surveys are linear in format with a large predetermined set of items. These questionnaires are digital conversions of print formats administered online to facilitate data collection. For example, the short form of the Student Satisfaction Inventory ™ 4-Year College and University (Schreiner & Juillerat, 1994) includes 100 items, each to be rated on importance and satisfaction via Likert scales. Inherent to the design of these questionnaires is the tradeoff between efficiency and the length of the questionnaire. Students often are frustrated with long questionnaires because of the time needed to complete them. They are less inclined to provide meaningful and useful data, thus defeating the intended purpose of the assessment.

Current design of typical exit surveys does not take advantage of computer technologies and statistical theories that allow adaptable instruments. Academic institutions need an exit instrument that is brief and easy to complete, with a built-in algorithm to focus on what is relevant and ignore what is not in a given content. The results and the item indices should be comparable across institutions. Advances in computer technology and statistical theories have facilitated the development of computer-adaptive assessment instruments in a number of domains, including ability achievement testing, language proficiency, reading comprehension, classification problems, and health outcomes (Wainer, 2000). These instruments are generally based on IRT frameworks (Hambleton, Swaminathan, & Rogers, 1991; Embretson & Reise, 2000) that target the location of an item to the latent trait of the person. Efficiency is realized by customizing the instrument to the individual. The process is adaptive to the individual and administers a subset of items to obtain an efficient and accurate estimate of the latent trait. Computer-adaptive questionnaires are self-paced and short, reducing students' fatigue and time normally associated with fixed-form questionnaires (Rudner, 1998; Linacre, 2000). Developing a computer-adaptive online exit survey based on IRT methodologies requires: (a) a secure and reliable technology infrastructure, (b) a calibrated item bank, and (c) an assessment algorithm.

Computer Technology Infrastructure

The computer technology for the online exit survey application discussed in this chapter is based on a three-tier architecture consisting of the client tier, middle tier, and the data storage tier (see "Appendix B: Exit Survey Three-Tier System Architecture"). It is intended to facilitate upgrades as requirements or technology change. Conceptually the three tiers can run on a single machine or on multiple machines depending on the scale of the operations. The user interface resides on the client workstation and is responsible for getting data from the user and presenting data to the user. The application logic is on the middle tier. It issues requests to the database server, performs business logic processing, and sends responses to the client. The data are stored on the database server which manages the data and performs operations on data upon requests from the application server. Security is implemented through the security firewall to prevent unauthorized access to institutional data and system resources. The system is also programmed to accept requests for system resources from trusted ports. An additional level of security is built through the user authentication system.

The feasibility of online exit surveys depends on both the technology infrastructure and the personnel to manage the system. Only a small percentage of post-secondary institutions in the U.S. may lack sufficient technology infrastructure and personnel to manage another online application such as the exit survey. For a majority of post-secondary institutions in the U.S., addition of another application will have a marginal effect on the system resources.

Item Bank

An item bank is a collection of calibrated items stored in a database operated and managed by the database management system (DBMS). In relational DBMSs, such as Oracle and Microsoft SQL, each item is described by multiple attributes, and a collection of items are organized into a table. The DBMS dictates the specifics of the cataloging and organization of items. It also manages user access to items from the item bank in the database. Construction of an item bank is a multi-step process and involves: (a) writing and pre-testing items, (b) item calibration, (c) coding the items, and (d) loading calibrated items to the database.

A major impediment to the computer-adaptive exit survey is the amount of time and resources required to develop a calibrated item bank (Rudner, 1998; Linacre, 2000). An item pool of 200 is recommended for an item bank (Rudner, 1998). For a satisfactory implementation of the exit survey, an item pool larger than 200 is needed to balance the content. One solution is to generate pools of items from alumni surveys, graduating senior exit surveys, and the instructor and course evaluation surveys. Content experts can help select and identify relevant items and the response formats from the surveys to match the constructs associated with recruitment and admissions, registration, orientation, student advising, student services, and the instructional environment. Each item is evaluated for relevance, clarity, conciseness, and cultural bias towards any sub-group.

Exploratory (EFA) and confirmatory (CFA) factor analysis procedures are needed to evaluate the construct validity of the instrument and test the unidimensionality of the latent variable (Hays, Morales, & Reise, 2000; Ware, Bjorner, & Kosinski, 2000). EFA with principal-axis factoring, followed by varimax and promax rotations, help determine the appropriate number of factors to retain. EFA is data driven and does not make any assumptions about the number of factors, which makes it a helpful tool to confirm loosely constructed models underlying data. According to Byrne (1998), EFA is limited in its ability to: (a) yield unique factorial solutions, (b) define a testable model, (c) assess the extent to which a hypothesized model fits the data, and (d) suggest alternative parameterization of model improvement. Measurement models from a structural equation perspective focus on the specification of measurement model. CFA based on structural equation modeling readily yields this information, thus providing a more powerful test of factorial validity (Byrne, 1998). The factor structures derived from EFA can be tested with the maximum likelihood estimation (MLE) procedures using the LISREL program. Because of the sensitivity of the chi-square measure to sample size, the goodness of fit of the hypothesized CFA model needs to be assessed on multiple criteria (Thompson & Daniel, 1996), reflecting statistical, practical, and theoretical considerations, including numerous fit indices (Byrne, 1998). A calibrated item bank is the basis for constructing individualized questionnaires. A large sample is required for item calibration, and sometimes it is split into calibration and validation samples. A measurement model is used to calibrate the items in the item bank. The calibration sample is used to estimate the item parameters and assess the model fit to the data.

IRT (Hambleton et al., 1991; Embretson & Reise, 2000) provides a methodology to describe the measurement properties of an item and determine the latent trait of the individual. It is based on a mathematical relationship between latent traits and item responses, and assumes that latent traits can be ranked along a continuum. IRT models are common in applications with dichotomous data in which a higher level of latent trait is associated with a higher item score. Individuals with a higher score are considered to have a higher level of proficiency relative to individuals with a lower score. The latent dimension of interest in the exit survey is the level of dissatisfaction or disagreement with institutional policies, procedures, and processes, in addition to personal factors that contribute to students' decisions to drop out. The goal is to measure the students' latent propensity to drop out by the responses to the items.

The graded response model (GRM), partial credit model (PCM), or the generalized partial credit model (GPCM) are generally proposed for applications with polytomous or Likert scale data, since these models also associate a higher level of latent trait with higher item score. Roberts and Laughlin (1996) proposed the unfolding IRT models as an alternative to the "cumulative" IRT models because graded disagree-agree responses are more consistent with an unfolding model of the response process rather than the cumulative model. In the unfolding IRT model, a higher item score indicates that the individual is close to a given item on the latent continuum. The most general of these models is called the Generalized Graded Unfolding Model (GGUM) (Roberts, 2001). According to Roberts (2000):

> *A single-peaked, nonmonotonic response function is the key feature that distinguishes unfolding IRT models from traditional, 'cumulative' IRT models. This response function suggests that a higher item score is more likely to the extent that an individual is located close to a given item on the underlying continuum. In contrast, cumulative IRT models imply that a higher item score is more likely when the location of the individual exceeds that for the item on the latent continuum.*

In the absence of a clear consensus regarding the choice of model, Ware et al. (2000) have suggested fitting the PCM model to the data in order to take advantage of the properties of Rasch models. If the item pool does not fit the data, then it is advisable to try a general IRT model like GPCM. If neither model fits the data, then one should try GRM or the unfolding model. The strategy is to select a model that fits the data instead of discarding the data to fit the model.

Conceptually the items for the exit survey will be organized by categories representing each of the institutional processes. Every item in the item bank will be described by a number of attributes such as item category, item description, Likert-scale score (whether the item is based on five-point or seven-point Likert scale), type of Likert scale (whether it is disagree/agree or satisfied/not satisfied type), number of item parameters, who created the item, and the date and time the item was created.

Assessment Algorithm

Adaptive assessment is a two-step process. At the core of this algorithm is the IRT estimation of students' latent traits and their match with IRT scale values of the items that dynamically determine the item selection process in response to each item. The algorithm in the first step includes a procedure for selecting an initial set of items and a scoring methodology. The second step includes an algorithm to determine the next item for the follow-up process, and a stop rule to terminate the session. The algorithm for assessing performance or ability is different than those for classification because of the distinct nature of these applications. In ability assessment, the goal is to spread the examinee across a continuum, whereas in classification the examinee is placed in one of the categories, thereby dictating a different logic between the two applications. In ability assessment applications, first an item of moderate difficulty is administered. Ability estimate is calculated based on the response to the item. Based on the current ability estimate, the next item to be administered is located from the calibrated item bank, avoiding items that do not provide any additional information, to determine the score. This process is continued until sufficient information is obtained for the predetermined stop rule to take effect. In the classification application, all candidates receive a unique but optimal set of items covering the content areas. The system is used to identify candidates for targeted interventions such as skills training or clinical care. The algorithm for applications with polytomous items is more challenging. It needs to consider a range of rating scales with a view to targeting the student at every level.

The computer-adaptive exit survey is efficient because items are selected in real time on the basis of ongoing responses without administering the same set of items. The goal is to obtain maximum information with a minimum set of items. The algorithm for the proposed computer-adaptive exit survey is a two-step process (see "Appendix C: Logic Chart"). The first step involves administering a representative set of items to all students. It includes an item from each category, and identifies and prioritizes categories in which the student has expressed concerns that resulted in the decision to drop out. Responses to this set will influence the selection of the next set of items. Items will need to be selected in those categories in which the student has expressed concerns that resulted in the student dropout decision. For the purpose of understanding the root causes of student attrition, additional information will not come from those categories in which the student has expressed no concerns. In this context such items will add very little to the information set. Items for step two will be selected based on the marginal contribution of the item to the information set. Suppose in step one, the student has expressed relatively higher satisfaction with the recruitment, teaching, and learning environment categories. Administering additional items from these categories will have a very insignificant contribution to the total information set. It will result in redundant and unnecessary questions, causing frustration and boredom to the student. The intelligent selection of items in step two is the key to making the questionnaire adaptive and efficient. It will increase the quality of responses from the student. The algorithm continually makes decisions on whether to administer another item and, if so, which item to administer next. The stop rule should be set such that the boundary of the instrument is neither too short nor too large, resulting in an accurate estimate of the latent trait. The logic of stop-rule can be based on the level of a precision indicator, a fixed set of items, time to complete the questionnaire, a target level of item score, or a combination of these factors.

Administering the Survey and Data Analysis

Any reliable data collection instrument must be free of administrative and methodological shortcomings. The administrative shortcoming of the exit survey is similar to any assessment initiative. It relates to not having a standard protocol to administer the survey, and not using the feedback from the survey (Garretson & Teel, 1982) to develop appropriate and timely policy interventions. To be useful, the exit survey needs to address these issues appropriately.

To be effective, an exit survey must be administered by an independent agency. Institutions with a separate division on evaluation and assessment, such as the Center for Teaching Excellence at the University of Illinois at Urbana-Champaign, can serve as objective third parties for administering institution-wide survey questionnaires and conducting data analysis. The exit survey should be administered by such a unit to help standardize the processes, data analysis, and reports. Outsourcing to an external third-party agency that specializes in conducting surveys is another option. It will increase the students' comfort and candor so that they are more open and honest about the reasons for dropout, resulting in richer and more useful data about attrition.

The exit survey should be administered within a short period of time following the student's choice to dropout in order to obtain objective responses and greater insights into the issues relevant to student dropout. The responses to the survey should be kept confidential, and steps should be taken to ensure confidentiality of the reports. The details students reveal about the processes can often be a catalyst for change. Multiple levels of analysis should be performed to identify trends and generate hypotheses about the underlying causes of student dropout.

There are many benefits to the online surveys. The online format of the exit survey offers students the opportunity to complete the questionnaire at their convenience, freeing the students of the time and location constraints. The anonymous nature of the online data collection process ensures candid feedback from the students. The online format also enables the institution to collect and analyze data in real time, thus saving the costs associated with data entry and data input errors.

Communicating to Students and Other Stakeholders

Academic institutions often make use of handbooks to communicate general responsibilities and expectations, as well as provide academic and non-academic information to the students. Since student attrition is a strategic issue, it should be included in the handbook. It offers a good forum to address any misgivings students may have about the exit survey. A brief statement stating the goals of the exit survey, the confidential nature of the data collection process, and the critical nature of students' feedback to develop efficient and timely policy interventions will motivate and increase participation in the assessment process. The trend analysis and reports should be submitted to an independent working group charged with the responsibility to implement effective and timely policy interventions. The analysis must be disseminated to the administrative units and instructional departments in a timely manner; otherwise, the institution would miss the opportunity to address the issue.

Culture of Retention

The exit survey process depends on honest, accurate, and unbiased perspectives regarding the attrition process from all the dropout students. Failure to receive honest and unbiased responses would compromise the validity of the responses, and would raise questions about the usefulness of the process. The institution can promote an environment for honest, accurate, and unbiased reporting (Filkins et al., 2001). There are a number of strategies that can help promote and cultivate the culture of retention. For example, a balanced emphasis on recruitment and retention will contribute toward a culture of retention. A framework that promotes and rewards quality advising services by the staff will reinforce the importance of advising and promote the culture of retention. A rewards structure that promotes quality teaching and quality research by the instructional staff contributes to enhancement of the culture of retention.

Conclusion

Retention as a strategic issue is beyond debate. Low retention rates question the quality and credibility of the institution and affect the stability of the institution. A marginal increase in retention results represents a significant gain in revenue to the institution. The instructor and course evaluation questionnaire, the program evaluation questionnaire, and the alumni surveys are not designed to uncover the root causes of retention. There is a need for a computer adaptive online exit questionnaire to help identify the root causes of student attrition, test the theoretical constructs, and contribute to bridging the gap between theory and practice. The spillover effects of the computer-adaptive exit questionnaire initiative will be felt in other areas of assessment. It would serve as an alternate model to redesign the instructor and course evaluation questionnaire, the program evaluation questionnaire, and the alumni surveys.

The start-up and maintenance costs of the technology infrastructure and the development and maintenance of sufficiently large item pools are major factors in the implementation of exit surveys. For many institutions, the infrastructure is already in place, so the additional cost will be mostly toward the development and maintenance of the item bank. Creating an initial pool of items from existing assessment questionnaires and adapting the items for the exit survey will save institutional resources. The testing algorithm for ability or proficiency testing applications has to operate with an additional set of constraints, such as content balancing and item exposure. Overexposure of an item jeopardizes the confidentiality of the item. Content balancing ensures that all examinees are tested in all the required content domains. Content balancing is not a requirement, and item exposure is not an issue in the development of exit survey questionnaire. Assessment instruments dealing with ability testing are proprietary. The exit survey questionnaire is not required to follow the proprietary model. On the contrary, academic institutions can benefit from inter-institutional collaboration to develop and share the item bank. It will reduce costs and benefit the collaborating partners.

Future Directions

The World Wide Web Consortium (W3C) provides Web content accessibility guidelines (WCAG) to promote accessibility and make Web content accessible to people with disabilities. The online exit survey application should be designed to meet the W3C guidelines so that it is not browser specific, but is free of external environmental constraints. The goal is to enable participation by all dropout students. With the current pace of advancement of digital technologies, mobile and handheld devices will substantially reduce the cost of delivering online assessment in the near future and make it even more accessible to the students. This will provide additional delivery modes and a new set of challenges to develop and administer online assessment instruments. With inter-institutional collaboration it will be feasible and cost effective to scale the calibrated item bank to regional or national levels, granting access to all academic institutions faced with similar challenges. Computerized adaptive exit surveys in the current form do not include the option to go back and review and possibly change any of the responses to previously administered items. Since this is not a high-stake questionnaire, the issue of item review should be researched and carefully reviewed for future implementation.

Retention decisions are the result of multiple factors involving different stakeholders in the institution. While the student group is the primary source of information on institutional policies, procedures, and processes that influence their dropout decisions, additional perspectives on student attrition are desirable to obtain a better understanding of the causes of the student attrition. Similar surveys need to be developed and administered to faculty, academic staff, administrative staff, and any other personnel associated with the student attrition process. From a methodological point of view, it is necessary to triangulate data from multiple perspectives to minimize individual biases.

References

Anderson, S., Halter, A., & Schuldt, R. (2001). Support service use patterns by early TANF leavers. *New Directions for Evaluation, 91,* 87-100

Bean, J.P. (1980). Dropouts and turnover: The synthesis and test of a causal model of student attrition. *Research in Higher Education, 12,* 155-187.

Bean, J.P. (1990). Why students leave: Insights from research. In D. Hossler (Ed.), *The strategic management of college enrollments* (pp. 147-169). San Francisco: Jossey-Bass.

Benkin, E., Beazley, J., & Jordan, P. (2000). Doctoral recipients rate their dissertation chairs: Analysis by gender. *Graduate Focus: Issues in Graduate Education at UCLA* (Eric Document ED 464 576).

Byrne, B.M. (1998). *Structural equation modeling with lisrel, prelis, and simplis: Basic concepts, applications, and programming.* Mahwah, NJ: Lawrence Erlbaum.

CSRDE (Consortium for Student Retention Data Exchange). (2001). Executive summary. 2000-2001 CSRDE report: The retention and graduation rates in 344 colleges and universities. Retrieved December 11, 2001, from *http://www.occe.ou.edu/csrde/index.html*

Cuseo, J. (2003). Academic advisement and student retention: Empirical connections and systemic interventions. Retrieved August 2, 2004, from *http://www.brevard.edu/fyc/listserv/remarks/cuseorentation.htm*

Department of the Army. (2004). Exit survey. Office of Assistant Secretary, Department of Army, Washington, DC. Retrieved December 10, 2004, from *http://cpol.army.mil/survey/exitsurvey/survey.html*

Draper, S.W. (2003). Tinto's model of student retention. Retrieved August 2, 2004, from *http://www.psy.gla.ac.uk/~steve/localed/tinto.html*

Eastfield College. (2004). Withdrawal/exit survey form. Retrieved December 10, 2004, from *http://www.efc.dcccd.edu/ARI/X-SURVEY.pdf*

Embretson, S.E., & Reise, S.P. (2000). *Item Response Theory for psychologists.* Mahwah, NJ: Lawrence Erlbaum.

Filkins, J.W., Kehoe, L.E., & McLaughlin, G.W. (2001). Retention research: Issues in comparative analysis. *Proceedings of the Annual Meeting of the Association for Institutional Research,* Long Beach, CA. Retrieved August 2, 2004, from *http://oipr.depaul.edu/open/general/air_paper_01.doc*

Garretson, P., & Teel, K.S. (1982). The exit interview: Effective tool or meaningless gesture? *Personnel Journal, 59*(40), 70-77.

Hambleton, R.K., Swaminathan, H., & Rogers, J.H. (1991). *Fundamentals of item response theory.* Newbury Park, CA: Sage.

Hays, R., Morales, S., & Reise, P. (2000). Item Response Theory and health outcomes measurement in the 21st century. *Medical Care, 38*(supplement II), 28-42.

Karp, R., & Parker, M. (2001). The literature of first year retention. Retrieved December 10, 2004, from *http://www.clarion.edu/admin/academicaffairs/ue/trans_1st.shtml*

Kearney, G., Townsend, N., & Kearney, T. (1995). Multiple-transfer students in a public urban university: Background characteristics and interinstitutional movements. *Research in Higher Education, 36*(3), 323-344.

Kielty, L. (2004). *Feedback in distance learning: Do student perceptions of corrective feedback affect retention in distance learning?* Thesis submitted to University of South Florida. Downloaded December 10, 2004.

Lajubutu, O., & Yang, F. (1998). *Predictive factors for students' success at a mid-sized rural community college.* Bel Air, MD: Hartford Community College (Eric Document ER 422 832).

Leys, J. (1999, December). Student retention: Everybody's business. *Proceedings of the 'Educators and Planners: Symphony or Discord' Meeting of the Australasian Association for Institutional Research Conference,* Auckland, New Zealand.

Linacre, J. (2000). Computer-adaptive testing: A methodology whose time has come. Retrieved December 12, 2004, from *http://www.rasch.org/memo69.pdf*

McLaughlin, G.W., Brozovsky, P.V., & McLaughlin, J.S. (1998). Changing perspectives on student retention: A role for institutional research. *Research in Higher Education, 39*(1), 1-18.

Native Elder Health Care Resource Center. (2004). NEHCRC exit survey. University of Colorado Health Sciences Center. Retrieved December 10, 2004, from *http://www.uchsc.edu/ai/nehcrc/nehcrcqs/*

Nelson, E., & Johnson, K. (1997). A senior exit survey and its implications for advising and related services *Teaching of Psychology, 24*(2), 101-104.

Noel-Levitz, Inc. (2004). Retention savings worksheet. Retrieved August 2, 2004, from *http://www.noellevitz.com/pdfs/RetSvgsWkst.pdf*

Porter, S. (1999). Including transfer-out behavior in retention models: Using the NSLC enrollment search data. *Proceedings of the 1999 North East Association of Institutional Research Conference,* Newport, Rhode Island.

Roberts, J.S. (2000). Free software to perform IRT unfolding analysis. Retrieved August 2, 2004, from *http://www.ncme.org/news/newsdetail.ace?ID=30&ArchView=y*

Roberts, J.S. (2001, April). Equating parameter estimates from the general graded unfolding model. *Proceedings of the Annual Meeting of the American Educational Research Association,* Seattle, WA (Eric Document ED 457 187).

Roberts, J.S., & Laughlin, J.E. (1996, April). *The graded unfolding model: A unidimensional item response model for unfolding graded responses.* Princeton, NJ: Educational Testing Service (Eric Document ED 403 276).

Robinson, D., Burns, C., & Gaw, K. (1996). Orientation programs: A foundation for students' learning and success. *New Directions for Students Services, 75,* 55-68.

Rovai, A.P. (2002). Building sense of community at a distance. *International Review of Research in Open and Distance Learning.* Retrieved August 2, 2004, from *http://www.unescobkk.org/ips/ea/eadoc/BuildingSense.pdf*

Rovai, A.P. (2003). In search of higher persistence rates in distance education online programs (electronic version). *The Internet and Higher Education, 6*(1), 1-16.

Rudner, L. (1998, November). An online, interactive, computer adaptive testing tutorial. Retrieved December 10, 2004, from *http://edres.org/scripts/cat/catdemo.htm*

Schreiner, L.A., & Juillerat, S.L. (1994). Student Satisfaction Inventory ™ 4-year college and university version. Retrieved August 2, 2004, from *http://survey.noellevitz.com/index.cfm*

Seidman, A. (1996). Retention revisited: RET = E Id + (E + I + C)Iv. *College and University, 71*(4), 18-20. Retrieved August 2, 2004, from *http://www.cscsr.org/article_retention_revisited.htm*

Shaik, N. (2003, November). An alternative theoretical framework to analyze failures in decision making: Application to student dropout in asynchronous learning environments. *Proceedings of the 9th Sloan-C International Conference on Asynchronous Learning Networks,* Orlando, FL.

Silver, S., & Nickel, L. (2002). *Surveying user activity as a tool for space planning in an academic library.* University of South Florida (Eric Document ED 468 929).

Thompson, B., & Daniel, L.G. (1996). Factor analytic evidence for the construct validity of scores: A historical overview and some guidelines. *Educational and Psychological Measurement, 56,* 197-208.

Tinto, V. (1975). Dropout from higher education: A theoretical synthesis of recent research. *Review of Educational Research, 45,* 89-125.

Tinto, V. (1982). Limits of theory and practice in student attrition. *Journal of Higher Education, 53*(6), 687-700.

Tinto, V. (1993). *Leaving college: Rethinking the causes and cures of student attrition.* Chicago: University of Chicago Press.

Tinto, V. (1997). Classrooms as communities: Exploring the educational character of student persistence. *Journal of Higher Education, 68,* 599-623.

Turner, A.L., & Berry, T.R. (2000). Counseling center contributions to student retention and graduation: A longitudinal assessment. *Journal of College Student Development, 41*(6), 627-640.

University of Illinois at Urbana-Champaign. (2004). Instructor and course evaluation system online catalog. Retrieved August 2, 2004, from *http://www.oir.uiuc.edu/dme/ices/catalog/*

Van Ry, V. (2002, January). Exit survey of teachers in Kern County, California. Kern County Superintendent of Schools. Retrieved December 10, 2004, from *http://wwwstatic.kern.org/gems/research/ExitSurveyFinal.pdf*

Wainer, H. (2000). *Computerized adaptive testing: A primer* (2nd edition). Mahwah, NJ: Lawrence Erlbaum.

Ware, J., Bjorner, J., & Kosinski, M. (2000). Practical implications of Item Response Theory and Computerized Adaptive Testing. *Medical Care, 38*(9), Supplement II, 73-82.

Whitehead, L., Hutchinson, N., Munby, H., Lock, C, & Martin, A.(1999, Spring). Exit evaluation of the pilot project for a restructured preservice teacher education program. *Teacher Education Quarterly, 26*(2), 79-88.

Appendix A:
Student Retention Components

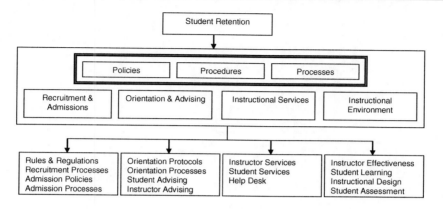

Appendix B: Exit Survey
Three-Tier System Architecture

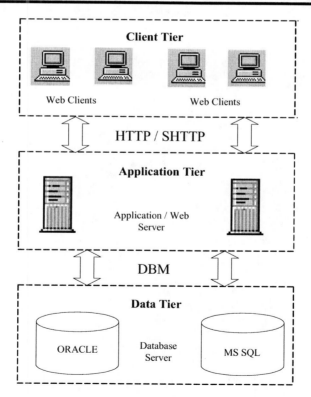

Appendix C: Logic Chart

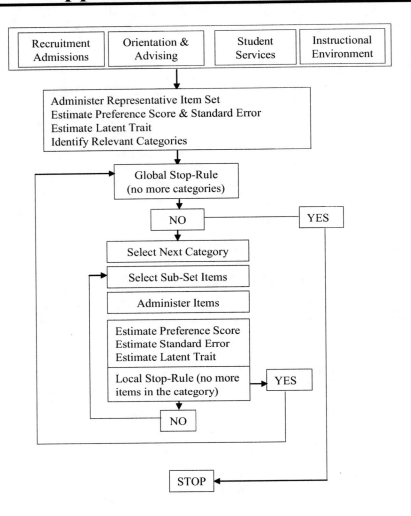

Chapter IV

Quality Standards for E-Learning:
The Demand-Driven Learning Model

Krista Breithaupt, American Institute for CPAs, USA

Colla J. MacDonald, University of Ottawa, Canada

Abstract

This study compliments the theoretical work that led to the development of a new e-learning model, termed the Demand-Driven Learning Model (DDLM), and describes the development of a survey that can be used to determine the quality of e-learning programs. Scores from the survey are intended to provide a useful indication of the extent to which e-learning programs provide evidence of quality defined by the DDLM. In this way, the DDLM represents a proposed standard for the quality of online learning. The authors also provide a description of the development and pilot study of the survey measure, and propose this survey as a means of assessing the quality of e-learning programs against this standard.

Introduction

The tension between improving employee skills and meeting the daily demands in the organization has led employers in many industries to endorse, fund, and even design and deliver alternative education and training programs. Internet, online or e-learning, is becoming a popular way to address this issue whereby staff can pursue higher credentials without interrupting their service to employers. However, a close examination of new e-learning programs has indicated a critical gap between the use of technology and sound pedagogical models (Khan, 1997; Salmon, 2000; Willis, 2000). Several researchers have written about the need for quality standards to ensure the integrity of e-learning programs (Benson, 2003; Carstens & Worsfold, 2000; DeBard & Guidera, 2000; Salmon & Speck, 2000).

This study complements the theoretical work that led to the development of a new e-learning model, termed the Demand-Driven Learning Model (DDLM), and describes the development of a survey that can be used to determine the quality of e-learning programs. Scores from the survey are intended to provide a useful indication of the extent to which e-learning programs provide evidence of quality defined by the DDLM. In this way, the DDLM represents a proposed standard for the quality of online learning. The authors also provide a conceptually sound tool (survey measure) that may be used to assess the quality of any application of e-learning against this standard. Specifically, research represented here describes the pilot study of the DDLM and survey tool used to assess three e-learning programs, and poses three research questions:

1.   Is there evidence of score validity and reliability?
2.   Is the expected relationship between constructs in the DDLM present in pilot study response data?
3.   How do the online programs in the pilot study compare based on the DDLM?

The development process that resulted in the DDLM required collaboration between academics and experts from commercial, private, and public industries. An early draft describing the DDLM was presented to a panel of industry experts. Present at this meeting were representatives from highly respected national and international commercial organizations influential in online technology and education, including Nortel Networks, Alcatel, Lucent Technologies, Cisco Systems, Arthur D. Little Business School, Learnsoft Corporation, and KGMP Consulting Services. These representatives reacted with enthusiasm and interest in the DDLM, and also provided recommendations for future refinement and utility. Specifically, the authors identified a need to reflect in the DDLM practical and logistic features required for success in e-learning. These elements were identified during the process of planning the pilot study, and continually defining and refining the DDLM survey through ongoing consultations with industry representatives over a two-year period.

After a brief introduction to the DDLM and the e-learning context, a short description of the initial development of the online survey is provided, followed by the results from the authors' pilot study with three e-learning programs. These results furnish some initial evidence for the validity of the DDLM and the utility of the DDLM online survey used to examine program quality. The model and survey are intended to support a confident evaluation of a wide range of e-learning programs.

DDLM

The DDLM is grounded within a constructivist framework and defined by five main components: the quality standard of superior structure; three consumer demands of content, delivery, and service; and learner outcomes. Further, it is framed within frequent opportunities for ongoing adaptation, improvement, and evaluation. Superior structure can be viewed as a standard of high quality attained only by e-learning programs that meet specific requirements. The elements of superior structure are required for excellence in content, delivery, and service. As a result, learner outcomes will be optimized (MacDonald, Stodel, Farres, Breithaupt, & Gabriel, 2001). The DDLM has the following distinguishing features that make it an appropriate quality standard for adult e-learning. The DDLM:

- emerged out of a concern for the lack of standards and validated models for e-learning, specifically e-learning for adults;

- was built specifically to address the needs and concerns of adult learners and educators in this climate of rapid technological advancement;

- was created with a specific purpose: to support and guide e-learning designers, developers, evaluators, and facilitators, and ensure the most significant challenges of e-learning are anticipated and met in practice;

- was developed through a collaborative process between academics and industry experts to ensure the model was relevant and practical for learners, secondary beneficiaries (employers), and educators (including program designers, developers, and evaluators); and

- includes an "outcomes" component to ensure a comprehensive evaluation of e-learning.

The dynamic relationship between DDLM constructs may be presented graphically (see Figure 1). The five central constructs in the DDLM are superior structure, content, delivery, service, and outcomes. These are organized in the graphic to emphasize the interplay between outcomes, content, delivery, and service as indicators of the more global quality standard, superior structure. Two unifying themes are represented as text on the left and right sides of the graphic to indicate the importance of ongoing monitoring and adaptation in establishing and measuring quality.

Utility of the model was a key principle in conceptualization of the DDLM, and in the identification of a means of evaluating e-learning programs against the DDLM standard. To ensure utility, it was considered essential that any measure of DDLM features must be easily applicable in a variety of e-learning programs. An online survey was developed to operationalize each construct to define the DDLM, because this mode of assessment fit well within the context of distance learning programs. The development of the survey and the pilot study in three e-learning programs is discussed in the final section of this chapter. A detailed research report is available in MacDonald, Breithaupt, Stodel, Farres, and Gabriel (2002).

Figure 1. Demand-Driven Learning Model (DDLM)

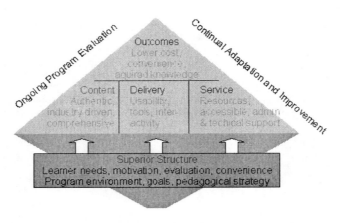

Demand -Driven Learning Model (DDLM)

Context of E-Learning

The rapid development of the Internet from a text-only medium to an expanding multimedia communication system has increased and diversified delivery mechanisms of quality education. These developments are challenging common conceptions of the teaching-learning process (Bonk & Cummings, 1998). Accompanying this increased use of technology is an increase in the expectations of all stakeholders (Baker & O'Neil, 1994). As a result, quality assurance, defensibility, and accountability in e-learning programs have become critical. Consumers and educators demand that e-learning programs be evaluated to determine and guarantee effectiveness and high quality.

Educators and researchers have voiced concern over the lack of appropriately rigorous evaluation studies of e-learning programs (e.g., Cheung, 1998; Lockyer, Patterson, & Harper, 1999; Reeves & Reeves, 1997). The dearth of e-learning evaluation efforts may be in part a result of competing priorities. Funding into the development and deployment of novel programs may be emphasized, while resources are not tagged to support expertise for evaluation (Wills & Alexander, 2000). In addition, evaluation methods used in more conventional programs may not be appropriate for e-learning courses and programs. New methodologies need to be devised (Zuniga & Pease, 1998).

Some researchers have made steps towards developing evaluation instruments to assess e-learning programs (e.g., Biner, 1993; Cheung, 1998; Stanford, 1997). Such instruments are most often developed to assess only specific program content and are not suitable for wider application. Perhaps this lack of generic utility is the reason these measures are usually not subjected to rigorous psychometric study. There appears to be a need in many fields of education for validated online measures with desirable psychometric properties.

Any study of the validity of a generic measure of the quality of e-learning must be referenced to an underlying theoretical framework. To this end, the DDLM was used as the basis for an evaluation measure that could be administered online to examine the effectiveness of e-learning programs from any discipline. The authors intend this measure to be applied easily for immediate feedback to program providers. This will permit rapid identification of strengths and weaknesses of various programs, and afford timely intervention and resource allocation. The purpose of sharing this work is to place this measure and the development effort under the scrutiny of educators and program researchers who might benefit from its use.

Online DDLM Survey Tool

While culling survey questions from a wide variety of sources, the authors sought to include only questions that are relevant, clear, and that elicit the expected information reflecting DDLM constructs. The survey must be as brief as possible, retaining a sufficient number of questions to gain a confident estimate of the underlying construct of interest. Close to two-thirds of the initial questions were dropped based on the authors' analysis of the pilot survey.

Once the short survey was constructed, tests of the hypothesized model and the relationship between included constructs were possible. This step of psychometric evaluation of any new survey usually requires extensive pilot testing. To date, attempts to develop online measures have had only limited success and sometimes lack scientific rigor.

The questions were targeted to elicit the learner's appraisal of the efficiency and ease of participating in the program, and the quality and relevance of curriculum content. Questions in the content, delivery, and structure sections were accompanied by five response options: never, rarely, sometimes, often, and always. Questions in the outcomes area were presented with four response options: strongly disagree, disagree, agree, and strongly agree. Higher scores were associated with positive responses (e.g., always = 5, strongly agree = 4). The original pilot instrument (long survey) is available from the authors. The short survey is appended here (Appendix A).

The survey is used to generate five scores based on the DDLM for content, delivery, service, outcomes, and superior structure. Based on the hypothesized relationships between these constructs, the superior structure scale acts as a holistic measure of desirable e-learning program features or as a high-quality standard. By contrast, the content, delivery, service, and learner outcomes can be viewed as indicators that have a logical predictive relationship to this goal.

The development work and pilot study of the DDLM survey provide appropriate initial evidence that the scores and interpretations of these scores are linked to a conceptually meaningful pedagogical framework. Practitioners may be confident in using the survey that it is explicitly based on a sound theoretical framework, and that there is evidence of score validity and reliability. Ideally, the survey could be used to evaluate any distance education program, and as the application is extended, our understanding of score properties will be improved. The DDLM is not limited to any content area, and may be used to evaluate e-learning courses and programs in any discipline.

Pilot Evaluation of Three Operational E-Learning Programs

The characteristics of participants involved in the pilot study are described in Table 1. Participants were considered eligible for the study if they were enrolled in online programs in which the program executives shared the authors' goal of gaining a better understanding of the features that make learning effective, relevant, and accessible. Participants were adult learners who were engaged in e-learning programs during the 2000-2001 academic school year. A total of 46% of learners in these programs completed the survey.

Is There Evidence for Score Validity and Reliability?

Evidence of the validity or reliability of scores derived from a survey or test can come from a variety of sources. A global definition of score validity has been offered by Messick (1993), Moss (1995), and others, whereby evidence may range from objective analyses of score properties (e.g., reliability indices, estimates of association, or dimensionality) to subjective expert reviews of the appropriateness of content. This global conception of score validity has been termed construct validity, and can be applied to the construction of and evaluation of measurement instruments (AERA, APA, & NCME, 1999). In this research, a variety of methods was used to assess the validity of interpretations that might be made from the DDLM survey. These began with the selection of questions by experts in practice and educational settings, and the theoretical work that determined the constructs intended for measurement. The pilot study afforded

Table 1. Pilot study sample demographic profile

Demographic	Program 1 N	Program 2 N	Program 3 N	Total N (%)[a]
Gender				
Male	7	14	33	54 (58)
Female	3	14	20	37 (40)
Education				
University	5	13	21	39 (42)
College	5	15	32	52 (56)
High school	2	-	-	2 (2)
Age				
<30 years	-	1	2	3 (3)
31 to 40	10	27	51	88 (95)
41 to 50	2	-	-	2 (2)
Marital Status				
Single	1	2	10	13 (14)
Single parent	1	2	1	4 (4)
Married with children	6	16	30	52 (56)
Married no children	2	8	12	22 (24)
Total Participants	12	28	53	93

an opportunity to refine the survey and also to examine some quantitative evidence for score validity.

Analysis methods were selected based on the limitations of our sample size (less than 100 participants were available for the pilot survey), and our expectation that some culling of survey items would be needed. An initial assessment of evidence of the relationship among underlying constructs in the DDLM was conducted based on the association between sub-scale scores, and with external demographic scores. The results from the pilot study, described here, can be understood as steps in survey development and as initial evidence to support the interpretation of scores from the DDLM. An independent research study would be required to support these assertions based on analysis of responses from a larger sample of students in other online learning programs.

An estimate of the strength of association between responses to an item and the total score on that scale was one criterion used to determine the contribution of items to meaningful changes in total scores. After elimination of less important items, a reliability assessment was conducted for total scores. Next, a factor analysis was used to determine which items contributed to measurement of the intended construct for each score. Less influential items were eliminated at this stage.

The original 196 items were reduced to a short survey of 59 items. The final number of items retained in each scale was: 24 items for structure, 10 items for delivery, 8 items for service, 8 items for content, and 9 items for outcomes. All scales had high reliabilities (the alpha estimate for internal consistency reliability ranged from .93 to .97 for scores on any construct). These high alpha values were confirmation that item eliminations led to greater unidimensionality of the underlying constructs. A mean score was then calculated for each of the five scales based on the short survey items.

Correlations of mean scale scores were calculated to determine if the dynamic relationship between DDLM constructs was supported. Based on the DDLM theory, it was expected that scale scores would have positive and significant correlation estimates. This expectation was met; the pattern of associations is presented in Table 2.

It is important to scale development to understand if irrelevant constructs may be contributing to the scores derived. One method of examining this possibility is by obtaining evidence of divergent validity. Divergent validity can be assessed by testing the hypothesis that extraneous indicators do not have a meaningful association with the scores on the intended construct. In our pilot study, divergent validity was tested by calculating Spearman correlations between DDLM mean scores and variables that would not be expected to have a strong association (education, age). Low non-significant correlations were found for education and age with DDLM scores. Only Program code was somewhat related to any DDLM score. The Spearman correlation was .248 for Program code, and the Content mean score. This is reasonable based on the finding that mean content scores do differ by program, and can be interpreted as support for the construct validity of DDLM scores.

Is the expected relationship between constructs in the DDLM present in pilot study response data?

Table 2. Correlations of DDLM mean scores[a]

Mean Scores	Delivery	Outcomes	Content	Structure
Delivery	1.0	.450	.459	.640
Outcomes	.450	1.0	.515	.589
Service	.359	.430	.344	.588
Content	.459	.515	1.0	.445
Structure	.640	.589	.445	1.0

[a] Pearson correlations reported here were statistically significant at p < .01. Included samples ranged from n = 70 to n = 93.

A predictive regression model was constructed to examine the direction and strength of relationships between content, outcomes, service, delivery, and superior structure scores. The first four constructs were specified as positive predictors of superior structure. The hypothesized model was statistically meaningful ($R^2 = .48$; df = 5,87; F = 16.3, $p < .01$). Delivery and service were the strongest (statistically significant) indicators of superior structure. Higher scores on these constructs resulted in higher scores on superior structure.

In addition, the data were examined to determine what construct might be used to most accurately classify programs based on the DDLM standard of high quality. Classes of structure were defined to represent traditional and transitional stages. Traditional structure classification was made if there was a superior structure mean score below 4. This response means the structure characteristic was present never, rarely, or sometimes. Mean structures at 4 or above represented ratings that meant the characteristic was present often or always, on average. A discriminant function analysis was conducted to determine the usefulness of content, delivery, and outcome mean scores in differentiating traditional from transitional programs. Results indicated the delivery score was the best differentiating variable for transitional or traditional structure, followed by content, service, and outcome scores. Based on analytic weights from this analysis applied to the construct scores, 85% of cases were correctly classified into traditional or transitional categories.

How Do the E-Learning Pilot Programs Compare Based on the DDLM?

An analysis of variance procedure was constructed to profile and contrast each e-learning program based on DDLM constructs. This analysis was conducted to test our expectation that DDLM scores were a useful way to profile differences in e-learning programs. Surprisingly, none of the scale scores were found to be a source of important differences between the three programs participating in our pilot study. However, Program 1 was highest on all mean scores, except outcomes, compared to Programs 2 and 3. Program 2 had highest mean outcome scores. The relatively small samples from each program might have reduced the statistical power and mediated some important differences that might exist. Program providers were supplied more detailed profile information representing their own achievement to inform their ongoing efforts towards high-quality e-learning standards.

Implications and Future Directions

This pilot study provided an opportunity to shorten the survey and retain desirable psychometric properties for scale scores. The short survey is intended for use with e-learning programs that have been tailored specifically to accommodate the adult learners who strive to retain their place in industry, while improving marketability and service to employers. Scores from the DDLM can be used to identify areas of strength and weaknesses (Outcomes, Content, Delivery, or Service sub-scores), or to derive a global index of program success (Superior Structure). Extending this initial study to evaluations of large e-learning programs would be essential in determining the potential scope of this contribution.

Some extensions of this pilot work have been undertaken, furnishing initial evidence that the model may be generalized. Since their conception, the DDLM and evaluation tool have been used to design, develop, deliver, and evaluate a variety of e-learning courses. The model is being used for educational programs in various healthcare and education institutions across Canada and the United States. Descriptions of these applications are available from MacDonald, Stodel, and Casimiro (in press), MacDonald and Thompson (2005), and more recently, Stodel and MacDonald (2005) and Thompson and MacDonald (2005).

Desirable qualities that comprise superior structure are consistent with the need for improved access to lifelong education opportunities for many adult learners. These adults require a combination of part-time or full-time study for retraining, advancement, career change, or response to downsizing. The DDLM quality standard is aligned with the needs of each program stakeholder; including industry sponsors and employers, learners, and academia. When superior structure is present, the program represents the balance required by working learners and their employers. The flexible online delivery structure also encourages the learner to apply skills back in the workplace between modules, as learners discuss experiences with instructors and peers online. By linking theory and practice in this way, e-learning ensures a genuine, long-lasting impact will occur in the workplace (MacDonald & Cousins, 1998).

A logical step for later studies might be to evaluate the pattern of growth in scale scores over time as e-learning programs strive to achieve superior structure. The e-learning programs that were assessed in this study appear to have similar results overall. It is likely that the e-learning programs in the authors' pilot study represent the upper level of superior structure (these groups actively partner with academics involved in moving knowledge and practice for e-learning forward). Therefore, it would be helpful to evaluate some e-learning courses and programs at earlier stages of development in order to determine the utility of the DDLM, given a variety of program limitations.

These findings provide practical insights into how to support adult learners with varying needs and capabilities as they engage in e-learning. Efficiency in meeting these needs fits the goals of both employers and learners. This knowledge will make a significant contribution to enhancing Internet-based educational programs. The DDLM is a unique and timely starting point for the implementation of meaningful quality standards for e-learning. This work may inform progress in a variety of ways, including: a) revision of business plans, management concepts, and program strategies to improve the experience and performance of adult learners in e-learning programs; b) specification of guidelines to reflect high-quality DDLM standards to allow formative evaluation of e-learning programs as they grow from traditional pedagogy and delivery; and c) creation of new e-learning programs aligned with DDLM constructs to exemplify the high-quality standard defined as superior structure.

Acknowledgments

This research is part of a three-year project funded by the Office of Learning Technologies (Department of Human Resources Development Canada, Government of Canada).

References

AERA, APA, & NCME (American Educational Research Association, American Psychological Association, & National Council for Measurement in Education). (1999). *Standards for educational and psychological testing.* Washington: AERA.

Baker, E.L., & O'Neil, H.F. (1994). *Technology assessment in education and training.* Hillsdale, NJ: Lawrence Erlbaum.

Biner, P.M. (1993). The development of an instrument to measure student attitudes toward televised courses. *The American Journal of Distance Education, 7*(1), 62-73.

Bensen, A. (2003). Dimensions of quality in online degree programs. *The American Journal of Distance Education, 17*(3), 145-159.

Bonk, C.J., & Cummings, J.A. (1998). A dozen recommendations for placing the student at the center of Web-based learning. *Educational Media International, 35*(2), 83-89.

Breithaupt, K., & MacDonald, C.J. (2003). Quality standards for e-learning: Cross-validation study of the Demand-Driven Learning Model (DDLM). *Testing International, 13*(1), 8-12.

Carstens, R.W., & Worsfold, V.L. (2000). Epilogue: A cautionary note about online classrooms. In R.E. Weiss, D.S. Knowlton, & B.W. Speck (Eds.), *Principles of effective teaching in the online classroom* (no. 84, pp. 83-87). San Francisco: Jossey-Bass.

Cheung, D. (1998). Developing a student evaluation instrument for distance teaching. *Distance Education, 19*(1), 23-42.

Conrad, D.L. (2002). Engagement, excitement, anxiety, and fear: Learners' experiences of starting an online course. *The American Journal of Distance Education, 16*(4), 205-226.

DeBard, R., & Guidera, S. (2000). Adapting asynchronous communication to meet the seven principles of effective teaching. *Journal of Educational Technology Systems, 28*(3), 219-230.

Gabriel, M.A., & MacDonald, C.J. (2002). Working together: The context of teams in an online MBA program. *Canadian Journal of Learning and Technology, 28*(2), 49-65.

Lockyer, L., Patterson, J., & Harper, B. (1999). Measuring effectiveness of health education in a Web-based learning environment: A preliminary report. *Higher Education Research and Development, 18*(2), 233-246.

MacDonald, C.J., Breithaupt, K., Stodel, E., Farres, L., & Gabriel, M.A. (2002). Evaluation of Web-based educational programs via the Demand-Driven Learning Model: A measure of Web-based learning. *International Journal of Testing, 2*(1), 35-62.

MacDonald, C.J., Stodel, E.J., & Casimiro, L. (in press). Online dementia care training for healthcare teams in continuing and long-term care facilities: A viable solution for improving quality of care and quality of life for residents. *International Journal on E-Learning.*

MacDonald, C.J, Stodel, E.J., & Coulson, I. (2004). Planning an e-learning dementia care program for healthcare teams in long-term care facilities: The learners' perspectives. *Educational Gerontology: An International Journal, 30*(10), 1-20.

MacDonald, C.J., Stodel, E.J, Farres, L.G., Breithaupt, K., & Gabriel, M.A. (2001). The Demand-Driven Learning Model: A framework for Web-based learning. *The Internet and Higher Education, 4*(1), 9-30.

MacDonald, C.J., & Cousins, J.B. (1998). Predictors and outcomes of successful product development projects. *Training Research Journal, 4,* 117-133.

MacDonald, C.J., & Gabriel, M.A. (1998). Toward a partnership model for Web-based learning. *The Internet and Higher Education, 1*(3), 203-216.

MacDonald, C.J., & Stodel, E.J. (2003). *E-learning in a team-based healthcare environment: Needs analysis report.* Unpublished manuscript.

MacDonald, C.J., & Stodel, E.J. (2004). *An e-learning dementia care program for healthcare workers in LTC facilities: Final evaluation report.* Unpublished manuscript.

MacDonald, C.J., & Thompson, T.L. (in press). Structure, content, delivery, service, and outcomes: Quality eLearning. *International Review of Research in Open and Distance Learning Journal.*

Messick, S. (1993). Validity. In R.L. Linn (Ed.), *Educational measurement* (pp. 13-103). New York: American Council on Education/Macmillan.

Moss, P.A. (1995). Themes and variations in validity theory. *Educational Measurement: Issues and Practice,* (Summer), 5-13.

Reeves, T.C., & Reeves, P.M. (1997). Effective dimensions of interactive learning on the World Wide Web. In B.H. Khan (Ed.), *Web-based instruction* (pp. 59-66). Englewood

Cliffs, NJ: Educational Technology Publications.

Salmon, G. (2000). *E-moderating: The key to teaching and learning online*. London: Kogan Page.

Stanford, S.W. (1997). Evaluating ATM technology for distance education in library and information science. *Journal of Education for Library and Information Science, 38*(3), 180-190.

Stodel, E.J., & MacDonald, C.J. (2005). *Furthering our understanding of online learning: The learners' perspectives of what is missing*. Manuscript in preparation.

Thompson, T.L., & MacDonald, C.J. (2004). *Designing quality e-learning: Challenges and implications*. Manuscript submitted for publication.

Willis, J. (2000). The maturing of constructivist instructional design: Some basic principles that can guide practice. *Educational Technology, 40*(1), 5-16.

Wills, S., & Alexander, S. (2000). Managing the introduction of technology in teaching and learning. In T. Evans & D. Nation (Eds.), *Changing university teaching: Reflections on creating educational technologies* (pp. 56-72). London: Kogan Page.

Zuniga, R.E., & Pease, P. (1998, May). Evaluating the virtual university: The Flashlight Project of International University. *Proceedings of the Annual Forum of the Association for Institutional Research,* Minneapolis, MN (ERIC Document Reproduction Service No. ED422829).

Appendix A: Short DDLM Survey

For the following questions, the following response options were available:
Never; Rarely; Sometimes; Often; Always; Undecided

[Content]
The content is...

1.   of appropriate depth and breadth

The content includes...

1.   readings which are relevant to the workplace
2.   the teaching of skills necessary to deal with authentic workplace problems
3.   strong links between business theory and workplace practice
4.   current industry problems
5.   realistically complex learning tasks which are similar to those faced in the workplace
6.   information which is applicable and adaptable to new situations
7.   current best industrial practices

[Delivery]
The online management system provides...

1.   tasks in a guided sequence (options, choices, inputs)
2.   relevant and appropriate use of technology
3.   reasonably fast download of images

Presentation of material on the site features...

1.   aesthetically pleasing graphics
2.   effective styles and displays
3.   uncluttered and concise presentation
4.   captions, labels, and legends for all visuals
5.   easy to find and use screen elements
6.   appropriate use of graphics
7.   information that stimulates imagination and curiosity

[Service]

Administrative and technical support . . .

1.   is provided by competent individuals
2.   is provided expediently

1.   Turn around time for assignments is quick.
2.   E-mails are responded to within a reasonable amount of time.
3.   Suggestions are quickly handled and responded to.
4.   Complaints are quickly handled by professors/learning facilitators.
5.   Suggestions are quickly responded to by professors/learning facilitators.
6.   Feedback is provided promptly by professors/learning facilitators.

[Superior Structure]

The course...

1.   meets my needs with respect to content
2.   employs suitable technological applications
3.   respects my experience and current knowledge
4.   meets my learning objectives

The course...

1.   engages me in the learning experience
2.   builds my confidence in problem solving and planning
3.   uses interactive technology
4.   is interactive

In the course...

1.   the learning facilitators are partners in the learning experience
2.   my opinions are considered

In the course, the professors/learning facilitators are...

1. empathetic to my needs
2. effective in creating a positive learning environment

In the course...

1. the content and learning activities support the course goals

The professor/learning facilitator...

1. facilitates self-directed learning
2. makes his/her expectations clear
3. embeds learning in realistic and relevant contexts
4. allows me to make choices with regards to my learning
5. provides sufficient practice opportunities
6. provides opportunities for support and self-reflection
7. provides opportunities for self-evaluation
8. supports exploratory learning

The assignments, tests, and evaluation exercises...

1. enhance my learning
2. highlight the steps I need to take to further my learning

1. There is access to online resources.

[Outcomes]

For the following questions, the following response options were available:
Strongly Disagree; Disagree; Agree; Strongly Agree; Undecided

The course is...

1. interesting
2. in line with my expectations

As a result of my participation in this course...

1.   I have gained more knowledge
2.   I have acquired proficiency in new techniques
3.   I have developed new skills
4.   My attitude has changed

As a result of my participation in this course, I have...

1.   applied new skills in the workplace
2.   applied new knowledge in the workplace
3.   initiated new ideas and/or projects

Chapter V

Online Course-Ratings and the Personnel Evaluation Standards

Susan J. Clark, Brigham Young University, USA

Christian M. Reiner, Purdue University, USA

Trav D. Johnson, Brigham Young University, USA

Abstract

Many institutions of higher education are considering the possibility of conducting student evaluations of teaching (course-ratings) online. Some campuses have already implemented online evaluation systems that collect, process, and report ratings data electronically. Information on the successes and challenges of these systems is beginning to emerge. This chapter outlines some of the most salient advantages and challenges of online student evaluations of teaching within the context of how they relate to The Personnel Evaluation Standards set forth by the Joint Committee on Standards for Educational Evaluation (JCSEE, 1988). The authors also provide suggestions for successful implementation of online evaluation systems.

Introduction

Ten more minutes and the class will be over. The professor rushes through the last two slides of the lesson, and then introduces the course-rating forms, while asking the students to give honest feedback. One minute later the professor leaves the room, and the only sound that can be heard is the scribbling of pencils as students fill in bubbles on the course-rating sheets.

Will this traditional picture of course-rating become as foreign to future students as the picture of a typewriter is to the current generation of computer-savvy students? The answer to this question will be determined in part by the degree to which the practice of rating courses online replaces traditional paper-based rating in college classrooms.

A considerable number of institutions have already partially or completely replaced their paper-based course-rating systems with an online system (Clark, 2003). Although the practice of rating courses online is still in its infancy (compared to the last 75 years of paper-based ratings), it seems appropriate to step back and review advantages and challenges associated with online course-rating. This chapter reviews online course-rating in view of how it compares to the traditional paper-based method. Because course ratings often influence faculty rank and status decisions, as well as course modification choices, this chapter is written in light of the personnel evaluation standards established by the Joint Committee on Standards for Educational Evaluation (JCSEE, 1988). Standards are included that have the most potential for highlighting differences between online and paper-based course-ratings. Also, this chapter provides a set of recommendations for those using or intending to implement online course-rating systems on their campuses.

Online Course-Rating Systems

Perhaps the most comprehensive volume to date dealing with online course-rating systems is the winter 2003 edition of *New Directions for Teaching and Learning* (Sorenson & Johnson, 2003). Within the chapters of this volume, online course-rating systems are compared to paper-based systems in five main areas: psychometric properties of ratings results; response rates; issues of security; logistics and confidentiality; and cost analysis. Based on results of various research and individual case studies, the authors list advantages of an online rating system: time savings, flexibility, quantity and quality of written comments, timelier reporting, and overall cost savings. Challenges in using an online system discussed in the volume include: low response rates, possible response bias, dependence on technology, high initial costs, data access issues, student perception of compromised anonymity, lack of control of conditions under which students complete ratings, and culture change. Evidences of these advantages and challenges are specifically cited within the subsections of this chapter as they relate to the personnel evaluation standards (JCSEE, 1988).

Paper-based course-ratings have been a vital part of instructor and course evaluation in higher education for many decades. Hoffman (2003) conducted a national survey "...to determine the extent to which institutions have adopted the Internet for data collection and reporting of student evaluations of instruction" (p. 25). In his study, Hoffman used a random sample of 500 U.S. institutions of higher education.. He found that "...paper-based evaluation remains the predominant method of data collection in face-to-face courses" (p. 28). Only 10% (26 of the 256) of those replying to the survey indicated that a campus-wide Internet system was the principal means of collecting student ratings data for all courses.

The three main functions of course-rating systems are collecting, processing, and reporting responses for student ratings of teaching. Online course-rating systems vary in the degree these functions are performed online and in the range of courses served by the system. For example, some institutions offer online course-ratings for *all* courses, while others use online course-ratings for particular departments or colleges. Some institutions collect and report student evaluations of teaching online; others only report evaluation results online, while still collecting rating data using paper forms administered in class. Online rating systems can be summarized according to the categories listed in Table 1.

The authors have identified a sample of 15 institutions with campus-wide online course-rating systems (type 5): Bates College, Lewiston, Maine; Brigham Young University, Provo, Utah; Carnegie Mellon University, Pittsburgh, Pennsylvania; Georgia Institute of Technology, Atlanta, Georgia; Hong Kong University, Hong Kong, China; Laval University, Quebec, Canada; Northwestern University, Evanston, Illinois; Polytechnic University, Brooklyn, New York; Smith College, Northampton, Massachusetts; Tel Aviv University, Tel Aviv, Israel; University of Idaho, Moscow, Idaho; University of North Texas, Fort Worth, Texas; Wellesley College, Wellesley, Massachusetts; Whitman College, Walla Walla, Washington; and Yale University, New Haven, Connecticut. In addition, many other institutions are experimenting with various aspects of online course-rating. At present, at least 25 institutions identified by the authors are using online course-rating systems for one or more academic department (type 4); more than 30 institutions use online systems to rate online and distance courses (type 3); at least 23 institutions use instructor-produced online ratings or provide online ratings for some courses, but not an entire department (type 2); other institutions only report course evaluation data online, for example, the Massachusetts Institute of Technology and the State University of New York at Buffalo (type 1) (Clark, 2003.). Profiles from institutions using online course-rating are being solicited on the OnSET (Online Student Evaluation of Teaching) Web site at *http://OnSET.byu.edu.*

Table 1. Online course-rating systems

Type	Basic System Functions		
	Data Collection	Data Processing	Results Reporting
1	Paper-based collection only	Scanned sheets	Online reporting of paper-based results
2	Limited to individual instructors' courses	Spreadsheet	NONE (instructor uses results only)
3	Online and distance courses only	Online	Online reporting of data collected online
4	At least an entire department participates	Online	Online results of department ratings
5	Campus-wide (100% of all courses offered)	Online	100% online

Issues and Recommendations

The Personnel Evaluation Standards (1988) offer a framework for evaluating online course-rating systems already in operation. These standards can also be used as guidelines when considering whether to develop an online system. There are 21 standards that fall into the following four main categories: propriety, utility, feasibility, and accuracy. Although each of the 21 standards can be used to evaluate online course-rating systems, this chapter will only address those standards where there is the greatest potential for differences between the use of online and paper ratings. Pertinent standards will be addressed under each of the four main categories.

Propriety

"The propriety standards require that evaluations be conducted legally, ethically, and with due regard for the welfare of evaluatees and clients of the evaluations" (JCSEE, 1988, p. 21).

> *Propriety Standard 4.* This standard relates to the emerging issue of access to online course-rating results. The standard states, "Access to reports of personnel evaluation should be limited to those individuals with a legitimate need to review and use the reports, so that appropriate use of information is assured" (JCSEE, 1988, p. 36).

This means that storing and accessing course-rating data online makes the data potentially more accessible to a broader group of people for a larger scope of purposes. Given these new possibilities for accessing the data, questions arise regarding who should have access to results or, in other words, who has a legitimate need to review and use the results from course ratings (Llewellyn, 2003).

Researchers are among those who might benefit from access to online course-rating data. However, if researchers use online-rating data for longitudinal studies, for example, the ethical question arises, when do students "…stop becoming students and start to become subjects of human research"? (Zimitat & Crebert, 2002, p. 764). Given the legal and ethical implications of conducting research that involves human subjects, colleges should clarify whether researchers can legitimately access and use results from course-ratings. Moreover, if researchers are allowed access to course-rating results, parameters should be established within which they can legitimately access and use the results. These parameters and procedures for gaining access should be communicated to all interested parties.

Students may also have an interest in accessing and using course-rating results. Some institutions already publish rating results so students can use the information to select courses (e.g., University of Colorado, Hong Kong University, University of Washington, Chicago Graduate School of Business, Northwestern University). This practice, however, is debated as an ethical and legal question encompassing such issues as free speech, academic freedom, security, and privacy (Haskell, 1997; Howell & Symbaluk, 2001). Colleges using online course-ratings should clarify whether students will be allowed to view and use course-rating results, and, if so, under what conditions.

Users of online course-ratings should not only consider what constitutes an authorized disclosure of course-rating results, but should also ensure that only those who are authorized actually access the reports. Security measures, such as firewalls and login passwords, should be in place to help deter unauthorized persons from gaining access (e.g., computer hackers and others who have no legitimate need to see the data). Moreover, special care must be taken to make sure the list of those with access is updated to reflect only currently authorized positions and individuals.

Propriety Recommendations

In summary, the following actions are recommended for those considering or implementing an online course-rating system:

1. Determine who should be authorized to access data and reports from course-ratings and for what purposes.
2. Secure the online course-rating system so that only authorized persons have access to data.
3. Communicate to relevant stakeholders (e.g., students, instructors) how confidentiality is assured.
4. Communicate to all stakeholders the criteria and processes for accessing data.

Utility Issues

"The utility standards are intended to guide evaluations so that they will be informative, timely, and influential" (JCSEE, 1988, p. 45). In comparison to paper-rating reports, online-rating reports have the potential to be more informative, timely, and influential.

> *Utility Standard 4.* This personnel evaluation standard focuses on report functionality: "Reports should be clear, timely, accurate, and germane, so that they are of practical value to the evaluatee and other appropriate audiences" (JCSEE, 1988, p. 64).

The usefulness of course-rating results depends to some degree on the timeliness of the results' availability. It often takes weeks or months before teachers receive the results of paper-based course-ratings. In a survey of the 200 most wired colleges in the United

States, 65.7% of the 105 participating colleges reported that, on average, it takes three weeks to two months before their faculty members receive paper-based course-ratings results (Hmielski, 2000). This turnaround time can be much shorter when using an online course-rating system. When turnaround time is shortened, reports can become more useful to instructors. If instructors receive the feedback before they begin their course for the next semester, they will have a chance to incorporate student feedback into the course.

The Georgia Institute of Technology has discovered some additional benefits of online reporting that can positively impact the relevance of course-rating data to its potential users (Llewellyn, 2003). Specifically, the university found the following:

1.   Specialized reports can be fairly easily programmed and made available to all users.

2.   Reports can be accessed from a personal computer.

3.   Reports are more accessible to a broader group of individuals (e.g., researchers).

4.   Data are more readily available for analysis across different types of classes and different sections.

5.   Reports can be made available immediately.

Compared to paper reporting, online reporting provides more flexibility and customization, which increases relevance to potential users and better addresses individual reporting needs.

> *Utility Standard 5.* This standard includes the follow-up and impact of the evaluation. It states: "Evaluations should be followed up so that users and evaluatees are aided to understand the results and take appropriate actions" (JCSEE, 1988, p. 67).

Online assistance for interpretation of course-rating reports may be implemented to aid users in understanding the course-ratings results. An example of an interactive sample of Brigham Young University's report is found online. In this example, users can point to a particular heading on the report to find an explanation of the statistics in that column. The interactive nature of this type of online report can facilitate interpretation of the results in a more user-friendly manner than might be accomplished through paper-based explanations.

Reports can also be used to facilitate the use of the online course-rating results for instructional improvement. Brigham Young University is preparing resources for improving instruction related to each item on the rating form and linking these resources to the rating report itself. Resource materials will be available to all faculty members and administrators. The resource materials are tiered: first are tips, second are explanations and examples, and third are original sources and other Web sites. When a faculty member is concerned about results of any particular rating item, he or she will be able to access resources immediately from the rating report. This type of direct access to resources from rating reports would be very difficult to accomplish using a paper-based reporting system. It is hoped that access and use of the resources will positively impact instruction on the Brigham Young University campus.

Online ratings lend themselves to efficient follow-up on written comments students provide on rating forms. Online ratings can help instructors effectively compile, summarize, and use students' written comments. Written comments that are typed online rather than written on paper can be searched and sorted electronically for patterns and analyzed to determine what action, if any, should be taken to improve instruction.

A survey conducted at Murdoch University in Western Australia revealed that their students' main concern regarding course ratings was what happened to rating results and whether staff made any use of the information (Ballantyne, 1999). The School of Physiotherapy at Curtin University, also in Australia, uses Course Evaluation on the Web (CEW) to process course-rating scores and collate qualitative information, enabling easier synthesis of feedback. Unit coordinators discuss the student feedback and their response to this feedback with a peer. Then a written response is posted online to show students how the school is responding to their comments (Straker & Smith, 2000). This process is facilitated by the online environment of the CEW system.

Utility Recommendations

The following actions are recommended to facilitate the utility of an online course-rating system:

1. Provide online reports of course-ratings as soon as possible after grades are posted.
2. Provide online help to assist users in understanding the ratings results.
3. Provide online resources to facilitate follow-up and use of rating results.

Feasibility Issues

"The feasibility standards call for evaluation systems that are as easy to implement as possible, efficient in their use of time and resources, adequately funded, and viable from a number of other standpoints" (JCSEE, 1988, p. 71).

> *Feasibility Standard 1.* This standard points to practical procedures of personnel evaluation. It states: "Personnel evaluation procedures should be planned and conducted so that they produce needed information while minimizing disruption and cost" (JSCEE, 1988, p. 72).

An online rating system can minimize disruption by freeing up valuable class time because, unlike paper-based course-rating, students can complete their ratings outside of class. Not only do instructors value this savings in class time, several studies have shown that students also tend to value the class time they gain through online ratings (Dommeyer, Baum, & Hanna, 2002; Johnson, 2001; Layne, DeCristoforo, & McGinty, 1999).

Having students complete the ratings outside of class not only minimizes disruption, but also tends to facilitate the production of needed information. When filling out paper forms in class, students must do so within a narrow time span (usually 10 to 20 minutes). In contrast, online ratings can be completed anytime over a period of weeks, and students can take as long as they like to complete individual rating forms. Several studies have shown that students using an electronic course-rating format of course-rating forms tend to provide longer and more frequent written responses than students using the paper-based system in class (Hardy, 2003; Hmielski & Champagne, 2000; Johnson, 2001; Layne et al., 1999).

The greater length and frequency of written responses may be due to students feeling less rushed in giving feedback, believing that typing responses is easier and faster than writing them, and understanding that their handwriting cannot be used to identify them (Johnson, 2001; Layne et al., 1999). Students have also pointed out that online course-ratings give them more time to consider their answers in order to provide more thoughtful written responses (Johnson, 2001; Ravelli, 2000).

An online course-rating system's capacity to minimize interruption also depends on the careful and thoughtful design and implementation of the system. Feedback from people using the system is crucial for minimizing interruption. Among other things, studies to date have shown that students value online course-rating tools that are easy to use and understand, and that can be readily accessed (Layne et al., 1999; Ravelli, 2000). In a study conducted at California State University, students pointed out that it took a considerable amount of time to complete the ratings online, that the log-on process was complicated, and that they experienced computer difficulties (Dommeyer et al., 2002). To minimize disruption, the online rating system and process should be easy and quick to access and navigate.

Online course-ratings are generally perceived to be cheaper than paper-based course-ratings. Automating the course-rating process (i.e., completely converting to an online system to collect and report data) eliminates the cost of paper forms and reduces personnel costs because human involvement in the processes of collecting, entering, and reporting course-rating data is minimized. One study suggests that conducting course ratings online leads to a savings of 97% over the traditional paper-based approach (see Hmielski & Champagne, 2000). However, the generalizability of this study is questioned because it "present[s] the best case for electronic data processing and the worst case for paper-based systems" (Theall, 2000, p. 62).

The cost for paper-based course-rating can vary significantly from college to college. In response to Hmielski's survey (2000), colleges reported costs for the paper-based method ranging from $.25 per student to $4.00 per student, with a mean of $1.45 per student. However, the information provided in the survey report is inadequate for making conclusions regarding *reasons* for the differences in cost.

In order to obtain usable and comparable data about the cost of the two different course-rating methods, the contributing factors must be clarified and uniformly applied to provide a basis for valid and reliable research. One such comparison of the actual costs of the former paper-based system and the current online course-rating system was conducted at Brigham Young University (Bothell & Henderson, 2003). Results of this cost-comparison study showed that overall (i.e., considering prorated development, operating, and miscellaneous costs), the online system costs were about half of the paper-rating system costs. In particular, although development costs were much higher for the online system, operating costs of the paper-based system were a great deal more over time. Calculations of annual costs revealed that paper-based course-ratings cost about $1.06 per rating form, while online course-ratings cost about $0.47 per rating form. A benefit analysis was not reported as part of the study. Although many studies have investigated various benefits of using an online rating system (e.g., Hardy, 2003; Hmielski & Champagne, 2000; Johnson, 2001; Layne et al., 1999; Llewellyn, 2003), a review of the literature produced no reports of single studies that analyze *both* cost and benefits of an online system compared to a paper-based course-rating system.

Feasibility Standard 1 not only requires personnel evaluation procedures to minimize cost and disruption, but to also "*produce needed information*" (JSCEE, 1988, p. 72, emphasis added). In light of this requirement, current and potential future users of online course-rating should carefully compare benefits and challenges associated with online course-rating systems in light of their particular needs to determine the degree to which such systems "*produce needed information.*" The most likely threat to the ability of an online system to yield needed information is the potential for low response rates. As will be discussed under Accuracy Standard 5, online course-ratings can yield adequate response rates when appropriate strategies are implemented.

> *Feasibility Standard 3.* This standard states: "Adequate time and resources should be provided for personnel evaluation activities, so that evaluation plans can be effectively and efficiently implemented" (JCSEE, 1988, p. 79).

Converting from paper-based course-ratings to an online course-rating system requires a considerable initial investment. Money invested this way is lost for other purposes. This can be problematic considering the tight budgets within which many schools must operate. Initial set-up costs may be reduced through savings in the long run depending on the difference in reoccurring costs between the online and the paper-based systems. Colleges considering the implementation of an online course-rating system should conduct a careful cost-benefit analysis to determine whether or not the advantages of online course-ratings outweigh the initial set-up costs and other challenges associated with online course-rating.

Another important decision to make before developing an online course-rating system is whether to purchase compatible commercial products and services or to build components of the system in-house. Purchasing an online rating system may be cheaper than developing a new system (Ha & Mars, 2003). Available commercial products boast features such as customized forms and reports, real-time results, and scalability (e.g., eCourseEvaluation™, WebFOCUS™, OnlineCourseEvaluations™). In contrast, the online course-rating system used campus-wide at Brigham Young University was developed onsite over a three-year period from pilot to full-scale implementation. This in-house rating system provided maximum flexibility and compatibility with other campus systems and databases; however, it also required high initial set-up costs and resulted in some periodic problems in service due to development glitches. In order to choose the best option for a particular institution, decision makers must weigh their university's needs and resources for developing and maintaining an online system with the costs and features of commercially available products.

Feasibility Recommendations

The following actions are recommended to help assure the feasibility of using online course-ratings.

1. Test the proposed system to insure its usability, efficiency, and accessibility.
2. Perform a cost-benefit analysis to determine the fiscal feasibility of the online system.
3. Determine whether the system should be developed in-house or acquired from an outside provider.

Accuracy Issues

"The accuracy standards require that the obtained information be technically accurate and that conclusions be linked logically to the data" (JCSEE, 1988, p. 83).

> *Accuracy Standard 4.* This standard emphasizes valid measurement: "The measurement procedures should be chosen or developed and implemented on the basis of the described role and the intended use, so that the inferences concerning the evaluatee are valid and accurate" (JCSEE, 1988, p. 98).

A valid measurement is one in which what was intended to be measured is actually measured. Accurate and valid data are determined in part by the attitudes respondents have regarding the anonymity and/or confidentiality of their responses. In comparison to paper ratings, online ratings provide some plusses and minuses in this regard. Anonymity and confidentiality are concerns of students completing course ratings. Because of these concerns, students' ratings and comments may be affected by their perceptions of possible compromises in response anonymity or confidentiality. When completing course ratings, students may experience a conflict of interest between providing honest feedback on the one hand and maintaining anonymity of their comments on the other. In a paper-based rating system, students may question the anonymity of written comments because of the possibility of instructors identifying respondents based on handwriting. This may explain why some students perceive anonymity as an advantage of online course-ratings—that is, because their handwriting cannot be used as a means of identifying them as respondents as it can be with paper-based systems (Layne et al., 1999).

However, as online course-ratings eliminate one threat to anonymity, they introduce another threat. Several studies have shown that students wonder if the origin of their online comments remains unknown because they are required to identify themselves when logging into the system (Dommeyer et al., 2002; Hardy, 2003; Layne et al., 1999). This perceived threat to anonymity may also compromise students' willingness to give honest feedback and to offer written feedback.

In order to avoid compromising the validity of online rating systems, institutions should use systems that ensure anonymity and/or confidentiality of student responses. In addition, student identification should not be linked in any way to student responses. Institutions should communicate to students how anonymity and confidentiality are secured in the system.

> *Accuracy Standard 5.* This standard deals with reliable measurement. It states: "Measurement procedures should be chosen or developed to assure reliability, so that the information obtained will provide consistent indications of the performance of the evaluatee" (JCSEE, 1988, p. 104).

Low response rates are a common concern for those using online course-rating. Response rates may be low for a number of reasons, including students' perceived lack of anonymity, lack of compulsion to complete ratings online, student apathy, inconvenience, technical problems, and time required to complete the ratings (Ballantyne, 2003; Dommeyer et al., 2002). Students are concerned that they and their peers are less likely to complete course ratings if they are asked to respond during their free time outside of class instead of during class (Hardy, 2003; Johnson, 2001; Layne et al., 1999). Response rates may also be low due to technology-related issues because the group of students responding to online course-ratings may exclude those who have poor computer skills, are limited in access to required technology, or dislike using computer technology.

Because of the often low response rates for online ratings, instructors are concerned sometimes about the reliability of data obtained via this method. They wonder to what degree the group of responding students is representative of the whole class and to what degree the results are generalizable. In other words, instructors are concerned about the impact of *response bias* on course ratings. This is an important concern given the frequent use of course ratings in determining faculty tenure and advancement.

Studies have shown that, in general, average ratings for paper-based ratings and online ratings may differ somewhat (Hardy, 2003; Johnson, 2003; Thorpe, 2002). However, there is no evidence that ratings submitted via paper are either consistently lower or higher than ratings submitted online. In the majority of cases, the average ratings for the two different methods differ between 0.1 and 0.5 points (Johnson, 2003). Ratings for the two methods can vary from course to course and from item to item for the same course (Hardy, 2003; Thorpe, 2002). Results of a study at Brigham Young University (correlating rating means and response rates of paper and online ratings) "…suggest that online ratings are much less susceptible to response-rate bias than paper-based ratings" (Johnson, 2003, p. 55).

Instructors are also concerned that the low response rates for online ratings may negatively bias written responses because students with negative opinions about the course or instructor may be more likely to respond than students with positive opinions. A study at Northwestern University, however, showed no predominance of negative comments in online ratings compared to paper-based ratings (Hardy, 2003). Nevertheless, more research is needed to clarify whether online course-rating introduces a systematic increase of negative written comments in comparison to the paper-based method.

Existing and new rating data should be analyzed to determine emerging patterns and trends of ratings over extended periods of time. For example, a teacher switching from paper-based course-ratings to online ratings may receive higher ratings using the new method. However, the higher ratings may simply be a continuation of an upward trend of the teacher's ratings over previous years. In such a case, the different ratings obtained through the two methods could be plausibly explained independent of the method used. Nevertheless, close attention should be paid to possible consistent patterns of rating differences between the two methods.

In addition to addressing the issue of possible response bias, users of online course-ratings should continue to explore and implement methods that may lead to increased response rates. Various strategies have been employed by institutions of higher learning in an attempt to boost online rating response rates. Among these are the practices of withholding students' early access to grades for those who do not complete ratings (e.g., Yale University, Wellesey College, Polytechnic University), giving students access to rating results (e.g., Northwestern University), or providing extra credit or other positive incentives to those that complete ratings. Institutions should also find ways to make the online system accessible and appealing to students who may currently not be able or willing to use it. Failure to do so will raise issues related to fairness, validity, and reliability.

Accuracy Recommendations

The authors recommend the following actions to help assure accuracy of course-ratings.

1.   Communicate to students and other users how anonymity and/or confidentiality are insured.

2.   Boost response rates with reminders, incentives, and encouragement.

3.   Analyze data from course-ratings to determine possible response bias and possible differences between online and paper-based ratings.

Future Trends

The authors expect an increased use of online course-rating in the future as more institutions convert from paper-based systems. More commercial online-rating systems will likely become available as a result of the popularity of online rating. More research is needed to adequately explore the issues related to online rating. Specific research may be conducted on online-rating results and processes. Future research may also concentrate on such issues as how procedures, results, or student comments in online ratings differ in campus-based and distance courses. Collaboration between universities and sharing of experiences will likely increase, benefiting those using or contemplating conversion to online ratings.

Although less obvious than the anticipated trends listed above, the following developments are also predicted:

1.   The use of online course-ratings for formative evaluation of instruction will increase.

2.   More institutions will elect to publish course rating results to students.

3.   Universities and colleges will provide students with more feedback on how the results of course ratings are used.

4.   Personnel evaluation standards may reflect more online course-rating issues in the future, supplying a more complete set of guidelines to decision makers.

The authors feel that collecting, processing, and reporting course-rating data online is a worthwhile endeavor for institutions that have considered propriety, utility, feasibility, and accuracy issues in their decision to convert from paper-based systems. By using the Personnel Evaluation Standards as guidelines, institutions of higher learning can make informed decisions regarding the development and implementation of their course-rating systems.

References

Ballantyne, C. (1999). Improving university teaching: Responding to feedback from students. In N. Zepke, M. Knight, L. Leach, & A. Viskovic (Eds.), *Adult learning cultures: Challenges and choices in times of change* (pp. 155-165). Wellington, Australia: WP Press.

Ballantyne, C. (2003). Online evaluations of teaching: An examination of current practice and considerations for the future. In D.L. Sorenson & T.D. Johnson (Eds.), *Online student ratings of instruction: No. 96. New directions for teaching and learning* (pp. 103-112). San Francisco: Jossey-Bass.

Bothell, T.W., & Henderson, T. (2003). Do online ratings of instruction make cent$? In D.L. Sorenson & T.D. Johnson (Eds.), *Online student ratings of instruction: No. 96. New directions for teaching and learning* (pp. 69-80). San Francisco: Jossey-Bass.

Brigham Young University. (n.d.). Sample online student ratings report. Retrieved from *http://www.byu.edu/fc/pages/tchlrnpages/samplereport.htm*

Clark, S.J. (2003, Summer). *Results on a Web search: Institutions of higher education reporting the use on online student ratings.* Provo, UT: Brigham Young University Faculty Center.

Dommeyer, C.J., Baum, P., & Hanna, R.W. (2002). College students' attitudes toward methods of collecting teaching evaluation: In-class versus online (electronic version). *Journal of Education for Business, 78*(1), 5-11.

Goodman, A., & Campbell, M. (1999). Developing appropriate administrative support for online teaching with an online unit evaluation system, Retrieved March 28, 2003, from *http://www.deakin.edu.au/~agoodman/isimade99.html*

Ha, T.S., & Mars, J. (2003). Using the Web for student evaluation of teaching (COSSET & OSTEI). Retrieved March 28, 2003, from *http://home.ust.hk/~eteval/cosset/qtlconf.pdf*

Hardy, N. (2003). Online ratings: Fact and fiction. In D.L. Sorenson & T.D. Johnson (Eds.), *Online student ratings of instruction: No. 96. New directions for teaching and learning* (pp. 31-38). San Francisco: Jossey-Bass.

Haskell, R.E. (1997a). Academic freedom, tenure, and student evaluation of faculty: Galloping polls in the 21st century. *Education Policy Analysis Archives, 5*(6). Retrieved April 5, 2002, from *http://olam.ed.asu.edu/epaa/v5n6.html*

Hmieleski, K. (2000). *Barriers to online evaluation: Surveying the nation's top 200 most wired colleges.* Unpublished manuscript report. Rensselaer Polytechnic Institute, USA.

Hmielski, K., & Champagne, M.V. (2000). Plugging in to course evaluation. *The Technology Source*. Retrieved March 28, 2003, from *http://ts.mivu.org/default.asp?show=article&id=795*

Hoffman, K.M. (2003). Online course evaluation and reporting in higher education. In D.L. Sorenson & T.D. Johnson (Eds.), *Online student ratings of instruction: No. 96. New directions for teaching and learning* (pp. 25-30). San Francisco: Jossey-Bass.

Howell, A.J., & Symbaluk, D.G. (2001). Published student ratings of instruction: Revealing and reconciling the views of students and faculty. *Journal of Educational Psychology, 93*(4), 790-796.

Johnson, T.D. (2001, September). Online student ratings: Research and possibilities. *Proceedings of the Online Assessment Conference,* Champaign, IL.

Johnson, T.D. (2003). Online student ratings: Will students respond? In D.L. Sorenson & T.D. Johnson (Eds.), *Online student ratings of instruction: No. 96. New directions for teaching and learning* (pp. 49-60). San Francisco: Jossey-Bass.

Joint Committee on Standards for Educational Evaluation. (1988). *The personnel evaluation standards: How to assess systems for evaluating educators.* Newbury Park, CA: Sage.

Layne, B.H., DeCristoforo, J.R., & McGinty, D. (1999). Electronic versus traditional student ratings of instruction (electronic version). *Research in Higher Education, 40*(2), 221-232.

Llewellyn, D.C. (2003). Online reporting of results of online student ratings. In D.L. Sorenson & T.D. Johnson (Eds.), *Online student ratings of instruction: No. 96. New directions for teaching and learning* (pp. 61-68). San Francisco: Jossey-Bass.

Online Student Evaluation of Teaching in Higher Education. (n.d.). Retrieved December 10, 2004, from *http://onset.byu.edu/OnSETinstitutions.htm*

Ravelli, B. (2000). *Anonymous online teaching assessments: Preliminary findings.* Calgary, Alberta, Canada: Mount Royal College (ERIC Document Reproduction Service No. 445069). Retrieved March 28, 2003, from *http://www.edrs.com/DocLibrary/0201/ED445069.PDF*

Sorenson, D.L. & Johnson, T.D. (Eds.). (2003). *New directions for teaching and learning: No. 96. Online student ratings of instruction.* San Francisco: Jossey-Bass.

Straker, L., & Smith, R. (2000, February 2-4). Course evaluation on the Web (CEW): A 'learning community' tool to enhance teaching and learning. In A. Herrmann & M.M. Kulski (Eds.), *Flexible futures in tertiary teaching. Proceedings of the 9th Annual Teaching and Learning Forum.* Perth, Australia: Curtin University of Technology. Retrieved from *http://lsn.curtin.edu.au/confs/tlf/tlf2000/straker.html*

Theall, M. (2000). Electronic course evaluation is not necessarily the solution. *The Technology Source,* (November/December). Retrieved March 28, 2003, from *http://ts.mivu.org/default.asp?show=article&id=823*

Thorpe, S. (2002, June). Online student evaluation of instruction: An investigation of non-response bias. *Proceedings of the 42nd Annual Forum Meeting of the Association for Institutional Research,* Toronto, Ontario, Canada. Retrieved March 28, 2003, from *http://airweb.org/forum02/550.pdf*

Zimitat, C., & Crebert, G. (2002, July 7-10). Conducting online research and evaluation. In A. Goody, J. Herrington, & M. Northcote (Eds.), *Research and development in higher education: Quality conversations* (vol. 25, pp. 761-769; electronic version). *Refereed Proceedings of the Annual International HERDSA Conference* (pp. 761-769), Perth, Western Australia. Canberra, Australia: Higher Education Research and Development Society of Australasia. Retrieved March 28, 2003, from *http://www.ecu.edu.au/conferences/herdsa/main/papers/ref/pdf/Zimitat.pdf*

Chapter VI

Case Study:
Developing a University-Wide Distance Education Evaluation Program at the University of Florida

Christopher D. Sessums, University of Florida, USA

Tracy A. Irani, University of Florida, USA

Ricky Telg, University of Florida, USA

T. Grady Roberts, Texas A&M University, USA

Abstract

To enhance quality, faculty and student satisfaction, and learning outcomes, an academic working group comprising University of Florida faculty members proposed a project to develop a valid, reliable course evaluation tool for distance education courses and programs. Components of the project included institutional benchmarking, stakeholder input, instrument development, and instrument testing. The project resulted in a course evaluation tool that is more reflective of the actual course experience than what was previously being used. The chapter concludes with a brief list of recommendations and lessons learned from the project.

Introduction

According to recent national data on distance education at postsecondary institutions, more than 68% of institutions of higher learning currently offer some form of distance education course or program (U.S. Department of Education, 2003). Growth in distance education has led to new opportunities to serve place-bound students who otherwise would not be able to access degree programs. This growth has also introduced new challenges. One major challenge is in addressing the need to reassess how distance education courses and programs are evaluated. Distance education courses, by their nature, incorporate instructional and technological components of instruction at a more synergistic level than traditional, live classes. This creates challenges for those academic units and the institution in terms of evaluation of faculty, since the technology component adds complexity to standard course evaluation techniques. As a result, academic unit administrators across the globe have been wrestling with the following questions:

1. Should student evaluations for distance education courses include items measuring the technology component?

2. How should evaluations be disseminated in a distance education course where instructors may not meet with students face-to-face?

3. Given that such courses may include diverse elements, such as multiple delivery technologies, remote sites, and use of facilitators and co-instructors, should evaluations be specific to the individual course situation? Should they be separate from the traditional class evaluations but be otherwise generic? Or should distance courses share the same evaluation form as traditional, live classes?

At many major institutions around the country, the current approved course evaluation form has been in place for many years, and as a consequence may not evaluate technology other than by a series of items focused on laboratory instruction (Roberts, Irani, Lundy, & Telg, 2004). Further, most course evaluation forms do not include questions to assess important distance education concepts, such as level of interaction, support, and facilitation. As a result, some academic units have developed their own instrumentation to evaluate their own distance education courses. From an academic and institutional standpoint, however, the utility, validity, and reliability of these instruments are questionable, and data from these instruments have typically not been reported by instructors seeking tenure and promotion.

Case Study in Course Evaluation

In December 2001, an academic working group at the University of Florida, composed of a distance learning administrator and two faculty members, proposed a project to develop a new university-wide distance education course evaluation instrument. This was in accordance with the Southern Association of Colleges and Schools' (SACS) regional accrediting guidelines for distance education program quality assurance. SACS's accrediting standards for distance education programs call for the following: (a) institutional assessment of student capability to succeed in distance education programs; (b) institutional evaluation of the educational effectiveness of its distance education programs, including assessment of student learning outcomes, student retention, and student satisfaction; and (c) institutional long-range planning, budgeting, and policy development processes that reflect consideration and evaluation of the resources essential to the viability and effectiveness of the institution's distance education program

Based on the above, the team proposed a project that would utilize academic rigor and appropriate research methodology to develop a valid and reliable course evaluation tool for distance education courses and programs. Components of the project were as follows: (a) institutional benchmarking of other institutions' efforts in student assessment and evaluation of distance programs; (b) stakeholder input, composed of a systematic program of focus groups and qualitative interviews, designed to collect data and develop buy-in from institutional stakeholders, while facilitating project development and implementation; (c) development of a distance education course evaluation instrument designed to be used for all university distance education courses; and d) instrument testing to determine reliability and validity of the instrument for use with desired student populations.

Rationale and Approach

Course evaluation can take many forms. Formative evaluation or assessment takes place during the educational activity and is used for continuous improvement, while summative evaluation or assessment is conducted at the conclusion of an educational activity to measure outcomes (Woolfolk, 1993). Educational evaluation and assessment can also be undertaken at four levels (Kirkpatrick, 1998):

1.   First-level evaluation attempts to determine student reactions.
2.   Second-level evaluation seeks to determine the amount of learning that has occurred.
3.   Third-level evaluation focuses on a change in student behavior.
4.   Fourth-level evaluation examines holistic results.

In the higher education setting, evaluating courses at the second, third, and fourth levels can be problematic, especially if course evaluation data is used for promotion and tenure decisions regarding instructors who are teaching the courses being evaluated. Given the broad range of courses offered at most institutions and the variance in academic rigor of these courses, it is nearly impossible to establish baseline data on the amount of student learning that has occurred or changes in student behavior. Thus, comparison of instructors across, or even within, disciplines would seemingly be difficult. Ehrmann and Zuniga (1997), developers of a well-known database inventory of questions for use in student evaluations of course technology, liken the problem to that of trying to find an elephant in a dark cave with a flashlight: "Seeing everything in the cave is impossible— it's too large and complex, and your flashlight (evaluation) is too weak" (p. ix).

In most higher education institutions, secondary research suggests courses are typically evaluated at the first level by assessing student reactions or attitudes toward a course they are taking. This is often achieved by a standardized evaluation instrument that is administered at the conclusion of a course for summative evaluation purposes. These instruments are often characterized by a series of Likert-type questions and may include a few open-ended questions. The challenge for the University of Florida and the project team, however, was to develop instrumentation in an academically rigorous way that would insure validity and reliability, and address course-specific elements, yet provide instrumentation that would be standardized to the point that generalizability at the institutional level was possible.

In January 2002, the University of Florida's Office of Distance, Continuing, and Executive Education authorized the project budget and timeline. With the allocated project funds, the project team was able to hire graduate assistant support, purchase equipment and software, and fund development costs and limited travel.

Phase 1: Institutional Benchmarking

The purpose of this phase of the project was to ascertain the distance education evaluation practices of peer institutions. In doing so, two groups of universities were identified as peers: land-grant universities, and Research I and Association of American Universities (AAU) universities. Additionally, an internal assessment was undertaken to determine the current practices of individual units within the University of Florida.

Land-grant institutions with active distance education programs were identified by their membership in the American Distance Education Consortium (ADEC). Although not a comprehensive list, it was deemed that ADEC member institutions were representative and could provide information necessary for this study. Given that the unit of analysis was the institution, it was necessary to identify a knowledgeable contact person for each institution. For ADEC member institutions, a list of primary contact officers (n = 57) was available and utilized for this study. Eighteen (32%) institutions responded. Participants represented a cross section of personnel involved in distance education and included instructional designers, faculty, and administrators.

Research I and AAU member institutions with active distance education programs were identified by their membership in *r1edu.org,* an organization that promotes distance education among the nation's elite universities. Membership in this organization requires Research I status, AAU membership, and participation in the Internet2 group. At the time of this study, 33 institutions were members of *r1edu.org.* Contact information was obtained for each of these universities by contacting the administrator at the provost or vice president level with responsibility for distance education. From this process, 24 individuals were nominated to participate by their respective administrators, of which 13 (54%) participated in this study. A list of participating institutions can be seen in Table 1.

Table 1. Participating universities

University of Arkansas–Pine Bluff (ADEC)	University of Maryland–Eastern Shore (ADEC)
University of California–Berkeley (R1)	College of the Menominee Nation (ADEC)
University of California–Irvine (R1)	University of Missouri–Columbia (ADEC)
University of California–Los Angeles (R1)	University of Nebraska–Lincoln (ADEC & R1)
University of California–Santa Barbara (R1)	New York University (R1)
Chief Dull Knife College (ADEC)	University of North Carolina–Chapel Hill (R1)
University of Colorado (R1)	University of Oregon (R1)
Delaware State College (ADEC)	The Pennsylvania State University (ADEC &
Florida A&M University (ADEC)	R1)
University of Idaho (ADEC)	Rutgers University (ADEC)
Indiana University (R1)	University of Tennessee (ADEC)
John Hopkins University (R1)	Texas A&M University (ADEC)
Kansas State University (ADEC)	University of Texas (R1)
University of Kentucky (ADEC)	Washington State University (ADEC)
Louisiana State University (ADEC)	West Virginia University (ADEC)

Table 2. Focus of distance education evaluation instrument(s)

Focus	Frequency	Percent
Instructors	30	97
Course Organization & Delivery	27	87
Support Services	22	71
No Evaluation Utilized	1	3

Participants were sent a questionnaire designed to ascertain their current practices in evaluating distance education. Of particular interest, participants were asked about the focus, administration, and development of their current distance education course evaluation instruments. In determining the focus of their evaluation efforts, participants were asked to indicate if they evaluated the instructor, course organization and delivery, and support services. Of the 31 institutions responding, 30 evaluated the instructor, 27 evaluated course organization and delivery, and 22 evaluated support services (see Table 2). One institution did not evaluate its distance education courses.

Participants were also asked to indicate the methodology used to administer their distance education evaluation instruments. Of the 31 institutions, 12 used only electronic

Table 3. Evaluation data collection methods

Method	Frequency	Percent
Electronically Only	12	39
Electronically & Mail	7	23
Mail Only	3	10
Electronically & In-Person	2	6
In-Person	2	6
No Evaluation Utilized	1	3
Not Indicated	4	12

Table 4. Instrument development method

Method	Frequency	Percent
Used On-Campus Evaluation Instrument	1	3
Revised On-Campus Evaluation Instrument	18	58
Designed Evaluation Instrument Specifically for Distance Education	10	32
No Evaluation Utilized	1	3
Not Indicated	1	3

means, seven used a combination of electronic and mail, three used mail only, two used a combination of electronic and in-person, and two used solely in-person methods (see Table 3). The majority of institutions (n = 21, 67%) utilized an electronic delivery method to administer the evaluation instruments.

Institutions were also asked about the method used to develop their evaluation instrument. Of the 31 institutions, one used the exact same evaluation form used in the on-campus courses, 18 revised their on-campus instrument, and 10 developed an instrument specifically for distance education courses (see Table 4).

Individual units that deliver distance education courses within the University of Florida were also asked to provide the focus, administration method, and development method of the evaluation instruments used in each of their respective programs. A list of contacts for each program (n = 7) was obtained from the Office of Distance, Continuing, and Executive Education. Six programs evaluated instructors, four evaluated course organization and delivery, and three evaluated support services (see Table 5).

University of Florida academic units were also asked to indicate the data collection method used to administer the instruments. Two programs utilized only electronic methods to administer the instrument, one used a combination of electronic and mail, and

Table 5. Focus of distance education evaluation instrument(s) (UF units)

Focus	Frequency	Percent
Instructors	6	86
Course Organization & Delivery	4	57
Support Services	3	43
No Evaluation Utilized	1	14

Table 6. Evaluation data collection methods (UF units)

Method	Frequency	Percent
Electronically Only	2	29
Electronically & Mail	1	14
Mail Only	0	0
Electronically & In-Person	1	14
In-Person	1	14
No Evaluation Utilized	1	14
Not Indicated	1	14

Table 7. Instrument development method (UF units)

Method	Frequency	Percent
Used On-Campus Evaluation Instrument	2	29
Revised On-Campus Evaluation Instrument	4	58
Designed Evaluation Instrument Specifically for Distance Education	0	0
Not Indicated	1	14

one used electronic and in-person (see Table 6). Four programs (57%) utilized an electronic method in some manner.

When developing the evaluation instruments, two UF programs used the same evaluation instrument as in on-campus courses, four made revisions to the on-campus evaluation instrument, and no programs developed an instrument specifically for distance education (see Table 7).

Phase 2: Stakeholder Input

The individual items that compose a questionnaire contribute directly to the validity and reliability of the instrument (Gall, Gall, & Borg, 2003). The "Stakeholder Input" phase sought to identify as many items as possible that contribute to student satisfaction with a distance education course. By maximizing the list of potential items, the possibility of omitting a pertinent item was greatly reduced. From an inductive perspective, this process was started without any preconceived notions of the items that must be included. It was reasoned that if at least one distance education student thought an item was important, then it was worth examining. A large-scale qualitative survey was utilized to generate these items.

The population used in this phase was all students enrolled in distance education courses during the Summer 2002 semester at the University of Florida (n = 1,269). This list was obtained from the contact person from each distance education program and represented students from six academic colleges. A random sample was drawn from this population for data collection purposes (n = 400).

Data was collected using a Web-based form. Given the geographic separation, students in the sample were contacted by e-mail, which included a link to the Web site containing the questionnaire. The Web site consisted of the informed consent and an open-ended statement: "List as many factors as you can that you personally believe could potentially affect the quality of a distance education course in any way. Please be as specific as possible." A text box was provided that allowed participants to include as many items as they deemed necessary.

In an effort to further enrich the data set, several follow-up e-mails were sent to all students in the sample to encourage their input. Data was collected until a point of redundancy in the data was achieved (Lincoln & Guba, 1985). Ultimately, 54% of the sample responded (n = 214).

The responses were analyzed to identify the maximum number of unique items. Consensus was reached that the data contained 85 relatively independent items. A broad diversity of items was generated. However, each item addressed a specific component of a distance education course.

Phase 3: Instrument Development

The next phase of this project was to identify the underlying dimensions within the 85 items identified in Phase 2. The grouping of these items into dimensions was necessary to allow for items that addressed similar components of a distance education course to be clustered together. This was especially important to allow the expert panel used to determine which items were essential and if necessary items were missing for each dimension. Consistent with the inductive nature of this project, the data were allowed to guide the creation of the dimensions without any preconceived notion of the dimensions that should be present.

The identification of underlying dimensions was undertaken independently by each of the researchers using a constant comparative method to group similar items (Glaser & Strauss, 1967). Each response was compared with the others and either placed into a category with similar responses or used to begin a new category. The results of each researcher were compared to form a consensus list of the nine underlying dimensions from the 85 items identified: Learner-Instructor Interaction, Learner-Learner Interaction, Content, Instructor, Course Organization, Support Services/Administrative Issues, Facilitator, Technical Support, and Delivery Method.

In an effort to reduce the number of items, a national panel of experts was used to determine which of the 85 items were truly essential for inclusion. Fifteen experts were identified, based on their experience with distance education. This panel included six instructional designers, six administrators, two distance education instructors, and one researcher, representing 15 different institutions. The average panel member had been involved in distance education for just over 10 years.

Panel members were mailed a questionnaire with the 85 items, separated into the nine dimensions. Using a five-point Likert-type scale (1 = Not Necessary, 5 = Essential), they were asked to indicate how essential each item was. They were also given instructions to modify the wording of any item or add additional items they deemed essential. All of the panel members returned the questionnaire for a 100% response rate.

Data collected from the Likert-type items was treated as interval data. Means and standard deviations were used in determining the degree to which an item was essential. The least essential item was "Face-to-face contact with the instructor was needed for this course," with a mean of 2.29. The most essential items were "The objectives for this course were clear" and "The assignments and tests in this course were appropriate for the objectives of the course," which both had means of 4.80.

Data were subjectively evaluated to determine which items to retain. Upon examining the data, a natural division was seen between items below and above 4.25. As such, it was decided that only items with a mean greater that 4.25 would be considered for development of the instrument. This eliminated 47 items. Panel members suggested a few wording changes on items and combining a few items, but did not add any additional items.

The next step in this phase was to compare the items recommended by the expert panel to the existing evaluation instrument utilized in on-campus courses. The objective of this process was to create a distance education evaluation instrument that was consistent with the current on-campus evaluation instrument, while reflecting the unique aspects of courses taught at a distance. Upon comparison of the two and using recommendations from the expert panel, an initial draft of the instrument was constructed that consisted of 20 questions, synthesizing and integrating the current with new items. These items were presented with an accompanying five-point Likert-type scale that ranged from "poor" to "excellent."

Phase 4: Instrument Testing

The distance education course evaluation instrument was pilot-tested twice. Five instructors representing three academic colleges were nominated by their respective administrators to test the first draft. The instrument was administered during the last two weeks of the Spring 2003 semester as a Web-based form, which was available for two weeks. Students were directed to the instrument by an e-mail with a link to the Web form. The researchers sent this e-mail to each instructor who then forwarded it to their students. To further enrich the data, these instructors were contacted post hoc for their opinions about improving the instrument and the data collection process. One-hundred-and-ninety-four students completed the first draft of the instrument. Students were also asked to indicate the amount of time they spent completing the instrument. Responses ranged from 30 seconds to 15 minutes, with a mean of just over four minutes. Anecdotal evidence suggests that students take a similar amount of time to complete the traditional in-class course evaluation instrument.

The collected data from the first pilot test were used to refine the instrument for the second pilot test. Based on input from the students and instructors in the first pilot test, a "not applicable" option was added to items that may not be pertinent to every course, and the general open-ended questions that are a component of the instrument used for on-campus courses were added. Additionally, demographic questions also were added. A complete list of items included in the final version of the instrument can be seen in Appendix I. Courses from 10 instructors, representing five academic colleges, were used for the second, final pilot testing. Data were collected from 112 students.

Table 8. Individual item alphas

Item	Alpha
Description of course objectives and assignments	.9504
Communication of ideas and information	.9493
Expression of expectations for performance in this class	.9497
Timeliness in responding to students	.9517
Timeliness in returning assignments	.9533
Respect and concern for students	.9506
Interaction opportunities with other students	.9583
Stimulation of interest in course	.9520
Coordination of the learning activities with the technology	.9518
Enthusiasm for the subject	.9529
Encouragement of independent, creative, and critical thinking	.9493
Overall rating of instructor	.9473
Overall, I rate this course as	.9499

Reliability of the instrument, as a measure of internal consistency, was evaluated using Cronbach's alpha. Items included in Part I and Part II of the instrument were treated as a construct and included in reliability analysis. The final version of the instrument yielded an alpha of .95. Individual item alphas can be seen in Table 8.

Several of the classes used in the final pilot testing of the distance education evaluation instrument also completed a traditional course evaluation instrument. Results of these evaluations were available through the University of Florida Registrar's Web site. To further establish the reliability of the instrument, similar items between the two instruments were compared. It is important to note that respondents to the distance education evaluation instrument were not randomly selected, so a statistical comparison was not possible. The results of these individual items can be seen in Table 9. Although not identical, similarities in the means for each item can be seen.

Table 9. Individual items from the on-campus and distance education evaluation instruments

Item	Course 1 (n = 26)		Course 2 (n = 213)	
	On-Campus Instrument (n = 17)	Distance Instrument (n = 14)	On-Campus Instrument (n = 200)	Distance Instrument (n = 36)
Description of course objectives and assignments	4.06	4.50	3.23	3.39
Communication of ideas and information	4.06	4.43	3.25	3.34
Expression of expectations for performance in class	4.06	4.29	3.27	3.33
Respect and concern for students	4.24	4.57	3.72	3.66
Stimulation of interest in course	4.12	4.00	3.48	3.57
Overall assessment of instructor	4.59	4.50	3.43	3.36

Table 10. Optional items

Focus	Item
Facilitator	The subject matter knowledge of the facilitator of this course
	The level of preparedness of the facilitator for each class session
	The accessibility of the facilitator
	The coordination of class activities between the facilitator and the instructor
Course Management Software (WebCT)	The organization of course materials in the course management software
	The use of message boards in this course
	The use of chat rooms in this course
Other Web-Based	The design of the course Web site(s)
	The accuracy of material on the course Web site(s)
	The level to which hyperlinks and other features on the course Web site(s) worked properly
	The quality of streaming video(s) used in this course
	The instructor's presentation skills in the streaming videos used in this course
Videotapes	The quality of video in the videotapes used in this course
	The quality of audio in the videotapes used in this course
	The accuracy of the videotapes used in this course
	The instructor's presentation skills in the videotapes used in this course
Synchronous Videoconferencing	The visual aids (slides, chalkboard, etc.) used by the instructor were easy to see.
	The video quality during videoconferencing in this course
	The audio quality during videoconferencing in this course
	The instructor's presentation skills during videoconferencing in this course
	The camera operator's ability to keep the appropriate object(s) on screen

Note: The scale for these items is Poor, Below Average, Average, Above Average, Excellent, and Not Applicable.

Optional Items

Through this research process, items specific to a distance delivery method were also identified. Although not included in the distance education evaluation instrument, they may be added as optional items if an instructor or administrator has interest in evaluating the specific delivery method(s) employed in the course. Items are available to evaluate facilitators, course management software (WebCT), other Web-based delivery modes (including streaming video), videotapes, and synchronous videoconferencing. Items may be selected as a group, or individually. A complete list of available items can be seen in Table 10.

Phase 5: Implementation

Results of this project clearly demonstrate that a reliable and valid instrument for evaluation of distance education courses has been developed which provides both functionality and flexibility to be used across the university's academic units. The optional items provide additional opportunities for instructors to utilize tested items to evaluate specific components of a distance education course. Testing also revealed that utilization of a specific instrument of distance education courses yields evaluations that are comparable to the State University System Assessment of Instruction (SUSAI), but more reflective of the actual course experience.

During the stakeholder phase of this project, faculty were asked to provide qualitative evaluative comments. Comments included the need for online Web-based delivery, authentication of respondents, concern about potentially lower course evaluations, and the desirability of keeping the instrument as close to the SUSAI as possible, while still reflecting the uniqueness of the distance setting. These questions and concerns have been addressed during the course of this project, and due to the academically rigorous way in which it was developed and tested, the resulting product is one that university faculty can have confidence in using to address their needs.

Recommendations

After the testing and research phase, project researchers developed several recommendations with respect to implementing a project similar to this one. These recommendations are based on lessons learned and are intended to serve as guidelines rather than hard, fast rules:

1. *Start on technology implementation sooner rather than later.* Since an online evaluation instrument has far-reaching effects on faculty tenure and promotion, it is no easy task making the technical aspects safe, secure, accurate, and user friendly. An early start on this side of the evaluation process will make implementation and use much easier in the long run.

2. *Be prepared to share data with faculty—but do so gingerly.* One of the important elements in establishing the credibility of the project and potential buy-in of faculty and administrators was the decision to approach the project as a formal research study, employing as rigorous a process and procedure as possible and relying on empirical research findings to guide the way. Faculty members were involved as participants and colleagues in all phases of the research process, and many were interested in the results of particular studies conducted with their students. Since the objective of the overall project was not to evaluate specific class situations, research data were compiled into a formal report, which was presented to the university-wide curriculum committee and summarized for all interested faculty. (A copy of the full report was also made available on the project Web site, *http:// deeval.ifas.ufl.edu/.*)

3. *Make friends with program administrators.* In many cases, distance learning program administrators are the gatekeepers to the faculty, and can either hinder or help you get the input and feedback you will need to build an effective evaluation tool.

4. *Take the long view.* The process of building and implementing a rigorous, fully supported evaluation takes time. Stakeholders need to be informed about the long-term, positive effects of evaluation. Plan to spend time educating faculty members and administrators about the value of assessment and evaluation, and how it can positively affect teaching, learning, retention, and recruiting efforts.

5. *Do not wed yourself to a one-size-fits-all mentality.* The evaluation tool developed by the University of Florida was designed to allow instructors to customize specific aspects of the evaluation, while maintaining a standard set of eight evaluation questions used on campus in face-to-face classes. The ability to adapt certain sets of questions to specific courses or academic unit needs allows for a greater sense of practicality and ownership by those constituents.

6. *Take advantage of faculty researching in this area (credibility) and your administrative structures.* The researchers on this project were social scientists based in the communication and education research disciplines. Faculty researchers in these disciplines can be found at most academic institutions, and some of them even conduct research in distance education as an application area. In addition to academic departments, distance education and communication technology task forces and committees are good places to find researchers with this kind of expertise.

7. *Buy-in at all levels must be built into the plan from the start.* From the beginning of this project, the researchers and project manager realized the importance of having buy-in from all levels of the university community. The project was initially conceived at the faculty level, then brought to the administration level. Once approved at the dean and provost level, the project was taken back to the faculty level through the faculty senate for approval and adoption. This process took many months and involved many meeting hours. However, it is worth noting that having advocates ("cheerleaders") at both the faculty and administrative level ultimately contributed to the adoption of the evaluation tool by the university community as a whole.

8. *Educate administration to the "costs" of quality distance education.* As at many institutions, initially, distance education was sold to administrators as a potential "cash cow." Once the reality of development costs and faculty time were factored in, it became apparent that the "cow" took a lot of resources to keep it going. Nevertheless, the opportunity to provide quality education for students around the globe was never forgotten. The University of Florida's distance education evaluation tool was ultimately adopted because faculty and administration saw the value in getting good student feedback regarding distance learning courses. Students are customers, in a sense, who can provide valuable product feedback. They let the instructors know what works, what does not work, and often have suggestions regarding how to make the course or product better. To ignore such important feedback would be foolish at best.

9. *Value of reflection.* Evaluation really is an act of reflection. Reflecting on how well teaching and learning are occurring in the class learning space is an important aspect of good practice. The distance learning evaluation tool allows instructors and administrators to draw conclusions from teaching and learning experiences. If these conclusions are reasonable and helpful, they can set the stage for future experiences.

Conclusion

Evaluation of instruction is an essential component of any educational enterprise. Not only does it enhance the teaching and learning process, it also provides reliable measures for quality and allows for continuous improvement of courses and programs. Many institutions offering distance education courses have developed their own systems and instruments to assess and evaluate the effectiveness of course delivery modes, including student outcomes. Although many have tried to apply their face-to-face instruments used in on-campus courses and programs, there are some obvious discrepancies that can cause faculty and administrators much grief. Distance education courses, by their nature, incorporate instructional and technological components of instruction at a more sophisticated level than traditional, live classes. This creates challenges for those academic units and the institution in terms of evaluation of faculty, since the technology component adds complexity to standard course evaluation techniques. The distance education course evaluation project outlined in this chapter is an attempt to bridge the gap created by the transition from face-to-face to online or distance teaching and learning modes.

References

Ehrmann, S.C., & Zuniga, R.E. (1997). *The flashlight evaluation handbook*. Washington, DC: Corporation for Public Broadcasting.

Gall, M.D., Gall, J.P., & Borg, W.R. (2003). *Educational research: An introduction* (7th ed.). Boston: Allyn and Bacon.

Glaser, B.G., & Strauss, A.L. (1967). *The discovery of grounded theory*. Chicago: Aldine.

Kirkpatrick, D.L. (1998). *Evaluating training programs: The four levels* (2nd ed.). San Francisco: Berrett-Koehler.

Lincoln, Y.S., & Guba, E.G. (1985). *Naturalistic inquiry*. Newbury Park, CA: Sage Publications.

Roberts, T.G., Irani, T., Lundy, L.K., & Telg, R. (2004). Practices in student evaluation of distance education courses among land-grant institutions. *Journal of Agricultural Education, 45*(3), 1-10.

Roberts, T.G., Irani, T., Lundy, L.K., & Telg, R. (2005). The development of an instrument to evaluate distance education courses using student attitudes. *The American Journal of Distance Education, 19*(1), 54-64.

U.S. Department of Education. (2003). *Distance education at degree-granting postsecondary institutions: 2000-2001*. Washington, DC: National Center for Education Statistics (NCES Publication No. 2003017).

Woolfolk, A.E. (1993). *Educational psychology* (5th ed.). Boston: Allyn and Bacon.

Appendix I: Distance Education Course Evaluation Instrument

Part I—Instructor	Poor	Below Average	Average	Above Average	Excellent
1. Description of course objectives and assignments	1	2	3	4	5
2. Communication of ideas and information	1	2	3	4	5
3. Expression of expectations for performance in this class	1	2	3	4	5
4. Timeliness in responding to students	1	2	3	4	5
5. Timeliness in returning assignments	1	2	3	4	5
6. Respect and concern for students	1	2	3	4	5
7. Interaction opportunities with other students	1	2	3	4	5
8. Stimulation of interest in course	1	2	3	4	5
9. Coordination of the learning activities with the technology	1	2	3	4	5
10. Enthusiasm for the subject	1	2	3	4	5
11. Encouragement of independent, creative, and critical thinking	1	2	3	4	5
12. Overall rating of instructor	1	2	3	4	5

Part II—Overall Evaluation	Poor	Below Average	Average	Above Average	Excellent
13. Overall, I rate this course as	1	2	3	4	5

Part III—Additional Questions	Poor	Below Average	Average	Above Average	Excellent	
14. Relationship between examinations and learning activities	1	2	3	4	5	n/a
15. Appropriateness of assigned materials (readings, video, etc.) to the nature and subject of the course	1	2	3	4	5	n/a
16. Timeliness in delivering required materials	1	2	3	4	5	n/a
17. Reliability of the technology(ies) used to deliver this course	1	2	3	4	5	n/a
18. Technical support's ability to resolve technical difficulties	1	2	3	4	5	n/a
19. Availability of necessary library resources	1	2	3	4	5	n/a
20. Convenience of registration procedures	1	2	3	4	5	n/a

Part IV—Student Background

21. Was this course required for your degree program?	Yes	No			
22. What is your overall GPA?	1.9 or less	2.0 – 2.2	2.3 – 2.7	2.8 – 3.3	3.4 – 4.0
23. What is your classification (e.g., 4AG, 3EG)?					
24. What grade do you expect to achieve in this course?		A / C	B+ / D+	B / D	C+ / E
25. How often have you been absent?	Never	1–5	6–9	10+	n/a

continued on following page

continued from following page

Part V—Open-ended Questions
1. What personal qualities or teaching practices of the instructor contributed to the success of the course?
2. What personal qualities or teaching practices of the instructor hindered the success of the course?
3. What is your opinion of the course, including the text(s) and materials?
4. Comment on the adequacy of the materials/equipment provided to conduct class/laboratory activities.
5. Add any other comments you wish.

Chapter VII

Online Program Assessment:
A Case Study of the University of Illinois at Urbana-Champaign Experience

Faye L. Lesht, University of Illinois at Urbana-Champaign, USA

Rae-Anne Montague, University of Illinois at Urbana-Champaign, USA

Vaughn J. Page, University of Illinois at Urbana-Champaign, USA

Najmuddin Shaik, University of Illinois at Urbana-Champaign, USA

Linda C. Smith, University of Illinois at Urbana-Champaign, USA

Abstract

Through case study, this chapter lends insight to ways online assessment can facilitate a holistic approach to the evaluation of distance education programs. In 2001, the University of Illinois at Urbana-Champaign transitioned from program evaluation methods that relied heavily on data gathering by postal mail to online instruments. While the transition was spurred by the need to evaluate the campus' first online degree program, online assessment methods are now used to review all off-campus degree programs. Results of this new assessment strategy have proven beneficial for continuous quality improvement across all modes of delivery.

Introduction

A holistic approach to program evaluation can be facilitated by online assessment as exemplified by the experience of the University of Illinois at Urbana-Champaign (UIUC). The need to assess online graduate-level degree programs led the campus to rethink and revitalize its longstanding approach to evaluation strategies of off-campus degree programs, replacing data gathering by mail with online assessment tools. Initial experience with the revised approach suggested that response rates were significantly higher than the postal-based method and participant response was received more quickly than in the past. In addition, meaningful interaction with stakeholders was more likely to occur, and online assessment enhanced the possibility of using results for continuous program improvement. Online program assessment may be applicable in the evaluation of a variety of off-campus programs (both site-based and online), and has implications for program reviews conducted by accrediting bodies and other entities. Furthermore, once the basic infrastructure to administer online surveys is in place, the method is a more economical way to gather and analyze responses to the assessment instruments.

This chapter takes a multiple-case-study approach, drawing most heavily on the first online master's degree program formally reviewed at UIUC, the Master of Science (MS) in Library and Information Science LEEP option, and comparing and contrasting the evolution of the online assessment instruments to the former approach that relied heavily on instruments sent and returned via postal mail. Although the focus of this chapter is on assessment strategies related to off-campus (including online) degree program assessment, it is important to note that during the period of the evolution from postal to online program-assessment strategies, the campus also developed and implemented an online course-assessment instrument. Used together, these online assessment instruments may provide a powerful vehicle for program evaluation and development.

The objectives of this chapter are to share what has been learned and gained through this transformation, the potential for using the generic assessment instruments in other settings, significant issues that emerged and how they were handled, and assessment issues on the horizon. By emphasizing a specific context, this case offers an opportunity for readers to consider the topic in depth and understand the complexities inherent within this authentic situation. The position of this chapter is that online program assessment, combined with interview data, provides an effective approach to evaluation of all off-campus programs (e.g., off-campus site-based, print-based by mail, video, online) because it encourages a holistic approach to program evaluation and lends itself well to continuous quality improvement. The UIUC experience and instruments presented in this chapter offer a model to other institutions interested in incorporating online program assessment.

Background

The University of Illinois was established in 1867. It is a state-supported institution with a threefold mission of teaching, research, and service with three campuses: Urbana-

Champaign, Chicago, and Springfield. As of Fall 2003, the largest campus, UIUC, has a student body of 38,864, of whom 9,210 (23%) are graduate students. UIUC is "one of the nation's great research universities, known for its distinguished faculty, its outstanding resources, and the breadth of its academic programs. It is deeply committed to educating its large, diverse student body and to engaging critical societal and scientific issues" (University of Illinois, 2004, p. 8).

Prior Evaluations and the Committee on Extended Education and External Degrees

The UIUC campus has a history of offering credit courses and degree programs throughout and beyond Illinois; it began using distance education technologies for instructional delivery in the 1930s. The profile of off-campus students differs from that of on-campus students: off-campus students tend to be older than their campus counterparts, complete degree programs on a part-time rather than a full-time basis, and typically do not receive financial support from the institution. Most off-campus students are engaged in post-baccalaureate degree programs; most on-campus students are pursuing baccalaureate degrees.

Because the campus prides itself on the quality of its research and teaching, it subscribes to the American Distance Education Consortium Guiding Principles for Distance Teaching and Learning (2004), and expects that the quality of off-campus programs will be comparable to that of on-campus programs. Although campus units are subject to periodic program reviews mandated by the state Board of Higher Education and campus administration, these reviews may be conducted by the academic units in which the programs are housed. This is not the case for off-campus programs. Since all of UIUC's off-campus degree programs are currently at the graduate level, the Graduate College has oversight of off-campus program reviews. These reviews are conducted by the Graduate College Committee on Extended Education and External Degrees (CEEED). This committee, established in the late 1970s, is charged with monitoring the quality of off-campus, graduate-level degree and certificate programs.

This charge includes approval of off-campus/online programs in order for them to be offered, as well as systematic program evaluation of each off-campus program on a rotating basis. Regular review is based on the assumption that "even the best designed or adapted distance delivered courses will likely require revision" (Willis, 1993, p. 70). Once initial CEEED approval is gained, programs are extensively reviewed every five years. Specifically, the evaluation is intended to provide: (a) a judgment of the quality of programs and a recommendation related to continuation or discontinuation, (b) suggestions or recommendations for improving programs, and (c) credibility or sanction of the programs.

In short, the emphasis is on proving and improving off-campus programs. This same standard is not in evidence on campus—at least not by an external review similar to the one conducted by CEEED. There seems to be a tacit assumption that it is more important to systematically assess the quality of off-campus/online programs than on-campus programs because the students are remote from campus, the faculty may be remote from campus, and the profile of the students differs considerably from the campus profile. Although additional policies and procedures to support quality assurance are desirable, the rationale for extra scrutiny in extension programs is likely connected to an additional (possibly unwarranted) burden of proof placed upon new or uniquely perceived programs, as described by Brown and Wack (1999).

CEEED was established to address the underlying question: How does a campus ensure the educational validity and reliability of programs that occur outside its walls? Although CEEED is charged with providing a summative evaluation for each program it reviews, the process also includes the provision of formative feedback and is based on the principles of continuous quality improvement, whereby:

> Continual institutional self-evaluation directed toward program improvement, targeting more effective uses of technology to improve pedagogy, advances in student achievement of intended outcomes, improved retention rates, effective use of resources, and demonstrated improvements in the institution's service to its internal and external constituencies is vital. (Johnstone, 2004, p. 378)

CEEED is composed of nine faculty members, representing disciplines that offer off-campus programs, along with the dean and associate dean of the Graduate College, and an administrator from Continuing Education. The committee is co-chaired by a member of the faculty and an administrator from Continuing Education.

Prior to 2001, program reviews conducted by CEEED consisted of print-based assessment instruments for students and faculty sent through the mail. In addition, program administrators responded to questions in written form. Contact between the committee and those responsible for the program under review was limited. Representatives might be asked to address the committee, but it was not required. At the end of the evaluation, a letter was sent by CEEED co-chairs to the department administrators whose program was under review, informing them of the results. In the event that a program was to be terminated, discussions took place between the dean of the Graduate College and the dean of the college where the program was housed.

Defining and Addressing the Need to Change

During the spring of 1996, CEEED approved the first online degree program offered by the campus, the Graduate School of Library and Information Science (GSLIS) LEEP option. LEEP, originally known as the Library Education Experimental Program, is primarily online with a 10-day orientation during the first summer of enrollment and campus visits once each semester thereafter. Since approving the LEEP program, the campus has approved nine additional online master's degree programs and several online certificate programs.

In the spring of 2001, CEEED was charged to consider how it would conduct a five-year evaluation of the first online degree program offered by the campus during the upcoming academic year. It was during these discussions that the idea of using online program assessment as an opportunity to reconceptualize the entire process of off-campus program evaluation began to unfold. As Moloney and Tello (2004, p. 201) note, "Assessment of online education presents unique challenges and unique opportunities that offer a powerful potential to transform student learning, programs, and institutions." With the growing use of technology on and off campus, it seemed plausible to the committee that even off-campus, site-based programs might in time benefit from an assessment instrument that would work, at least in part, for all reviews, regardless of how the program or assessment instruments were delivered.

One question that emerged during the committee's initial evaluation redesign was: "Why do we do this type of program evaluation at all?" Discussions about the utility of CEEED's role in program evaluation included three issues:

1.   The campus culture is heavily research oriented.

2.   Programs at a distance are disadvantaged by concerns stemming from an "out of sight, out of mind" attitude that may generate doubts about their quality.

3.   These programs might be jeopardized if a formal system were not in place to justify their quality and importance to the campus mission and to society.

The committee recognized the need for online assessment instruments for online programs and also discussed the potential of using these instruments for all reviews in the future. At the same time, concerns were raised regarding access for those not involved in online programs. Would it be possible and beneficial, in the future, to conduct all program reviews online? Would the cost of developing online instruments be worthwhile?

Stakeholder Considerations

In order for evaluation processes to be effective, the investment of key stakeholders must be secured (Fitzpatrick, Sanders, & Worthen, 2004). The committee carefully considered whom to include in the assessment process. In the past, the instruments were sent to all students enrolled in courses offered by the program under review. Was this still appropriate? Or might it be advisable to assess only those who had been admitted to the program within the five-year period under review, including those who dropped out, those who were alumni of the program, and those currently enrolled in the program? In the past, faculty members who had taught for the program were included even if they had only taught once and at the beginning of the review cycle. Should this remain the case? Program administrators were asked to respond in writing to a series of written questions. Would it add to or detract from the process to invite program administrators to a meeting of the committee as part of the data collection process? Were there other stakeholders who should be included? For instance, the committee considered whether employers should be sent an assessment instrument (given that most of the students in these programs are professionals working in the public and private sectors).

Also discussed were issues pertaining to committee expectations of the amount of time that should be spent completing the respective assessment instruments and how much time should be allowed for responses. The instruments should be concise and yet allow for in-depth responses to open-ended questions. The time for response was limited to two weeks. The committee thought that those receiving the instruments would either respond immediately (or within a short time) or not at all. At the same time, CEEED noted that the faculty response rate in the past was "generally dismal." It was hoped that an online review might catch their attention and result in higher rates of return.

The best way to contact student and faculty participants was also considered. The existing instruments were sent to home or office addresses, which might not be current but typically did not change as frequently as e-mail addresses. Since the committee wanted to send the instruments electronically to participants in online and site-based programs, the issue of contacting participants in a reliable way became critical. Furthermore, since online programs tend to be heavily scrutinized in their early stages, there was a concern about how the evaluation instruments would be received by the already heavily assessed student group. Would they understand the nature of this request for participation and how it differed from earlier evaluations in which they may have participated?

Another issue emerged relating to program administrators. Although some administrators were pleased to be part of a formal review and saw it as an opportunity to enrich data needed for other purposes (e.g., accreditation reviews), others were less enthusiastic. On a campus where online programs are still a relatively recent phenomenon and therefore heavily examined aside from formal review processes, CEEED's process took on renewed significance for key stakeholders. On the one hand, it was used to enhance the credibility of the online programs offered by UIUC; on the other hand, it raised concern at times among program administrators unfamiliar with the review process and already feeling the effects of multiple justifications of online education as an effective instructional delivery method. For example, some administrators expressed concerns about the timing of the reviews. Due to budget constraints experienced campus-wide, many programs were under close scrutiny by their respective colleges. A review that was less than stellar might jeopardize a program's future.

Instrument Design

Since the existing assessment technique relied heavily on instruments sent through postal mail, among the first issues was how to design online instruments so they would be user friendly, easily accessible, and easy to complete and yet maintain the committee's standards. Also, the existing instruments had been used with little modification over a number of years. The committee wanted to design separate online instruments for students and faculty that would have core questions that applied across programs while also enabling sets of program-specific questions, pending committee approval. What questions needed to be retained from the existing instruments? What questions should be modified or added? How might this sense of collegial engagement with program administrators be obtained so they could actively participate in the process without compromising the committee's position as ultimate decision maker on the final outcome of the evaluation? The process was initiated using a basic approach to instrument design, as described by Coffman (2004, p. 7), incorporating an "understanding of survey methodology, sensitivity to the group or population being surveyed, and good questions that make sense and can be answered."

Data Analysis, Interpretation, and Reporting

The historic instruments served a dual purpose. One was to gather information in order to evaluate the program; the second was to serve as a survey instrument to gather demographic information. In the past, analysis of the data was limited to frequency statistics, and responses to open-ended questions were included verbatim. The committee wanted to improve upon past practice by extracting more focused and more detailed information from the online assessments. In addition, the committee wanted to use the data from online instruments to inform its discussion with program administrators. The committee wished to receive the data in a form that would make the task of assessing program strengths and weaknesses straightforward. The committee discussed ways of handling data analysis and reporting, along with instrument design to facilitate its work.

Solutions and Recommendations

CEEED's Approach

The design of assessment instruments and the overall administration of the evaluation process are guided by: incorporation of widely accepted standards of quality education, such as the Sloan-C *Five Pillars of Quality Online Education* (Lorenzo & Moore, 2002); building on the work of the Joint Committee on Standards for Educational Evaluation (1994); and reflecting the values of the faculty and staff appointed by the Graduate College to serve on CEEED and, to a lesser extent, the values, standards, and questions of department heads and departmental faculty and staff involved in the program review process. The complete list of criteria that shaped the questions to be answered and the measures used to provide those answers include the following:

- perception of department commitment to the program

- effectiveness of the administrator/coordinator

- extent and quality of support services

- quality of technical support

- perspective on student learning

- quality of students and comparison with on-campus students

- rigor of courses and program

- effective use of faculty time
- personal and professional satisfaction with involvement in the program

At the same time, responses to the instruments reflect the values of the students and program alumni as well as faculty who have taught in the programs under review.

Through discussion pertaining to the rationale for conducting periodic program reviews, CEEED endorsed the view that evaluation leads to quality improvement by providing an "impetus for this change" (Rovai, 2003, p. 123) and that this particular process would be beneficial in terms of:

- judging quality
- providing credibility
- providing feedback and recommendations to programs under review
- serving a policy function for the campus (especially related to program continuation or discontinuation)
- providing the link between off-campus and on-campus

As for applicability of online assessment across programs, the committee members took an iterative approach. They began by using the same basic instrument across programs, administering the instruments online for those in online programs and by postal mail for off-campus, site-based programs. Over time, the committee moved to sending letters to student participants in off-campus, site-based programs with the URL for the online instruments. However, faculty instruments were routinely administered online for all programs. Due to response rates that were comparable, and in some cases better than the postal mail method, by the academic year 2003-2004, the committee administered the assessment instruments online for students in all programs under review, regardless of mode of delivery.

Involving Stakeholders

The committee decided to limit the sample to students who had been admitted to the degree program under review, rather than to all students who had enrolled in a program-related course as in the past. This included stop-outs, alumni, and current students—provided they had engaged in coursework within the five-year review period. All current and former instructors who taught courses in the program over the past five years were also included. Unlike in the past, the committee decided to involve the program administrators in verifying the list of students and faculty and assisting with contact information. However, CEEED would not allow program administrators to alter the participant lists unless a person was known to be deceased or incapacitated.

Involving program administrators in the process was deemed to be highly beneficial. They were able to lend insight into the questions, reframe questions to suit their needs, include questions that would be valuable to them in the future (e.g., accreditation visits), and participate actively in the process. At the same time, it allowed the committee an opportunity to address concerns early on in the process. For example, it enabled the committee to provide reassurance to coordinators as necessary that the process is intended to strengthen existing programs and, where weaknesses exist, to provide guidance on program improvement.

Experience proved that concerns regarding response time were unfounded. Surprisingly, the committee received requests from the student group to extend the deadline to enable more thoughtful responses to the questions. For LEEP, faculty response was a surprising 100%.

One criterion used in designing the instruments was that the process should be collegial and yet allow the committee to take appropriate action as necessary, even if this action meant recommending discontinuation of a program. The review was designed to reflect the mission of CEEED—program quality rather than individual course quality. For example, CEEED accepted the request from a program coordinator to include a question that allowed faculty to compare the performance of off-campus students to on-campus students, but rejected this question on the student instrument related to reading assignments: *I complete reading assignments: (a) all the time, (b) most of the time, (c) infrequently, or (d) not at all.*

In this way, the committee reinforced its expectation that the purpose of each review is to focus on the quality of the total program (or summative experience) rather than on individual courses, students, and faculty. Although CEEED solicits items from program administrators and often includes their questions verbatim, it also retains the right to decide if a question fits in with the purpose of the review. The committee decided not to include employers in the review process, considering that area as being distinct from the main concern related to program quality.

Assessment Instruments

Two online assessment instruments were designed, one for student participants and one for faculty (Appendixes A and B). Student participants include program alumni, current students, and students who began study but stopped out or withdrew prior to completing their degree. Also, the committee designed an interview guide shared with administrators prior to the in-person interview with CEEED to discuss the program (Appendix C). The guide contains questions pertaining to the history of the program, student characteristics, administrative issues, and program success and impact. CEEED also has a set of questions to which it refers in order to probe more deeply in areas related to program health and future directions for the program. Over time, CEEED realized that some of the questions on the online instruments could be perceived as ambiguous or did not elicit the intended information. For instance, as the question on advising was seen as too broad and responses might result that would be difficult to interpret, that question was modified. Rather than include it as part of items related to "quality of instructional components," the advising question was included in the "quality of student support services" section, that is, Student Services (e.g., advising, library, financial aid, career services, and admissions).

CEEED wanted instruments that would collect enough relevant data to enable it to gauge a program accurately. At the same time, the instruments could not be so long to complete as to discourage participation. The committee wanted a uniform set of instruments so that trends could be compared across programs over time. Consequently, it was decided that instruments would need to be similar, even if some were administered online and others were sent through the mail to accommodate the off-campus, site-based programs. The instruments were designed to:

- be administered in paper-and-pencil or online formats
- be used by any department within CEEED's purview
- allow individual departments to add items specific to their needs
- include items related specifically to online courses
- be easily adapted for either online or off-campus, site-based programs

The survey items include both Likert-scale and open-ended items. Throughout the design phase, it became apparent that some CEEED members had special areas of interest regarding the evaluation process. Some of these special interests presented a unique view of the criteria and ways to address them, and were incorporated into the instruments. Others, however, delved into areas that did not fit the overall goals of the evaluation process or focused on areas outside of the criteria. In those instances, it would not have been appropriate to include items that addressed those issues. It was important to ensure that those individuals whose suggestions would not be used still felt included rather than excluded from the process. One way this was accomplished was to focus on what worked in the instruments to accomplish CEEED's goals.

Prior to dissemination, program administrators were sent the online instruments for their review and comments. At this point, the administrators were invited to include questions of special interest to them; however, the committee retained the right of final approval so that all questions on the instruments were judged by CEEED as addressing the established criteria. Examples of questions included by departmental request on the student instrument relate to "cost as a factor in enrolling," "convenience of an online program in the decision to enroll," "access to equipment and facilities," and specific questions regarding mentoring and responsiveness on the part of the departments. There were fewer departmental questions on the faculty instruments; additional questions pertained to benefits of the program related to new research and service opportunities as a result of teaching in the online programs, as well as ways "participating in the online program impacted your classroom teaching methods."

Interpreting and Reporting Results

CEEED reviewed and interpreted the online assessment data prior to administrative interviews. The committee used the data to help guide further discussion with program administrators prior to releasing its final report. The in-person discussion with program administrators usually lasted between 45 and 60 minutes, and focused on program viability and future directions. All the data were synthesized and used as part of a final report organized to highlight actionable recommendations. Along with a summary letter, the report includes the same data reviewed by the committee.

Prior to the online assessment process, program review data were gathered by committee support staff and results were reported in frequencies, along with noted qualitative comments. Initially, for the revised process, an advanced doctoral student conducted the data analysis. Mean and standard deviation were calculated for each scaled item using the raw-score method. An iterative process was used to analyze the qualitative data. The open-ended responses for both faculty and students were sorted by item and transcribed. The transcripts were analyzed using qualitative data-presentation and content-analysis methods. Major themes were identified along with cross-data tables of similar responses per item. Themes were presented in table format that included the frequency with which each theme occurred. Frequency was presented by the number of respondents who mentioned each theme, as well as the percentage of the total number represented. Select, representative quotes from respondents accompanied each table. The report includes two parts, one pertaining to students and one pertaining to faculty.

Emerging Trends

As more institutions include online courses and degree programs in their portfolios (Allen & Seaman, 2003), wired campuses gain in popularity, and emphasis on student outcomes continues to grow (Shavelson & Huang, 2003), the need for effective online assessment strategies will become even more important to institutions of higher education in the future. As at UIUC, institutions across the country may begin to use online assessment instruments for course as well as program evaluation.

For example, UIUC recently implemented an online course evaluation system, Evaluation ONline (EON), as a tool for student feedback on instruction. Although response rates still fall short of 100%, the fact that the forms can be completed online for a period of about two weeks at the conclusion of a course has led to higher response rates than was achieved with mailed forms for online programs. In this way, online assessment may enhance opportunities for continuous program improvement.

One program exemplifying this model is LEEP. For example, GSLIS subscribes to the notion that "success is remaining open to continuing feedback and adjusting the program accordingly," as stated by McNamara (1999). Throughout the development of LEEP, GSLIS faculty and administrators have been very attentive to assessing outcomes of individual courses, student success, faculty satisfaction, and performance of the program overall. Such monitoring has been integral to gauging success and guiding improvements. Approaches to evaluation and quality assurance have included: external evaluation of the program; CEEED five-year comprehensive review; accreditation reviews; inviting student comments on what is and is not working via community bulletin boards and other interactive approaches; a LEEP retreat in Summer 2002 involving faculty, staff, students, and alumni; formal research related to the online program; ongoing examination of student retention and completion statistics; and end-of-course evaluations.

The results of the CEEED evaluation were of particular value because they provided data from key stakeholders—students, alumni, full-time faculty, adjunct faculty, and program administrators. Because program administrators participated in the development of the instruments used to survey students and faculty, the resulting data served as a means of identifying existing program strengths as well as areas in need of improvement. The latter have been addressed as part of the continuous program improvement efforts that characterize the LEEP program. In this way, online assessment strategies become part of, rather than apart from, the larger context of program development.

In the future, research conducted to study factors that facilitate and/or inhibit continuous program improvement using online assessment tools may lend further insight into online program assessment as part of a holistic approach to educational program evaluation.

Furthermore, once a common set of metrics on key issues and program indicators has been identified by the stakeholders, and standard instruments are used, intra-program and inter-program comparisons may be made. For example, over time, research comparisons may be made within and across programs related to participant response rates, program quality, satisfaction, demographic changes, and evolution of assessment instruments. Studies are also needed related to the economics of online assessment, including ways that online assessment can be scalable over time.

Conclusion

Based on experience at UIUC, online assessment can facilitate a holistic approach to program evaluation and continuous program improvement. Online program assessment as part of an overall evaluation process may also promote consistency within and across institutional evaluation procedures. In this way, data from course and program assessments may inform the process of continuous program improvement.

Although the response rates for the LEEP review were extraordinarily high (especially the 100% response from faculty) compared to response rates of past reviews, response rates for the other programs were satisfactory. It may be premature to compare the response rates between the traditional and the online methods of assessment, but it seems that response rates are at least comparable and the entire review process (including disseminating instruments and collecting and analyzing data) is significantly faster. In the past, a second notice or extension of deadline was routine. With the online version, extensions have been the exception or at the request of participants.

In the UIUC experience, start-up costs for online program assessment, including initial hardware, programming, and analytical skills, are outweighed by the benefits. Benefits of online assessment include increased access and response rates, ease of instrument refinements, reduced postal costs, and a common set of questions that allow intra-program and inter-program comparisons. Moving to online program assessment provided an opportunity to rethink and significantly improve the entire evaluation process. Another important outcome at UIUC was the opportunity to reinforce the evaluation process as a collegial endeavor that would be useful to departments being evaluated, campus evaluators, as well as accrediting and other groups to whom institutions of higher education are accountable.

References

Allen, I.E., & Seaman, J. (2003). *Sizing the opportunity: The quality and extent of online education in the United States, 2002-2003*. Needham, MA: Sloan-C. Retrieved December 5, 2004, from *http://www.sloan-c.org/resources/sizing_opportunity.pdf*

American Distance Education Consortium. (2004). *Guiding principles for distance teaching and learning.* Retrieved December 5, 2004, from *http://www.adec.edu/admin/papers/distance-teaching_principles.html*

Brown, G., & Wack, M. (1999). The difference frenzy and matching buckshot with buckshot. *The Technology Source,* (May/June). Retrieved December 5, 2004, from *http://ts.mivu.org/default.asp?show=article&id=459*

Coffman, J. (2004). Internet surveys: Back to the future. *The Evaluation Exchange, 10*(3), 6-7. Retrieved December 5, 2004, from *http://www.gse.harvard.edu/hfrp/eval/issue27/index.html*

Fitzpatrick, J.L., Sanders, J.R., & Worthen, B.R. (2004). *Program evaluation: Alternative approaches and practical guidelines* (3rd ed.). Boston: Allyn-Bacon.

Johnstone, S.M. (2004). Program evaluation. In A. DiStefano, K.E. Rudestam, & R.J. Silverman (Eds.), *Encyclopedia of distributed learning* (pp. 374-379). Thousand Oaks, CA: Sage Publications.

Joint Committee on Standards for Educational Evaluation. (1994). *The program evaluation standards: How to assess evaluations of educational programs.* Thousand Oaks, CA: Sage Publications.

Lorenzo, G., & Moore, J.C. (2002). The Sloan Consortium report to the nation: Five pillars of quality online education. Retrieved December 5, 2004, from *http://www.sloan-c.org/effective/pillarreport1.pdf*

McNamara, C. (1999). *Basic guide to program evaluation.* Retrieved, December 5, 2004, from *http://www.mapnp.org/library/evaluatn/fnl_eval.htm#anchor1581634*

Moloney, J., & Tello, S. (2004). Achieving quality and scale in online education through transformative assessment: A case study. In J. Bourne & J.C. Moore (Eds.), *Elements of quality online education: Into the mainstream* (pp. 197-211). Needham, MA: Sloan Center for OnLine Education.

Page, V.J. (2003). *An evaluation of the Graduate School of Library and Information Science's LEEP3 master's degree program at The University of Illinois at Urbana-Champaign.* Unpublished manuscript, University of Illinois at Urbana-Champaign, USA.

Rovai, A.P. (2003). A practical framework for evaluating online distance education programs. *Internet and Higher Education, 6*(2), 109-124.

Shavelson, R.J., & Huang, L. (2003). Responding responsibly to the frenzy to assess learning in higher education. *Change, 35*(1), 11-19. Retrieved December 5, 2004, from *http://www.aahe.org/change/shavelson.pdf*

University of Illinois. (2004). *2004 pocket facts: The University of Illinois never sleeps.* [Online Brochure]. Retrieved December 5, 2004, from *http://www.uillinois.edu/about/pubs/facts04.pdf*

Willis, B. (1993). *Instructional development for distance education.* Syracuse, NY: Syracuse University.

Appendix A

SAMPLE

Evaluation Instrument (Student)

Committee on Extended Education and External Degrees

Graduate College of the University of Illinois at Urbana-Champaign

	Item	Very Low	Low	Average	High	Very High	Not Applicable
	Quality of Instructional Components of the Program						
1.	Program curriculum (including relevance to practice)	O	O	O	O	O	O
2.	Instruction	O	O	O	O	O	O
3.	Instructors' use of students' past work experiences	O	O	O	O	O	O
4.	Instructional materials	O	O	O	O	O	O
5.	Learning assignments	O	O	O	O	O	O
6.	Grading methods	O	O	O	O	O	O
7.	Feedback from instructors	O	O	O	O	O	O
8.	Overall program quality	O	O	O	O	O	O
	Quality of Student Support Services						
9.	Advising	O	O	O	O	O	O
10.	Student services	O	O	O	O	O	O
11.	Library services	O	O	O	O	O	O
12.	Technical support	O	O	O	O	O	O
13.	Information regarding course schedules	O	O	O	O	O	O
14.	Information regarding program requirements	O	O	O	O	O	O
15.	Information regarding technical requirements	O	O	O	O	O	O
16.	Information regarding student support services	O	O	O	O	O	O

Instructional Delivery Methods		Not very appropriate			Very appropriate		
17.	The delivery methods used were	O	O	O	O	O	O
		Very unreliable			Very reliable		
18.	Distance education delivery was	O	O	O	O	O	O
		Detracted from the program			Enriched the program		
19.	Site-based face-to-face opportunities	O	O	O	O	O	O
		Detracted from the program			Enriched the program		
20.	Synchronous live session opportunities	O	O	O	O	O	O

Overall Quality of the Program		
21.	What are the program's major strengths?	
22.	What are the program's major weaknesses?	
23.	What impact has the program had on your career?	
24.	What impact has the program had on your work-related performance?	
25.	If you could make changes to this program, what would you propose?	
26.	What course(s) made particularly effective use of the technology?	
27.	For what purposes are you seeking or did you seek a graduate degree (e.g., improve knowledge, improve skills, enhance career opportunities)?	
28.	Other comments	

Demographic Information	
29.	During which term (summer, fall, spring) and year did you begin this program?
30.	Have you completed this program? __Yes __ No If so, when? _____
31.	Are you an Illinois resident? __ Yes __ No
32.	Age Group __ 20-29 __ 30-39 __ 40-49 __ 50 and over
33.	Sex __Male __ Female

Appendix B

SAMPLE

Evaluation Instrument (Faculty)

Committee on Extended Education and External Degrees

Graduate College of the University of Illinois at Urbana-Champaign

Demographic Information:

My faculty status is ____ Full-Time ____ Adjunct

Years of teaching experience _____

Number of times taught a course in this program _____

Number of different course(s) taught in this program _____

(continued on following page)

Appendix B. (cont.)

	Item	Strongly Disagree	Disagree	Neutral	Agree	Strongly Agree	Not Applicable
1.	Our academic unit is very committed to this program.	O	O	O	O	O	O
2.	People in my academic unit view this program as second-class.	O	O	O	O	O	O
3.	The coordinator of this program is very committed to the success of this program.	O	O	O	O	O	O
4.	The coordinator is very effective in planning this program.	O	O	O	O	O	O
5.	The coordinator is effective in motivating me and other faculty to participate in this program.	O	O	O	O	O	O
6.	Access to technical support personnel was good.	O	O	O	O	O	O
7.	Sufficient technical support was provided.	O	O	O	O	O	O
8.	It was easy to access the technology needed to deliver courses.	O	O	O	O	O	O
9.	I was given adequate support in designing or transforming my course.	O	O	O	O	O	O
10.	I received adequate technical support during delivery sessions of my course.	O	O	O	O	O	O
11.	I think that students learn as well in my course in this program as they do on campus.	O	O	O	O	O	O
12.	I receive personal satisfaction from being involved in this program.	O	O	O	O	O	O
13.	I receive professional recognition for being involved in this program.	O	O	O	O	O	O
14.	I will continue to teach in this program if given the opportunity.	O	O	O	O	O	O
15.	I had access to adequate equipment for development and delivery of my course.	O	O	O	O	O	O
16.	I think students benefit from this program by helping them advance in jobs and career.	O	O	O	O	O	O
17.	I think the employers of program's students benefit from this program.	O	O	O	O	O	O
18.	This program makes our academic unit's overall program stronger.	O	O	O	O	O	O
19.	Support from the library was good.	O	O	O	O	O	O
20.	Electronic reserve support for my course was good.	O	O	O	O	O	O
21.	Document delivery support for students in my course was good.	O	O	O	O	O	O
22.	Overall this is a very good program.	O	O	O	O	O	O
23.	Students devote appropriate levels of time and effort to the program.	O	O	O	O	O	O

	Item	Less Than	Same As	Greater Than
24.	Compared to on-campus students, the performance of off-campus students in this program is:	O	O	O
25.	The rigor of online courses in this program compared to on-campus courses is:	O	O	O
26.	The quality of online courses in this program compared to on-campus courses is:	O	O	O
27.	My expectation of online students compared to on-campus students is:	O	O	O
28.	The amount of time I spend on my online course compared to a similar on-campus course is:	O	O	O

Overall Quality of the Program	
29.	The program's overall strengths are:
30.	The program's overall weaknesses are:
31.	What impact, if any, has the program had on your career?
32.	What impact, if any, has the program had on you?
33.	If you were able to, what changes would you make to this program?
34.	Other Comments

Appendix C

SAMPLE

Administrator Discussion Guide

Committee on Extended Education and External Degrees

Graduate College of the University of Illinois at Urbana-Champaign

1.   History and Description of the Program
- Changes in the program since last review
- Fit with the overall mission and goals of the department
- Current course offerings and trends

2.   Student Characteristics
- Target audience of the program
- Current demand for the off-campus program
- Current enrollment and number of limited status students
- Retention rate
- Contributors to student retention

3.   Administrative Issues
- Time to degree of students
- Cost of instruction
- Department support for the program
- Person responsible for updating

4.   Program Success and Impact
- Highlight program success and shortcomings
- Criteria used to determine the program's continuation
- Perceived value of the program within the unit
- Planned changes

Section III

Student Feedback

Chapter VIII

Cybercoaching:
An Emerging Model of Personalized Online Assessment

Ni Chang, Indiana University - South Bend, USA

Naomi Jeffery Petersen, Indiana University - South Bend, USA

Abstract

This chapter introduces cybercoaching, an emerging model of online formative assessment. This model emphasizes the process of development rather than a procedure for evaluation. Personalized feedback is provided by the instructor through the Internet/cyberspace using accessible technologies of electronic mail and word processing. Unlike mechanical responses that are not individually tailored, the instructor offers the students detailed information for improvement. Included also in this chapter are practical suggestions, including a detailed discussion of rubrics and their uses.

Introduction

This chapter presents *cybercoaching*, an emerging model of paperless formative assessment. This tutorial approach rests on the coaching role of monitoring and adjusting instruction to match student learning needs, the coaching tools of the least sophisticated

Table 1. Components of the cybercoaching model

Component	Characteristics	Features
Cyberspace	Commonly available online technology	E-mail
		Microsoft Word
+ Coaching	Personalized monitoring and instructing during the process of refining skills (tutoring)	Rubrics
		Personal Relationship
		Monitor & Adjust
= Cybercoaching	Paperless, goal-oriented feedback with an opportunity to revise before summative evaluation	Online Feedback

and most accessible computer technology, and the coaching technique of personalized, objective-related feedback (see Table 1). The feedback is for the purpose of improving student performance and self-regulation. The theory and research behind the use of online technology (cyberspace), the instructor's coaching role, and the feedback techniques discussed here may apply to any paperless assessment process, but cybercoaching is specifically intended for personalized feedback appropriate for higher levels of thinking, that is, analysis and synthesis (Anderson et al, 2000).

The Cybercoaching Model

Cyberspace

The simple speed of online or electronic communication is of such great value that a new culture of immediate response has developed. According to the 2003 National Survey of Student Engagement, 80% reported assignments requiring interaction via Internet and various forms of computer technology (Zhao & Kuh, 2004). In addition, word processing programs are now almost universally readable, even by competing operating systems (i.e., Mac vs. PC). Instructors and students need to have compatible online technology and word processing tools, through which both parties can improve. Students can learn more and instructors can teach better. The technology serves the relationship between students and instructors for continuous improvement, identified here as a coaching relationship.

Coaching

Coaching is defined here to include a tutorial function of monitoring student progress to provide feedback for improvement. The term 'coaching' has been used outside of sports. For instance, Nelson, Apenhorst, Carter, Mahlum, and Schneider (2004) observed that a *coach* "questioned and prompted reflective practice in building confidence and critical thinking" (p. 32). In a similar way, the focus of coaching in the classroom is on the process of giving feedback in order to develop performance before the final assessment (Clark, 2004). A coach, unlike a referee or a spectator or even a player, looks for skills to develop rather than errors committed or goals scored. Athletic coaches work closely with their athletes, developing skills through practice and feedback before a final game or competition (Gilbert & Trudel, 2004), whereas academic coaches work closely with their students, developing concepts, skills of logic, and expression in written products (Petersen, 2004a).

It is important to recognize the personal relationship that develops between the coach and the individual being coached. A coach who responds with the same automatic response to every player is not really coaching for improvement so much as monitoring activity. We offer our model for instructors who are interested in developing complex skills needed for proficient performance, which means that judgment on the part of the coach is required and subsequent change on the part of the student is expected.

Cybercoaching

Cybercoaching is a way to use readily available technology for the purpose of coaching. This chapter does not intend to defend online technology. Rather, it argues that technology can be used to achieve a difficult task more efficiently. Cybercoaching works when the student's product can be communicated via cyberspace.

The "cyber" part of cybercoaching refers not only to online technology or cyberspace through which the coaching occurs, but to the organization of the relationship that encourages feedback. The study of communication and control between man and machine was introduced as cybernetics (Smith & Smith, 1965), a theory of individual and organizational learning based on the need for feedback to adjust the momentum and direction of progress. Current theory and research in cognitive science have influenced standards of teaching to include the need for students to receive feedback in a timely manner. Zimmerman and Kitsanas (2003) reported that social feedback "has been consistently linked with higher achievement and greater motivation to learn" (p. 662).

Providing feedback to students is a process of scaffolding, which reflects the core concept of the 'Zone of Proximal Development', or ZPD (Vygotsky, 1978). From Vygotsky's perspective, learning takes place in a social context. A learner observes and is assisted by a more skilled learning partner (Lindblom-Ylanne & Pihlaijamaki, 2003). The guide, or helper, detects the need of the learner and renders assistance accordingly. The cybercoaching model is consistent with Vygotsky's theory of development. The instructor offers feedback based on the pre-stated objectives when assessing learners' written products. The learner must observe and then rehearse. This is a cornerstone of student-centered "best practice" (Danielson & McGreal, 2001; Lambert & McCombs, 1997): the instructor uses techniques that facilitate the learner's learning. Providing feedback is, therefore, a process of instruction and must be included in the course design.

Figure 1 represents a teaching-learning cycle with the cybercoaching elements added to it. The instructional decisions are in a cyclical sequence: first the learning targets are identified, then the teaching activities are designed—which often involve learning activities at the same time. These learning activities provide the focus for the instructor to assess the student's understanding. It is through feedback regarding these activities that the coaching occurs. These decisions must align with each other; otherwise the communication is not meaningful for learning.

The teaching-learning cycle is well established as a process of continuously monitoring and adjusting effective instruction. This is the difference between formative and summative assessment. Formative assessment is the coaching feedback provided before the summative, or final, evaluation. The assessment of student learning is then used by the instructor to self-assess the effectiveness of all the instructional decisions. The interior arrow of the loop signifies formative assessment, through which the teacher monitors whether the stated objectives have been mastered. The teacher then returns to the teaching activity because feedback is an opportunity to extend and personalize instruction. This completes the harmonic loop.

As with all instructional designs, cybercoaching requires thoughtful organization of teaching activities and learning activities. These activities are structured to promote self-regulated learning so that the harmonic cycle predicts a continuous learning habit for the individual student long after the teacher's immediate influence.

Teaching Activities

Teaching activities are the specific ways students will get new information directly or indirectly. Because the teaching is done by the teacher, any communication, regardless of whether it is written or in person, is a teaching activity as long as the content is directly related to learning objectives. Traditionally, this means lecturing, explaining text material, and designing inquiry exercises. However, within the cybercoaching model, this includes feedback inserted into the students' work. When the objective of the course is to develop more advanced thinking than simple memory or comprehension, or when the student lacks confidence in making creative decisions, feedback is certainly warranted. The feedback may direct the student to instructional materials or elaborate on previous instruction. Feedback provides additional scaffold for students' continued learning.

Learning Activities

As mentioned above, effective instruction includes interaction between instructor and student, and among students. Specific to cybercoaching, the learning activities feature the submission of early drafts or completed work for feedback. The assigned learning activities may include any step of the development process: to develop projects, to submit drafts, to respond to feedback, to revise drafts, or to reflect on the process and formally self-assess progress according to an agreed-upon set of criteria. These activities all promote long-term, self-regulated learning for a more thoughtful transfer of knowledge and skills to new situations. The short-term achievement required for success in the class is not as important as the long-term usefulness. This requires independent decisions by the student to use that learning.

Self-Regulated Learning

The cybercoaching model addresses a core belief that students, and especially those becoming professional educators themselves, must develop skills of analysis and dispositions of self-improvement. A key objective for developing self-regulation (Zimmerman & Schunk, 2002) is the strategy of **metacognition** (Bandura, 1997), that is, looking at one's own understanding and performance, and analyzing it according to criteria. When these criteria have been described in concrete terms along a continuum from unacceptable to ideal, a rubric has been articulated (for details, see "Rubrics: The Coach's Tool of Choice for Feedback" below).

Distinctiveness of the Cybercoaching Model

Computer technology has increased the speed of communication and simplified record-keeping. Students acknowledged through a survey study conducted through the first-year biology classes at the University of Sydney by Peat and Franklin (2002) that one of the most favored aspects of the computer-delivered and graded quizzes was instant feedback. In contrast, a survey study conducted by Angulo and Bruce (1999) focused on the degree of satisfaction of traditional students in five courses representing disciplines in the humanities, social sciences, and natural sciences. WebCt (*http://www.webct.com/software*) was used as a supplemental element for various purposes as designed by five different instructors. These instructors taught the courses ranging from a large freshman lecture course to a small graduate seminar. The participants completed online assignments besides checking for grades and retrieving lecture notes. On the basis of the analysis of surveys, the researchers found that the participants generally were neither strongly satisfied nor strongly dissatisfied with the Web-based instruction (WBI) supplement, despite their improved skill level in the use of technology.

The 2004 National Survey of Student Engagement (NSSE) concluded that almost 90% of faculty reported there was prompt feedback to academic performance. However, this result was agreed to by less than 60% of students. NSSE's report therefore supported the survey result conducted by Angulo and Bruce (1999). It is apparent that instant feedback generated by the machine alone does not "win" the hearts of the students. Students expect more than instant feedback in the assessment process. To understand what more is needed, let us first consider the technical options of computer-assisted responses.

Mechanical Reponses

Most universities provide some online platforms, such as Blackboard (*http://www.blackboard.com/*), WebCt (*http://www.webct.com/software*), or their own variety, such as OnCourse (*http://www.iu.edu*) developed by Indiana University Bloomington.

These online platforms all have features that allow the course instructor to design online quizzes or exams. Computer-assisted assessment—that is, the use of computers to deliver, mark, and analyze assignments or examinations—has a place (Rudner & Gagne, 2001), but they may only be used when there are simple solutions, or 'one right answer' (Stiggins, 2005). This means that computer-based tests, however helpful, are limited to testing lower levels of thinking (see Starko et al., 2003). In addition, quiz items may lead students to misinterpret quiz questions because of vagueness or errors made by the instructor in designing those questions. Although mechanical corrections do provide welcome information (Peat & Franklin, 2002), they constitute a pre-designed "one-shot deal." It is an end in itself that is insensitive to idiosyncratic expression from students and further development of their thoughts. For the instructor, mechanical corrections may not provide adequate information to analyze obstacles to student success.

Personal Attention

The distinguishing characteristic of the cybercoaching model affirms the personalized feedback based on the harmonic teaching-learning cycle (see Figure 1). Current theory, research, and pedagogical standards support student-centered 'best practice' for more effective learning (Danielson & McGreal, 2001; Lambert & McCombs, 1997). At the university level, student satisfaction is seriously considered. Personal attention from instructors is expected by university students as tuition-paying consumers, as evidenced by the fact that many items on typical student surveys concern student-instructor interaction and students' active engagement. In fact, the NSSE survey (*http:/*

Figure 1. The harmonic feedback loop

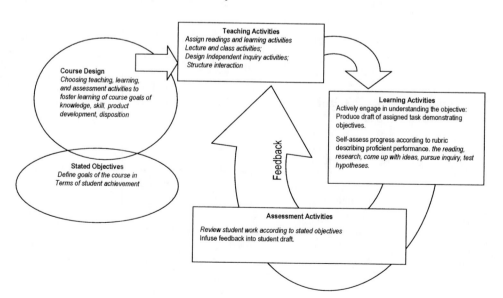

/websurvey.indiana.edu/nsse2004/submit.cfm) specifically asks students to rate how available, helpful, and sympathetic their instructors are. For example, one question asks how frequently the student has "received prompt feedback from faculty on your academic performance (written or oral)." In addition to the speed and frequency of feedback, though, the instructor must also consider the type of response that is communicated. These differ greatly in form as well as purpose. The purpose of most interest to cybercoaching is communication that strengthens the coaching relationship. It is helpful, then, to consider different types of responses and how they serve to provide personal attention from the instructor.

Difference Between Two Types of Responses

There is a big difference between tasks that have one right answer and tasks that are more complex. The first are often selected response items (i.e., true/false, multiple choice, matching, fill-in-blank) or else strictly mandated formats. Instead of a coach, these require only a referee to make a call of in or out, fair or foul, correct or incorrect. In contrast are tasks that demonstrate more than one objective. This means there is more than one criterion for success and more than one way of demonstrating proficiency. Whether the student is writing a research proposal or designing a lesson plan or generating a graph or charting a path, there are many skills involved, each benefiting from specific feedback.

Richard Stiggins (2005) called essay assessment 'subjective and powerful', compared to 'flexible and efficient' selected response items. Essays are not the only tasks to have more than one way to be right and more than one dimension of quality. Having more than one right answer is a characteristic of all assignments that require the creative combination of many elements for understanding one topic. For instance, maps are visual essays. Football plays add a time element to the spatial. In teacher education, the most common such task is the design of a lesson plan or instructional unit. Just like an essay, it has a conventional structure and identified purpose.

Selected response items have only one criterion, accuracy, while essay-type tasks have many criteria. The complexity is not just a matter of quantity, but quality, because accuracy is fairly concrete while many of the other criteria of excellence are vaguely defined. The challenge is to convert the subjective into the objective, and this is done by analyzing the writing in order to focus on separate traits while maintaining a perspective of the whole.

Tailored Responses

Many online platforms familiar to universities, such as Blackboard (*www.blackboard.com*) facilitate individualized instruction. The comments provided by the instructor are varied based on different responses made by students. The instructor's informed judgment is made at the moment the student requires feedback, which is specific to an individual learner's weaknesses or misunderstandings. Feedback tailored for each individual encourages the student to reflect upon his or her work, and to develop a higher level of thinking and understanding.

One of the authors conducted a study over five semesters of teaching an upper-division course at a Midwestern school of education (Chang, 2003a). Students received online feedback on lesson plans and essays, and were allowed to make revisions before the final evaluation. Participants (n = 110) were asked in an open-ended question to list reasons for their preference for or against the online feedback format and revision policy. These responses were analyzed for commonality. The following were the most common responses in favor of the online feedback format: (a) furthering learning opportunities (36 participants); (b) receiving more personal feedback in electronic classroom than in traditional instruction (31 participants); (c) receiving quick responses (24 participants); and (d) keeping in constant communication with the course instructor (15 participants). These responses suggest that the students were more interested in learning than in grades. Surprisingly, only five participants revealed that they liked the fact that they were allowed to revise their work because it could raise their grade. It is important to note that the participants experienced this feedback procedure several times; apparently feeling they were helped and supported by the instructor. One student noted in the survey: "It really helps to have feedback consistently from you [the instructor] to help keep us on the right track and to help further explain concepts." Another student expressed:

> *I never thought of it till now, but emailing back and forth was very nice—if I would have had class all the time I might no[t] have ask[ed] so many questions—this style we did was much more comfortable for me. Immediate feedback allowed me to be able to fix my mistakes in a timely manner.*

This is an encouraging response in light of the concerns regarding the dehumanization in utilizing computer technology to teach and learn (Bothel, 2002).

In another study, Chang (2003b) examined her students' perceptions toward online teaching and learning communication. The participants (n=27) were students in a general methods course for preschool and elementary teachers. After meeting face-to-face during the first two weeks of the semester, all the instruction and learning were structured online. At the end of that semester, students' perceptions were surveyed, and all 27 participants responded positively to the immediate feedback component of the course, and felt that they were supported and cared for by the instructor.

Assessment Aligned with Objectives

The harmonic feedback loop (see Figure 1) shows that all the teaching and learning activities must be related directly to the course objectives; assessment activities determine whether the objectives are reached. The instructor must decide what and how to communicate the assessment to best serve the student's readiness to develop further. The American Association of Higher Education developed nine principles of good practice for assessing students, including Principle 3: "Assessment works best when the programs it seeks to improve have clear, explicitly stated purposes. Assessment is a goal-oriented process" (Astin et al., 2004, para. 3). The authors agree with this principle, and therefore emphasizes the importance of clear objectives to be assessed (Wiggins & McTighe, 1999) and their use in feedback (Miller, 2003).

Formative vs. Summative Assessment

The cybercoaching model is a form of assessment. It is important to distinguish formative assessment from summative assessment. The former is intended to adjust the instruction and learning in response to the student's performance, while the latter is used to evaluate the student's mastery. Formative assessment involves monitoring the student's progress and then inserting focused mini-lessons that direct the student to particular skills required for adequate performance of the assignment.

Summative assessment is a final evaluation, after which the instructor does not expect to influence student learning. Online communication contributes an important opportunity to summative assessment for students who report liking to check their course grade as their separate assignments develop. The limit to this value is that once a grade is recorded, students tend to see it as a permanent indication of their value or potential. Cybercoaching is therefore concerned with techniques for self-assessment and formative assessment in order to inspire growth before any formal summative evaluation is conducted.

Rubrics: The Coach's Tool of Choice for Feedback

Cybercoaching involves a dialogue between the teacher and the student, prompted by directions from the teacher. The teacher, or coach, initiates the conversation with a 'prompt' that must be logically related to the objectives of the course. This may be a simple question or direction to which the student is expected to respond. The subsequent interaction will support the development of thinking. According to Bloom's taxonomy of cognitive development, the quality of thought progresses from simple memory of facts to more complex analysis and synthesis (Anderson et al., 2000). The lower levels of thinking tend to be concrete. They provide the knowledge base for the higher, more abstract, levels of thinking.

The abstract concepts of the course goals must be translated into concrete and recognizable products. The objectives of the course become the criteria articulated in the rubric, which, in turn, helps students understand the task. The rubric describes the whole integrated product at each level of proficiency; an analytic rubric describes each criterion, typically organized in a matrix to show gradual changes in quality (Mertler, 2001). A rubric is an established list of the criteria used to decide the quality of a performance. The gradual development from weak to strong performance may be described holistically or analytically.

Table 2. Example of a holistic rubric

Quantity of Online Participation	Score
The student contributed regularly.	4-5
The student's level of contribution was acceptable/of average value.	3
The student hardly contributed.	1-2
The student did not contribute at all.	0

Holistic Rubrics

A naïve or holistic rubric will be a single scale describing the general characteristic of each level, as shown in Table 2. These holistic rubrics could be refashioned using more specific criteria, such as factual knowledge, conceptual knowledge, procedural knowledge, and metacognitive knowledge, again using the revised Bloom's model of cognition (Anderson et al., 2000). To repeat the point made earlier about aligning activities with objectives, none of these criteria are appropriate unless they were established as objectives of the course.

Analytical Rubrics

A more specifically articulated rubric would describe the range from unacceptable to exemplary performance in concrete terms that students could recognize. Table 3 is an example of a comprehensive rubric for undergraduate writing assignments (Petersen, 2004b) using six traits as developed by the Northwest Regional Educational Laboratory (1998; see also Spandel, 2000; Stiggins, 2005). This sort of articulated, or analytical, rubric is a key tool for online assessment, beginning with the fact that the student is already familiar with it before the feedback exchange. Students are asked to self-assess their work by looking for descriptors that apply to their draft; students read each others' work and provide feedback using the language of the descriptors in order to avoid less helpful comments of bland approval. These pleasant but trite comments are informally referred to as 'attaboys'.

The last part of the rubric, 'next steps', emphasizes a metacognitive element of goal-setting. The student needs to make a decision to build on needed concepts and/or skills. This may be frustrating for a student who is accustomed to "spoon-fed" assessment (Kohn, 1999) and overly simplified targets. However, the instructor's timely assistance, encouragement, or support, available through e-communication, may help foster self-assessment and self-regulated learning. This is the part of the uniqueness of the cybercoaching model that promotes a personal relationship through dialogues between the instructor and student rather than interactions between the student and a device.

Table 3. Example of an analytical rubric

Trait	Emerging	Competent	Proficient	Professional
Organization	Random list	Logic within paragraphs	Clear intro and conclusion	Flows smoothly
Ideas	Few; superficial treatment; isolated concepts; no support	Some development; little connection between ideas; some support	More idea development; more theory and practice connection	Separate sections labeled with appropriate titles
Word Choice	Slang, colloquialisms, contractions, inaccuracies, misuse of jargon	No unconventional English usage; appropriate use of jargon	Fluent use of professional vocabulary	Helpful use of appropriate titles to summarize sections
Sentence Fluency	Fragments, comma splices, run-ons; choppy or rambling	Mostly complete thoughts with some attention to variety for emphasis	Smooth transitions as ideas develop; no clichés or empty phrases	Inspired turns of phrase
Voice	Completely casual or extremely mechanical	Scholarly tone with consistent point of view	Scholarly with personal point of view	Scholarly with personal point of view and experience
Conventions	Trends of mistakes in mechanics and usage	Few errors of mechanics or usage	No errors of mechanics or usage; skilled use to improve meaning	Fluent, skilled mechanics and usage to improve reading
Presentation	No title page or numbering, in consistent or distracting style choices	Mostly consistent, with adequate identification; few distractions due to format	Font and format enhances readability; no distractions of style	Professional presentation: visually inspired, easy-to-read format

Next steps:

Teaching on an Individual Basis

The advantage of a completely articulated analytic rubric that describes each criterion in concrete terms for recognizing insufficient to proficient work is that the teacher has a common language for discussing the issue with students (Andrade, 2000). Asking about the meaning of a rubric descriptor is a completely different dynamic in the relationship between instructor and student than challenging a grade. The rubric, therefore, becomes a versatile tool for the learning environment because it fosters clarity and independence as the student begins to recognize the descriptions as applying to his or her own work.

The rubric alone is a teaching tool as well as an assessment tool, because each time the concepts in it are referred to, those concepts are newly considered. Ultimately, the student will use rubrics to organize information and, in addition to using them, will construct them.

Practical Considerations

Using Neutral Language

One important consideration when developing the rubric is to avoid language that implies right or wrong compared to developmental criteria. This means that critical language is avoided. Instead, simple observations are made, which indicate a point in the sequence from novice to expert. This may be seen in Table 4, which highlights just one row, or criterion, from the full rubric of Table 3. The descriptors communicate an observation of fact rather than a judgment. This language encourages the student to analyze the performance rather than focus on the instructor's approval. It models the self-assessment that is the hallmark of continuous improvement.

Table 4. Developmental rubric

CATEGORY	Emerging	Competent	Proficient	Exemplary
Conventions	Unconventional English usage and mechanics are frequent enough to distract and establish doubt regarding minimum skills.	There may be one or two errors of usage or mechanics.	No errors of spelling, mechanics, or usage.	Not only are there no errors, but there is thoughtful use of format features.

Inserting Portions of the Rubric

The instructor uses the rubric while reading a draft, leaving it open in another browser while reading the student's work. After identifying a criterion from the rubric as a focus topic for some aspect of the draft, the instructor can select one row of developmental growth in that trait and paste it into the student's draft. This requires keeping more than one Word document open and toggling back and forth. Simply cutting and pasting a section of the rubric and highlighting the degree of proficiency with, say, yellow fill, will communicate enough. The instructor does not have to write an original note for each interaction. In yet another activity that does not require original messages, the instructor merely highlights problematic areas in the draft. The student is then given the task of analyzing which of the criteria are related to each of the highlighted sections.

Putting the Person in Personalized Feedback

Regarding the coaching function and the powerful influence of positive interaction, feedback should include minimum social courtesies of the student's name and mention of some aspect of the student known through shared experience. Like a letter, it should have an opening and a closing; and however long it takes to write them, contents must respect the need of the person to feel acknowledged as a living human being.

One of the easiest strategies is simply to write the student's name at least three times: once in a salutation, at least once within the text as part of a feedback item, and once in the closing. The comments may be as simple as "Thanks for turning this in early, Dennis" or "What an interesting topic, Andrea" or "An important point, Angelo." They should focus on the author's decisions relative to the assignment, rather than personal approval (Kohn, 1999). However, it is important to include details that establish a personal relationship. Some experience from a class session could be mentioned, thereby cementing the instructor's awareness of the student as a full participant in their community of learning. A future event or due date can be included to suggest the instructor's intention to continue the relationship.

The instructor will indeed have a similar relationship with most of the students, and will be able to refer to the same experience. If the instructor tries to compose varied comments every single time, there is a risk of repetition to the same student. Therefore, it is a good strategy to select routine remarks likely to apply to most students at any given point of feedback; then copy and paste the comment. This is not impersonal, but rather focused and efficient. Although these comments are generic, the instructor will not use them if they do not apply. Finally, the descriptors from the rubric can be inserted. Another helpful routine is to note which students do *not* receive the generic comments targeted for a particular assignment. This may reveal why they have difficulty achieving some minimum standard, an important aspect of the coaching role. The use of database software is beyond the scope of this article, but it is certainly not beyond the scope of the average classroom teacher.

Organizational Issues

Apart from the speed and flexibility of electronic files, there is a perennial problem of cluttered inboxes and endless lists of similarly named files. For this reason, the instructor needs a system of labeling that will take advantage of the computer's sense of order. Petersen (2004 a, 2004b) suggested an APA-style format of name and date bracketed by parentheses followed by the topic, like so: (Pooh, 15 Aug 04) Honeypot draft . This formula can also be used for e-mail subject lines. For student-instructor interaction, the label mentions the course, too, for example: (Eeyore, 30 Aug 04) 325 Exam Question . With this habit in place, new drafts will automatically appear in sequence with previous drafts. This is also a helpful convention for e-mail message subject lines, because scrolling through the inbox will still reveal the content and urgency of each message.

Word Processor Functions

There are many software programs that allow instructors to insert comments directly into the student's documents, such as the Microsoft Word Track Changes tool that allows for the automatic color change of deleted, added, or reformatted text. This has an advantage of instantly showing changes, but it can become confusing if the same draft goes back and forth several times. Newer versions remove the deleted text to margin notes, which simplifies the reading. Given that word processors and electronic mail are nearly universal among university students and instructors, it simply remains for the instructor to decide on some system to signal inserted information. The least defined approach is to simply read the student's work carefully and respond judiciously in order to encourage revision. Figure 2 is a sample from a student draft showing the use of Microsoft Word Track Changes to edit and coach.

Notice that the underlined text is added and the strike-through text was removed. Some of the text was simply moved. The final comment is bracketed with double asterisks to indicate it is not a change in text, but a comment about the writing process or assignment. At its simplest, it is proofreading and minor editing; at its most sophisticated it will inspire an understanding of the deep structure of the composition.

Figure 2. Feedback imbedded in Microsoft Word document using Track Changes tool

To avoid being dismissed raise the achievement of their students, educators must are encouraged to incorporate strategies based on scientific research that have been proven effective based on scientific research. The focus of proven strategy proposed in this paper is using is the use of homework as a tool to increase academic achievement of with twelfth grade U.S. Government students to meet the state proficiency level. **Mention the 'proven' part: add (author, date).**

Imbedded Feedback Cautions

The above figure is an example of imbedding comments in order to distinguish them from the original text. This technique is appropriate for directly coaching a particular thought development, or in this case, choosing more accurate or appropriate words—that is, "word-smithing." To advance the student to self-assessment, it would be helpful to include reference to some criteria of success already discussed. In this case, Word Choice (explained in the *Analytical Rubric*) would be a logical trait to explain the suggestions. This technique can be confusing or even anxiety-provoking for students if there is too much colorful adjustment. The student will not be able to see that his or her own words are still there, but simply rearranged. For this reason, instructors should be very selective, choosing one or two examples of the same concept if there is a trend in the paper.

Another caution is that once the instructor is skilled with this model of feedback, opportunities for teaching, as opposed to correcting, may be missed. The instructor should not provide all direct answers or the student may just wait for direction and change things accordingly, with no more thought than a word processor. Rubrics are used to translate abstract concepts into concrete descriptors. Using rubrics will encourage students to self-assess and help them recognize the objectives of the exercise. If the rubric makes no sense or cannot be applied competently, then the student should seek additional help.

Evaluation Cautions

Grades constitute snapshots of success at given points, not descriptions according to some standard used to judge, or evaluate, the student's performance. It is important to note that grades are sometimes used to monitor task completion or to compare students. Grades are useful to communicate measures of proficiency. The focus of cybercoaching is on the individual student's proficiency, or mastery of the course objectives, based on the criteria described in the rubric. The descriptions of each criterion should extend to a future proficiency to help the student predict continued progress. Therefore, the target is not to exhaust the rubric, but to reach the level of proficiency considered appropriate for that particular course.

A particular degree of proficiency could be targeted for successful completion of a course that is in a longer program sequence. For instance, the 'competent' level in either Table 3 or 4 might be the target for an introductory course, but the proficient level might be expected by graduation. The grade given for the paper would be based on the target within the rubric. In this way, the rubric can establish a stable range of quality while respecting the progression toward the highest possible achievement. Expectations can rise with experience, and students may avoid the pitfall of thinking the target within the course is the final goal. This is particularly useful for performance tasks that are expected to improve gradually, such as a philosophy statement, and to continue improving long after the course is over.

Table 5. Low-tech keyboard stroke indicators for feedback

Keyboard Stroke	Feedback Meaning	Keyboard Stroke	Feedback Meaning
< or >	*Move to a different place*	+	*Add*
~	*Suggest a different term*	^	*Format change*
[[ ]]	*Remove*	**	*Sidebar comment*

Color Options

Unlike the versatility of some systems, many e-mail programs do not have special formats of color or font. It is helpful for the imbedded feedback conventions to be able to work in both situations, such as those in the analytical rubric of Table 3. Each item of feedback should be bracketed to signal beginning and end. Microsoft Word options allow these changes to be color-coded, so the final comment could be highlighted to indicate a sidebar. Although text can be read through the color options on screen, most printers render all but yellow too dark to read on the hard copy. Black-and-white printers will obscure the text with a gray field. Therefore, before using color options, the instructor must understand and troubleshoot the recipients' situations. This naturally assumes that the instructor is asking for feedback regarding the use of the coaching features; acknowledging the students' reaction is a form of respect compatible with a coaching role.

Low-Tech Options for Editorial Feedback

Standard comments deserve a system much like editorial conventions written on hard copy, as suggested in Table 5.

In a straight substitute for the editor's classic red or blue pencil, the instructor can insert keystrokes to communicate suggestions. There must be a way to distinguish these additions from the student draft. One of the authors uses a standard double asterisk (**) to bracket all imbedded comments.

Future Trends in Cybercoaching

We anticipate several ways the cybercoaching model of online feedback may benefit learners and teachers. These are all important in light of society's increasing demand for personal attention as well as higher standards of performance, often associated with improved technology.

Equity and Excellence of Instruction

One social concern is the economic divide among students defined by access to advanced technology and access to campus resources; extending this is the problem of adjunct professors with limited access to resources which then place their students at a disadvantage. Support for underprepared and disadvantaged students as well as beginning or adjunct faculty may improve the quality of instruction and the community of learning. Cybercoaching is a manageable model for support at all levels of learning.

Quality and Frequency of Communication

Access to online communication technologies has become so widespread that the standards of communication are already rising. The traditional method of handing in a hard copy and waiting for a professor to read it and return it, which necessarily reduced the opportunity to revise before the end of a course, is now unnecessarily slow and cumbersome. A future trend will undoubtedly be that every face-to-face course will have an online component (Raschke, 2002). Student-instructor interaction will be defined more specifically to include feedback; future teachers will be taught to design systems of communication that use electronic messages. One special topic of communication is assessment, which will continue to increase in importance.

Quality and Frequency of Assessment

The trend toward regulation of jobs will mean greater demand for evidence that a candidate is qualified to do the job. This will mean that assessments must be clearly aligned with goals and standards. The process of identifying targets, describing performance, and giving feedback to encourage students' efforts to develop greater proficiency will not change, but the standard for analyzing each step will. As part of the trend of accountability, we may expect the quality of assessment to continue to rise, with students demanding syllabi and articulated rubrics for their complex assignments (Shavelson & Huang, 2003).

Continuous Professional Development

There is great demand for flexible and personal instruction as workers must update their skills or change careers. This often involves dispositional knowledge more than techni-cal skills. Related to this, in response to increased violence and sophisticated piracy, there is also an increasing demand for ethical behavior, best fostered through close communication. The cybercoaching model provides a framework for the reflective and tutorial functions required to develop personal paradigm shifts.

Increased Research on Formative Assessment

Current models of teaching and assessment that emphasize feedback need more study. However, its personalized nature makes it less standardized and therefore more difficult to measure. Much of the literature so far is limited to survey research concerning student opinion, for instance, Peat and Franklin's (2003) finding that although students saw value in formative assessment opportunities, there was no significant difference in summative assessment outcomes based on their use. There is compelling reason to study the relationship between formative and summative assessment techniques, course content, nature of tasks, and student characteristics.

Summary

Cybercoaching, an emerging model of online formative assessment, was introduced in this chapter. The coaching role connects with the new online technology. It works when the product under development can be transmitted via cyberspace. Computer technology may speed communication and simplify record-keeping, but it does not improve a poorly designed course nor compensate for a poorly prepared student. It does, however, provide a means to establish a supportive coaching relationship through which the student may expect personal attention and guidance.

We used a harmonic cycle to illustrate the circular process of teaching, learning, and assessment to emphasize the process of development rather than the procedure for evaluation. Formative assessment, or the monitoring of achievement in progress, rather than summative assessment (i.e., the evaluation at a checkpoint), is thus the purpose of this model. Cybercoaching promotes self-assessment with the use of rubrics that describe performance according to each criterion at various stages of development. Finally, further research was suggested in order to understand the dynamics of the teaching and learning process through formative assessment.

To summarize, these are the salient components of successful cybercoaching:

- Foster a coaching relationship with each student.

- Design rubrics that describe novice to expert performance of each criterion of success.

- Establish a routine of immediacy for feedback, and respond to feedback from students.

- Encourage revision for mastery, separating feedback from grades.
- Respect the limitations of both the word processing and e-mail software.
- Prepare for an increasingly paperless culture.

Cybercoaching is presented here as a model for promoting more student-centered interaction by using readily available technology. The authors sincerely hope that this serves to encourage faculty who have not adopted a coaching role to consider its merits for teaching, and to encourage faculty who have not become adept at using e-mail and word processors to consider their advantages for both efficiency and effectiveness. Finally, we hope that the increased use of technology is always considered a means to improving student-instructor engagement within the teaching and learning cycle.

References

Anderson, L., Krathwohl, D., Airaisian, P., Cruikshank, K., Mayer, R., Pintrich, P., Raths, J. & Wittrock, M. (2000). *A taxonomy for learning, teaching, and assessing: A revision of Bloom's taxonomy of educational objectives.* Boston: Allyn & Bacon.

Andrade, H.G. (2000). Using rubrics to promote thinking and learning. *Educational Leadership, 57*(5), 13-18.

Angulo, A.J., & Bruce, M. (1999). Student perceptions of supplemental Web-based instruction. *Innovative Higher Education, 24*(2), 105-125.

Astin, A.W., Banta, T.W., Cross, K.P., El-Khawas, E., Ewell, P.T., Hutchings, P., Marchese, T.J., McClenney, K.M., Mentkowski, M., Miller, M.A., Moran, E.T., & Wright, B.D. (2003). 9 principles of good practice for assessing student learning. Retrieved July 15, 2004, from *http://www.aahe.org/assessment/principl.htm*

Bandura, A. (1997). *Self-efficacy: The exercise of control.* New York: W.H. Freeman.

Bothel, R.T. (2002). Epilogue: A cautionary note about online *assessment. New Directions for Teaching & Learning, 91,* 99-105.

Chang, N. (2003a, April). Students' perspectives of online individualized instruction and learning. *Proceedings of the 5th Annual Midwest Conference on the Scholarship of Teaching and Learning,* South Bend, IN.

Chang, N. (2003b, October). What are preferences of students? Constructivist pedagogy. *Proceedings of the 2003 Conference of the Mid-Western Education Research Association,* Columbus, OH.

Clark, K. (2004). What can I say besides sound it out? *Reading Teacher, 57,* 440-450.

Danielson, C., & McGreal, T. (2001). *Teacher evaluation to enhance professional practice.* Alexandria, VA: Association for Supervision and Curriculum Development.

Gilbert, W., & Trudel, P. (2004). Role of the coach: How model youth team sport coaches frame their roles. *Sport Psychologist, 18,* 21-44.

Kohn, A. (1999). *Punished by rewards: The trouble with gold stars, incentive plans, A's, and other bribes.* Boston: Houghton Mifflin.

Lambert, N., & McCombs, B. (1997). *How students learn: Reforming schools with learner-centered education.* Washington, DC: American Psychological Association.

Lindblom-Ylanne, S., & Pihlaijamaki, H. (2003). Can a collaborative network environment enhance essay-writing processes? *British Journal of Educational Technology, 34,* 17-31.

Mertler, C.A. (2001). Designing scoring rubrics for your classroom. *Practical Assessment, Research & Evaluation, 7*(25). Retrieved August 10, 2004, from *http://PAREonline.net/getvn.asp?v=7&n=25*

Miller, S. (2003). How high- and low-challenge tasks affect motivation and learning: Implications for struggling learners. *Reading & Writing Quarterly, 19,* 39-58.

Nelson, J., Apenhorst, D., Carter, L., Mahlum, E., & Schneider, J. (2004). Coaching for competence. *MEDSURG Nursing, 13,* 32-46.

Northwest Regional Educational Laboratory (NWREL). (1998). Toolkit98. Retrieved February 20, 2004, from *http://www.nwrel.org/assessment/ToolKit98.asp*

Peat, M., & Franklin, S. (2002). Supporting student learning: The use of computer-based formative assessment modules. *British Journal of Educational Technology, 33*(5), 517-526.

Peat, M., & Franklin, S. (2003). Has student learning been improved by the use of online and offline formative assessment opportunities? *Australian Journal of Educational Technology, 19,* 87-99. Retrieved August 10, 2004, from *http://www.ascilite.org.au/ajet/ajet19/peat.html*

Petersen, N.J. (2004a, April). Rubrics for the reflective record: Tools for coaching the development and use of professional portfolios. *Proceedings of the Annual Meeting of the American Educational Research Association,* San Diego, CA.

Petersen, N.J. (2004b, July 17) Using performance assessment to promote imagination. *Proceedings of the 2nd International Conference on Imagination and Education,* Vancouver, British Columbia.

Raschke, C.A. (2002). *The digital revolution and the coming of the postmodern university.* New York: Routledge/Falmer.

Rudner, L., & Gagne, P. (2001). An overview of three approaches to scoring written essays by computer. *Practical Assessment, Research & Evaluation, 7*(26). Retrieved August 10, 2004, from *http://PAREonline.net/getvn.asp?v=7&n=26*

Shavelson, R.J., & Huang, L. (2003). Responding responsibly to the frenzy to assess learning in higher education. *Change Magazine,* (January/February). Retrieved from *http://www.aahe.org/change/shavelson.pdf*

Smith, K.U., & Smith, M. (1965). *Cybernetic principles of learning and educational design.* New York: Holt, Rinehart & Winston.

Spandel, V. (2000). *Creating writers through Six-Trait Writing assessment and instruction* (3rd ed.). Boston: Allyn & Bacon.

Starko, A.J., Sparks-Langer, G.M., Pasch, M., Frankes, L., Gardner, T.G., & Moody, C.D. (2003). *Teaching as decision making: Successful practices for the elementary teachers* (3rd ed.). Upper Saddle River, NJ: Merrill-Prentice-Hall.

Stiggins, R. (2005). *Student-involved assessment FOR learning* (4th ed.). Upper Saddle River, NJ: Merrill.

Vygotsky, L. (1978). *Mind in society: The development of higher psychological processes*. Cambridge, MA: Harvard University Press.

Wiggins, G., & McTigue, J. (1999). *Design for understanding*. Alexandria, VA: Association of Supervision and Curriculum Development.

Zhao, C., & Kuh, G.D. (2004). Adding value: Learning communities and student engagement. *Research in Higher Education, 45*, 115-138.

Zimmerman, B., & Kitsanas, A. (2003). Acquiring *writing* revision and self-regulatory skill through observation and emulation. *Journal of Educational Psychology, 94*, 660-668.

Zimmerman, B.J., & Schunk, D.H. (Eds). (2002). *Educational psychology: A century of contributions*. A Project of Division 15 (Educational Psychology) of the American Psychological Association. Mahwah, NJ: Lawrence Erlbaum.

Chapter IX

Testing the Validity of Post and Vote Web-Based Peer Assessment

Bruce L. Mann, Memorial University, Canada

Abstract

Two tests of validity were conducted with undergraduate education students on a method of online peer assessment called post and vote. Validity was determined by calculating a Pearson product-moment correlation and corresponding coefficient of determination that compared the average grade assigned by the pre-service teachers with the grade assigned independently by the course instructor. Results of both studies showed that post and vote Web-based peer assessment was valid with these groups, and generalizable to undergraduate classes engaged in similar tasks.

Introduction

Post and vote is a method of collecting and analyzing peer assessment data using off-the-shelf Web tools. This approach emerged in the late 1990s, at a time when colleges, universities, and training organizations had already adopted a Web-based training platform and were becoming acquainted with the features provided in the Web tools. The Web tools included: a bulletin board for posting and replying to discussions, a student viewing area, a questionnaire tool, a message compiler, online chat, student progress tracking, group project organization, student self-evaluation, grade maintenance and distribution, access control, navigation tools, auto-marked quizzes, electronic mail, automatic index generation, course calendar, student homepages, and course content searches.

Today colleges, universities, and training organizations around the world are using Web-based training platforms to offer students an online education. Since these tools are customarily grouped together under a course name and protected by a password, they can be treated as elements of a "system," a "Web course management system" (WCMS) (Mann, 1999a, 1999b, 2000a), consistent with systems theory, and the post and vote model is a subsystem, or more accurately a modeling subsystem of the WCMS. More discussion follows about post and vote as a system.

Trial-and-Error Learning and Bulletin Board Data

Throughout the late 1990s and 2000, publicity and sales promotions in print and on the Web claimed that their Web tools required minimal technical skill, and said they preferred to let educators apply their own methods of course design to their Web courses (Mann, 1998a, 1998b, 1998c). Consequently: (1) the bulletin board tool was overused, with high volumes of student data being saved in the discussion board for reading and grading; and (2) a trial-and-error method of learning Web tools became the de facto method of preparing instructional materials for student learning on the Web, a method which was later re-defined as "an instructor's gradual phasing-in to Web course management behavior" (Mann, 2000a, p. 23).

Instructional Design Inertia

Around the same time that most of us were sifting through hundreds of student discussions and learning Web-tools by trial and error, familiar models and theories of instructional design were slowly being abandoned by practitioners, and when they were used, were regularly misapplied (Gros, Elen, Kerres, van Merrienboer, & Spector, 1997). According to some experts, instructional design models and theories had become static (Boshier et al., 1997), inert (Yang, Moore & Burton, 1995), unusable (Wild & Quinn, 1998), and simply not workable (Winn, 1997) for prescribing interactive learning.

In sum, this was a busy time for instructors, a lack of enthusiasm for applying familiar models and theories of instructional design to Web-based learning, little real Web tool assistance to count on, and hundreds of board postings to read and analyze.

Phase Theory and Post and Vote

It was under these conditions that two frameworks were introduced to help to better explain the situation. First, "phase theory" was published, a descriptive framework for analyzing the Web tools and strategies that an instructor already knows how to use. A detailed explanation of phase theory is available in Mann (1999a, 1999b, 2000a). Second, "post and vote model" appeared to help reduce the perceived instructional design inertia and overuse of the bulletin board tool, and settle in to learning a few specific Web tools. A more systematic method of collecting and analyzing the data was needed to manage the high volume of student postings in the discussion board. A key component of the post and vote model was using more of the Web tools together as a system of tools and strategies for the purpose for which they were intended. Another key component was student involvement in the assessment process, which already had a 30-year history and was becoming more prominent (see Falchikov & Goldfinch, 2000; Sluijsmans, Saskia, & van Merriënboer, 2002).

Peer Assessment: The Benefits and Limitations

Student peer assessment is the process where students evaluate one another's work (Topping, Smith, Swanson, & Elliot, 2000). Peer assessment requires that students exchange assignments, discuss responses, and rate one another's work using scoring systems or rating scales devised by the teacher (Airasian, 2001).

Benefits of Peer Assessment

The peer assessor learns from critically analyzing and evaluating other students' work. The student that is assessed learns from their peer's feedback. Peer assessment has the following advantages in face-to-face learning settings (Blumhof & Stallibrass, 1994):

- Helps develop evaluative thinking skills.

- Helps focus on criteria that improve the learning outcomes.

- Helps to motivate students' own sense of assessment as a result of:

  - Negotiating and agreeing on criteria

  - Understanding the system

  - Having a share in the marking.

- Provides an opportunity to judge their own work and hence improve their own performance because of raised self-awareness of how assessment is undertaken, and what is assessed.

- Heightens the awareness of the teacher's skills that students might otherwise not notice.

- Enhances concentration and increases the learning potential in a situation because students are intimately involved in the processes. By intimate we mean that emotions and values are engaged in an analytic task. The process includes planning and reflection.

- Provides a built-in emphasis on planning and reflection that is of particular value to reflective learners.

Many studies show that peer assessment can help learners develop critical, evaluative, and analytical skills (Anderson, Howe, Soden, Halliday, & Low, 2001; Falchikov, 1986; Pond, Rehan, & Wade, 1995; Searby & Ewers, 1997; Topping et al., 2000). Peer assessment that involves students' ability to make value judgments, analyze responses, and provide reasoned arguments on other students' work is beneficial for both the peer assessor and the student being assessed (Falchikov, 1995; Freeman, 1995). Anderson et al. (2001) found that college students who were involved in peer-based critiquing exercises showed significant improvement in their oral and written work in terms of providing justification of their arguments, compared to those in the control group. Falchikov (1986) reported that undergraduate science students involved in peer assessment found that the assessment process "made them think more, learn more, and become more critical and structured" (p. 161). Searby and Ewers (1997) stated, "The most significant reason for the introduction of peer assessment is that it helps students to think critically and to take control of their learning so that they are less dependent on the instructor" (p. 372). In sum, peer assessment that involves students' ability to make value judgments, analyze responses, and provide reasoned arguments on other students' work is beneficial for both the peer assessor and the student assessed (Falchikov, 1995; Freeman, 1995; O'Donnell & Topping, 1998).

Limitations of Peer Assessment

Although peer assessment can facilitate many positive outcomes, it can also raise issues of personal anxiety and exposure. *In face-to-face teaching conditions, students have said they felt that peer assessment was threatening* (Blumhof & Stallibrass, 1994):

- *Changes the culture.* Students expect the teacher to be the expert and judge, as this is what they have come to expect in their educational experience. Peer assessment is seen to be changing a well-worn and tried 'traditional system' and shifting the balance of power from course instructor to students. Though the shift at present is absolutely minimal, the change in culture makes it destabilizing.

- *Challenges the contract.* In economic terms, the informal contract for many students is that they agree to pay their fees and do a reasonable amount of work, and the course instructor will design a course, teach it, and pass a high proportion of students. Some feel badly treated when the contract is changed.

- *Causes personal anxiety.* Some students have reported that they did not feel they had the appropriate skills to undertake the assessment, and this increased their anxiety.

- *Raises problems of exposure.* Students are not trained in our social relations to give and take constructive criticism without it feeling like a personal attack on them as individuals. Students dislike the exposure of publicly offering critical feedback as much as they fear receiving it. The main fears that they have heard voiced are that:

  - *Peer pressure.* If you give offence, there is the fear that you may be ostracized from the group.

  - *Friendship marking.* Questions can be raised about the fairness of the marking scheme. Marks may be skewed through friendships or hostilities. Peer assessors also have a tendency to "over-mark"—assign higher marks relative to the course instructor-assigned marks—students' work (Falchikov, 1986; Kelmar, 1993; Pond et al., 1995; Mowl & Pain, 1995; Rushton, Ramsey, & Rada, 1993; Sluijsmans, Moerkerke, Dochy, & van Merriënboer, 2001).

- *Makes more visible the inherent difficulties in all marking schemes.* These difficulties include:

  - The tendency to mark the more easily measurable.

  - A tendency to mark towards the middle to avoid obvious offence. Peers are reluctant to indicate weaknesses (critical comments) in their assessment of other students' work (Falchikov, 1995, 1996; Topping et al., 2000).

  - The tendency to be affected by stereotyping and expectations without the safety valve of anonymity marking.

  - Exposing the subjectivity of marking schemes by trying to decide on, and weight, criteria.

These inconsistencies in peer marking may affect the reliability of the peer assessment process. It was under these conditions that that the post and vote model of Web-based peer assessment was introduced, a systematic method of using Web tools and strategies together to collect and analyze student peer assessment data (Mann 1999a, 1999b, 2000a).

Post and Vote

Post and vote is a partially open, four-step system of Web-based peer assessment. In this research, the post and vote model is both a focal system of peer assessment itself, as well as a subsystem of the Web course management system (WCMS). As the focal system of Web-based peer assessment, the post and vote model readily employs generic, off-the-shelf Web tools provided in most WCMSs, such as *BlackBoard* (Pittinsky & Chasen, 1997), *WebCT* (Goldberg & Salari, 1996), or any one of a number of others (Mann, 1999a). For a current listing of WCMSs, consult the EduTools Web site (WCET, 2003). This model requires no extra computer programming, patches, add-ons, or third-party software.

Figure 1 shows a graphical representation of the four steps in post and vote, described as a "partially open system" of Web-based peer assessment. The arrows show the direction of input, output, and throughput (processing) between the four elements in the post and vote system. The dashed line surrounding Figure 1 separates the elements "inside the system" from those "outside the system" (in the environment, other systems).

According to systems theory, every system strives toward equilibrium as it constantly fluctuates between too much and too little information. For this reason, every system is necessarily concerned with the communication and control of variety inside and outside itself. "Variety" in this sense is a measure of the number of distinct states a system can be in at any given time. A system can thrive, barely survive, or even die from its variety. "Requisite variety" is a measure of capability inside and outside the system. The more variety of actions available to a system, the larger the variety of perturbations it is able to compensate for from elements inside and outside itself.

"Systems" are either "closed," "open," or "partially open" (Heylighen, Joslyn, & Turchin, 2002). A WCMS is a "partially open system," only partially open because access to its data and Web tools is protected by a password, making the WCMS "closed" to the general public; yet learning in a WCMS is usually dependent on hypertext links to the

Figure 1. A graphical representation of the steps in post and vote of Web-based peer assessment

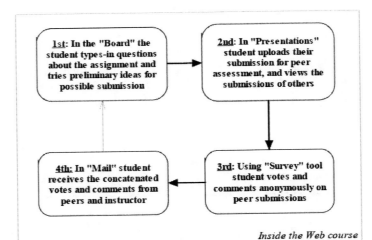

outside Web sites or tools, or access to e-mail systems, chat, or other communication tools on other servers. As a partially open system, students and instructors will sometimes require tools from the parent WCMS or those from other Internet systems to improve requisite variety. Filters such as the discussion board and survey tools help to limit the variety entering the system; amplifiers such as e-mail, ftp, and instant messaging help to increase variety, leaving the system for other systems outside itself (in its environment).

The best test of an educational system is the benefit it brings to students and instructors using it. The survival of the post and vote system of peer assessment depends on the requisite variety among the peers working with the WCMS; that is to say, the variety of knowledge and skill of instructor and student assessors together must be greater or at least equal to the variety in each student assignment being assessed. Using another educational metaphor, a teacher working in a school system must possess the requisite variety of knowledge and skill to thrive or at least survive within the variety of knowledge and skill of her students. Group work and role-playing are two well-known filters for maintaining the teacher's requisite variety in the classroom. Useful amplifiers for increasing teacher variety and maintaining requisite variety inside and outside the classroom include photocopies, homework Web sites, and class e-mail lists. Details on requisite variety and other systems concepts can be accessed from the Principia Cybernetica Web site.

Step 1: Typing into the Board

Figure 1 shows that the student's first step in using post and vote is to access the discussion board tool, type-in questions and comments about the assignment, and tryout preliminary ideas for possible submission. Even at this early stage, student contributions or "participation grades" can be assigned, their postings to online conferences (the discussion board tool) evaluated using any one of a number of methods of analyzing the discourse. Henri (1992), for example, developed a widely used content analysis model. Five key dimensions were identified for analysis of online discussions, namely: (1) participation rate (e.g., raw number and timing of messages); (2) interaction type (e.g., direct response, "in response to the posting…"); (3) social cues (e.g., "It's my birthday today"); (4) cognitive skills (e.g., judgment "I disagree with…") and depth of processing (surface-level or deep-level processing); and (5) meta-cognitive skills and knowledge (e.g., providing examples and relating to situations). Hara, Curtis, and Angeli (2000) paralleled Henri's (1992) recommendations of content analysis in online discussions and proposed more elaborate guidelines to analyze electronic conversations. Their study focused on the social and cognitive processes demonstrated by the students during online discussions. Rose (2002) and Brown (2002) used Henri's content analysis model in their doctoral research. There are other models, however. For a recent overview of issues and trends in Web-based discourse analysis research, see Rourke, Anderson, Garrison, and Archer (2001).

Step 2: Student Uploads

The second step for the student using the post and vote model is to upload their html-ed assignments into a common viewing area for subsequent viewing by other students. Most WCMSs support individual or group uploads and allow the designer to designate group membership. Alternatively, the WCMS can automatically divide the class into groups, given the desired group size. Students might collaborate (using the e-mail and document-sharing tools) to critique a flow chart or write a research paper or proposal, then "html it" and electronically upload the html file into their student viewing area. Only group members can edit their own content. Once all the papers are uploaded into the student viewing area using the appropriate tool, students are requested to read the submissions of their classmates. Each student uses the survey tool to anonymously grade and comment on other students' presentations. Student peer assessors can be made "accountable," told in advance that the instructor will be grading the quality of their peer assessments, and that this grade will be counted toward their final mark. In a recent experimental comparison of accountability (more accountable vs. less accountable) and anonymity (anonymous vs. named) in Web-based peer assessment, Wadhwa, Mann, and Schulz (2004) found that more accountability improved the quality of student peer comments.

Step 3: Student Votes and Comments

Student "voting" is the third step for the student using the post and vote model. Student "voting" in this context means "assigning a number and writing a comment." The process of assigning a mark occurs as follows: First, individual students view each uploaded assignment in the student viewing area. Once the individual student views an uploaded assignment (e.g., a student Web site developed, a case analyzed, a research paper critiqued, etc.), they open the survey tool to assign a mark and justifying comment to the assignment. Likewise, the instructor independently views the uploaded assignment, and then opens the survey tool to assign a mark and justifying comment to the assignment.

Step 4: Concatenated Votes and Comments

The fourth step for the student using post and vote peer assessment is to wait for the concatenated votes and comments from instructor and peers in e-mail. Meanwhile the

Figure 2. The post and vote formula for calculating a student's grades on a Web-based assignment

$$\text{Student Grade} = \frac{\text{Instructor or T.A.} + \dfrac{S1+S2+S3+S4}{4}}{2}$$

instructor uses the compile tool in the WCMS to display the students' concatenated votes and justifying comments. If the class has small numbers, the instructor can highlight and paste the entire page of student peer assessments (grades and justifying comments) into a word processor, and attach the file to the submitting student's e-mail.

The "final mark" on the assignment is determined as the average of the instructor's and students' marks. Figure 2 shows the post and vote formula for calculating a final grade for a student's educational Web site based on the course instructor's and student peer assessments. Interpretations of validity, reliability, and generalizability from the data are presented later in this chapter.

Two important components of successful application of the post and vote model are peer anonymity and peer accountability. Anonymity and peer accountability in the post and vote model have been found to reduce peer over-marking and improve the quality of peer comments (Wadhwa et al., 2004).

Anonymity in Peer Assessment

In using post and vote, student peer assessors as well as those being assessed can either be anonymous (their names replaced by numbers) or can remain named. Some studies suggest that anonymous peer assessment may reduce social pressure, resulting in peers providing marks that are more accurate and critical comments (Bostock, 2000; Davis, 2000; Falchikov, 1995; Haaga, 1993; Tsai, Liu, Lin, & Yuan, 2001).

There are several different types and degrees of anonymity: *complete anonymity*, where all participants are completely anonymous to each other; *one-way anonymity*, where one of the participant's identities is concealed; and *social anonymity,* where the absence of social presence depersonalizes individual's identity. Therefore, an individual's identity need not be concealed to create anonymity.

The absence of social presence in written electronic communication can lead to social anonymity (Berge & Collins, 1993; Brodia, 1997; Bump, 1990; Liu et al., 2001; Jonassen & Kwon, 2001). However, in graduate online educational courses, students may know each other from another face-to-face course or another online course. Therefore, in graduate online educational courses, social absence may not cause social anonymity. Hence, the effect of friendship and social interactions resulting in peer over-marking and reluctance in providing critical comments remains about the same in a face-to-face and online peer assessment. Whereas peer assessment in an online learning environment can encourage students to provide more comments, it may also invite social loafing that can affect the quality of those comments. Zhao (1998) found anonymity to be a "double-edged sword in collaborative learning." He concluded that while anonymity allowed participants to be more critical, it made them less diligent.

Peer Accountability in Peer Assessment

Incorporating peer accountability into post and vote may reduce social loafing, as defined elsewhere (Davis, 2000; Tsai et al., 2001). Tetlock (1983) defined accountability as "a special type of transmission set in which one anticipates the need not only to communicate one's opinions, but also to defend those opinions against possible counterarguments." Topping (2000) suggested that assigning a greater sense of accountability and responsibility on peer assessors may affect the quality of peer comments. Studies on the effect of accountability on student responses has shown that participants put in more cognitive effort in their responses when they are asked to justify their comments or when others review their decision (Gordon & Stuecher, 1992; Price, 1987). Davis (2000) reported that peer assessors took greater care in marking, since they (peer assessors) knew that they were being assessed on their ability in marking other students' work (p. 351). In Tsai's (2001) study for example, quality of peer comments was reviewed and graded by the instructor. This was done to encourage assessors to provide helpful comments. Gordon and Stuecher (1992) examined the differences in students' responses on teacher evaluation based on degree of accountability imposed by the instructor.

The real proof of post and vote Web-based peer assessment will reside in its testing. Two tests of validity were conducted with undergraduate education students (pre-service teachers) on the post and vote model of Web-based peer assessment.

Study 1

Participants

The participants in Study 1 were pre-service teachers (n = 39) enrolled in a core course on the Bachelor of Education (Primary/Elementary) program at the largest Canadian university in the Atlantic region. The program was designed to prepare K-6 teachers in a specific discipline, as well as pedagogy courses over five years. A core course on this program was called "Computers and Learning Resources for Primary/Elementary Teachers" with the purpose of teaching pre-service teachers how to integrate computer software and other learning resources into their teaching. Laboratory components were scheduled so that students would learn how to use and implement communications, applications, and curricular software.

Materials

These students used modern computing facilities over a high-speed network designed to maximize the computing experience. A learning resources library provided students with the textual and supplementary materials they required for their course work, including current school texts, as well as teachers' curriculum guides, children's literature, resource books, and educational software. Students also had access to a variety of media equipment, educational videos, and multimedia kits. Students were expected to attain high performance levels. This teacher preparation program encouraged examination and discussion of significant educational issues within a framework of critical reflection and analytical practice. Under these conditions, each participant was required to develop a educational Web site of five Web pages, in accordance with two sample educational Web sites and the course instructor's rubric.

Research Design

In this study, the correlation pre-experimental ex post facto research design described in Cohen, Manion, and Morrison (2000) was implemented to test the validity of the post and vote model of Web-based peer assessment by pre-service teachers. Validity was determined by Pearson product-moment correlations and corresponding coefficients of determination. Working from a rubric, each student developed a paper-based mock-up for an educational Web site, then a five-page online prototype from the mock-up, followed by four peer assessments of other student-made Web sites. The post and vote model was tested with peer assessments of student-made Web sites.

Instrumentation

The instrument for collecting data was a class assignment completed by students as part of their regular course work. The students' used a rubric for peer assessment of student-developed Web sites developed from other rubrics that had been designed for a similar purpose (e.g., Schrock, 2004). Students were asked to score four of their peer's Web sites using this rubric out of a maximum score of 30: content and ideas (/10), organization (/5), language use (/5), presentation (/5), technical (/5). Student-assessors were required to use the WebCT Survey tool to enter their peer assessments. Student assessors were made "accountable," told in advance that the instructor would grade the quality of their peer assessments, and that this grade would be counted toward their final mark. Student accountability in Web-based peer assessment can improve the quality of peers' comments (Wadhwa et al., 2004).

Procedure

The procedure in Study 1 lasted just under six weeks, and was conceptualized in three distinct steps, namely: (1) the paper-based mock-up, (2) the five-page online prototype from the mock-up, and (3) peer assessment.

Step 1. The paper-based mock-up. First, each student created a "paper-based mock-up" of a educational Web site, essentially Web page frames on paper, as outlined in Brown and Mann (2001). These paper frames were intended to help them think through their educational Web site design, to provide a platform for active discussion and debate about the content. A "Web page frame" is the appropriate chunk of information for presentation to their students at one time. In the computer lab, students were shown how to make the opening frame for their educational Web site, add Web page frames, each one with a title zone, a graphic zone, a text zone, a zone of hypertext links, and a mail zone. Students were advised that the "name, title zone" of their educational Web site should attract and hold their student's attention. Students were encouraged to include an interesting picture or drawing to evoke curiosity in their students. A "picture or drawing zone" should appear at the top or side of the screen, far above the need to scroll. An "instructional content zone"—also called "task-oriented directions zone"—should provide a goal, learning objective, or challenge for their students. Students were told that it was very important that their educational Web site include a zone for "hints, fault-free questions, or partial answers" to one or two questions, and that their "links zone" should contain only one idea that required the student to click to get a partial answer. An "e-mail or chat zone" close to the bottom of each Web page should get their students sharing information about the content or task with one another in class or from home.

During this time, these students were encouraged to think creatively about educational Web site development. They were encouraged to access the Bulletin Board, post their questions and comments about the assignment, and tryout preliminary ideas for possible submission. Contribution or "participation" grades were also assigned at this stage of the process. Student postings to online conferences were evaluated using the widely used content analysis model by Henri (1992).

Step 2. The five-page online prototype from the mock-up. Next, students were required to transform their paper mock-up into an "five-page online prototype from the mock-up" by developing html documents from paper frames, and uploading them to the Web. Each student uploaded his or her submission for peer assessment using the ftp program provided in the WCMS. Most WCMSs will support individual student uploads and allow the designer to designate group membership. Once all the submissions were uploaded into a public viewing area, students were requested to read the submissions of their classmates.

Step 3. Web-based peer assessment. Step 3 had each student assess four of their colleague's educational Web sites, working from a rubric that was adapted from the university regulations:

Excellent performance with clear evidence of: comprehensive knowledge of the subject matter and principles treated in the course, a high degree of originality and independence of thought, a superior ability to organize and analyze ideas, and an outstanding ability to communicate. (Section 8.2 University Calendar, 2004-2005)

Using a survey tool, each student voted and commented anonymously on four peer submissions. To clarify: "voting" in this sense meant "assign a mark." Similarly, the course instructor independently assigned a mark and justifying comment to each submission using the "Survey" tool. Again, everyone was anonymous—student peer assessors, their names replaced by numbers, and those being assessed. Student assessors were also accountable, told in advance that the quality of their peer assessments would be graded by the course instructor and their grade counted toward their final mark. Students were informed of their peer's grades and comments in a word file attached to an e-mail from the course instructor. Using the "Compile" feature, the course instructor concatenate individual student's votes and justifying comments. The course instructor pasted the entire results page for each submission (i.e., the final mark and justifying comment) into a word processor and attached it as an attachment to each student's e-mail.

Data Collection and Analysis

In Study 1, the survey data from the peer assessors were generated from individual students clicking on the Web-based survey tool and entering a grade and comments for four classmates. Their student ID number identified them as peer assessor and the student being assessed, so that the assessor and the assessed were unknown to one another (in the context of peer assessment). All students in the study were told that the course instructor would grade their assessments on the quality of feedback on the students' assignment. Figure 2 shows the Post and Vote formula for calculating a final grade for a student's educational Web site based on the course instructor's and student peer assessments.

Results and Inter-Rater Reliability

Results of the analysis of Study 1 are summarized in Table 1. The correlations between the course instructor's scores and the average student peer assessment scores of educational Web sites (n = 39) was very high, at $r = 0.745$, $p. = .000$, with almost 56% of shared variance explained.

Inter-rater reliability between the course instructor and an independent coder was assessed by Pearson Product Moment correlation and found to be significant with the course instructors at $r= 0.961$, $p=.000$. Coding reliability was determined by having a different coder trained to the coding rubric, and then independently code 25% of educational Web sites. The rater was a Fellow of the School Graduate Studies whose thesis in peer assessment had won the 2004 College Teachers Scholarship.

Table 1. Correlations of course instructor and average peer assessments using the Post and Vote method of peer assessment in Study 1

Assessment Content	Assessment Rubric	Course Level & Sample	Agreement and Shared Variance
Educational Web site development	Instructor's rubric	Pre-service teachers (n = 39)	$r = 0.745**$ $r^2 = 0.555$

Study 2

Participants

The participants were an entire class (n = 66) from the same population of pre-service teachers enrolled in a Teacher Education program described in Study 1.

Materials

The materials given to participants in Study 2 were similar to those in Study 1, in that these studies were assigned the same sample educational Web sites and the same course instructor's rubric. The task assigned to students in this study was more challenging than Study 1 because, in addition to developing an educational Web site consisting of five Web pages, each student had to explain how they developed their Web site on Explorer video.

Research Design and Instrumentation

Study 2 used the same pre-experimental correlation *ex post facto* research design that was implemented in Study 1, except that students assessed one another's verbalizations about how they were developing their educational Web sites. Working from an instructor-made rubric, each student assessed four of their colleague's Explorer videos, according to the procedure recommended in Mann (1998, 1997, 1996). Explorer videos are video footage generated by students at their Explorer Center. An Explorer Center is a self-instructional computer workstation with a microphone linked to a videotape recorder through a thin wire.

Procedure

Study 2 used a procedure similar to Study 1, except that students assessed one another's Explorer videos, instead of their Web sites. The procedure in Study 2 lasted eight weeks and was conceptualized in four distinct steps, namely: (1) the paper-based mock-up, (2) the five-page online prototype from the mock-up, (3) student-videotaped verbal explanations and demonstrations of how they had developed their educational Web site, and (4) peer assessment. Student assessors were also accountable, told in advance that the quality of their peer assessments would be graded by the course instructor and their grade counted toward their final mark.

Data Collection and Analysis

In Study 2, as in the first study, survey data were generated from individual students clicking on the Web-based survey tool, and entering a grade and comments for four classmates. Their student ID number identified them as peer assessor and the student being assessed, so that the assessor and the assessed were unknown to one another (in the context of peer-assessment).

Results

Summary results of the analysis of Study 2 are shown in Table 2. Analysis of the data revealed that the strength of agreement between course instructor's scores and student peer assessment scores of the Explorer videos (n = 66), was highly significant, at $r = 0.701$, $p. = .000$, with over 49% of shared variance explained.

General Discussion

Results indicated that the computed average of grades and justifying comments assigned by students highly correlated with grades assigned independently by the course instructor. The statistical reliability of this research was high. The calculations were a

Table 2. Correlations of course instructor and average peer assessments using the post and vote method of peer assessment in Study 2

Assessment Content	Assessment Rubric	Course Level & Sample	Agreement and Shared Variance
Explorer video of verbalizations	Course instructor's rubric	Pre-service teachers (n = 66)	$r = 0.701**$ $r^2 = 0.491$

measure of inter-rater reliability insofar as different independent judges or raters evaluated the student work. Most researchers report one of four different methods of determining inter-rater reliability, either: Cohen's Kappa, Kendall's coefficient of concordance, the intra-class correlation, or the Pearson product-moment correlation (Huck, 2004, p. 84). Rourke et al. (2001), for example, make an argument for using the Cohen's Kappa chance-corrected measure of inter-rater reliability over other statistics. Cohen's Kappa would be a good choice for analysis of the nominal data in Step 1 of post and vote, where raters would have to classify each bulletin board discussion into one of Henri's (1992) five key categories of online discussion, either: participative, interactive, social, cognitive, or meta-cognitive. At Step 4 of post and vote however, the judges' ratings are all raw scores from 0 to 30, and therefore best analyzed by the Pearson product-moment correlation, the most frequently used correlational procedure in educational research (Cohen et al., 2000; Huck, 2004). Reliability is a necessary, but insufficient condition for validity. Validity refers to the degree to which the research accurately reflects or assesses the specific concept that the researcher is attempting to measure. Three types of validity are considered below: face, construct, and content.

The face validity in both studies was high. Face validity is concerned with how a measure or procedure appears. Relative to other methods mentioned earlier, post and vote Web-based peer assessment was a reasonable way to gain assessment information. The interactivity required in the post and vote model answers Schuttler and Burdick's call (2006) for a faculty model that promotes a facilitative relationship, and an interactive environment for students that can enable a sense of *closeness* that supersedes distance. Furthermore, the formative feedback aspect of the post and vote model fits Morgan and O'Reilly's criteria (2006) that a model should provide for student input and negotiation in assessing products and processes. Post and vote is also consistent with Popham's (2004) view of assessment as "a formal attempt to determine student status with respect to educational variables of interest" (p. 6). "Student status" in this context was their ability to peer assess their classmates online in the same way they would in a classroom setting—"to make structured judgments about the quality of the work produced by members of your own peer group (such as classmates) and, through raised awareness, increase their ability to self-assess" (Blumhof & Stallibrass, 1994, p. 4).

Construct validity was good in both studies, meaning close agreement between the theoretical concept under investigation and the specific measuring device or procedure. In Study 1, the theoretical concept was "the student-developed Web site," Web pages completed by students as part of their regular course work, following a procedure published in Brown and Mann (2001). Web site development occurred at Steps 1 and 2 of the post and vote model (see Figure 1). As an educational activity, developing Web sites are believed to have value.

> *Building Web pages is among the most constructivist activities that learners can be engaged in, primarily because of the ownership that students feel about their products and the publishing effect.* (Jonassen, Peck, & Wilson, 1999, p. 28)

The specific measuring device used by students at Step 2 of post and vote was a rubric for assessing student-developed Web sites that was developed from other rubrics that had been designed for a similar purpose (e.g., Schrock, 2004). In Study 2, the theoretical concept was the student verbalizations self-recorded on Explorer Center videos, and Explorer Centers the specific measuring device or procedure. Explorer Centers have been found to be less intrusive than individual workstations, a means of collecting verbal protocols in the absence of the investigator's tape recorder, and more accurate than conventional transcriptions of observations (Mann, 1998, 1997, 1996).

Finally, content validity was assured. Content validity is the extent to which the measurement reflected the intended content domain. The content domain in this research was limited to "the process of developing a student-developed Web site" (Study 1) and "student verbalizations and demonstration of the process of developing Web sites captured on Explorer video" in Study 2.

Research Design Limitations

A limitation of the correlation *ex post facto* research design was that models of online peer assessment could not be directly compared, and therefore claims could not be made about post and vote relative to any other methods of assessment or learning. Further analyses of these data should include experimental comparisons of post and vote with MUCH, NetPeas, and especially an "All-in the-Discussion Board" condition. Other quantitative studies should look at "grading-over-time intra-rater agreement," the relationship between the grades and the comments assigned by a peer on a student's assignment, while carrying out non-anonymous peer-assessment. Qualitative studies could explore "comment-grade intra-rater agreement," the relationship between the grades and the comments assigned by a peer on a student's assignment, while carrying out anonymous peer assessment.

Conclusion

Both studies in this chapter supported the stated hypothesis, namely: that post and vote Web-based peer assessment would be valid with these groups and generalizable to undergraduate classes engaged in similar tasks. Furthermore, post and vote was shown to be a direct way of using a variety of Web tools suited to the tasks for which they were designed, with the result of high validity of student assessment and democratization of the assessment process. Finally, it appears that familiar models and theories of instructional design are now being augmented by research in cognitive load theory (Paas, Renkl, & Sweller, 2003) and multimedia learning (Mayer, 2003; Mayer & Moreno, 2003). It seems that in general educators are becoming more socialized to the new tools and strategies of the trade. It appears too that we may soon count on better Web tool assistance from platform developers.

The other hypotheses, however, will certainly be tested at another time, both experimentally and in the court of public opinion. Other hypotheses will be observed under ex post facto conditions. The advent of evolving hardware and software will surely give us more adaptive and nonlinear interactions, and a capacity for more sophisticated Web-supported assessment. In any case, it seems likely that student assessment of Web-based learning will always be a busy time for instructors.

References

Airasian, P.W. (2001). *Classroom assessment: Concepts and applications* (4th ed.). New York: McGraw-Hall.

Anderson, A., Howe, C., Soden, R., Halliday, J., & Low, J. (2001). Peer interaction and the learning of critical thinking skills in further education students. *Instructional Science, 29*, 1-32.

Berge, Z.L., & Collins, M. (1993). Computer conferencing and online education. *The Arachnet Electronic Journal on Virtual Culture, 1*(3). Retrieved August 19, 2003, from *http://www.emoderators.com/papers/bergev1n3.html*

Blumhof, J., & Stallibrass, C. (1994). *Peer assessment.* Hatfield, UK: University of Hertfordshire Press.

Boshier, R., Mohapi, M., Moulton, G., Qayyum, A., Sadownik, L., & Wilson, M. (1997). Best and worst dressed Web lessons: Strutting into the 21st century in comfort and style. *Distance Education, 18*(1), 327-349.

Bostock, S.J. (2000, May). *Computer-assisted assessment—experiments in three courses.* Workshop, Keele University. Retrieved August 19, 2003, from *http://www.keele.ac.uk/depts/cs/Stephen_Bostock/docs/caa-ktn.htm*

Boud, D., & Holmes, H. (1995). Self and peer marking in a large technical subject. In D. Boud (Ed.), *Enhancing learning through self-assessment* (pp. 63-78). London: Kogan Page.

Brown, E., & Mann, B.L. (2001). Effects of pre-computer Web site framing on student recall and knowledge restructuring. *International Journal of Educational Telecommunications, 7*(2), 129-163.

Brown, K. (2002). A case study describing online discussion in a tenth-grade biotechnology class. (PhD, University of Virginia). *Dissertation Abstracts International,* (DAI-A 63/03), 909.

Bump, J. (1990). Radical changes in class discussion using networked computers. *Computers and Humanities, 24*, 49-65.

Clark, R.E. (2001). *Learning from media: Arguments, analysis and evidence.* Greenwich, CT: Information Age Publishing.

Cohen, L., Manion, L., & Morrison, K. (2000). *Research methods in education* (5th ed.). Taylor & Francis.

Davis, P. (2000). Computerized peer assessment. *Innovations in Education and Training International, 37*(4), 346-355.

Falchikov, N. (1986). Product comparisons and process benefits of collaborative peer group and self-assessments. *Assessment and Evaluation in Higher Education, 11*(2), 146-166.

Falchikov, N. (1995). Peer feedback marking: Developing peer assessment. *Innovations in Education and Training International, 32,* 175-187.

Falchikov, N. (1996). Improving learning through critical peer feedback and reflection. *Higher Education Research and Development, 19,* 214-218.

Falchikov, N. (2001). *Learning together: Peer tutoring in higher education.* London: Routledge Falmer.

Falchikov, N., & Goldfinch, J. (2000). Student peer assessment in higher education: A meta-analysis comparing peer and teacher marks. *Review of Educational Research, 70*(3), 287-322.

Freeman, M. (1995). Peer assessment by groups of group work. *Assessment and Evaluation in Higher Education, 20,* 289-300.

Goldberg, M., & Salari, S. (1996). *WebCT.* [Computer software]. Vancouver: University of British Columbia.

Gordon, R.A., & Stuecher, U. (1992). The effects of anonymity and increased accountability on the linguistic complexity of teaching evaluations. *Journal of Psychology, 126*(6), 639-649.

Gros, B., Elen, J., Kerres, M., Merrienboer, & Spector, M. (1997). Instructional design and the authoring of multimedia and hypermedia systems: Does a marriage make sense? *Educational Technology.*

Haaga, D. (1993). Peer review of term papers in graduate psychology courses. *Teaching of Psychology, 20*(1), 28-32.

Hara, N., Bonk, C., & Angeli, C. (2000). Content analysis of online discussions in an applied educational psychology course. *Instructional Science, 28*(2), 115-152.

Henri, F. (1992). Computer conferencing and content analysis. In A.R. Kaye (Ed.), *Collaborative learning through computer conferencing* (pp. 117-136). Berlin: Springer-Verlag.

Heylighen, F., Joslyn, C., & Turchin, V. (2002). Principia Cybenetica Web. Retrieved January 5, 2005, from *http://pcp.lanl.gov/DEFAULT.html*

Huck, S.W. (2004). *Reading statistics and research* (4th ed.). Boston: Pearson Education.

Jonassen, D., Peck, K., & Wilson, B. (1999). *Learning with technology: A constructivist perspective.* Englewood Cliffs, NJ: Merrill-Prentice-Hall.

Kelmar, J.H. (1993). Peer assessment in graduate management education. *International Journal of Educational Management, 7*(2), 4-7.

Mann, B.L. (1996). Preservice applications of explorer centers for general computing. In J. White (Ed.), *The technology and teacher education conference annual 1996.* Needham, MA: Allyn & Bacon.

Mann, B.L. (1997). Evaluation of presentation modalities in a hypermedia system. *Computers and Education: An International Journal, 28*(2), 133-143.

Mann, B.L. (1997, September 17-19). Explorer centers (ECs): Good practice and assessment for teacher education. *School Education in the Information Society: Proceedings of The Open Classroom II Conference,* Crete, Greece.

Mann, B.L. (1998). Motor learning, metacognition and teacher competencies: Critical competitors in educational technology. *The Morning Watch: Educational and Social Analysis, 25,* 3-4.

Mann, B.L. (1998a, November). Working through phases: Instructional design in WebCT. *Proceedings of the Meeting of the School of Communications and Multimedia,* Edith Cowan University, Perth, Australia.

Mann, B.L. (1998b, October). Three phases of Web-based instructional development. *Proceedings of the State Conference of the Educational Computing Association of Western Australia (ECAWA),* Notre Dame University. Fremantle, Australia.

Mann, B.L. (1998c, June). Instructional design for online learning: A case study of WebCT developers. Universities in a Digital Era: Transformation, Innovation and Tradition. *Proceedings of the 7th Annual European Distance Education Network (EDEN) Conference,* University of Bologna, Italy.

Mann, B.L. (1999a). Web course management. *Australian Educational Computing, 14*(1).

Mann, B.L. (1999b). Web course management in higher education. *Bulletin of the Canadian Society for the Study of Higher Education.*

Mann, B.L. (2000a). Phase theory: A teleological taxonomy of Web course management (pp. 3-26). In B.L. Mann (Ed.). *Perspectives in Web course management.* Toronto, ON: Canadian Scholar's Press.

Mann, B.L. (2000b). WebCT: Serving educators in Newfoundland and Labrador. *The New Morning Watch: Educational and Social Analysis, 28*(1/2).

Mann, B.L. (Ed.). (in press). *Selected styles in Web-based educational research.* Hershey, PA: Idea Group Publishing.

Mann, B.L., Whitmore, M., & Bussey, W. (2000). Network-intensive research at Memorial University. *The New Morning Watch: Educational and Social Analysis, 28*(1/2).

Mayer, R.E., & Moreno, R. (2003). Nine ways to reduce cognitive load in multimedia learning. *Educational Psychologist, 38*(1), 43-52.

Mayer, R.E. (2003). The promise of multimedia learning: Using the same instructional design methods across different media. *Learning and Instruction, 13,* 125-139.

Morgan, C., & O'Reilly, M. (2006). Ten qualities of assessment online. In M. Hricko, S. Howell, & D. Williams (Eds.), *Online assessment and measurement* (vol. 1). Hershey, PA: Idea Group Publishing.

Mowl, G., & Pain, R. (1995). Using self and peer assessment to improve students' essay-writing: A case study from geography. *Innovations in Education and Training International, 32*(4), 324-336.

Paas, F., Renkl, A., Sweller, J. (2003). Cognitive load theory and instructional design: Recent developments. *Educational Psychologist, 38*(1), 1-4.

Pittinsky, D., & Chasen, D. (1997). *BlackBoard,* [Computer program]. Washington, DC: BlackBoard Inc.

Pond, K., Rehan U., & Wade. W. (1995). Peer review: A precursor to peer assessment. *Innovations in Education and Training International, 32*(4), 314-323.

Popham, J. (2004). *Classroom assessment: What teachers need to know* (4th ed.). Pearson.

Principia Cybenetica Web. (1998). System variety. Retrieved January 1, 2005, from *http://pcp.lanl.gov/VARIETY.html*

Rose, M. (2002). Cognitive dialogue, interaction patterns, and perceptions of graduate students in an online conferencing environment under collaborative and cooperative structures. (EdD, Indiana University). *Dissertation Abstracts International,* (DAI-A 63/04), 1249.

Rourke, L., Anderson, T., Garrison, D., & Archer, W. (2001). Methodological issues in the content analysis of computer conference transcripts. *International Journal of Artificial Intelligence in Education, 12.*

Rushton, C., Ramsey, P., & Rada, R. (1993). Peer assessment in a collaborative hypermedia environment: A case study. *Journal of Computer-Based Instruction, 20*(3), 75-80.

Schrock, K. (2004). Teacher helpers: Assessment and rubric information. Retrieved December 13, 2004, from *http://school.discovery.com/schrockguide/assess.html*

Schuttler, R., & Burdick, J. (2006). Creating a unified system of assessment. In M. Hricko, S. Howell, & D. Williams (Eds.), *Online assessment and measurement* (vol. 1). Hershey, PA: Idea Group Publishing.

Searby, M., & Ewers, T. (1997). An evaluation of the use of peer assessment in higher education: A case study in the school of music. *Kingston University, 22*(4), 371-383.

Sluijsmans, D., Moerkerke, G., Dochy, F., & van Merriënboer, J.J.G. (2001). Peer assessment in problem-based learning. *Studies in Educational Evaluation, 27*(2), 153-173.

Sluijsmans, D., Saskia B, & van Merriënboer, J.J.G. (2002). Peer assessment training in teacher education: Effects on performance and perceptions. *Assessment and Evaluation in Higher Education, 27*(5), 443-454.

Tetlock, P.E. (1983). Accountability and complexity of thought. *Journal of Personality and Social Psychology, 45,* 74-83.

Topping, K.J., Smith E.F., Swanson, I., & Elliot, A. (2000). Formative peer assessment of academic writing between postgraduate students. *Assessment and Evaluation in Higher Education, 25*(2), 149-169.

Tsai, C.C., Liu, E.Z., Lin, S.S.J., & Yuan, S. (2001). A networked peer assessment system based on a vee heuristic. *Innovations in Education and Teaching International, 38,* 3.

Wadhwa, G., Mann, B.L., & Schulz, H. (2004). *Effects of anonymity and peer-accountability during peer assessment in a graduate Web-based education research methods course.* Paper Session on Teaching Educational Research, Measurement, and Research Methodology, Division D, American Educational Research Association, San Diego.

WCET. (2003). Course management systems. Retrieved December 15, 2004, from *http://www.edutools.info/course/index.jsp*

Wild, M., & Quinn, C. (1998). Implications of educational theory for the design on instructional multimedia *British Journal of Educational Technology, 29*(1), 73-82.

Winn, W. (1997). Advantages of a theory-based curriculum in instructional technology. *Educational Technology,* (January/February).

Yang., C., Moore, D., & Burton, J. (1995). Managing lessonware production: An instructional theory with a software engineering approach. *Educational Technology Research and Development, 43*(4), 60-70.

Zhao, Y. (1998). The effects of anonymity on computer-mediated peer review. *International Journal of Educational Telecommunications, 4*(4), 311-345.

Chapter X

Online Assessment in a Teacher Education Program

Charles W. Peters, University of Michigan, USA

Patricia Ann Kenney, University of Michigan, USA

Abstract

In this chapter the authors describe how they have incorporated a constructivist view of learning into their approach to online assessment. The context of their discussion is within an accelerated (12-month) teacher education program at the graduate level for preservice secondary teachers. At the heart of the authors' view of assessment is an attempt to capture through the use of online techniques how their preservice teachers are progressing toward becoming effective teachers through engagement in authentic situations that are experience based and problem oriented. The authors present three examples of how they use online assessment to encourage elaborated discussion, metacognitive thinking, and critical reflection.

Introduction

Why should we educators be interested in assessment, and in particular assessment that is carried out in an online environment? The short answer is because assessment approaches need to change so that they are more aligned with current views of learning.

As critics of traditional assessment point out (e.g., Popham, 2003; Shepard, 2001; Wiggins, 1998), behaviorist views of assessment are still the norm, and instances of these views can be seen in the use of tests to determine if students have learned isolated bits of knowledge, in the tight sequencing of curriculum so that concepts are taught hierarchically from simple to complex, and in the view of performance on tests as being isomorphic with learning. While many aspects of traditional assessment approaches are worth retaining and for good reasons (Terwilliger, 1997), there is little evidence that forms of assessment that reflect a more constructivist view of learning have gained prominence in K-16 education. When examined in light of constructivist principles and ideas, the current view of assessment provides a rather limited way to gather information about students' understanding, especially at the more complex levels. We posit that the use of online assessment can serve as a model for beginning to move the continuum of assessment toward a more balanced approach, and one that is more consistent with a constructivist view of learning.

What differentiates a constructivist approach to learning and assessment from a more traditional behaviorist approach? According to Shepard (2001), the constructivist approach includes qualities such as: (a) learners constructing knowledge and understandings within a social context; (b) self-monitoring by learners of their own understandings as they develop; (c) learning that is applied in authentic contexts beyond the walls of the classroom; and d) a focus on deep understanding that supports transfer to new settings. In addition, a number of scholars have contributed their ideas to advancing what a constructivist approach to learning and assessment might look like in the classroom. For example, Newmann and his colleagues (e.g., Archbald & Newmann, 1988; Newmann & Associates, 1996; Newmann, Marks, & Gamoran, 1996; Newmann, Secada, & Wehlage, 1995) have included important characteristics of constructivism within their ideas on *authentic achievement*, a term that embodies the alignment among curriculum, assessment, and instruction in ways that highlight their interactive nature. To Newmann et al. (1996), authentic achievement "stands for intellectual accomplishments that are worthwhile, significant, and meaningful" (p. 23). In the context of schooling, authentic achievement is defined through three criteria: construction of knowledge by learners, disciplined inquiry characterized by deep understanding and elaborated communication, and learning that has value and meaning beyond school. Other educators, researchers, and theorists have added their own ideas to the constructivist view of learning, including the importance of mediated instruction (Vygotsky, 1978), the notion of scaffolding toward higher levels of achievement and knowledge (Wood, Bruner, & Ross, 1976), and the importance of deep understanding and how students can achieve it (Onosko & Newmann, 1994; Perkins, 1993).

This focus on constructivist learning has important implications for assessment, and especially for online assessment. Many scholars and researchers have proposed that this view of learning requires a different way of thinking about assessment so that it is more closely aligned with curriculum and instruction (Paris et al., 1987; Peters & Wixson, 1989; Peters, Wixson, Valencia, & Pearson, 1993; Valencia, Hiebert, & Afflerbach, 1994; Wixson & Peters, 1987). For example, adopting Newmann's model for authentic achievement necessitates the creation and use of assessment tasks that embody construction of knowledge, disciplined inquiry, and value beyond the classroom. When these criteria become integral to the assessment process, the resulting assessment tasks must go far beyond paper-and-pencil testing of isolated concepts. Assessment tasks must be able to document how students acquire deep understanding, capture how they engage in elaborated communication, and demonstrate how they document their own learning. We contend that online assessment offers a way to capture some of the important characteristics of the constructivist approach to learning in ways that traditional assessment techniques have not.

In the sections that follow we describe how we have incorporated a constructivist view of learning into our approach to online assessment. The context of our discussion is within an accelerated (12-month) preservice teacher education program at the graduate level. At the heart of our view of assessment is an attempt to capture through the use of online techniques how our preservice teachers are progressing toward becoming effective teachers through engagement in authentic situations that are experience based and problem oriented.

Our View of Assessment

As we mentioned above, our view of assessment is based on a constructivist model of learning, teaching, and assessment, one in which assessment is centered on the *purpose*, not merely on the techniques or tools of assessment. Therefore, assessment is central and not peripheral to curriculum and instruction. To implement this approach we have incorporated four characteristics of constructivist theory into our online assessment model: (a) the social construction of knowledge, (b) a focus on deep understanding, (c) the engagement in reflection and metacognitive thinking, and (d) the use of scaffolding as the basis for structuring assessment tasks.

Within our view of assessment, feedback is integral to student learning; in fact, feedback must be both concurrent and continuous, and it must lead to improvement in the learner's performance level and understanding (Wiggins, 1998). When feedback is concurrent and continuous, the comments provided to the learner are not ends in themselves, but rather they become a bridge to other important learning opportunities. The key for us is how each of the four characteristics and the type of feedback we provide are manifested in our assessment activities and tasks—especially those that are based on electronic means such as online discussions, electronically based feedback provided to fostering instructor-student interactions, and the analysis of electronic records to monitor the preservice teachers' progress toward becoming effective teachers.

Social Construction of Knowledge

Central to the social constructivist model for learning is the idea that intellectual abilities are developed and the acquisition of knowledge occurs within a social context (Heath, 1983; Langer, 1991; Newmann & Associates, 1998; Shepard, 2001; Wixson & Peters, 1984). The kind of knowledge acquired within a social context has the potential to go beyond mere facts to include conceptual, procedural, and metacognitive knowledge.

Most conceptualizations of knowledge construction involve the learner being mediated by a more experienced person such as a teacher, a mentor, or a more capable peer. This is the model proposed by Vygotsky (1978) concerning the existence of the zone of proximal development, or the distance between the learner's actual level of development and his or her potential level of development. With appropriate guidance from a more experienced person or from peers working together in a group setting, a learner can be led toward a higher level of potential development than he or she might achieve if left alone.

These ideas of social construction of knowledge have significant implications for assessment. In particular, if assessments are to capture the social context of learning, they need to include a variety of tasks that require students working together to organize, synthesize, interpret, or evaluate complex information—all of which are components of higher-order thinking. In addition, the tasks should require students to consider alternative solutions, strategies, and/or perspectives. Finally, one aspect of assessment that is not always captured is an opportunity for students to engage in elaborated conversation that shows their understanding, explanation, or conclusions. These components lend themselves very well to the online assessment environment in ways that are not possible with more traditional assessments. For example, in our preservice teacher education program, we create a myriad of opportunities for our students to work together on a series of engaging activities such as producing graphic organizers (e.g., concept maps), sharing their work on a class Web site, and then having both class-based and online discussions about the topic at hand. The feedback element comes into play as students provide commentary to one another and as faculty join in the online discussion by providing evaluative and constructive comments.

Deep Understanding

Another attribute that we found to be critical to include in our view of assessment involves deep understanding. More than just mastery of facts or concepts, deep understanding involves robust learning that generalizes and transfers to new situations (cf., Darling-Hammond & Snyder, 2000; Newmann & Associates, 1996; Newmann et al., 1995; Wiggins, 1998). In particular, Newmann (Newmann & Associates, 1996; Newmann, et al., 1995) contends that deep understanding is best obtained from authentic situations and instruction that have value beyond school. Perkins (1993) also takes a performance perspective: "understanding a topic…is a matter of being able to perform in a variety of thought-demanding ways with the topic, for instance to: explain, muster evidence, find examples, generalize, apply concepts, analogize, represent in a new way, and so on" (p. 29).

Determining if and how students are acquiring deep understanding requires special assessment techniques. Perkins (1993) makes the point that acquiring deep understanding is not an instantaneous process, but instead results from "making learning a long-term…process" (p. 31). Assessing the acquisition of deep understanding over time necessitates a view of assessment that is not dependent on conventional forms such as quizzes, exercises, and essays that occur only at the end of a unit and focus only on providing the means to assign students a grade. Much of the deep understanding is captured in our electronic portfolio (called the "Teaching e-Portfolio") where students document their growing knowledge and understanding as they progress toward becoming an effective teacher. We also have students submit a series of assignments in electronic format which affords us the opportunity to provide feedback on the assignments via a "comments" function in Microsoft Word, and this provides the student with the chance to reply to our comments. Once established, such an electronic dialogue between student and teacher can continue, thus providing documentation of the journey toward deep understanding.

Reflection and Metacognitive Thinking

Reflection and metacognitive thinking comprise the third component of our view of assessment. Metacognition is important because it provides a window into how students' understanding of and control over their own cognitive processes play an important role in learning (e.g., Bransford, Brown, & Cocking, 1999; Sternberg, 1985; Zimmerman & Schunk, 1998). For example, Perkins and his colleagues (Perkins, 1993; Perkins, Tishman, Ritchhart, Donis, & Andrade, 2000) acknowledge that reflection and metacognition have an important effect on what is learned, how much is learned, and how much of that learning is retained and utilized. Specific to teacher education, the research literature suggests that critical reflection enables teachers to develop the habit of continually learning by standing back from their own experience and framing the problems of practice in light of multiple perspectives, and then critiquing and reframing problems within a broader context (e.g., Darling-Hammond & Snyder, 2000; Whipp, 2003).

Evidence of reflection and metacognitive thinking are not often captured in more traditional approaches to assessment. What is important in our approach is that we attempt to incorporate some aspects of reflection and metacognition within our online assessment tasks. Specifically, students are asked to reflect on their learning across a number of tasks and within an online environment, and this allows us to provide immediate feedback to our students and to monitor their growth in the capacity to reflect and the quality of that reflection over time. These tasks range from a series of written reflections on how our students read and write within their respective content areas (e.g., English, mathematics, history, biology) to a more comprehensive reflection on their year-long experience within our teacher education program.

Scaffolding

An important component of the constructivist model of learning is that external factors often augment learning, and one of these factors is *scaffolding*, which Ritchhart (2002) describes as a way to "help students to activate their thinking and make appropriate decisions about next steps" (p. 160). For example, when some students have difficulty engaging in more sophisticated forms of analogical reasoning, scaffolding helps to break down more sophisticated and complex forms of reasoning into smaller components so the learner better understands what the steps are in the process of reasoning through analogies. Scaffolding also has important ties to the cognitive apprenticeship model (Collins, Brown, & Newman, 1989) in which experts scaffold learning experiences for novice learners. We have adapted this view to our model of assessment by purposefully designing assessment tasks so that they are linked with one another, a characteristic of the "designing down" principle advocated by Wiggins and McTighe (1998). At the heart of this principle is the notion that apprentice teachers learn how to "think like assessors," which means they learn to develop a clear vision of the learning goals for their students and how they will achieve these goals. This process produces an instructional "roadmap" that details how the various elements of instruction are linked. Thus, designing down promotes the alignment of assessment and instruction, and provides the necessary support in terms of scaffolding to model for students how to achieve the learning goals.

It is important that our preservice teachers see connections among the tasks, and that the tasks be structured so as to lead the students through simple, directive activities to more complex learning. Our online techniques offer an effective way to provide assessments that are scaffolding learning experiences for students. In particular, we begin with a simple assessment task that is very directive and prescriptive, and that sets forth our goals for the student. By submitting a written response online, the student can then receive feedback on his or her work, and suggestions for the next stage. The next assessment task may increase in complexity but decrease in directiveness, until the student understands the requirements of the larger task and can undertake it successfully. In our program the most obvious use of scaffolding is our use of a series of Reflective Writing Tasks (RWTs) that culminate in our students' e-Portfolios; briefly, these are a series of assessment tasks that help students understand how to collect and provide evidence of their own learning related to becoming an effective teacher.

Examples of How We Use Online Assessment in Our Teacher Education Program

In operationalizing our view of assessment within our teacher education program, we have made extensive use of online assessment as a way to encourage social construction of knowledge, deep understanding, reflection and metacognitive thinking, and implementation of various scaffolding techniques. Additionally, providing feedback via electronic means carries with it an element of immediacy that written feedback cannot match. To us, then, online assessment fits well with our view of learning and teaching; in fact, using online assessment is essential to our efforts in the MAC A cohort.[1] To illustrate how we use online assessment within our program, we have selected three different examples that we believe demonstrate the importance of this kind of assessment. These three examples are: (1) online discussions, (2) the Literacy Journal, and (3) Teaching e-Portfolio and Reflective Writing Tasks (RWTs).

Online Discussions

Our first example of online assessment involves the use of online discussions. Such discussions align well with our view of assessment, and the online nature of the discussions provides valuable enhancements. First, discussion encourages the social construction of knowledge. Because we use a cohort model in our program—in that a group of 25 or so preservice secondary teachers remains together in many classes throughout the MAC A experience—it is important that we create learning situations that encourage socialization through discourse. Such socialization helps to acculturate our students into the language that allows them to participate in the profession of teaching at multiple levels—as student teachers, colleagues, students, and community members. By talking to one another and through mediation by one of the faculty members, our students begin to build understandings about important concepts and ideas as they learn to be effective teachers.

Second, such elaborated discussions, when conducted over time and if structured properly, can lead to the acquisition of deep understanding, which is another aspect of the constructivist paradigm that is essential to our view of assessment. In the MAC A experience, we encourage discussions that are structured in a number of different ways. For example, two techniques that are modeled at the beginning of the program are substantive conversation (Newmann et al., 1995) and the Socratic seminar (Tredway, 1995). At times we videotape these discussions so that we can evaluate our progress as a cohort as we engage in these kinds of discussions; however, because we do not videotape or audiotape all such discussions, the substance is often lost and is not available for analysis or reflection by ourselves or by our students. In order to preserve a record of a non-videotaped discussion so it can be analyzed over the course of the program, we create opportunities for our students to have online discussions on a local system called CTools.[2] Many of these discussions are directly linked to ones that begin in class and are then continued online. To our way of thinking, this is a good use of online assessment because a written record of the discussion is preserved for later analysis.

One of our first online discussions is a concept mapping activity.[3] This activity is completed in stages, with the first stage requiring each of our students to produce a concept map on their own based on a foundational reading. The concept maps are drawn using a software package called *Inspiration*. The second stage of the activity involves a small-group, in-class discussion on the concept maps and the eventual production of a consensus concept map that represents the group's shared understanding once the discussion is over. The social construction of knowledge about the topic at hand begins in these small groups. The third stage, which is actually the beginning point for our online assessment, involves each group posting its consensus concept map on CTools, and then having each student view the collection of maps and engage in an online discussion in which they compare and contrast the features of the maps. This stage facilitates feedback from a number of sources: students providing feedback to one another on the merits of the posted concept maps, and faculty providing feedback both on the quality of the concept maps and on the quality of the ensuing discussion. Because the concept maps are posted in electronic format and the discussion surrounding them is preserved in written form electronically, this affords us with the opportunity to analyze how our students construct understanding and how that understanding changes as the discussion unfolds. A specific example of the concept mapping activity follows.

For an introductory lesson on assessment terminology, our students did a concept mapping activity based on a chapter from Horn (2004). The goal of the activity was to form reasonable connections among the terms shown in Figure 1. During class, students met in small groups to discuss their concept maps and to agree on a single concept map that represented the best thinking of the group about the assessment terms. Part of our plan for this activity was to have the students continue the discussion online after class, with the discussion shifting to a commentary on the set of consensus concept maps that were posted on CTools. The students were instructed to view the concept maps, and to comment on their merits and shortcomings as part of an online discussion within the CTools environment.[4] Some very interesting discussions emerged from this activity, and the one we chose to include illustrates the value of online discussion as part of online assessment.

During the online discussion and at a point where all six co-constructed concept maps had been presented with a full range of student comments, one student whom we call Lyle, posted the comments that follow about the set of concept maps:

From: Lyle

Message: While all these concept maps are valiant efforts, I am going to be stubborn and stick to my guns on what I like in a concept map. My ideas certainly created controversy within my own group, so please feel free to respond to what I have to say.

First, although all these concept maps contain a significant number of links, none are thorough enough to satisfy me. When I originally read the assignment, I thought that we were supposed to connect every concept with every other concept. And I did this in my concept map. [Authors' note: Lyle's concept map appears in Figure 2.]

A good example of this is the tendency to not link the various test formats (t/f, multiple choice, etc.) to more than one "higher order." In other words, most groups connected these terms to one blanket term, such as "variety of assessment," while in reality, they are applicable to several terms, including SAT,

Figure 1. Terms used in the concept mapping activity

1. Models of Assessment	9. Essay Test
2. Holistic Assessment	10. Rubrics
3. Criterion-Referenced Test	11. SAT
4. Standardized Tests	12. MEAP (Michigan Educational
5. Variety of Assessments	Assessment Program)
6. Analytic Assessment	13. Constructed Response
7. Multiple-Choice Test	14. Projects
8. True/False Test	15. Norm-Referenced Test

MEAP, analytic, standardized test, criterion referenced, norm referenced, etc. Being thorough in this manner leads to a web-like concept map instead of the neat, hierarchical models that most of you provided.

Hierarchical models also create difficulty when some terms are applicable in more than one "higher order" category. For example, one group listed "t/f, mult choice, etc." twice, under two different headings. This is correct, in that these terms should be recognized under both conditions; however, listing terms twice on a concept map somewhat changes the terms themselves. The uses of the terms can change under different circumstances, but by listing them separately, their qualities are also separated in a sense. To me, it makes more sense to only list them once, with links going to each category, for both the sake of simplicity and consistency.

That's my take. I like messy, complicated webs of tangled terms and links, as long as it's thorough.

Figure 2. Lyle's concept map

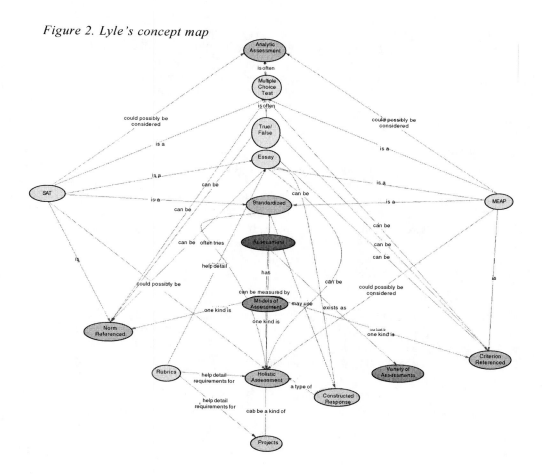

What followed was a very animated online discussion, with about a dozen students from the cohort responding to Lyle, Lyle responding back, and so on as the discussion progressed. Because the online discussion produced a record of the comments, we were able to assess the discussion and identify some important components. First, the text of the online discussion illustrated how Lyle and the other responders were working together to construct a deepening understanding about assessment terminology. This exchange between Evan and Lyle illustrates how they were extending their thinking about the interrelatedness of different kinds of assessment:

From: Evan

Message: Lyle, you commented that when some terms are applicable in more than one "higher order" category, they should not be listed twice, under two different headings. You then went on to say that "listing terms twice on a concept map somewhat changes the terms themselves. The uses of the terms can change under different circumstances, but by listing them separately, their qualities are also separated in a sense." This is completely true and why I think that they should be listed twice. You can't have a question on a test that is both holistic and analytic. In order to be in both categories, they must take on different qualities. Although they can still be the same basic "type" of question, they have to be different. In order to show that they are different in their approach, I think that listing them twice is crucial. I might have a skewed thinking on this, but that is my take.

From: Lyle

Message: You're right, a single test item cannot be both holistic and analytic. The problem is that here, we are not speaking in terms of specific examples, such as a specific question on a particular exam. Also, it is not that something can be BOTH one thing and another, but rather that it can be EITHER one thing or another. We have to look at the concept itself, and in this view, for example, an essay test can certainly be EITHER holistic or analytic, and thus links should be drawn from a single "essay test" bubble [on the concept map] to both "analytic" and "holistic" bubbles.

Here, Evan and Lyle discuss the important concepts of analytic and holistic assessments, and Lyle offers a shared understanding of the terms based on the example of an essay test that could be either holistic or analytic. Through this interchange, both students extended their understanding of assessment terms and how they are operationalized within a test.

Second, there is evidence within the discussion that the MAC A students were thinking deeply about the process of concept mapping as a graphic organizer. At the heart of this discussion was the issue of complexity—should concept maps be simple or complex?—or as Kendle put it:

Is the goal of concept mapping to make the most obvious connections between the various concepts or is it a web where every potential link should be considered (which seems to be your interpretation)? I believe it simply depends on our perspective. So, I guess I disagree with you only because my interpretation of concept mapping is to create the main relationships between the terms and not all conceivable ones.

Responding to this idea from Kendle that concept maps should be a simplification of ideas based on including only the main relationships, Lyle offers these questions: "My only problem is, how does one determine what is the 'main relationships'? When does a relationship stop being 'main' and thus should not be shown on the concept map?" He goes on to contend that drawing an exhaustive concept map in which all links appear has the potential "to lead to a more thorough understanding of the concepts involved." The discussion around concept mapping became truly interactive and spirited, with most students in favor of simplicity. This response to Lyle from Iris is typical of these responses:

From: Iris

Message: I agree with you (Lyle) if I am making a concept map for my own personal use to understand a subject and how everything is connected. However, I think a concept map needs to be more simple if others will be using it. If you are using the map as a way to introduce an idea or subject, I feel it is best to make it hierarchical—at least to begin with. Then as students begin to learn more about the subject, more arrows may be drawn in to show connectedness. If someone were to introduce a subject to me with a concept map that was a tangled mess of arrows, etc., I wouldn't even know where to begin. But again, for my own personal use, when I need to fully understand an idea and how all parts are connected and related, my maps end up pretty tangled too.

And Lyle's reaction to Iris and the other the advocates of simplicity? He "stuck to his guns" and wrote:

I simply don't agree [with a simple concept map]. By actively constructing a complicated map, students are bound to more thoroughly understand the complete meaning of a given concept. In what medium would the complete meaning of ideas be explored after a map has been constructed? I can see a teacher perhaps starting students off in class with a few simple connections, but I would then encourage students to get after it and let their links explode. Iris, you're right about introducing a complicated map to new learners. However, I was a new learner to the concept of assessment when I did this map. By engaging myself with the construction of the map, I was able to, one at a time, understand the concepts in a thorough manner. I think the greatest potential of learning from concept maps is not from reading them as a completed product, but instead in their actual construction, where decisions on links and concepts is actively and *constructively* made.

This online discussion on the simplicity vs. complexity of concept maps was not resolved either online or during the next class, where the discussion continued and involved nearly the entire class. The students wanted to continue to debate the pros and cons of creating intricate concepts maps that might indeed show the complexity of the interconnected assessment ideas, but that might be too involved to be understandable.

An online activity like production and discussion of the concept maps provided us with more insight into student thinking than a traditional assessment possibly could. First, it allowed for an assessment of how well students understood the information presented in a reading. Because each student posted an individual, electronic version of his or her concept map on CTools, we had an opportunity to check for depth of understanding or misconceptions or other misunderstandings in advance of the class in which the maps would be discussed, and thus we could better anticipate the needs of our students.

Second, it allowed us to introduce the content-related reading strategy of concept mapping that encourages deep understanding. To construct a concept map, students had to identify the key concepts and the relationships between and among them, thus requiring synthesis of ideas as opposed to merely defining each term separately or connecting only two or three concepts. A concept map, then, provided a venue in which students had to demonstrate how the key terms were interconnected and linked. Using the concept map in an online assessment task provided an archival record of students' thinking and reaction to what their fellow students presented, and it afforded us a way to gauge how their understandings changed and deepened as discussion unfolded.

Third, the activity served as an introduction to online discussion and furthered our students' foray into construction of knowledge through elaborated conversation. This is the first of many online discussions that we conduct over the course of the year-long program, and the first of many opportunities for us to gain important information about our students' understanding through online assessment.

Literacy Journal

Our second example of how we use online assessment in the MAC A cohort showcases an assignment we call the Literacy Journal. The Literacy Journal is representative of many of the assignments that are required of our preservice secondary teachers in that it asks them to reflect in writing on a particular topic and then to apply their ideas to their own teaching. We discuss this assignment here because it illustrates another characteristic of our constructivist approach to assessment—the use of metacognitive knowledge in helping students to realize why and how they "know what they know" about their own literacy skills. The Literacy Journal assignment asks our students to reflect on the cognitive demands that are placed on them as they read and write about topics they may have little background knowledge on. Some guiding questions that we ask our students to think about as they write their Literacy Journals are:

1.　　When reading difficult material in your subject area, what strategies do you use? What happens when the strategies you select do not work?

2.　　How does the purpose of the reading (e.g., researching a topic, preparing for class, reading for pleasure) and the context (e.g., school, home, vacation) influence how you read?

3.　　How do you approach writing assignments? What accounts for differences in your approach?

4.　　When you find yourself struggling to put your thought down on paper or on the computer screen, what do you do to get beyond the struggle?

The Literacy Journal, then, can be thought of as a think-aloud activity designed to make the *covert* more *overt* to our preservice teachers—in this case a well-developed set of reading and writing strategies. Moreover, the assignment promotes self-monitoring, an important aspect of metacognition (cf. Anderson & Krathwohl, 2001), and the unpacking of complex processes so that they can be examined in light of what the preservice teachers do when they read and write, why they do it, and how they might teach their students to be strategic readers and writers.

Because the Literacy Journal entries are submitted electronically, we have the opportunity to capitalize on the convenience and timeliness that providing online feedback affords. According to Wiggins (1998) feedback can fall into three categories depending on when it is given (during, after, and between learning tasks), and it is this third category that is critical and well suited for online assessments, because it provides us with an excellent opportunity to provide feedback that permits the MAC A students to make adjustments in their learning between assignments. The goal for our students is improved performance, and our feedback allows them to better understand standards of excellence. Feedback helps them think about how they can apply some of the comments they receive to future assignments, such as the second Literacy Journal that comes later in the term, thus allowing them to adjust their learning.

The example that follows is an excerpt from the first Literacy Journal assignment that was completed during the six-week summer term. A student whom we call Sibyl submitted her journal as an electronic document and made these comments about her writing strategies:

> Whereas reading is fun and easy for me, writing is often a painful process. Talking about how I write is an easier task for me, since I have thought a lot about the way that I write. However, I don't necessarily know how to break my writing method down into concrete steps or strategies. I would think that many of the writing strategies that I will be teaching my students will be different from the strategies I use when I write. I know that you are "supposed" to use brainstorming, outlines, rough drafts, editing, and final drafts. However, I cannot use any of these methods **[CP1]**. For some reason, I cannot write unless I combine all of these functions into one process: as I put the words down on the page, I am brainstorming, crafting language, making connections to what I've written and what will come next, and editing.

The **[CP1]** within the text represents a comment that the first author (Peters) inserted into Sibyl's Literacy Journal at the point where the comment is most relevant. The text of Peters' comment follows:

> It is fine to share this information [about how you write] with your students, because writing strategies vary and not all people use the same ones. However, there are some general understandings that students need to be aware of when approaching a writing assignment. For example, knowing the type of **text** you are creating, e.g., poem, essay, lab report, the **purpose** for writing, e.g., notes taking, test, review for test, and the **audience**, e.g., professor, friend, public forum, all influence your strategies and students need to understand this because they tend to write everything the same way.

The electronic commenting has important advantages over merely writing comments on a printed version. First, the comment is inserted electronically at the most relevant place in the text and there is no restriction on how long the comment can be. To view the comment, all the student needs to do is either to click on it or to hold the cursor over it and the comment appears in a on-screen window. In the case of paper copies, oftentimes long comments would have to be written on the back of a page or on a separate sheet of paper, and consequently they might be far removed from the sentence or paragraph that sparked the need for the comment.

Second, and more importantly, electronic commenting opens the opportunity for a dialogue between the instructor and the student that might not happen otherwise. As he read Sibyl's musings, Peters was able to assess her understanding of the writing process and to insert a comment reassuring her that it was "ok" that her writing strategies were idiosyncratic, but also pushing her to think about general understandings that students need to know about writing, such as type of text, purpose, and audience. This commentary did not go unheeded, as shown by the e-mail note that Sibyl sent to Peters about the **[CP1]** comment:

> This comment in particular was very helpful: "…there are some general under-standings that students need to be aware of when approaching a writing assignment. For example, knowing the type of text you are creating, e.g., poem, essay, lab report, the purpose for writing, e.g., notes taking, test, review for test, and the audience, e.g., professor, friend, public forum, all influence your strategies and students need to understand this because they tend to write everything the same way." That's good to think about as a way to guide my students in writing: type, purpose, and audience—I wouldn't have thought about that. I like the idea of presenting the possible strategies to my students— like brainstorming, outlining, concept mapping—having them practice each one, and then having them reflect on what works best for them.

> Thanks, Charlie, that feedback was really helpful. I would like to talk more about literacy practices with you soon.

This type of online assessment has some very valuable features. First, the feedback possible from online assessment is designed to lead to improved performance. Peters gave feedback to Sibyl so that it encouraged her to think more deeply about her own literacy practices and how she can use them to better anticipate the needs of her students and to plan for instruction more effectively. Another impact of this type of feedback is that students extend their dialogue beyond the assignment. In Sibyl's case, she expressed a desire to improve her own metacognitive thinking related to her literacy practices, and she and Peters had a number of subsequent face-to-face discussions about it. Peters gave Sibyl several texts that described in more detail how she could improve her literacy strategies, as well as how to apply what she learns to her own instructional practices.

Second, the Literacy Journal models authentic assessment practices for our preservice teachers, an important characteristic of a constructivist approach to assessment. They are asked to reflect on their own reading and writing skills so that they can apply these skills to their own student teaching. One of their responsibilities as effective teachers is to help students achieve success in acquiring subject matter knowledge. This means finding strategies that will work, and the Literacy Journal is one way to begin by having the preservice teachers examine their own strategies as expert learners. This requires them to engage in reflective thinking, which goes to the heart of this assignment; metacognitive thought is fundamental to the assignment and, more generally, to becoming an effective teacher. By the end of the assignment, our goal is that the preservice teachers will better understand how metacognitive knowledge works and why it is important to include as part of the assessment process. Most assessment tasks are devoid of a metacognitive component, and for this reason it is important for us to model this process for our students so they can begin to think about how they can employ some of the same strategies in their own assessments.

Third, because this is an online assessment, the feedback provided allows the preservice teachers to better understand how they can improve as they strive to become effective teachers. Specifically, the instructor can offer suggestions for improvement of reading and writing that are tailored to individual needs. For example, because many of the preservice teachers did not offer specific examples of how they approached reading within their subject areas (e.g., reading a short story; reading a mathematics or physics problem; reading an historical document), one of the frequent comments made to Sybil was to think more deeply about what they were actually *doing* while reading—for example, using headings and subheadings, identifying new vocabulary or mathematical symbols, or relating the text to what they had read before.

When the preservice teachers did provide examples of what they did while reading, the feedback would frequently ask them about specific strategies: for example, if they used underlining as a strategy, and how it is they knew which words, phrases, and sentences to underline and which ones to skip? In other words, how were they able to distinguish between important and unimportant information? The explicit message in the feedback was that the MAC A students need to unpack their thoughts, so they will be better prepared to meet the needs of their own students. The impact of this type of feedback is that students extend their dialogue beyond the assignment. Returning to the Sibyl example, she was one of several students who talked to the faculty about wanting to improve their own metacognitive thinking related to their literacy practices. Because it was an online assessment and the comments encouraged students to think beyond the assignment to how they could improve, students reacted very differently; they wanted to improve, not merely to get a grade.

Teaching E-Portfolio and Reflective Writing Tasks

Our third example of how we use online assessment in the MAC A cohort involves our culminating project: the Teaching Electronic Portfolio (e-Portfolio) and the Reflective Writing Tasks (RWTs) that serve as a way to scaffold the MAC A students' preparation for writing the e-Portfolio. This project, which is due in the final months of the MAC A experience, encompasses deep understanding, reflection and metacognitive thinking, and scaffolding. Feedback is also central to the e-Portfolio and the RWTs, and the project as designed necessitates the use of online assessment in a comprehensive way. In fact, we cannot imagine how we would accomplish this project without the features that online assessment affords.

The purpose of the e-Portfolio is to document growth toward becoming an effective teacher at the secondary level. Moreover, as they write about the ways in which their teaching has changed over the 12 months of the MAC A experience, our students must provide concrete evidence of this growth. The evidence can be in the form of lesson plans, assignments, analyses of student work, conversations with their mentor teachers, videotapes of themselves teaching, and so forth. In order to produce the e-Portfolio, the MAC A students must engage in critical reflection across all aspects of their experiences such as readings, assignments, coursework, classroom observations, a myriad of student teaching experiences, conversations with their mentor teachers, interviews with students, and so forth. High-quality critical reflection cannot occur just before the students begin in earnest to compile their e-Portfolio, because such reflection would be superficial at best. Instead, we encourage our students to begin to reflect on their experiences in a variety of ways at the outset of the program, which in our situation means 10 months before the e-Portfolio is due. For example, through online discussions and assignments such as the Literacy Journal that we have discussed earlier in this chapter, we create situations in which our students must engage in reflection as they move through the various stages of the MAC A experience.

Because nearly all of these experiences are designed to be online assessments, the students have an electronic record of their reflections as well as comments that we provide as feedback, and these records are the kind of evidence that can be used in the e-Portfolio. Having access to this information allows our students to use it in a variety of ways to clarify and deepen their understanding of what is expected in the e-Portfolio. It is their examination of and reflection on their work that permits students to gain deeper and richer understandings of their own practice. Also, because our students are new to the profession,[5] they need to be directed toward engagement in critical reflection about the art and craft of teaching. It is through this process that we are able to lead them to a deep understanding of how to assemble an extensive document like the e-Portfolio[6] that captures their transition from students to teachers.

At the heart of this transformation are our RWTs, which are designed as online assessments that provide each student with a scaffolding experience leading up to the e-Portfolio. The RWTs are informal essays submitted as electronic files that require the MAC A students to supply information about how they are incorporating important aspects of effective teaching into their practice and to provide evidence that supports their claims. The students complete about a dozen RWTs across a four- to five-month period of time, while they are doing their full-time student teaching in secondary classrooms. Each RWT focuses on one or more of the five Standards and their associated benchmarks[7] that we have established for MAC A. We created the standards and benchmarks as a way for our students to gain a more concrete understanding of what it means to be an effective teacher. The RWTs are used to help our students reflect on their practice as they progress through their student teaching. To help guide them through this reflection process, the RWTs scaffold the experience.

To recapitulate, what differentiates the examples used in this section from those in the previous sections of this chapter are two important features. First, the RWTs are systematically sequenced so they provide us with specific types of information over an extended period of time. Second, we expect our students to implement some changes that are recommended in the feedback that is provided; therefore, the RWTs allow us to document student progress in an ongoing manner.

As we just noted, the RWTs are sequenced and structured in specific ways that provide us with continuous opportunities to help our students not only gain deeper insights into their own teaching. but also to demonstrate how those insights lead to improvements in their classroom performance. Our suggestions are coupled with those from other people such as the students' mentor teachers who are also evaluating their teaching. In particular, we structure the set of RWTs so that the early ones are very directive and the later ones become much more open-ended and allow the students to actually use them as sections of the e-Portfolio. For the first few tasks, we specify the standard and a few benchmarks associated with that standard, and the students must write about their experiences with the topic as specified and include appropriate evidence to support their statements. We sometimes include focus questions that must be answered in the RWT. This initial sequencing guides our students in a direct manner so they consider the specific benchmarks and provide examples as evidence. The later RWTs are more like the sections of the e-Portfolio in that we allow the students the freedom to select the standard and the associated benchmarks that align more directly with what is actually going on in their classroom. These RWTs are also longer and thus require more documentation, a feature that is ideal for online assessment.

We include an example to illustrate how the sequence and structure of the RWTs helped our students gain deeper insights into their own teaching. In one of his first RWTs on assessment, a student we call Frederick was asked to comment on and provide specific examples, which were electronically posted, of how he approached assessment in his own classroom. The examples he used in response to the focus questions (e.g., What kinds of assessment formats have you tried?) were very traditional: true/false, short answer, and multiple-choice formats which primarily focused on lower-order thinking. After gaining additional experience in the classroom and after receiving feedback and sugges-tions from those with whom he shared his first RWT, Fredrick began to rethink his views on assessment. In his second RWT dealing with assessment, it was evident that Frederick's approach to assessment was changing. For example, he reported that he was experimenting with a variety of assessment formats such as essays and projects. By the time he wrote about this topic in his e-Portfolio, it was evident he was using a greater variety of assessments such as performance assessment tasks, classroom conversations, and authentic writing tasks, all of which were evaluated using rubrics. Thus, Frederick had moved from depending upon assessments that were dominated by lower-order thinking tasks to adopting a more balanced approach. Through the use of online assessment, Frederick was able to demonstrate how his approach to assessment significantly changed over the course of five months. The online assessment record also demonstrated how Frederick's ability to reflect on his teaching had improved; he clearly was able to comment in greater depth and with more specificity about his teaching practices.

Through sequencing our RWTs, we are able to focus on an important feature of our e-Portfolio, the type and quality of the evidence offered to support the claims our students made about their progress toward effective teaching. The evidence can be in the form of documents (e.g., lesson plans), pictures or other graphics (e.g., photos of their students and their mentor teacher; copies of student work), audiotapes (e.g., interview with their mentor teacher), and videotapes of themselves teaching a lesson, and all forms of evidence can be stored in electronic formats through scanning, streaming video and audio, and electronic documents. For example, if the RWT were submitted as a Word document, then there could be hyperlinks embedded within it as "hot buttons" that, when clicked on, would result in the appearance of another document, a videoclip, picture, or other artifact that serves as evidence for the statements in the text. Students even embed links within the linked documents so the reader could better understand the point they were making. In one example, a student who used a hyperlink to a PowerPoint presentation included additional links within the PowerPoint slides that further elaborated upon the point the student was making, a feature that is just not possible with a more traditional paper portfolio.

However, just because a student included many links to documents, pictures, videoclips, and other kinds of evidence, this did not mean that the links effectively supported the claims made about growth in his or her teaching practice. Evaluating the *quality* of the evidence is another feature that online assessment afforded us. At first, our students were somewhat puzzled about what would constitute evidence of growth toward becoming an effective teacher; and as a consequence, most did not include many, if any, electronic links in their first few RWTs. If links were included, there often was not a clear connection between the linked document and the text. The e-Portfolio readers could make suggestions about appropriate links to include and how they could be couched in terms of demonstrating growth. If links were included in these early RWTs, then the readers could comment on them and suggest improvements. This way we did not have to wait until students submitted a final product to discover problems. By using online assessments we were able to improve the overall quality of each student's e-Portfolio. It also provided us with a record that we could examine in order to ascertain how well students attended to the feedback we provided. What follows is an example of how this process worked.

In an early RWT based on the Standard 4 Classroom Environment, Natalie talked about how she worked to create a "comfortable classroom environment":

As an initial step, I believe the first few days should be devoted to creating a comfortable classroom environment. I plan to dedicate the first few class periods to fun introduction to public speaking. This activity is explained in detail in a handout I prepared for **[CP1] lesson planning**. [Author note: Text of this link is in Figure 3]. The text of the link highlighted in yellow shows how I tried to make my students more comfortably when they spoke in front of the class. Hopefully, by allowing students to perform silly, child-like tongue twisters, students will be able to let their defenses down and likewise gain a foundation for what is expected of a public performance in my classroom. **[CP2]**

In reacting to the text and the corresponding link to evidence, the first author (Peters) in comment **[CP1]** provided feedback that confirmed Natalie's use of the lesson plan excerpt as evidence:

> This is a nice example of an electronic link and the highlighted portion of the text you to which you referred me better helps me focus on the intent of the evidence you provided. You also do a nice job of explaining the connection between the link and the ideas it supports in your RWT.

The last comment about explaining the connection between the link and the text that it supports refers to a common area for which students had difficulty presenting quality evidence. Frequently, they would merely use a hyperlink and then not explain what it supports. The online feedback gave us an opportunity to clarify problems, and then through our monitoring of their subsequent RWTs, we could check to see if they were using our suggestions to improve their presentations. As in Natalie's case, we could also confirm that students were using links appropriately and providing the kinds of explanations that we expected.

Figure 3. Excerpt from a link with Natalie's Reflective Writing Task (RWT)

Dr. Seuss Visits the Classroom
Overcoming the barriers of oral speech

Description: Students practice and ultimately perform excerpts from Dr. Seuss books in order to improve their confidence, communicative skills, and become aware of dramatic devices.

Rationale: When faced with reading texts out loud in class, such as drama, poetry, or novels, students often feel intimidated. They can feel silly, inarticulate, and sometimes lack confidence. This lesson provides an introductory exercise that enables students to overcome the social boundaries of a typical classroom. By utilizing Dr. Seuss, a fun, silly, over the top, known entity, students can interact with texts in a non-threatening environment. This lead-in will make it easier for students to then work with more challenging texts.

Context: This is the perfect introductory lesson to any type of performance or oral reading unit. This activity can also be used to remove barriers standing in the way of a cohesive classroom community. It enables students who do not typically praise for participation (class clowns, silent students) to engage in the lesson and receive recognition. This is a change from traditional classroom norms and students feel at ease to laugh at their mistakes.

In the second comment [CP2], Peters offered some advice about an activity that could provide additional evidence:

> One thing you might want to consider after you complete this lesson is to ask students what their reaction was to it, especially given your goal. You might also ask them for suggestions about other activities that might help to establish that comfort zone you want to create in your classroom. This information would provide evidence that your ideas worked, or it might provide information on what you might need to change in a future lesson.

In subsequent RWTs, Peters was able to use online assessment to monitor Natalie's use of links and to evaluate their quality as evidence of growth toward effective teaching. We found that for all of our students, the online assessment feature of feedback improved the quality of the evidence and consequently the quality of the RWTs from the first to the final one and ultimately to the e-Portfolio itself.

The e-Portfolio that grew out of the scaffolded RWTs was the epitome of online assessment in our program, and our students adapted remarkably well to its technical requirements, many of which were new to them (e.g., electronic links, burning CDs, scanning documents, streaming video, creating Web sites). In particular, the e-Portfolio became a student's online self-assessment of his or her growth toward becoming an effective teacher. While it is impossible here to demonstrate the scope and content of an entire e-Portfolio, we include an excerpt from a sample portfolio produced by Nita, a science major and one of two students who submitted a Web-site-based e-Portfolio. The excerpt, which is in the Appendix, documents how Nita's views of assessment changed over time. She provided evidence of using feedback from a previous RWT to refine how she designed her assessments based on her instructional goals, and not as an after-thought. The excerpt also demonstrates her use of evidence to support her statements. For example, in the e-Portfolio she included an audioclip of an interview with a student. This is only one example of how by using online feedback the overall quality of the e-Portfolio changed. Both by systematically structuring the RWTs so they clearly scaffolded student thinking, learning, and practice, and by providing students with continuous feedback that gave them an explicit picture of our intended goals and the standards we used for determining the quality of their work, our students were able to produce a higher quality e-Portfolio.

Conclusion

In this chapter we have articulated how we have incorporated our view of assessment based on constructivist principles of learning into our use of online assessment in our teacher education program at the University of Michigan. Online assessment has provided an appropriate venue in which we can monitor our students as they construct knowledge and understanding together, work toward the acquisition of deep understanding of important topics, engage in metacognitive thinking, and accomplish tasks that are scaffolded toward higher-order thinking. The feedback option that online assessment offers is especially important as we establish a concurrent and continuing dialogue between ourselves and our preservice teachers.

As of this writing, online assessment was still a relatively new phenomenon. We have much to learn about how it fits within the larger view of assessment and how advances in technology might affect online assessment techniques in the future. We conclude this chapter with some thoughts about online assessment specifically and assessment more generally.

1. *Online assessment must continue to be based on a model that is theoretically consistent with existing views on learning.* Regardless of the environment in which assessment is placed, we must begin with a view of assessment that is based on sound theories and principles of learning. For our model we chose constructivist ideas and principles, not as the only method but as an approach that helps establish a bridge between more traditional views of assessment and more current approaches to assessment.

2. *Online assessments should be designed in ways that take full advantage of the technology.* The online component adds features to assessment tasks that may not be accomplished in any other way. Online assessment offers a means by which to expand our thinking about what can be included as part of a repertoire of assessment tasks. For example, it may mean rethinking how feedback is provided or it may mean including videotape or other types of documentation that are not possible with more traditional forms.

3. *Online assessment provides the opportunity for using more authentic methods for assessing student knowledge, skills, and dispositions.* Online assessment techniques offer an excellent way for including more complex intellectual performances in assessment tasks than approaches that place more emphasis on assessment procedures. Online assessments often require significant intellectual accomplishments through the use of disciplined inquiry that pose issues, problems, and questions that have some meaning beyond the classroom. In our situation we used the Teaching e-Portfolio that captures a variety of aspects of effective teaching (e.g., videotapes of teaching).

4. *Online assessment tasks should scaffold to more complex understandings.* Online assessments afford us an excellent opportunity to use a variety of assessment tasks that provide a supportive pathway to more complex understandings. In the case of the MAC A experience, the Reflective Writing Tasks (RWTs) were such a vehicle. They provided flexibility and versatility that offered our students a means for better understanding how to assemble evidence for their own classroom experiences that demonstrated they were becoming more effective teachers. Because we used online assessment, we had access to a wide range of documentation of the preservice teachers' progress toward effective teaching.

5. *Online assessment is an excellent means for providing students with an opportunity to engage in metacognitive reflection of their own learning.* Because

metacognitive knowledge is difficult to assess in simple pencil-and-paper tests, online assessment offers a better way to capture this type of knowledge. One reason is that it provides a means for more closely examining students' awareness of their own knowledge and thought. In our particular approach to online assessment, we use metacognitive reflection to determine how well students use a variety of pedagogical strategies by asking them to apply them to their own teaching and then evaluate how effective they were. Here students often compare their approaches with other students in the cohort or use the feedback offered by their cooperating teacher or field instructor. With this approach we were able to successfully determine whether students selected and applied the most appropriate evidence to document their growth as an effective teacher.

6.   *Online assessments provide a means for capturing a wider range of cognitive complexities.* Online assessments have the potential to provide a variety of methods for documenting a range of cognitive complexities. Paper-and-pencil assessments often limit themselves to a narrow range of cognitive dimensions such as recalling, interpreting, classifying, summarizing, comparing or analyzing ideas, concepts, principles, and theories. Online assessments have the capability for assessing deeper levels of understanding that often require evaluating, critiquing, and producing new insights on the part of the learner. In our approach to online assessment, we used online discussions, an electronic teaching portfolio, and assignments that required students to apply what they were learning in class to their own classroom experiences in the schools, all of which meant engaging the faculty in online discussions that demonstrate a deeper understanding of important concepts that is not typically possible with more conventional assessment techniques. By integrating online assessment tasks with more traditional measures of student performance, we were able to document more complex student understanding of critical domain-specific knowledge.

References

Anderson, L.W., & Krathwohl, D.R. (Eds.). (2001). *A taxonomy for learning, teaching, and assessing: A revision of Bloom's taxonomy of educational objectives* (abridged edition). New York: Longman.

Archbald, D.A., & Newmann, F.M. (1988). *Beyond standardized testing: Assessing authentic achievement in the secondary school.* Reston, VA: National Association of Secondary School Principals.

Bransford, J.D., Brown, A.L., & Cocking, R.R. (1999). *How people learn: Brain, mind, experience and school.* Washington, DC: National Academy Press.

Collins, A., Brown, J.S., & Newman, S.E. (1989). Cognitive apprenticeship: Teaching the craft of reading, writing, and mathematics. In L.B. Resnick (Ed.), *Knowing, learning, and instruction: Essays in honor of Robert Glaser* (pp. 453-494). Hillsdale, NJ: Lawrence Erlbaum.

Darling-Hammond, L., & Snyder, J. (2000). Authentic assessment of teaching in context. *Teaching and Teacher Education, 16*, 523-545.

Heath, S.B. (1983). *Ways with words: Language, life, and work in communities and classroom.* New York: Cambridge University Press.

Horn, R.J. (2004). *Standards primer.* New York: Peter Lang.

Langer, J.A. (1991). Literacy and schooling: A sociocognitive perspective. In E.A. Hiebert (Ed.), *Literacy for a diverse society: Perspectives, practices, and policies* (pp. 9-27). New York: Teachers College Press.

Newmann, F.M., & Associates. (1998). *Authentic achievement: Restructuring schools for intellectual quality.* San Francisco: Jossey-Bass.

Newmann, F.M., Marks, H., & Gamoran, A. (1996). Authentic pedagogy and student performance. *American Journal of Education, 104*(4), 280-312.

Newmann, F.M., Secada, W.G., & Wehlage, G.G. (1995). *A guide to authentic instruction and assessment: Vision, standards, and scoring.* Madison, WI: Wisconsin Center for Education Research.

Novak, J.D., & Gowin, D.B. (1984). *Learning how to learn.* Cambridge, UK: Cambridge University Press.

Onosko, J.J., & Newmann, F.M. (1994). Creating more thoughtful learning environments. In J.N. Mangieri & C.C. Block (Eds.), *Creating powerful thinking teachers and students: Diverse perspectives.* New York: Harcourt Brace.

Paris, S.G., Calfee, R.C., Filby, N., Hiebert, E.H., Pearson, P.D., Valencia, S.W., & Wolf, K.P. (1987). A framework for authentic literacy assessment. *The Reading Teacher, 46*(2), 88-98.

Perkins, D. (1993). Teaching for understanding. *American Educator, 17*(8), 28-35.

Perkins, D.N., Tishman, S., Ritchhart, R., Donis, K., & Andrade, A. (2000). Intelligence in the wild: A dispositional view of intellectual traits. *Educational Psychology Review, 12*(3), 269-293.

Peters, C.W., & Wixson, K. (1989). Smart new reading tests are coming. *Learning, 17*(8), 42-44, 53.

Peters, C.W., Wixson, K.K., Valencia, S.W., & Pearson, P.D. (1993). Changing statewide reading assessment: A case study of Michigan and Illinois. In B.R. Gifford (Ed.), *Policy perspectives on educational testing* (pp. 295-391). Boston: Kluwer.

Popham, W.J. (2003). *Test better, teach better: The instructional role of assessment.* Alexandria, VA: Association for Supervision and Curriculum Development.

Ritchhart, R. (2002). *Intellectual character: What it is, why it matters, and how to get it.* San Francisco: Jossey-Bass.

Shepard, L.A. (2001). The role of classroom assessment in teaching and learning. In V. Richardson (Ed.), *Handbook of research on teaching* (pp. 1066-1101). Washington, DC: American Educational Research Association.

Sternberg, R. (1985). *Beyond IQ: A triarchic theory of human intelligence.* New York: Cambridge University Press.

Terwilliger, J. (1997). Semantics, psychometrics, and assessment reform: A close look at "authentic" assessments. *Educational Researcher, 26*(8), 24-27.

Tredway, L. (1995). Socratic seminar: Engaging students in intellectual discourse. *Educational Leadership, 53*(1), 26-29.

Valencia, S.W., Hiebert, E.H., & Afflerbach, P.P. (1994). Realizing the possibilities of authentic assessment: Current trends and future issues. In S.W. Valencia, E.H. Hiebert, & P.P. Afflerbach (Eds.), *Authentic reading assessment: Practices and possibilities* (pp. 286-300). Newark, DE: International Reading Association.

Vygotsky, L.S. (1978). *Mind in society: The development of higher psychological processes*. Cambridge, MA: Harvard University Press.

Whipp, J.L. (2003). Scaffolding critical reflection in online discussions: Helping prospective teachers think deeply about field experiences in urban schools. *Journal of Teacher Education, 54*(4), 321-333.

Wiggins, G. (1998). *Educative assessment: Designing assessments to inform and improve student performance*. San Francisco: Jossey-Bass.

Wiggins, G., & McTighe, J. (1998). *Understanding by design*. Alexandria, VA: Association for Supervision and Curriculum Development.

Wixson, K.K., & Peters, C.W. (1984). Reading redefined: A Michigan Reading Association position paper. *Michigan Reading Journal, 17*, 4-7.

Wixson, K.K., & Peters, C.W. (1987). Comprehension assessment: Implementing an interactive view of reading. *Educational Psychologist, 22*(3-4), 333-356.

Wood, D., Bruner, J., & Ross, G. (1976). The role of tutoring in problem solving. *Journal of Child Psychology and Psychiatry, 17*, 89-100.

Zimmerman, B.J., & Schunk, D.H. (Eds.) (1998). *Self-regulated learning: From teaching to self-reflective practice*. New York: Guilford Press.

Endnotes

[1]   "MAC" stands for Master of Arts with Certification, and the "A" designates one of two cohorts of preservice teachers. The MAC A preservice teachers earn both a master's degree and become certified to teach at the secondary level within a 12-month timeframe.

[2]   CTools is a Web-based system designed at the University of Michigan for coursework and collaboration. It is similar to commercially available systems such as Blackboard, and allows students to post assignments, download handouts, participate in online discussions, etc.

[3]   Concept maps are graphic organizers that "represent meaningful relationship between concepts in the form of propositions" (Novak & Gowin, 1984, p. 15) and appear as a network or web of ideas. If a person can draw a concept map, then he or she understands the hierarchical relationship among the ideas—the central

ideas, key ideas, the supporting ideas—presented in the text. Thus, a concept map is one way to assess a student's deepening understanding of a particular concept or topic.

[4]   Discussions in CTools are not done in an "instant messaging" environment. Instead, they can be "threaded"; that is, one person can begin the discussion and another person can choose to respond to that person's comments or make a new comment, or both.

[5]   The students in the MAC A cohort have undergraduate or graduate degrees in areas other than education such as English, mathematics, the sciences, and the social sciences. Some students have degrees in the professions such as engineering, business, law, and medicine. Most have little or no teaching experience before entering the program.

[6]   The e-Portfolios submitted as text files with electronic links can be over 60 pages in length. Some students choose to submit their e-Portfolios as Web sites, which have five or six menu bars and many links to other documents and Web sites.

[7]   Our five Standards are: Standard 1—Planning and Preparing for Instruction; Standard 2—Designing and Using a Variety of Assessments; Standard 3—Implementing Instruction; Standard 4—Creating and Maintaining an Effective Classroom Environment; and Standard 5—Fostering Relationships Within and Outside of School. Accompanying each Standard is a set of 9 to 12 benchmarks that provide details about the kinds of skills and understandings necessary for effective teaching. For example, Benchmark 1.3 in Standard 1 is: "The teacher activates and builds on students' prior knowledge within and across lessons by linking new ideas in the unit to already familiar ideas."

Appendix

Excerpt from Nita's Teaching E-Portfolio

In February, I gave my students a quiz that I wrote after we were already engaged in the Unit. I got so wrapped up in preparing the Unit that I didn't take the time to sit down and go over what exactly I wanted the students to get out of the lessons. My teacher reminded me that it had been awhile since I had given my students a quiz, so I felt pressured into coming up with something on the fly.

I had written the quiz and the review for the quiz separately, and the results were not what I intended. I learned a lot about why backwards design (designing down) is so important. If you try to teach a subject and then write the quiz based on what you thought you had taught, there is definitely going to be a gap between what you wanted the students to learn and how you assess that they have learned it. The **quiz** *(Author's note: This is a* *link to a copy of the quiz itself)* was on DNA, Proteins, and Enzymes. I analyzed the questions based on **Anderson and Krathwohl** *(Author's note: This is a link to the taxonomy table in the Anderson and Krathwohl book. In an RWT on assessment, her portfolio reader suggested that she use this source in thinking about her assessment practices.)* and determined that most of the questions were low on the taxonomy and tested factual, recall knowledge. The average grade on this quiz was 19/25 or 76%. I definitely used this as an opportunity to reflect on my teaching to try and figure out what went wrong. Since the questions weren't really testing higher-order thinking skills, I had to assume that the students just weren't getting the factual knowledge. Perhaps I covered the material too quickly, or didn't give them enough time to practice/demonstrate their understanding before quizzing them on it. I most certainly realized that an effective teacher MUST align their instructional objectives with the way in which they assess student understanding.

I also looked back at another quiz I had given them prior to this one. This **quiz** *(Author's note: This is a link to a different quiz.)* was on Mendelian genetics and had many of the same types of questions, primarily testing factual knowledge with some conceptual and procedural questions. The students did very well on this quiz, but struggled with the matching vocabulary at the beginning. This really surprised me because I had given them a review sheet that had all of the vocabulary terms on it, so I figured they would know it really well. Apparently, from **feedback** *(Author's note: This is a link to an audiotape excerpt from an interview that Nita did with one of her students. This is a particularly good example of the power of online assessment and the electronic record that it supports. Her e-Portfolio reader was able to go back to a previous RWT and see how much had changed. One of the suggestions in that RWT was that Nita use feedback from her students. Because the information was presented online and was preserved, we could see that she not only followed the advice about interviewing students, but we could also listen to an excerpt from the interview.)* that I got from one of my students, I found out that because I had included vocabulary on the review sheet and allowed them to turn that in for a little extra credit, my students thought that meant that I wouldn't quiz them on it. What I have learned is that you have to be very careful with what type of review sheet you give students. If you are not careful, they will use that as the sole template for studying. I have noticed that many of my students completely forget to review their lecture notes, homework assignments, and in-class work.

Section IV

Tests

Chapter XI

Variations in Adaptive Testing and Their Online Leverage Points

Roy Levy, University of Maryland, USA

John T. Behrens, Cisco Systems, Inc., USA

Robert J. Mislevy, University of Maryland, USA

Abstract

This chapter builds on foundational work on probabilistic frames of reference and principled assessment design to explore the role of adaptation in assessment. Assessments are characterized in terms of their claim status, observation status, and locus of control. The relevant claims and observations constitute a frame of discernment for the assessment. Adaptation occurs when the frame is permitted to evolve with respect to the claims or observations (or both); adaptive features may be controlled by the examiner or the examinee. In describing the various combinations of these characteristics, it is argued that an online format is preeminent for supporting common and emerging assessment practices in light of adaptation.

Introduction

The digital revolution has brought dramatic shifts in the activities and conceptualizations of modern life by providing easily transformable digital representation, dramatic computing power for calculation and decision making, and the use of large-scale databases. Internetworking technologies are having a similarly impressive impact by allowing geographically and computationally distributed combinations of this representational, computing, and database power. Having inherited many of our current conceptualizations and tools from pre-digital and pre-networked times, it is prudent to reexamine our understandings and language in light of these new possibilities. In the context of a globally linked digital world of computation, representation, and data, one area of potentially great benefit is that of computer-adaptive testing. Online presentation is greatly affected by the simulation and display technologies that continue to emerge; task selection is greatly affected by the availability of computing power and the availability of databases that may need to be remote from the user.

As the assessment community moves forward in harnessing these opportunities, it is important that discussion not only occur in the language and dimensions inherited from a pre-digital era, but that we re-examine the language and categories available to us to take advantage of the wide range of possibilities at hand. The focus of this work is to lay out a conceptual framework and taxonomy of adaptive assessment based on discussion of probabilistic frames of reference (Shafer, 1976), and dimensions of evidentiary reasoning that serves as the foundation for modern assessment (Mislevy, Steinberg, & Almond, 2003). This will be addressed in the context of a pragmatic delivery model (Almond, Steinberg, & Mislevy, 2002) that has been embedded in industry computing standards and in large-scale online assessment systems (Behrens, Collison, & DeMark, in press; Behrens, Mislevy, Bauer, Williamson, & Levy, 2004).

There is no shortage of ways to classify assessments. One may consider assessments in terms of: classical test theory (CTT) vs. item response theory (IRT), linear vs. adaptive, large scale vs. small scale, high stakes vs. low stakes, diagnostic/formative vs. summative, and of course, computer-based vs. paper and pencil. Building from Shafer's (1976) conception of a "frame of discernment" in probability-based inference and Mislevy et al.'s (2003) work on "evidence-centered" assessment design, we propose a taxonomy that differentiates assessments along the three dimensions of: (a) *observation status*, (b) *claim status*, and (c) *locus of control*. This foundation allows us to highlight the inferential roles that adaptivity can play in assessment. It offers a principled perspective for examining advantageous features of various adaptive testing models such as reduced time and increased precision in adaptive observation assessments and diagnostic capability in examinee-controlled assessments. In detailing the taxonomy, we point out ways in which online assessment enables or enhances these features.

Conceptual Foundations

Frames of Discernment

In his 1976 treatise, *A Mathematical Theory of Evidence*, Glen Shafer defines a frame of discernment as all of the possible subsets of combinations of values that the variables in an inferential problem at a given point in time might take. The term *frame* emphasizes how a frame of discernment effectively delimits the universe in which inference will take place. As we shall see in the next section, the frame of discernment in assessment comprises student-model variables and observable variables. The former concern aspects of students' proficiencies such as knowledge, skill, ability, strategies, behavioral tendencies, and so on; the latter concern aspects of things they say, do, or make that provide clues about their proficiencies. The term *discernment* emphasizes how a frame of discernment reflects purposive choices about what is important to recognize in the inferential situation, how to categorize observations, and from what perspective and at what level of detail variables should be defined.

A frame of discernment depends on beliefs, knowledge, and aims. Importantly, in everyday inferential problems as well as scientific problems, frames of discernment evolve, as beliefs, knowledge, and aims unfold over time. The need for vegetable dip for a party may begin with the inferential problem of whether or not there is any on hand, and evolve to determining where to go to make a purchase and which brand and size to buy. People move from one frame of discernment to another by ascertaining the values of some variables and dropping others, adding new variables or refining distinctions of values of current ones, or constructing a rather different frame when observations cause them to rethink their assumptions or their goals.

Evidence-Centered Assessment Design

Evolving complexities in many aspects of assessment, from development and administration to scoring and inferences, have rendered many popular terms as ambiguous or limited in scope at best and irrelevant at worst. Expressions such as "item," "answer," and "score," which on the surface appear to be quite general, are, in fact, limited in their application and do not suffice for describing or designing complex, innovative assessments (Behrens et al., 2004). Assessments that are innovative, either in terms of how they are developed and administered and/or what they demand of the examinee, are better served by a richer, more general terminology. The language of evidence-centered design (ECD; Mislevy et al., 2003), a descriptive and prescriptive framework for assessment development and implementation, provides such a terminology. A full explication of ECD and its components is beyond the scope and intent of this chapter. This section provides a brief description sufficient to introduce terms relevant to the taxonomy.

Evidentiary and Inferential Language

A *claim* is a declarative statement about what an examinee knows or can do. Claims may be broad (the examinee can subtract) or specific (the examinee can subtract negative improper fractions). The level of specificity of the claim(s) is often tied to the purpose of the assessment. Formative assessments often refer to highly specific claims, while summative assessments tend to have broader claims. Claims are hypotheses about the examinee; addressing these hypotheses is the goal of the assessment. Information pertinent to addressing the claims is accumulated in terms of student-model variables, which are typically latent variables representing the underlying construct(s) of interest. The student-model variables represent examinees' knowledge, skills, or abilities, and are therefore the targets of inference in an assessment.

In order to gain information regarding the student-model variables and the claims to which they are relevant, *observations* must be collected to serve as evidence. The conceptual assessment framework addresses the components of the psychometric models; the components are assembled to manage the collection and synthesis of evidence in an operational assessment, including student-model variables and observable variables. It includes an assembly model that contains the logic used to choose tasks to provide observations.

A Language and Model for Assessment Delivery

The four-process delivery system (Almond et al., 2002) provides a description of the interaction among processes for delivering tasks, characterizing performance, updating belief about examinees, and, when appropriate, selecting subsequent tasks in light of what has been learned thus far.

Task Selection is the first of these four processes and consists of activities designed to determine which task should be presented to the examinee. In simple cases this might be a non-deterministic rule such as "show the next question" or may consist of a complex selection algorithm optimizing (or minimizing) values to make choices along a number of dimensions.

Task Selection leads into the **Presentation Process**, which consists of the presentation of task materials to the examinee. The result of the task/examinee interaction results in a record that is called a **Work Product**. Many assessment practitioners refer to this result as an answer; however, answer implies a question and in many situations, there is no question, but rather a task to be completed. Consider for instance an examinee that is asked to draw a painting or perform a dance. In this case there is presentation (the instructions and the stage); and the dance or painting is the Work Product.

The third process in the model consists of examining the Work Product and characterizing the Work Product in terms of one or several variables or observables. These observables are the computing instantiation of the observations desired from an inferential perspective. This transformational process is called either **Evidence Identification** or Response Processing. Here again, the language is extremely flexible. A more traditional language might talk about scoring a question. This is one way to look for characteristics of the

Work Product (the correct answer), but is overly restrictive. The four-process terminology allows what is being looked for in the Work Product to be any desired characteristic. Perhaps efficiency or the presence of a particular strategy are relevant features of a Work Product.

Evidence Accumulation is the fourth process. This refers to statistical processes (however simple or complex) that are used to synthesize or accumulate data from the observables to estimate values for the student-model variables that inform our knowledge of the claims we want to make.

Each of these processes requires data and a database to keep the data. Information about task difficulty and task domain is generally needed in Task Selection. Increasingly complex presentation (video, simulation) requires increasingly large databases, and scoring and statistical computing require unique computing resources as well. The four-process model refers to a "task/composite" library as a location for such information.

The four-process model is especially relevant to assessment computing in the current online age because its language allows for great complexity throughout the assessment delivery process. In this scheme, the unit of analysis is observables of any value, rather than integer values associated with questions. Accordingly, complex tasks can lead to multiple observables, which may load on multiple student-model variables. As the complexity of computer-based assessment expands, the language of the four-process model has already provided a framework to describe it.

At an architectural level, the four-process model suggests that each of the different processes can occur in different locations. For example, in the early versions of the NetPASS, a computer network troubleshooting assessment (Behrens et al., 2004), Task Selection was made by students at any Web browser throughout the world, while presentation came from a remote computer network in the eastern United States, and Evidence Identification and Evidence Accumulation happened in a data center in the western United States. As illustrated in this application, appropriately delivered online assessment has the possibility of bringing the best computational, representational, and data resources to bear on the assessment task as needed.

Integration of Epistemic, Inferential, and Delivery Languages

Combining these multiple languages allows us to reframe the discussion regarding adaptive testing at a number of levels. In this scheme, the student-model variables and observable variables in play at a given point in time entail a frame of discernment, which is here characterized as being fixed or adaptive. Here, *fixed* conveys that a particular aspect (i.e., claims or observations) of the frame of discernment is set *a priori* and is not subject to change. *Adaptive* means that the frame of discernment may evolve in response to unfolding information as assessment proceeds. A fixed-claim adaptive-observation assessment is one in which the claim(s) to be investigated is (are) set in advance and not subject to change, but the set of observations that will be collected to bring to bear on a claim may change during the assessment. In an adaptive-claim assessment, the inferential goals or targets are subject to change; the hypotheses of interest that are investigated may change as new information (from observations) is incorporated.

An important aspect of what are characterized as adaptive assessments is the role of feedback in the task selection or claim selection mechanisms. Feedback into the assessment system (usually to the examiner, possibly also to the examinee) may serve as an aid or as guidance as to how the assessment evolves. For example, it is common practice in computerized adaptive testing to use correctness of response to aid in choosing the next task on the basis of maximizing information regarding a student-model variable. While the majority of adaptive assessments discussed in this chapter involve feedback, there are assessments that are characterized as adaptive that do not involve feedback. These points are further elaborated in a later section in the context of an example of one such assessment.

Fixed tests, varieties of existing adaptive tests, and other configurations not in current use can all be described in these terms. Our main interest will be in the areas of Task Selection and the Presentation Process, though along the way aspects of Evidence Identification and Evidence Accumulation for updating beliefs about examinees will become indispensable.

The Taxonomy

The authors propose a taxonomy of assessment that classifies assessments based on: (a) whether the claims are fixed or adaptive, (b) whether the observations are fixed or adaptive, (c) the control of the claims, and (d) the control of the observations. As will be seen, these dimensions can be understood in terms of how the frame of discernment evolves (or does not) over the course of an assessment. Traditionally, the examiner (or a proxy thereof) has control of the assessment, specifically, what claims to make and what observations to collect. In what follows the authors discuss these familiar situations and departures from them. The taxonomy is represented in Figure 1 (where short descriptors of examples are given for the most interesting cells). The 16 cells represent the possible combinations of claim status (fixed vs. adaptive and examiner- vs. examinee-controlled for both cases) and observation status (fixed vs. adaptive and examiner- vs. examinee-controlled for both cases).

Before discussing the components of the taxonomy, general properties of assessments are noted that motivate the organization of the presentation. First, to say an assessment has adaptive claims implies that it has multiple claims. Assessments with single claims are necessarily fixed-claims assessments. Multiple-claims assessments may be fixed or adaptive. As such, the discussion will generally follow the logical progression of fixed, single-claim assessments to fixed, multiple-claim assessments to adaptive, multiple-claim assessments. While it is logically possible to have single observation assessments and therefore a structure of fixed single-observation, fixed multiple-observation, and adaptive multiple-observation assessments, the vast majority of assessment systems employ multiple observations. The authors confine this discussion to assessments with

Figure 1. Cell by cell layout of all combinations

Observation status

		Fixed		Adaptive	
		Examiner	Examinee	Examiner	Examinee
Fixed	Examiner	1. Usual, linear test	2.	3. CAT	4. SAT
	Examinee	5.	6.	7.	8.
Adaptive	Examiner	9. MMPI— examiner decides how to pursue analysis	10.	11. Examiner chooses target, Multidim CAT	12. Examiner chooses target, Multidim SAT
	Examinee	13. MMPI— examinee decides how to pursue analysis	14.	15.Examinee chooses target, Multidim CAT	16. Examinee chooses target Multidim SAT

Claim status (row label on the left side)

multiple observations, though it is noted that single-observation assessments are just a special case of fixed-observation assessments.

The presentation is organized as follows. In proceeding through the various combinations, the order will follow the rows of Figure 1. For each row, common features that apply to all assessment types in the row will be presented. Distinctions between the assessment types in each row will be more specifically addressed in subsections.

Fixed, Examiner-Controlled Claims

The most familiar types of assessment are of this kind. The claims are fixed in the sense that inferences are made regarding the same claims for each examinee; the assessment is developed to arrive at (estimates of) values of the same student-model variables. The claims are examiner controlled in that the examiner, rather than the examinee, determines the targets of inference. Examples of these types of assessments discussed below include fixed linear assessments, computerized adaptive tests, and self-adaptive tests.

Cell 1) Fixed, examiner-controlled observations. Traditional assessments in which the tasks presented to each examinee are determined by the examiner *a priori* are of this kind.

The sequence of tasks may also be determined by the examiner a priori or it may be random, such as in cases where there is concern for test security. Regardless, the observables are fixed in the sense that evidence for the values of the student-model variables come from values of the same observables for all examinees. The observables are examiner-controlled in the sense that the examiner, rather than the examinee, determines the tasks, possibly also including the sequence of tasks, that are presented. In Shafer's terms (1976), the examiner has determined a frame of discernment, encompassing the same fixed set of student-model variables and observable variables for all examinees. Neither the frame of discernment nor the gathering of evidence varies in response to realizations of values of observable variables or their impact on beliefs about student-model variables.

An example of these assessments is a fifth-grade spelling test that asks students to spell the same words in a sequence devised by the teacher such that the teacher can make inferences about the same proficiency for each examinee. Another example is a statewide math assessment where the same set of IRT-scaled tasks are given to all examinees in the same order to obtain estimates of the latent mathematics ability of each student. This classification may include assessments that vary with respect to any number of striking and often important dimensions, such as high stakes vs. low stakes, summative vs. formative, online vs. paper and pencil, CTT-based vs. IRT-based. What's more, this classification subsumes the configuration that is popularly misperceived as encompassing all possible assessments: a set of tasks is developed, given to all examinees, and scored to make inferences/decisions about the same qualities of the students.

Assessments of this type were developed long before the invention of computers. Gains from online administration of this type may be in terms of improved test security; a reduction in coding, scoring, and associated measurement errors; increased data storage; and immediate score reporting (Bunderson, Inouye, & Olsen, 1988). In terms of supporting the assessment argument (i.e., the warranted inference regarding the claim), the use of an online administration does little; indeed, this class of assessments was developed and refined before the advent of online assessment and, therefore, does not involve features of other assessment systems that rely on an online format.

One notable advantage that may be achieved by an online administration in even this class of assessments is the possibility of innovative task types. Tasks that involve moving parts or audio components typically cannot be administered without a computer. They almost certainly cannot be administered in a standardized way absent a computer. To the extent that innovative tasks enhance the assessment, in terms of the content and construct validity (for an inference regarding a particular claim), an online administration can potentially provide a considerable advantage over other administration formats. Quite aside from the inferential course that the assessment traverses, the substance of the assessment argument can extend to both student-model and observable variables that are difficult to address with static and paper-and-pencil modalities of testing (Behrens et al., 2004; Williamson et al., 2004).

As more and more complex assessment systems are described below, however, the emphasis in this presentation will be placed on features of those assessments for which an online administration is recommended to enhance assessment argumentation. Since the use of innovative task types is a potential advantage of online administration in even this, the most basic of assessment systems, it is also a potential advantage of online assessments for *all* assessment systems discussed in this chapter. Though the use of innovative task types will not be listed under each classification in the taxonomy, the reader should note that the potential benefits in employing an online administration that supports such task types applies to all cases.

Cell 2) Fixed, examinee-controlled observations. Traditional assessment with fixed, examiner-controlled claims and tasks affords little opportunity for the examinee to control the observations. Examples of this type include an examinee's freedom to work on different tasks in the same test section, choose the order to proceed through a section, revisit responses, and decide to omit responses to some tasks. These affordances do not play major roles in the examiner's reasoning, but they do introduce intertwined positive and negative effects: They provide the examinee with flexibility to achieve a higher level of performance if they are used well, but at the same time introduce construct-irrelevant variance among examinees to the extent they are not used well.

Cell 3) Adaptive, examiner-controlled observations. This class is similar to the traditional assessments in that the inferences are made about the same student-model variables for all examinees, and the examiner (or in many cases, a proxy for the examiner) controls the tasks. In contrast to traditional assessments, the observables are not constant across examinees. Examinees do not necessarily see the same tasks, and those that do might not see them in the same order. In other words, the frames of discernment the examiner works through with different examinees do not evolve with regard to student-model variables, but they do evolve, in some optimal manner, with regard to observable variables.

The most common example of this type of assessment is univariate IRT-based computerized adaptive tests, or CATs (Hambleton & Swaminathan, 1985; Wainer & Mislevy, 1990). In these assessments, a task is administered and the response, typically in conjunction with an initial estimate of the student-model variable, is used to update the estimate of the student-model variable. The next task is then selected from among the available tasks, administered, and leads to a revised estimate of the student-model variable. Algorithms for updating the student-model variable vary and may be based on maximum likelihood or Bayesian procedures (Wainer et al., 1990). Likewise, selection of the next task may be based on many features in addition to the current estimate of the student-model variable (e.g., task characteristics, frequency of task administration). Typically, the task to be presented next is (at least in part) a function of the current estimate of student-model variable and the psychometric properties of the tasks. For example, a task is selected that provides maximum information at the point of the current estimate of the student-model variable. Similarly, in a Bayesian framework, the task is selected on the basis of minimizing the expected variance of the posterior distribution for the examinee's student-model variable. In this way, the assessment is examiner controlled (via a proxy), and tasks are presented adaptively to facilitate better measurement in that the tasks any one examinee encounters are ideal or near-ideal. The result is greater measurement precision for a fixed amount of testing time and reduced bias in estimates of the student-model variable (Lord, 1983; Samejima, 1993).

Not all fixed-claim, adaptive-observation, examiner-controlled assessments employ IRT or require online administration. A century ago, Binet developed tests that called for the examiner to adapt the tasks long before the development of computers or IRT. To take another example, a five-question attitude survey may direct examinees that answered positively to question 1 to respond to questions 2 and 3, while directing examinees that answered negatively to question 1 to respond to questions 4 and 5. Such an assessment could be administered via paper and pencil as well as online. Important distinctions between these examples of examiner-controlled, adaptive assessments involve the number of observation adaptations (i.e., one for the attitude survey vs. many for item-level CAT), the number of tasks in the pool (i.e., five in the attitude survey vs. thousands for item-level CAT), and concern for test security (i.e., whether examinees will have access to tasks other than those that they are asked to complete). It is not feasible to present an examinee with a booklet of thousands of tasks and then direct them to respond to different tasks on the basis of their set of responses, particularly in high-stakes assessments where task security is a concern. We note these various possibilities and emphasize that the larger the task pool, the more adaptations required (both of which may be related to size of examinee pool), and the greater the concern for test security, the less and less feasible static assessments become.

Though the most common applications involve univariate IRT as a measurement model, the claim space may be multivariate (Segall, 1996). In a fixed, multiple-claims assessment with examiner-controlled adaptive observations, tasks are administered to provide observable variables that serve to update values of student-model variables that address the claims of interest. The assessment starts out focusing on a claim of interest and its associated student-model variable (for simplicity, assume there is a one-to-one relation between claims and student-model variables). Tasks are presented and observations are collected to statistically update the student-model variable; the tasks are presented adaptively, namely, on the basis of (at least) the current student-model-variable estimate and the psychometric parameters of the task. At some point, the assessment shifts focus to another claim and its associated student-model variable. As above, tasks are presented adaptively to update the estimate of the student-model variable, until at some point, the assessment shifts to another claim. This continues until the final claim is addressed, and the assessment concludes. As in the univariate-claim-space situation, the examiner controls the selection of subsequent tasks, which may vary over examinees.

In addition, the point at which the assessment shifts from one claim to another is also controlled by the examiner. Options for determining such a point include shifting the focus when: (a) the tasks appropriate for a particular claim are exhausted, (b) a predetermined level of statistical precision in the estimate of the student-model variable is reached, or (c) a certain time limit has been reached. The decision to shift may be influenced by the purpose of assessment and the particular claims involved. For high stakes claims and decisions (e.g., will hiring this applicant make the firm vulnerable to an expensive lawsuit?), greater precision may be required for the relevant student-model variables before a shift in the assessment is warranted.

After the shift to a different claim, we are again faced with a decision regarding the initial task. In addition to the options discussed earlier, selection of the initial task for the second (or subsequent) claim might be informed by the examinee's performance on earlier tasks. For example, if the examinee has performed well on the set of tasks pertaining to the first claim, and there is reason to believe the skills involved with the claims are positively related, the initial task for the second claim might be more difficult than if the examinee performed poorly on the first set of tasks.

A number of existing large-scale assessments fall into this category. For example, the Graduate Records Examinations General Test (Mills, 1999) consists (at present) of verbal, quantitative, and analytical sections. Though the total claim space is multidimensional, unidimensional IRT is employed in each section. Tasks for each section inform upon a student-model variable localized to the particular section. For each section, the examiner, who also controls the shifting and the stopping of the assessment, adaptively selects the tasks.

Adaptive IRT allows for higher-ability examinees to be given tasks suitable for them; they are not presented too many easy tasks that may lead to boredom or carelessness. Likewise, lower-ability examinees are given tasks suitable for them; they are not presented with too many difficult tasks that may lead to frustration or an ability estimate that is influenced by lower-ability examinees' tendencies to guess on inappropriately difficult tasks. The details of these and other mechanisms for Task Selection are beyond the scope and intent of this chapter. For current purposes it is sufficient to note that the necessary calculations involved in estimating student-model variables and shifting the assessment focus, even when approximations to such calculations are employed (e.g., the use of information tables), are computationally intensive enough that they require a computer.

Cell 4) Adaptive, examinee-controlled observations. In contrast to the examiner-controlled adaptive assessments just described, this family of assessments permits the examinee to select the tasks—or given a fixed initial task, permits the examinee to select subsequent tasks—on the fly. The frame of discernment does not evolve with regard to the student-model variable(s), which is (are) fixed and controlled by the examiner, but it does evolve with respect to observable variables, in a manner controlled by the examinee. This shared responsibility for the evolution of the frame of discernment immediately raises the question of the principles on which tasks are selected. As mentioned above, rules for examiner-controlled adaptive observations involve comparisons of the tasks. Implicitly, knowledge of the task properties is required; Task Selection algorithms typically involve maximizing information or minimizing expected posterior variance regarding the student-model variable(s). Furthermore, these algorithms are often subject to constraints regarding task content, structure, exposure, and so forth. Without question, it is unreasonable to demand examinees to make such decisions on these criteria on the fly as the decisions involve overly burdening computation. What's more, setting aside the properties of the tasks, selecting in this manner requires being aware of all the tasks. Though examinees are often familiar with types of tasks (especially in large-scale, high-stakes assessments), it is not the case that they have seen all the tasks from which to select. Clearly, if examinee-controlled, adaptive-observation assessments are to exist, they are to have a considerably different essence than that of the examiner-controlled, adaptive-observation assessments. In what follows, we describe two flavors of examinee-controlled, adaptive-observation assessments for a fixed-claim space.

Consider an assessment where tasks are developed to provide evidence for a single claim. Suppose, as occurs in assessments in a number of disciplines at the undergraduate and graduate levels, the examinees are presented with all the tasks and informed as to the order of difficulty of the tasks and how their work will be evaluated. A natural scoring rule would have a correct observable worth more than an incorrect observable, and harder observables would be worth more. For example, Wright (1977) describes a self-adaptive test in which a student chooses items one page at a time from a relatively short test booklet, scoring is based on the Rasch model, and correct responses to harder items induce likelihoods that are peaked at higher levels of the latent ability variable. The examinee then selects a finite number of tasks to complete and submit. Examinees will then not necessarily have values on the same observable variables; each examinee individually determines which variables will have values. Such an assessment model is easily generalizable to multiple claims.

This example illustrates the case where an assessment is adaptive (in terms of the observations), and yet there is no feedback provided to the examinee for the process of selecting the next task. The assessment is adaptive in the sense that the frame of discernment varies across examinees. Each examinee's frame of discernment, the collection of student-model and observable variables, is not fixed *a priori*, but rather is determined as the assessment unfolds.

There are two concerns with this type of examinee-controlled, adaptive testing—one practical and the other statistical. Practically, such assessments would have to consist of a task pool small enough for the examinees to review and select from among all the tasks, and the assessments would not be appropriate if task security was a concern. Statistically, care would need to be taken to avoid the bias incurred by not-answered questions that Rubin (1976) called non-ignorably missing. (A simple example is filming yourself attempting 100 basketball free throws, making 20, and editing the film to show the completed baskets and only five misses.) This can be accomplished by allowing choice among items that differ as to ancillary knowledge, but all demand the same targeted knowledge. For example, an examiner can ask for a Freudian analysis of a character in a Shakespearean play and let students choose a play that was familiar to them. This focuses evaluation on the Freudian analysis, while assuring familiarity with the character.

Another type of fixed-claim, examinee-controlled, adaptive-observation assessment is self-adaptive testing, a variant of more familiar (examiner-controlled) computer adaptive testing. To date, all self-adaptive tests (SATs) have employed IRT to achieve adaptation. In SATs (Rocklin & O'Donnell, 1987; Wise, Plake, Johnson, & Roos, 1992), tasks are grouped into a finite number (typically six or eight) of bins based on difficulty, namely the b parameter in IRT. Upon completion of each task, examinees choose how difficult the next task will be by choosing among the bin from which the next item will be selected. Once the examinee selects the difficulty level, a task from that bin may be selected randomly or on the basis of maximizing information. The latter case represents a hybrid of examiner- and examinee-controlled assessments. Input is necessary from both agents to select the next task.

Similarly, other considerations lead to hybrid assessments. In cases where the examinee repeatedly selects tasks from one difficulty bin, the examinee may exhaust the tasks in that bin before the assessment is complete (Wise et al., 1992). Or, if the selected bin is far from an examinee's ability level, ability estimates will be biased (Lord, 1983; Pitkin & Vispoel, 2001; Samejima, 1993). To control for these possibilities, the Task Selection algorithm may be constrained so that examinees are forced to select tasks from different bins, particularly if they are repeatedly correct (or incorrect) in their responses to tasks from a particular bin (Vispoel, 1998). Again such an alteration results in a hybrid of examiner- and examinee-controlled assessment.

Several studies have shown that SATs can lead to reduced test anxiety and higher ability estimates, as compared to examiner-controlled CATs (e.g., Rocklin & O'Donnell, 1987; Wise et al., 1992), though some studies have found these effects to be negligible or nonexistent (for a review, see Pitkin & Vispoel, 2001). Several theories for how SATs might counter the effects of test anxiety on performance exist. See the discussion in Pitkin and Vispoel (2001) and the references therein for a full review.

What is of greater concern in this work is an understanding of the convergent and divergent aspects of examinee-controlled SATs and the more traditional examiner-controlled adaptive-observation tests and the implications for test use. As Vispoel (1998) notes, the potential advantage of reducing construct-irrelevant variance (e.g., anxiety) via SATs does not come without a price. In particular, there is a loss in precision, as standard errors of ability estimates are higher for SATs (Pitkin & Vispoel, 2001; Vispoel, 1998), and a loss in efficiency, as SATs require more time (Pitkin & Vispoel, 2001). This result is to be expected when we recognize that examiner-controlled CATs are built to maximize precision. To the extent that the tasks selected deviate from those that would result in maximum precision (as will almost surely be the case in SATs), there will be a loss in the precision, or, in the case where the stopping criterion is based on precision of the estimate of the student-model variable, an increase in testing time.

In terms of use, we follow Pitkin and Vispoel (2001) in noting that possible bias, loss of precision, sensitivity to test-wiseness, and increased costs in item-pool development and management are some of the difficulties involving the use of SATs in high-stakes assessments. Further, we follow Pitkin and Vispoel (2001) in lamenting the fact that the effects of reducing test anxiety might be most pronounced and desirable in high-stakes assessments. Nevertheless, SATs may be appropriately used for low-stakes diagnostic purposes. In particular, SATs with feedback (Vispoel, 1998) may offer ideal properties for diagnostic assessments. Feedback given to examinees may be as simple as whether they completed the task correctly and may aid the examinee in selecting a task bin that is more appropriate (i.e., closer to their ability level), which would result in observed increase in precision in SATs with feedback vs. those without (Vispoel, 1998). An SAT with feedback is a step in the oft-desired but rarely achieved direction of an integration of assessment and instruction via a computer-based assessment system (Bunderson et al., 1988).

Reporting whether the task was completed correctly only scratches the surface of the level of feedback that may be given. That is, if the tasks are constructed appropriately, features of the Work Product (above and beyond "right" or "wrong") may serve as evidence regarding the examinee's cognitive abilities. This may be the case even if the task is as simple as the selection of a particular option in a multiple-choice question. For example, when solving problems in physics, students may employ principles derived from Aristotle, Newton, or Einstein (among others). If distractors are constructed to be consistent with incorrect frames of thinking, then the selection of those distractors by an examinee might be able to pinpoint the extent to which the examinee understands (or fails to understand) the relevant principles of physics. Such information would be relevant to examinees in a diagnostic setting or to examiners in both diagnostic and summative settings; an online administration permits immediate feedback to examinees and examiners.

Extensions to multiple-claims assessments are straightforward. The assessment commences with a task regarding one claim and the examinee selects subsequent tasks after completing each one. At some point, the assessment shifts to tasks that provide evidence for another claim, and the same process occurs. After completing an initial task (initial to this new claim), the examinee chooses the difficulty bin for the next task. Theoretically, there is no limit on the number of claims that can be addressed in this way.

Several decisions, some more implicit than others, are necessary in administering such an assessment. A number of options exist for selection of the first task. Since examinees will choose between harder and easier tasks, a sensible choice would be somewhere in the middle of the difficulty distribution. Alternatively, one could start with a comparably easier task, with the expectation that most examinees will then opt for a more difficult task.

In the case of multiple-fixed claims, specifying the change point and the initial task for a new claim may be accomplished in a number of ways, as discussed in the preceding section. With all the computation involved in selecting an initial task, accepting examinee input in terms of the bin to use, and selecting a task from the bin (either randomly or to maximize information), even the simplest SAT can only be administered online. With the increased complexity in hybrid algorithms for Task Selection and, in the case of multiple-claim assessments, shifting the focus to another claim—particularly when the shift is based on an achieved level of precision—the need for an online administration becomes even more evident.

Fixed, Examinee-Controlled Claims

Akin to the situation in **Cell 2**, it makes little sense to say the claims are fixed, and therefore not subject to evolve over the course of the assessment, and yet controlled by the examinee. This reasoning applies to *Cells 5, 6, 7,* and *8* in the taxonomy. In passing, it is noted that *Cell 6* states that both claims and observations are fixed yet controlled by examinees, and is therefore doubly nonsensical.

Adaptive, Examiner-Controlled Claims

In adaptive claim assessments, the claim space is necessarily multidimensional. All the classes of assessments discussed in this and subsequent sections are adaptive and hence multidimensional. They are adaptive in the sense that the inferences drawn may vary across examinees. The assessments are examiner controlled in the sense that the choice of the claim to consider, and the choice of when to move to another point in the claim space, are controlled by the examiner, rather than the examinee. The distinctions among these assessments, discussed in the following subsections, have to do with the status of the observations.

Cell 9) Fixed, examiner-controlled observations. This class of assessments is defined by examinees responding to the same tasks, the selection and presentation of which are in control of the examiner, while the inferences drawn vary across examinees. That is, examinees all encounter the same tasks, but the inferences drawn may be at different points in the claim space. An example of this includes analysis of a Rorschach test in which examinees are all presented with the same stimuli, but the responses lead the clinician to create an individualized interpretation that can involve different claims for different examinees.

Another example may be drawn from the Minnesota Multiphasic Personality Inventory–2, or MMPI–2 (Butcher, Dahlstrom, Graham, Tellegan, & Kaemmer, 1989). An examinee taking the full MMPI–2 sees hundreds of tasks that are fixed and examiner controlled. The examiner may then form different scales from these, adapting what is formed in light of the examinee. Though the observations are fixed, the frame of discernment alters as the claim of interest changes.

Two features of this type of assessment are noteworthy. First, as discussed above, that a claim space can be adaptive indicates that it is multidimensional. Second, given that they are multidimensional, fixed-observation assessments are in many cases inefficient. If the claim space is multidimensional and fixed, an appropriate number of tasks can be (constructed and) selected *a priori* for each claim (in which case it will be a fixed-claim, fixed-observation assessment described in *Cell 1*) or the tasks can be selected on the fly (i.e., a fixed-claim, adaptive-observation assessment described *Cell 3*). However, if the claim space is multidimensional and adaptive, a part of the goal is to allow the assessment to adjust the focus—the inferential target—during the assessment. Since observables that are optimal for certain claims are most likely not optimal for other claims, moving around the claim space adaptively calls for the selection of the observables to be adaptive as well. The authors take up adaptive-claim, adaptive-observation assessments in subsequent sections.

Cell 10) Fixed, examinee-controlled observations. As in the discussion of *Cell 2,* it offers little to an understanding of the analysis of argumentation to dwell on those marginal situations in which the observations are fixed but yet controlled by examinees.

Cell 11) Adaptive, examiner-controlled observations. In an assessment where summative inferences may be sought for multiple claims, an adaptive-claim, adaptive-observation assessment with examiner control of both claims and observations is ideal. To introduce this type of assessment, we begin by generalizing the more familiar (examiner-controlled) fixed-claim, examiner-controlled, adaptive-observation assessments (see *Cell 3*).

In *Cell 3,* fixed-claim, adaptive-observation assessments were discussed, and common procedures for adapting the observations were mentioned. The main purpose of adapting is to provide an assessment that is optimal for each examinee. Implicit in the discussion was the constraint that the inferences to be made were, for all examinees, with regard to the same claim(s). In adaptive-claim assessments, this constraint is released; the inferences made from an adaptive-claim assessment may vary across examinees, not only in their values (i.e., this examinee is proficient in math, this examinee is not proficient in math), but in the variables as well.

Results from the assessment might lead to inferences for an examinee regarding proficiency in one area of the domain (with an associated claim or set of claims), while inferences for another examinee would concern proficiency in a *different* area of the domain (with its own separate claim or claims). As an examinee proceeds through the assessment, evidence is gathered. As evidence is gathered, certain hypotheses are supported while others are not, which leads to questions about other hypotheses; these questions may differ between examinees. In fixed-claim, adaptive-observation assessments, the evidence differs between examinees, but the inferential question asked is the same. In adaptive-claim assessments, the inferential questions differ as well.

For example, consider an assessment in which tasks are constructed such that examinees may employ one of possibly several cognitive strategies in approaching or solving the tasks. The assessment could then adapt the claims on the basis of examinee performance. If performance on tasks early in the assessment indicates the examinee is employing a particular strategy, the assessment claim can be defined or refined to focus on that strategy, and tasks may be adapted accordingly, so as to provide maximum information regarding that claim for that examinee. Another examinee, employing a different cognitive strategy, will have the assessment routed to focus on a claim regarding that strategy, and will encounter appropriate tasks to obtain evidence for that claim. For both examinees, as information regarding a particular claim is incorporated, new questions regarding other claims may result. The assessment then shifts to address those claims, adaptively administering tasks to provide observable evidence regarding student-model variables for those claims. This process continues until the end of the assessment. Though the assessment may be broadly labeled with a general term, the results of the assessment will yield different inferential targets.

For example, a developing line of research has investigated the cognitive strategies employed by students in tackling problems of mixed number subtraction (de la Torre & Douglas, 2004; Mislevy, 1996; Tatsuoka, 2002; Tatsuoka, 1990). Under one strategy, a set of attributes is necessary to successfully complete the tasks, while under another strategy, a different (though possibly overlapping) set of attributes is necessary. One could devise an assessment that seeks to identify which strategy an examinee is employing in addressing the problems at hand and then select tasks that are most informative for that particular strategy. For examinees choosing a particular strategy, the assessment provides information relevant to claims associated with the attributes necessary for that strategy; it cannot speak to claims associated with attributes that are not part of that strategy. Though the assessment may be broadly labeled "mixed number subtraction," the actual inferential targets vary over examinees on the basis of their cognitive strategies.

As argued earlier, if the observations are to be adapted between examinees, an online administration is all but required. All the computational complexity is increased when both the claims and the observations are free to vary between examinees. Facilitation of individualized inferences using optimally selected tasks can only be accomplished via an online administration.

Cell 12) Adaptive, examinee-controlled observations. These assessments might be thought of as slight changes to either the assessments described in *Cell 11* or *Cell 4.* Similar to those in *Cell 11,* these assessments involve multiple claims that are controlled by the examiner. In *Cell 11,* the examiner adapts the observations. Here, the observations are adaptive but controlled by the examinee. Likewise, in *Cell 4,* the examinee controlled the observations related to a fixed (set of) claim(s) set out by the examiner. Here, the examinee controls the observations; the claims, though still controlled by the examiner, vary over examinees.

Recognizing that *Cell 11* builds off the CATs described in *Cell 3* by permitting there to be multiple claims, and that *Cell 4* builds off the CATs described in *Cell 3* by granting control of the observations to examinees, the current category can be seen as the combination of those changes. The focus of the assessment, though controlled by the examiner, varies over examinees; the observations also vary, as determined by the examinees. In a sense, these assessments are SATs with multiple claims that are controlled by examiners. The features, benefits, and drawbacks of examinee-controlled observations (see *Cell 4*) and examiner-controlled adaptive claims (see *Cell 11*) are combined.

Again, suppose tasks have been constructed such that examinees may employ one of possibly several cognitive strategies in approaching or solving the tasks. The assessment could then control the claims on the basis of examinee performance, all the while permitting examinees to have input into what tasks (within the family of tasks for that claim) are selected. If performance on tasks early in the assessment indicates the examinee is employing a particular strategy, the assessment claim can be defined or refined by the examiner to focus on that strategy, while the difficulty of the tasks would be controlled by the examinee, say by binning items and prompting the examinees for which bin to select from, as in conventional SATs.

Recent advances in intelligent tutoring systems include the development of innovative assessment models to support intelligent tutoring customized to the examinee's knowledge and problem solution strategy. Andes, an intelligent tutoring system for physics (Gertner & VanLehn, 2000) dynamically builds student models as the student proceeds through the tasks. Once a student selects a task, Andes loads the solution graph, a network representation of the relevant knowledge, strategies, and goals involved in successfully solving the problem. The solution graph is automatically converted into a student model in the form of a Bayesian network (Conati, Gertner, VanLehn, & Druzdzel, 1997; for more on Bayesian networks, see Jensen, 2001; Pearl, 1988; Almond & Mislevy, 1999; Martin & VanLehn, 1995; Mislevy, 1994). For each task in Andes, there is a Bayesian network containing nodes for all the relevant facts, rules, strategies, and goals. As the student solves the task, nodes may be fixed to certain values, other nodes may be added dynamically, and others may be updated in accordance with what the student does via propagation of evidence through the network.

Once the student selects a new task, the nodes relevant to the old task are discarded and the nodes relevant to the new task are added. Nodes relevant to both tasks are retained. In this way, the information from previous tasks is brought to subsequent tasks—the state of the nodes after the previous task becomes the prior distribution and initializes the model for the new task. Over the course of the assessment, as evidence regarding student knowledge of facts, familiarity with rules, and use of strategies enters the model, the assessment automatically moves around the claim space. In addition to the values of the student-model variables being updated, the contents of the student model—the variables themselves—change as beliefs about the student's knowledge, abilities, strategies, and goals change.

In Shafer's terms (1976), the frame of discernment adapts on the fly for each examinee as they proceed throughout the system. From task to task, the student model changes, and information regarding the examinee addresses some hypotheses and brings to light others that remain to be addressed.

What is key for the current purpose is recognizing that the additional complexity of adaptive claims, moving throughout the claims space and adjusting the target of inference, essentially requires an online administration. In addition to the computational requirements for storing and presenting the various tasks, the adaptation of the claims also depends on computational power.

Adaptive, Examinee-Controlled Claims

This class of assessments differs from all those previously discussed in that the examinee is in control of target of inference. As an adaptive claim assessment, the claim space is multidimensional and the inferences may vary across examinees. Here, the decisions regarding which claims to address and when to shift from one claim to another is in control of the examinee.

Cell 13) Fixed, examiner-controlled observations. Assessments of this sort may be described as slight changes to those in *Cell 9.* Recall the example of the MMPI–2, in which an examinee encounters hundreds of tasks that are fixed and examiner controlled. In *Cell 9,* the exploration of the scales that can be formed was controlled by the examiner. Here, the examinee chooses the scales to explore. As in *Cell 9,* having a fixed set of observations may be inefficient for adaptive-claims assessments.

Cell 14) Fixed, examinee-controlled observations. As in sections discussing *Cells 2, 6,* and *10,* little is gained toward the end of explicating the structures of assessment arguments by consideration of those situations in which the observations are fixed yet controlled by the examinee.

Cell 15) Adaptive, examiner-controlled observations. These assessments might be thought of as slight changes to the assessments described in *Cell 11.* Similar to *Cell 11,* the observations vary between students and are obtained based on examiner-controlled task presentation. In addition, the claims may vary between examinees. In contrast to *Cell 11,* control of the claims is in the hand of the examinee. Thus the focus of the assessment is controlled by the examinee. In short, the examinee chooses the target of interest (i.e., the claim) and then the examiner controls what tasks are presented. The assessment is ideally suited for diagnostic assessments in which the examinee determines the area of focus, say, regarding certain areas in which the examinee would like some feedback concerning their achievement level. Once the focus is determined, the examiner presents tasks to obtain maximal information employing the methods already described.

Again, the complexity involved with having libraries of tasks relevant to possibly many claims only adds to the computational requirements of adapting the tasks on the basis of previous performance. As with simpler assessments that involve adapting in simpler ways, any large scale application is feasible only with an online administration. The assessments described here are well-suited for diagnostic purposes under the guidance of each examinee. As such, possible situations for employing these systems are longitudinal diagnostic assessments. In the course of an instruction period, students could engage in the assessment, selecting the focus of the assessment while the examiner selects the most appropriate tasks. At a later time, the examinee could engage with the assessment system again; selection of the same claim(s) would lead to current estimates of the examinees' proficiencies with regard to that claim. This provides a natural way for the student to track his or her own progress over time.

Although we are not aware of any educational assessments in this cell, there is an analogue in Internet sites that helps people explore what cars, careers, books, or movies they might like (e.g., ETS's SIGI PLUS career planner). Standard questions about what the user likes to do, what is important to the user, how the user makes proffered choices, and so forth help the user figure out classes or properties of cars, careers, books, or movies to investigate more deeply. With examiner-adaptive observations, answers to earlier questions can influence what questions will be asked next. One site for helping elementary school children find books they might like is Book Adventure (1999-2004). Of course librarians also do this in person with students. The problem is that even though all the information is available in the library, it overwhelms young students. Only the students "know" what the ultimate claims of interest will turn out to be. A program's frame of discernment uses examiner-created observables and student-model variables, and as an interview proceeds, the frame of discernment is increasingly under the control of the student.

Cell 16) Adaptive, examinee-controlled observations. The final category consists of assessments that allow examinees to control both the claims and the tasks to yield observations for those claims. The examinee selects the claims to focus on and then has input into the observed data, for example in the manner of SATs described above.

Information-filtering and user-modeling systems involve these types of assessments of this class (e.g., Rich, 1979; this source is a bit outdated in terms of current cognitive theory, but the beginning is excellent in terms of laying out the situation as an inferential problem that is aligned with the taxonomy proposed here). For example, a central problem in information systems involves the retrieval systems in libraries that organize materials and search terms that try to help patrons find the information they might want, without knowing what it is that any new patron might want.

Consider a simple case where a user's query results in a list of documents, possibly structured by some criterion such as perceived relevance. The user then selects some of the documents from the list for further consideration. A great deal of observable information can be collected from such a process. Which documents were viewed? In what order? How much time did the user spend reading each? These only scratch the surface of what data could possibly be collected. In these systems, the user is in control of the claim space, via the query, and the observables, via the actions taken with respect to the produced list of documents.

A more refined example comes from NetPASS, a computer-based interactive assessment in the domain of computer networking containing tasks targeted towards the related but distinct aspects of network design, implementation, and troubleshooting (Behrens et al., 2004; Williamson et al., 2004). Upon selecting one of these areas of the domain, examinees select the desired level of difficulty (easy, medium, hard) of a task. Thus, the examinees control both the claims and observations. For each task, there is a Bayesian network fragment containing all relevant student-model and observable variables (Levy & Mislevy, 2004). As tasks are completed, values for the observables are entered and information is propagated throughout the network, updating the student-model variables. When a new task is called, the variables associated with the previous task that do not pertain to the new task are dropped, and previously unused variables relevant for the new task are included. In this way, variables are docked into or dropped out of the network, as needed (Mislevy, Almond, & Steinberg, 1998). Here, as is the case with Andes, the use of a Bayesian network for information propagation supports the adaptation and the flexibility it provides.

In *Cell 15,* it was argued that an assessment in which the examinee controls the focus was more suited for diagnostic than summative assessment. Likewise, in *Cell 4* it was argued that assessments in which the examinee controls the observations are likely to be inefficient for estimation of parameters pertaining to the claims and thus may be inefficient as summative assessments. Assessments in this final class combine the examinee-controlled features of *Cells 4* and *15,* and are ideally suited to diagnostic assessment. As with the other classes of assessments that involve adaptation of observations, the need for an online administration is clear. And, as in the classes that involve adaptation of claims as well as observations, the need for an online administration is increased.

Discussion

The focus of this work is to detail different ways an assessment system can operate in terms of the targets of inference and the tasks presented to examinees. The taxonomy described here classifies assessments in terms of the claim status, observations status, and the controlling parties. Well-known univariate IRT has been employed to facilitate both examiner-controlled and examinee-controlled, fixed-claim assessments. The advantages of an online administration, namely, high-speed computations regarding Evidence Accumulation and Task Selection, make adaptive-observation assessments feasible. More complex assessments involving adaptive claims have yet to achieve the prominence of adaptive-observation assessments.

We propose two reasons for this. First, the majority of traditional paper-and-pencil assessments were fixed-observation assessments. Limitations of fixed-observation assessments (e.g., inefficiency in terms of appropriateness of tasks) were known before the advent of online administration. Thus the capabilities of an online administration were first used to combat these limitations via adapting the observations, rather than extending to multiple, adaptive claims. Second, in order for the examiner-controlled, adaptive-claims assessments described here to actually be effective, considerable work must be done up front. In the case of an assessment system that adapts to the examinee's chosen strategy for solving subtraction problems, cognitive studies on the reasoning patterns employed by students must be done, and the tasks must be constructed and calibrated such that they are consistent with this cognitive work. This work will most likely need to be done domain by domain. Only recently has the cognitive groundwork necessary for such complex assessments been laid in certain domains (for an example in the domain of computer networking, see Williamson et al., 2004). In efforts to extend assessment in these directions, research and experience in the fields of user modeling in such domains as consumer preferences, adaptive software engineering, and information sciences should prove useful.

To summarize, adaptation enhances the validity argument for the assessment. This holds both for adapting the observations (e.g., increased measurement precision, decrease in bias, decrease in test anxiety) and adapting the claims (e.g., identification of cognitive strategies, individualized diagnostic feedback for both examiners and examinees). Assessment systems with adaptation all but require an online administration, especially for large-scale assessment. What's more, in providing increased security, decreased scoring errors, faster score reporting, and the opportunity for innovative task types, an online administration can be advantageous even in situations without adaptation.

No declaration is made about the taxonomy presented here being exhaustive. Already we have mentioned settings in which the locus of control for either the claims and/or the observations would be a hybrid of examiner- and examinee-controlled assessments. Further refinements in the future are eagerly anticipated. Nevertheless, framing assessments in terms of the observation status, claim status, and the locus of control for these aspects proves useful in: (a) designing/aligning an assessment with the purpose at hand, (b) understanding what options are available in terms of assessment design and operationalization, (c) documenting strengths and weaknesses of assessments, and (d) making explicit the features of the assessment argument. Though not described here, the taxonomy also proves useful for designing or selecting an appropriate statistical measurement model. Future work in this area will include aligning various existing statistical models with the taxonomy and suggesting the possible advantages (and disadvantages) of both more complex statistical models and adaptive reconfigurations of simple models.

References

Almond, R.G., & Mislevy, R.J. (1999). Graphical models and computerized adaptive testing. *Applied Psychological Measurement, 23,* 223-237.

Almond, R.G., Steinberg, L.S., & Mislevy, R.J. (2002). Enhancing the design and delivery of assessment systems: A four-process architecture [Electronic version]. *Journal of Technology, Learning, and Assessment, 1*(5).

Behrens, J.T., Collison, T.A., & DeMark, S.F. (in press). The seven Cs of comprehensive assessment: Lessons learned from 40 million classroom exams in the Cisco Networking Academy Program. In S. Howell & M. Hricko (Eds.), *Online assessment and measurement: Case studies in higher education, K-12, and corporate* (Vol. III). Hershey, PA: Idea Group.

Behrens, J.T., Mislevy, R.J., Bauer, M., Williamson, D.W., & Levy, R. (2004). Introduction to Evidence-Centered Design and lessons learned from its application in a global e-learning program. *International Journal of Testing, 4,* 295-301.

Book Adventure. (1999-2004). Retrieved December 10, 2004, from *http://www.bookadventure.com/ki/bs/ki_bs_helpfind.asp*

Bunderson, C.V., Inouye, D.K., & Olsen, J.B. (1988). The four generations of computerized testing. In R. Linn (Ed.), *Educational measurement* (3rd ed.). New York: Macmillan.

Butcher, J.N., Dahlstrom, W.G., Graham, J.R., Tellegen, A., & Kaemmer, B. (1989). *Minnesota Multiphasic Personality Inventory–2 (MMPI–2): Manual for administration and scoring.* Minneapolis: University of Minnesota Press.

Conati, C., Gertner, A.S., VanLehn, K., & Druzdzel, M.J. (1997). Online student modeling for coached problem solving using Bayesian networks. *Proceedings of UM-97, 6th International Conference on User Modeling* (pp. 231-242). Sardinia, Italy: Springer.

de la Torre, J., & Douglas, J. (2004). Higher-order latent trait models for cognitive diagnosis. *Psychometrika, 69,* 333-353.

Gertner, A. & VanLehn, K. (2000). Andes: A coached problem-solving environment for physics. In C. Frasson (Ed.), *Proceedings of ITS 2000* (pp. 131-142). New York: Springer.

Hambleton, R.K., & Swaminathan, H. (1985). *Item response theory: Principles and applications.* Boston: Kluwer-Nijhoff.

Jensen, F.V. (2001). *Bayesian networks and decision graphs.* New York: Springer-Verlag.

Lord, F.M. (1983). Unbiased estimators of ability parameters, their variance, and their parallel forms reliability. *Psychometrika, 48,* 233-245.

Martin, J.D., & VanLehn, K. (1995). A Bayesian approach to cognitive assessment. In P. Nichols, S. Chipman, & R. Brennan (Eds.), *Cognitively diagnostic assessment* (pp. 141-165). Hillsdale, NJ: Lawrence Erlbaum.

Mills, C.N. (1999). Development and introduction of a computer adaptive Graduate Records Examinations General Test. In F. Drasgow & J.B. Olson-Buchanan (Eds.), *Innovations in computerized assessment* (pp. 117-135). Mahwah, NJ: Lawrence Erlbaum.

Mislevy, R.J. (1994). Evidence and inference in educational assessment. *Psychometrika, 59,* 439-483.

Mislevy, R.J. (1996). Test theory reconceived. *Journal of Educational Measurement, 33,* 379-416.

Mislevy, R.J., Almond, R.G., & Steinberg, L.S. (1998). A note on the knowledge-based model construction in educational assessment (CSE Tech. Rep. No. 480). Los Angeles: University of California, National Center for Research on Evaluation, Standards, and Student Testing (CRESST).

Mislevy, R.J., Steinberg, L.S., & Almond, R.G. (2003). On the structure of educational assessments. *Measurement: Interdisciplinary Research and Perspectives, 1,* 3-67.

Pearl, J. (1988). *Probabilistic reasoning in intelligent systems: Networks of plausible inference.* San Mateo, CA: Kaufmann.

Pitkin, A.K., & Vispoel, W.P. (2001). Differences between self-adapted and computerized adaptive tests: A meta-analysis. *Journal of Educational Measurement, 38,* 235-247.

Rich, E. (1979). User modeling via stereotypes. *Cognitive Science, 3,* 329-354.

Rocklin, T.R., & O'Donnell, A.M. (1987). Self-adapted testing: A performance-improving variant of computerized adaptive testing. *Journal of Educational Psychology, 79*(3), 315-319.

Rubin, D.B. (1976). Inference and missing data. *Biometrika, 63,* 581-592.

Samejima, F. (1993). The bias function of the maximum likelihood estimate of ability for the dichotomous response level. *Psychometrika, 58,* 195-209.

Segall, D.O. (1996). Multidimensional adaptive testing. *Psychometrika, 61,* 331-354.

Shafer, G. (1976). *A mathematical theory of evidence.* Princeton, NJ: Princeton University Press.

Tatsuoka, C. (2002). Data-analytic methods for latent partially ordered classification models. *Journal of the Royal Statistical Society Series C (Applied Statistics), 51,* 337-350.

Tatsuoka, K. (1990). Toward an integration of item-response theory and cognitive error diagnosis. In N. Frederiksen, R. Glaser, A. Lesgold, & M. Safto. (Eds.), *Monitoring skills and knowledge acquisition* (pp. 453-488). Hillsdale, NJ: Lawrence Erlbaum.

Vispoel, W.P. (1998). Psychometric characteristics of computer-adaptive and self-adaptive vocabulary tests: The role of answer feedback and test anxiety. *Journal of Educational Measurement, 35,* 155-167.

Wainer, H., & Mislevy, R.J. (1990). Item response theory, item calibration and proficiency estimation. In H. Wainer, N.J. Dorans, R. Flaugher, B.F. Green, R.J. Mislevy, L. Steinberg, & D. Thissen (Eds.), *Computerized adaptive testing: A primer* (pp. 65-102). Hillsdale, NJ: Lawrence Erlbaum.

Wainer, H., Dorans, N.J., Flaugher, R., Green, B.F., Mislevy, R.J., Steinberg, L., & Thissen, D. (1990). *Computerized adaptive testing: A primer.* Hillsdale, NJ: Lawrence Erlbaum.

Williamson, D.M., Bauer, M., Steinberg, L.S., Mislevy, R.J., Behrens, J.T., & DeMark, S.F. (2004). Design rationale for a complex performance assessment. *International Journal of Testing, 4,* 303-332.

Wise, S.L., Plake, B.S., Johnson, P.L., & Roos, L.L. (1992). A comparison of self-adapted and computerized adaptive tests. *Journal of Educational Measurement, 29*(4), 329-339.

Wright, B.D. (1977). Solving measurement problems with the Rasch model. *Journal of Educational Measurement, 14,* 97-116.

Chapter XII

Using Messick's Framework to Validate Assessment Tasks in Online Environments:
A Course in Writing Effectively for UNHCR

Valerie Ruhe, University of Maine, USA

Bruno D. Zumbo, University of British Columbia, Canada

Abstract

Messick (1988) maintained that technology-based delivery methods would transform both our conceptions of teaching and learning, and also our methods for evaluating student learning. Designed 100 years ago (Crocker & Algina, 1986), classical approaches to assessing test quality are unsuited to the contemporary context of technology-based learning (Messick, 1988). We will discuss evolving conceptions of validity and show how Messick's (1989) framework is an improvement over traditional conceptions. We will then apply Messick's framework to the evaluation data from the globally delivered, hybrid "A Course in Writing Effectively for UNHCR." Our results will show how Messick's framework provides a comprehensive assessment, based on evidence, values, and consequences of the merit and worth of contemporary assessment tasks.

Introduction

In his (1988) article on validity, Messick discussed how technology-based delivery methods would transform widely held conceptions of teaching, learning, and assessment. Traditional approaches to assessing the quality of assessment tasks are ill-suited to technology-based environments, which measure knowledge, skills, and strategies in adaptive, pluralistic, and dynamic ways. Messick (1988) predicted that, in these new environments, traditional evidence-based approaches to validity and validation would give way to a comprehensive approach to validation practice based not only upon evidence, but also upon values and consequences. Although Messick's (1989) framework was developed to validate standardized paper-and-pencil tests, there is an increasing interest in its application to distance education (Bunderson, 2003; Chapelle, Jamieson, & Hegelheimer, 2003; Ruhe, 2002b, 2002c).

This chapter will be organized in the following sections. First, we will summarize Messick's (1988) argument that technology, by its very nature, will render a classical approach to validation untenable. Next, we will give an overview of our objectives, then we will give a brief history of validity and validation practice, and show how the emergence of technology-based assessment is forcing a rethinking of conventional conceptions of validity, which were designed for pencil-and-paper environments. After that, we will present Messick's (1989) contemporary conception of validity, followed by an adapted version for technology-based assessment tasks, and finally we will demonstrate how the adapted Messick's framework performs when used to guide the validation practice of an assessment task in an authentic distance education course, "A Course in Writing Effectively for UNHCR." In this exercise, we will cycle through the adapted framework and show the various aspects of merit and worth which emerge around the assessment task of writing a UNHCR field report.

An Emerging Practice

Validity refers to the merit and worth of an assessment task, and *validation practice* refers to the collection and analysis of evidence to assess validity (Messick, 1989). In the classical literature of educational measurement, validity has traditionally been conceptualized as a "unitary" construct, and statistical tests were used to "measure" a single aspect of validity. For example, content validity coefficients measure the "match" of the test items to the course content, criterion-related validity coefficients relate test items to authentic tasks in the "real world," and item bias rates are the percentage of items which reflect gender, language, or cultural bias. In addition, the focus of classical validation efforts has been on large-scale, paper-and-pencil tests, and not on small-scale assessments, that is, "classroom" tests. These classical, "unitary" approaches were designed for pencil-and-paper-based environments 100 years ago (Crocker & Algina, 1986). Although our conception of validity has gradually moved from a "unitary" towards a multifaceted conception of validity, the practice of validation *still* tends to be based largely upon tradition, "creating a persistent "gap between psychometric theory and research practice" (Hubley & Zumbo, 1996, p. 215). Messick (1988) maintained that technology would render this "persistent disjunction" between validity theory and validation practice "no longer tenable," thereby unifying theory and practice.

Over 15 years ago, Messick (1988) maintained that these classical procedures to validation practice are unsuited to technology-based assessment, and that technology would usher in a comprehensive, multifaceted approach to validity and validation practice. As the authors shall demonstrate, Messick's (1989) four-faceted approach is better suited to the complex nature of technology-based assessment. Today, assessment tasks can be delivered to hundreds of learners around the world, thereby blurring the distinction between small-scale, classroom assessment and large-scale assessment (Chapelle et al., 2003; Ruhe, 2002). Secondly, technology changes the very nature of assessment by giving rise to "an increased premium on the adaptive measurement, perhaps even the dynamic measurement, of knowledge structures, skill complexes, personal strategies and styles as they interact in performance and as they develop with instruction and experience" (Messick, 1989, p. 33). For both reasons, the value of technology-based assessment tasks goes beyond a single validity coefficient to include diverse aspects of value, such as learner satisfaction, cost-benefit, underlying values, theories and ideologies, and unintended consequences. As the authors will demonstrate, Messick's (1989) four-faceted framework of validity provides a conceptual guide for conducting a comprehensive assessment of merit and worth which includes all of these aspects of value.

Objectives

In this chapter, we have two purposes: (1) to provide a theoretical treatment of validity, and (2) to report the results of an empirical experiment using Messick's (1989) framework. Our second purpose is not to merely provide a "demo," but to leverage deeper insights into the validation process, and obtain a deeper theoretical understanding of the framework by applying it to authentic evaluation data from "A Course in Writing Effectively for UNHCR," a hybrid online/print course delivered by the Commonwealth of Learning in Vancouver, British Columbia.

The authors understand that bringing values and consequences into the discussion of validity is controversial. This controversy lies along a continuum from one extreme— Popham (1997), Wiley (1991), and Maguire, Hattie and Haig (1994), who maintain that values and consequences are not part of the discussion of validity—to Shepard (1997), who says that consequences are more important than construct validity. However, we are not interested in this debate or in who is right or wrong. The debate question should not be: Are values and consequences present in technology-based assessment tasks? We, the authors, are in the middle of the continuum, along with Messick, who is also a moderate. Like Messick, we believe that values and consequences are always present in testing, but hidden in the background. In this chapter, our purpose is to use Messick's framework to shine a light into the shadows, and bring values and consequences into the foreground. The issue is not whether unintended consequences "are positive or negative, but how the consequences came about and what determined them" (Messick, 1992, p. 1494). In distance education, a validation study that includes values and consequences can help to provide specific directions for course improvement. The final question is who is responsible for bringing consequences to the foreground? We believe that it is the community of scholars which bears this responsibility.

History of Validity and Validation Practice

In the early days, the American Psychological Association (1966) conceptualized four distinct types of validity: *construct validity, content validity, criterion validity,* and *concurrent validity. Construct validity* refers to how well a particular test can be shown to assess the construct that it is said to measure. *Content validity* refers to how well test scores adequately represent the content domain that they are said to measure. *Predictive validity* is the degree to which the predictions made by a test are confirmed by the target behaviors of the tested individuals. *Concurrent validity* is the extent to which individuals' scores on a new test correspond to their scores on an established test of the same construct. In traditional validation practice, each of these aspects of validity is measured by a statistical calculation based on test scores, yielding a validity coefficient which measures a single aspect of validity. Many of these procedures are based on logical or mathematical models that date from the early twentieth century (Crocker & Algina, 1986). Messick (1989) describes such procedures as fragmented, unitary approaches to validation. Hubley and Zumbo (1996) describe them as "scanty, disconnected bits of evidence…to make a two-point decision about the validity of a test" (p. 214).

Over the last 60 years, however, theoretical conceptions of validity have changed considerably (Angoff, 1988; Hubley & Zumbo, 1996). By the mid-'70s, the focus had shifted from validity as a property of tests to the validity of tests in specific contexts or applications (Angoff, 1988). In the American Psychological Association, American Educational Research Association, and National Council on Measurement in Education's (1974) Standards for Educational and Psychological Tests, traditional conceptions of content validity shifted from a representative sample of content knowledge to a representative sample of behaviors (Messick, 1989). The focus for validation also shifted from validating the test to validating responses, and then to validating inferences and actions based on test scores (Angoff, 1988). In addition, standards for test *use* and social impact of tests came to be endorsed as aspects of validity (Messick, 1989).

"The purpose of the contemporary view of validity, as it has evolved over the past two decades, is to expand upon the conceptual framework and power of the traditional view of validity" (Zumbo, 2005, p. 5). In the 1985 Standards, "validity" was defined as the "appropriateness, meaningfulness, and usefulness of the specific inferences made from test scores" (p. 9). "Validity is no longer a property of the measuring tool, but of the inferences made from scores" (Zumbo, 2005, p. 5). Construct validity is at the core of validity, which is no longer defined as four types but as an "elaborated theory and supporting methods" (p. 5). There is also momentum to consider the role of values and consequences, the latter in the sense of the consequences of "normal" test use, when the test is used exactly as intended. Although the inclusion of unintended social consequences in the "nomological net" of validity has generated a great deal of controversy (e.g., Green, 1998; Messick, 1998; Popham, 1997; Shepard, 1997; Wiley, 1991), it will "regain momentum in the current climate of large-scale test results affecting financing and staffing...in the United States and Canada" (Zumbo, 2005, p. 6). Finally, as for the relationship between validity and reliability, "reliability is a question of data quality, whereas validity is a question of inferential quality" (p. 6).

In sum, our theoretical conceptions of validity shifted from many distinct types to a unified conception with multiple aspects which closely resembles that of Messick (1989). Despite these theoretical advances, however, actual validation practice still tends to be based on classical conceptions of validity, creating a persistent "gap between psycho-metric theory and research practice" (Hubley & Zumbo, 1996, p. 215). Messick (1988) maintained that it was technology-based assessment that would finally overcome this persistent disjunction between validity theory and validation practice, thereby unifying both theory and practice.

The Problem:
Validating Assessment Tasks in
Technology-Based Environments

Theory and practice in evaluation in distance education have tended to evolve independently from the field of educational measurement (Tennyson, 1997; Ruhe, 2002), and evaluation concepts have come into distance education "through the back door," through concepts which do not deal with distance education directly, but were perceived as applicable (Bourdeau & Bates, 1997; Tennyson, 1997). Validation has been recognized as important for large-scale assessments delivered via the Internet, for example, but the procedures used tend to be classical (Bennett, 2001).

Yet classical conceptions and practices are becoming less applicable in contemporary environments. As Messick (1988) predicted, technology has ushered in complex, innovative assessment tasks which are pluralistic, adaptive, and individualized. These new assessment strategies include performance-based checklists for scoring online discussions (Marttunen, 1997), Web- and Internet-based strategies (Collis, 1998; Haughey & Anderson, 1998; Hiltz, 1990; Hudspeth, 1997; Laffey & Singer, 1997; Schacter, 1997; Thorpe, 1998), online summary statistics to track students' content coverage (Harasim, Hiltz, Teles, & Turoff, 1996), and new pluralistic assessment tasks based on multimedia (Baumgartner, 1999).

This complex, adaptive, and dynamic nature of technology-based assessment tasks, coupled with the increasing geographical reach, is blurring the distinction between large-scale and small-scale, or classroom, assessment. Small-scale assessments can now be delivered to hundreds of learners around the world, which creates a need for validation studies. Scholars are searching for alternatives to traditional methods of validation designed for pencil-and paper-based tests (Chapelle et al., 2003). A new model of validity is needed which is suitable for technology-based assessment tasks, and which can be applied to many different kinds of complex environments.

The Solution:
An Adapted Version of Messick's
Framework for Distance Education

According to Messick (1989), validity is "an integrated evaluative judgment of the degree to which empirical evidence and theoretical rationales support the adequacy and appropriateness of inferences and actions based on test scores or other modes of assessment" (p. 13). Messick's (1989) four-faceted conception of validity is usually referred to as a "framework" because, as a set of concepts organized in a schematic diagram, this term describes Messick's conception more closely than the terms "model" or "approach." The framework represents the unification of four facets formed by crossing the evidential with the consequential bases of test interpretation and use (Figure 1).

The *outcomes* dimension includes the categories of *test interpretation* and *test use* (the ways in which the test is actually used). The *justification* dimension includes the *evidential* and *consequential bases*. The *evidential basis* is an appraisal of psychometric data, relevance and utility or cost-benefit. In contrast, the *consequential basis of validity* is the value implications and the social impact of test use, especially issues of bias, adverse impact, and distributive justice (Messick, 1989).

Messick's (1989) framework, which was designed to validate standardized, paper-and-pencil tests comprises: (1) evidence, or a classical appraisal of psychometric data, including content- and criterion-referenced validity; (2) relevance to the "real-world" *and* utility, or cost-benefit analysis; (3) value implications (value labels, theory, and

Figure 1. Messick's (1989) unified conception of validity

Justification	Outcomes	
	Test Interpretation	Test Use
Evidential Basis	Construct Validity (CV)	CV + Relevance/ Utility (RU)
Consequential Basis	CV + RU + Value Implications (VI)	CV + RU + VI + Social Consequences

ideology); and (4) unintended social consequences of test interpretation and use, including issues of bias, potentially harmful impact, and distributive justice. The framework represents a departure from traditional conceptions of validity, which are based on psychometric evidence alone. By including values and consequences as aspects of validity, Messick's framework offers a comprehensive approach to the evaluation of merit and worth.

Messick's framework is a progressive matrix; in other words, the four facets are not distinct, but overlapping and dynamic. Issues around consequences, for example, are not distinct from issues around relevance or cost-benefit. Similarly, consequences can be either positive or negative, and must therefore be intertwined with values (Messick, 1989). Scientific evidence, then, cuts across all four facets, and values and consequences are always present in scientific analysis, but hidden in the background. This tension between evidence and consequences is the tension between facts and values which underlies all scientific inquiry (Messick, 1989).

To make Messick's framework more applicable to the distance education context, the authors have adapted the framework for this new context (Figure 2).

In Figure 2, the evidential basis of test interpretation is composed of construct validity, feedback, grading, completion rates, and learner satisfaction. Because of the relationship to learner motivation, perseverance, and success, learner satisfaction has been an important rationale for distance delivery since its inception (Varnhagen & Zumbo, 1990). The evidential basis of test use is composed of relevance and authenticity of the assessment tasks, and cost-benefit analysis, including economies of scale. The consequential basis of test interpretation is composed of underlying values, theory, and ideology, and their implications for assessment standards and practices. The consequential basis of test use is composed of an analysis of unintended instructional and social consequences. In other words, the evidential basis of the framework encompasses traditional evidence, while the consequential basis encompasses values and consequences. Finally, construct validity (CV) is included in all four facets to show the progressive nature of the matrix, as well as the overlap of each facet with all the other

Figure 2. The adapted Messick's framework

	Outcomes	
Justification	Test Interpretation	Test Use
Evidential Basis	Construct Validity (CV) Feedback and Grading Learner Satisfaction Completion Rates	CV + Relevance to Needs/Cost-Benefit/ Utility (RU)
Consequential Basis	CV + RU + Value Implications (VI)	CV + RU + VI + Unintended Consequences

facets. As we shall see from our analysis, each facet of value is not distinct, but tends to overlap with the other facets.

As for validation practice, evaluators can be guided by the adapted Messick's framework, which functions as a conceptual "road map" to guide a practical study of the merit and worth of a specific assessment task. In applying the framework to data, evaluators analyze all sources of evidence, both quantitative and qualitative, bearing on functional worth, value, or quality. This approach resembles program evaluation, where multiple sources of evidence are marshaled to determine merit and worth (Cronbach, 1982, 1989). In fact, Messick treats a test *as if* it were a program, and cost-benefit, relevance, values, and unintended consequences are recurring categories across Stufflebeam's (2001) 22 professional program evaluation models.

Applying the Adapted Messick's Framework to "A Course in Writing Effectively for UNHCR"

"A Course in Writing Effectively for UNHCR" is a technical writing course for native and non-native speakers of English, delivered by print and e-mail by the Commonwealth of Learning (COL) from Vancouver, British Columbia. The course ran for the first time in April 2000. Within two years, almost 570 UNHCR employees dispersed in 70 countries across 10 time zones had taken the course. Almost all learners had English as their second or third language, and English language skills varied widely.

The printed UNHCR course manual consisted of three modules. All learners were required to study Module 1, which dealt with principles of effective communication, reader analysis, and paragraph organization. In Module 1, learners were assessed on a reflective composition about their own strengths and weaknesses. They then had a choice of Module 2, office correspondence, or Module 3, field reports. In Module 2, they were assessed on a memo, fax, letter, diplomatic note, and minutes of a meeting, and in Module 3, on a field report. Assignments were e-mailed to tutors, who made footnoted comments on each draft and sent them back for revision. Learners had three attempts to resubmit, and six months to complete the course. There were three final grades: Pass, Incomplete, or Unsatisfactory.

In 2001, COL commissioned Ruhe's (2002) evaluation study to investigate geographical reach, "paperless" administration, and learner response to the course. Interviews were conducted with eight learners, two course administrators, and five tutors. Responses to a learner satisfaction survey were also obtained from 116 respondents from December 2000 to September 2001. We, the authors, will now apply the adapted Messick's framework to these qualitative and quantitative data from Ruhe's (2002) report, used with written permission from UNHCR and COL. We will now cycle through the four facets of Messick's framework, using them as coding categories to obtain an in-depth understanding of the multiple aspects of value provided by "A Course in Writing Effectively for UNHCR."

The Evidential Basis of Test Interpretation

Construct Validity

Construct validity refers to the "fit" between the assessment tasks and the course objectives, course content and learning activities. To assess construct validity, the authors analyzed and compared these course components and made a reasoned judgment of their "fit." (Alternatively, traditional content validity coefficients could have been calculated.) The objective of the course was to bring the written workplace correspondence of UNHCR employees "closer" to the style and format of standard UNHCR written English, as shown by the model correspondence in the course manual. The assessment tasks were closely linked to this objective and to the curriculum, so the UNHCR course performed well on construct validity. Next, inter-rater reliability coefficient could have been calculated to determine whether two independent tutors would give similar feedback and assign the same grade to the same learner on the same assignment. What is most interesting with this course, however, is that COL *extended* this traditional conception of inter-rater reliability into a quality assurance mechanism called the Tutor-Marked Assignment (TMA), which actually *reduced* rater error and *standardized* tutor feedback. We will return to this discussion in the next section on feedback and grading.

Feedback and Grading

The focus of tutor feedback and grading was on overall communications, with details such as grammar and word choice flagged only when they affected meaning. Both field reports and office correspondence were evaluated on a list of criteria which included organization, clarity, relevant content, interpretive, and summarizing skills (Appendix A). Using "tracked changes," tutors wrote detailed footnotes to address issues such as insufficient background information, acronyms, inconsistent verb tenses, missing topic sentence, wordiness, or discriminatory language. For example, in response to "Though it do not hit its targets, but the projectile lands sometimes in wheat farms which cause damaged to farm products," the tutor would use tracked changes to write a footnote about reader confusion, subject-verb agreement, and misuse of conjunctions. She would suggest an improved version such as: "Though they did not hit their targets, the projectiles (missiles) sometimes landed in wheat fields, causing damage to farm crops and equipment." With three chances to submit their assignments, learners had the opportunity to work through the suggested revisions, and understand them by referring back to the course manual. Some tutors also provided their own teaching materials to supplement the course manual, and shared these with other tutors during COL's monthly tutor conference.

To improve the quality of tutor feedback, COL evaluated tutors on the basis of their feedback to learners. All TMAs were submitted to the course administrator. With each cohort, the course administrator selected two of each tutor's marked assignments at random, and reviewed and scored the tutor's comments. Tutors were then ranked on their scores, and these rankings were used as the basis for assigning future contracts. Expectations were high, and from March 2001 to June 2001, the mean TMA score for all tutors combined improved from 6.6 to 7.1.

The tutor interviewees said that this quality control mechanism was a major strength of the course, and although one tutor found it "disconcerting," they agreed that it was important to establish consistency (Ruhe, 2002). Moreover, 100% of learners surveyed said they found the tutor feedback helpful to their learning all or most of the time. Assigning future contracts on the basis of TMA scores helped to reduce variability and "standardize" tutor feedback. In sum, the traditional conception of inter-rater reliability, which is the percentage of agreement among raters, was extended by this mechanism, which reduced rater error and promoted high-quality feedback.

Learner Satisfaction

In "A Course in Writing Effectively for UNHCR," the emphasis of the student assessment tasks was formative, and tutor feedback was directed towards the improvement of student learning. The next step in validation practice, then, was surveying learners about their satisfaction with the assessment tasks and tutor feedback (Appendix B). One hundred percent of UNHCR learners who responded to the survey said the assignments helped them to improve their writing skills, and 91% said the feedback was helpful all or almost all of the time (Ruhe, 2002). In their interviews, learners said they appreciated the high standards of the course manual and the lessons on UHHCR terminology, discriminatory language, grammatical structures, and concise language. One tutor said, "The biggest improvement is clarity…[and] better paragraphing and major and minor points" (p. 40).

Completion Rates

Although course participants had six months to finish their course assignments, their workloads were often heavy and unpredictable, so course extensions were granted on a case-by-case basis. Almost all learners who did not complete were caught up in circumstances beyond their control, for example, war, floods, pregnancy, illness, surgery, electricity blackouts, abrupt and overwhelming changes in workload, and job transfers (Ruhe, 2002). In Afghanistan, some learners studied even as the bombs were falling, or rode on horseback into Pakistan to deliver their assignments from an Internet café. In the December 2000 and March 2001 cohorts, course completion rates averaged around 76%, which, given these circumstances, was remarkable (Ruhe, 2002).

To increase completion rates, COL designed the Monthly Progress Report (MPR), which tutors were required to submit on each learner to the COL administration (Appendix C).

The MPR contained the dates of all e-mails and assignments sent and received, grades earned, and comments on student performance. All instances of delays and non-response were documented and reviewed. Biweekly reminder letters were sent out, and learners were informed that first assignment submissions would not be accepted during the last two weeks of the course. As a result of this diligent and detailed progress tracking system, tutors were aware of student activity on a weekly basis, sent students biweekly e-mails when they were inactive, and were able to take pre-emptive action to motivate students to finish their assignments on a timely basis. Because of the Monthly Progress Reports, few students left their assignments to the end of term, and completion rates were high.

The Evidential Basis of Test Use

Relevance

The evidential basis of test use has two aspects: relevance and cost/benefit. The Module 3 field reports were on topics of local interest assigned by their supervisors. One course participant, for example, wrote a funding proposal for an HIV/AIDS and Family Planning Project in Central Africa to promote curative, preventative, and reproductive health. Another wrote a report to evaluate several potential sites for new refugee camps in western Africa. A third wrote about a UNHCR program to provide elementary school education for girls, all of Kurdish descent, in refugee camps in the north and south of Iraq. The field reports were authentic, with up-to-date electronic UNHCR letterheads. To guide their writing, learners followed the organization, content, and format of the sample field reports in the UNHCR course manual. Language and content were integrated, as recommended by Mohan and Beckett (2003), and there were no traditional, de-contextualized grammar lessons. Ninety-five percent of learners surveyed said that the course content was highly relevant to their work at UNHCR (Ruhe, 2002).

Cost/Benefit

The final aspect of the evidential basis of validity is *utility* or cost/benefit. "A Course in Writing Effectively for UNHCR" was developed to reduce costs. Online delivery was less expensive than flying learners from remote field offices to a central location for face-to-face classes. Although Ruhe's (2002) report has no information on investment, the course would have presumably required more "up-front" investment, but operating costs would have been lower in the long run. Paperless delivery also reduced costs of paper, postage, and shipping, and enabled prompt feedback and turn-around times. (Delays in receiving course manuals were rare, but serious when they did occur, and for some cohorts, horseback rides across borders also increased costs, a situation created by the Taliban's opposition to the Internet.) In sum, the assessment tasks for the UNHCR course did well on all aspects of the evidential basis of validity: construct validity, feedback, grading, learner satisfaction, completion rates, relevance, and cost-benefit.

The Consequential Basis of Validity

Value Implications

In our analysis, striking issues emerged around value implications, which include value labels, theory of learning, and underlying ideology. UNHCR commissioned COL to design a course to teach "standard" UNHCR discourse, as defined by Headquarters in Geneva. The course objectives, then, reflected a single standard, or a unitary approach to values. However, with over 40 different language backgrounds from Eastern Europe, Africa, Asia, and South America, learners came into the course with widely varying English writing skills, multiple varieties of local English, and diverse cultural expectations. The challenge was finding a way to resolve this "tension" between unitary values, which held learners to high standards of professional writing, and pluralistic values that honored diversity.

COL resolved this tension by "aligning" tutor feedback and grading with UNHCR standards, *and* by assessing learners relative to where they began, not relative to each other. The focus of feedback was on the "macro" level, for example, organization, eliminating wordiness and coherence. There was a tolerance for errors at the word and sentence level, and correcting these details was not the tutors' primary focus. This pluralistic, individualistic approach is content-based, not a traditional grammar-based approach, and rests on the theory that second-language learners may require many years to achieve native-like proficiency (Mohan, & Beckett, 2003). In this way, the course design balanced UNHCR's prescriptive standards with respect for diversity.

In their interviews, tutors mentioned the impact of cultural differences on standards, deadlines and the granting of extensions. One recurring concern was that local standards sometimes differed considerably from "Geneva" standards, and some course participants believed that their assignments should be evaluated against *local* standards. One learner from Myanmar said that COL's educational methods were very different from those of his country, which was an education in itself. One participant in Africa said the assignment deadlines did not "fit" with African culture, which placed family obligations above work obligations. A third went so far as to say that the very notion of deadlines was "euro-centric" and "racist." These cultural value differences impacted on tutors' decisions about feedback, assessment, course extensions and grading.

As shown by the high learner satisfaction ratings (Ruhe, 2002), the pluralistic assessment standards of "A Course in Writing Effectively for UNHCR" successfully balanced the needs of diverse learners with the goal of teaching a standard professional discourse in a way that was fair and equitable. We have also shown how Messick's framework brings issues around values to the foreground, that underlying values have implications for assessment, and that these underlying values are an important aspect of the validity of assessment tasks.

Unintended Instructional and Social Consequences

The final aspect of value is unintended instructional and social consequences. First, non-response was sometimes a problem because technology was difficult to access or unreliable in the developing countries where UNHCR learners were situated. Some learners worked from "hub" addresses, that is, e-mail addresses shared by several people; this sharing of e-mail addresses sometimes resulted in confusion, and accidental deleting or misfiling of e-mails. Others worked with slow and unreliable line connections, sometimes without failure notices when e-mails were undelivered (C. Carigi, personal communication, June 13, 2002). In the monthly tutor conference, tutors said they noticed a sharp spike in undelivered or lost e-mails in the months after September 11, 2001.

Despite these technical problems, most learners tended to stay on track and complete the course. However, this outcome was hardly accidental, but the result of foresight and careful course design and implementation. The authors believe that the course designers *anticipated* unintended consequences in the design phase, and built various control mechanisms into the course to *minimize* unintended consequences. These mechanisms included the tutor welcome letters, biweekly reminder letters, the Monthly Progress Reports, the "buddy system," and the Tutor Marked Assignment reviews. The welcome letters set out expectations, a calendar of deadlines, and suggestions for working with the materials. In this way, learners were guided through the process, told which activities to send in and which to do on their own. Because of the participants' demanding workloads, tutors also sent out bi-weekly e-mails, drawn from a pool of sample letters, to remind them of their responsibilities and of the number of weeks left in the course. These mechanisms appeared to be very effective in reducing the number of rushed assignments submitted near the end of the course.

In addition to the welcome letter, reminder letters, and the MPRs (which we have already discussed), another innovative mechanism was the buddy system. In 2001, the first Afghan-based participants signed up for the course. Several of these course participants had no access to a non-radio-based e-mail system capable of receiving/sending e-mails with attachments, which was the primary means of communication with tutors. To overcome this obstacle, a buddy system was established whereby each learner identified "a buddy" in the closest regional office who had reliable, non-radio-based e-mail access. This person then became the liaison point between the learner and the tutor, with assignments and correspondence delivered by land via UNHCR's pouch delivery system. Because of the extra time involved, participants were given a six-month extension to complete the course. Unfortunately, when the Taliban later declared the Internet to be "un-Islamic," communication with course participants was discontinued to protect their safety.

Finally, another unintended consequence is that tutors who failed to score high enough on the Tutor Marked Assignments could lose their jobs. Although some readers might question this practice, COL had an obligation to deliver a quality product to its clients. The recent expansion into providing similar courses for other organizations such as the World Health Organization, shows that COL's approach to instruction and assessment was very successful. Indeed, this expansion of business was a positive unintended consequence of the success of "A Course in Writing Effectively for UNHCR."

Summary of Issues in Validation Practice in "A Course in Writing for UNHCR"

In summary, by cycling through the adapted Messick's framework, the authors have demonstrated that validation of online assessment tasks is a rhetorical art, an "argument-based approach" (Cronbach, 1982) based on multiple sources of evidence. First, we investigated traditional content and criterion-related validity. Then, we investigated whether learners were completing their assignments, if they were satisfied with them, when they were completing them, and how well they performed. Next, we investigated the cost savings of online delivery and the rapid turnaround time made possible by paperless recordkeeping. We also analyzed whether the skills being tested were relevant to the skills needed by the modern workplace, as recommended by Irby (1999). All of these are aspects of Messick's evidential basis of the value of online assessment tasks. The evaluator looks for both positive and negative unintended consequences, either of which may be present in a distance education course. In this chapter, we are emphasizing positive unintended consequences because they are a strength of distance education course designs.

The consequential basis of value includes the underlying values (value labels, theory, and ideology) of the assessment task. This analysis brought to the foreground the post-modern, pluralistic approach to assessment which balances a unitary UNHCR standard with the multiple languages, English skills, and cultural values of UNHCR learners. The fourth aspect of value is unintended consequences, which are absent in this course, probably because of the innovative mechanisms built into the course to minimize them. The monthly progress reports, bi-weekly reminders, and Tutor Marked Assignments were very effective in reducing non-response, keeping learners on track and enhancing completion rates.

The authors have shown that the value of online assessment tasks should no longer be based solely on traditional notions of construct, content, or criterion-related validity, which for example do not capture the value of the quality assurance mechanism that forces tutors, upon pain of future unemployment, to provide a common standard of high-quality feedback. The online assessment tasks overlap with the value of the course components, and for this reason, online assessment tasks need to be validated in the broader context of the course as a system. As we have demonstrated, the adapted Messick's framework provides a comprehensive assessment of merit and worth, which is better suited than a traditional analysis of validity to technology-based assessment tasks.

Conclusions and Future Trends

Using data from "A Course in Writing Effectively for UNHCR," we have shown that Messick's framework provides a conceptually elegant, practical, and easy-to-use approach to validation which is well-suited to online environments. We have shown how applying the adapted Messick's framework brings values and unintended consequences from the background, where they are hidden, into the foreground, thereby expanding traditional conceptions of merit and worth. We have shown that the value of the assessment tasks in "A Course in Writing Effectively for UNHCR" depends not only on content or relevance, but also on values and consequences, both positive and negative. If we had investigated only the psychometric evidence, we would have missed much of the hidden aspects of the value of the course, which are brought to the foreground by a comprehensive assessment of merit and worth based on evidence, values, and consequences.

We also believe that using Messick's framework to guide the validation of assessment tasks in technology-based environments is an emerging practice in distance education. Ruhe (2002b) showed how the framework performed when used to validate assessment tasks in a distributed, multimedia foreign language course. Messick's framework has also been used to evaluate distance education programs (Ruhe, 2002a). Bunderson's (2003) Validity-Centered Design is another adaptation, but the author provided no empirical evidence of the kinds of issues which emerge from applying the framework to authentic data. Chapelle et al. (2003) used Messick's framework to guide the validation of a Web-based ESL test, but limited their investigation to construct validity, authenticity, interactivity, and intended impact. In effect, they investigated only the evidential basis of Messick's framework, which is a classical approach to validation. Chapelle et al. (2003) also predicted more research on the theory, the argument, and the unintended consequences of assessment in distance contexts.

The findings in this chapter, along with the work of the previously cited authors, herald an emerging practice, that is, using Messick's framework to guide validation practice in technology-based education. Our findings support Messick's prediction that technology-based assessment will close the gap between validity theory and validation practice. In the future, readers can expect to see more of these applications in diverse delivery methods, and a growing awareness that: a) online assessment tasks should be validated, and b) technology-based environments call for a comprehensive approach to validity and validation based on evidence, values, and consequences.

References

American Psychological Association. (1966). *Standards for educational and psychological tests and manuals*. Washington, DC: American Psychological Association.

American Psychological Association, American Educational Research Association, & National Council on Measurement in Education. (1974). *Standards for educational and psychological tests*. Washington, DC: American Psychological Association.

American Psychological Association, American Educational Research Association, & National Council on Measurement in Education. (1985). *Standards for educational and psychological testing*. Washington, DC: American Psychological Association.

Angoff, W.H. (1988). Validity: An evolving concept. In H. Wainer & H.I. Braun (Eds.), *Test validity* (pp. 19-31). Hillsdale, NJ: Lawrence Erlbaum.

Baumgartner, E. (1999, April). Embedded assessments using simulations and visualizations tools. *Proceedings of the Annual Meeting of the American Educational Researchers,* Montreal, Canada.

Bennett, R.E. (2001). How the Internet will help large-scale assessment reinvent itself. [Electronic version]. *Education Policy Analysis Archives, 9*(5).

Bourdeau, J., & Bates, A. (1997). Instructional design for distance learning. In S.N. Dijkstra, F. Seel, F. Shott, & R.D. Tennyson (Eds.), *Instructional design: International perspectives: Volume 2* (pp. 369-397). Mahwah, NJ: Lawrence Erlbaum.

Chapelle, C.A., Jamieson, J., & Hegelheimer, V. (2003). Validation of a Web-based ESL test. *Language Testing, 20*(4), 409-439.

Collis, B. (1998). Building evaluation of collaborative learning into a WWW-based course: Pedagogical and technical experiences. *Indian Journal of Open Learning, 7*(1).

Crocker, L., & Algina, J. (1986). *Introduction to classical and modern test theory.* Toronto, ON: Holt, Rinehart & Winston.

Cronbach, L.J. (1982). *Designing evaluations of educational and social programs.* San Francisco: Jossey-Bass.

Cronbach, L.J. (1989). Five perspectives on validity argument. In H. Wainer & H.I. Braun (Eds.), *Test validity* (pp. 3-17). Hillsdale, NJ: Lawrence Erlbaum.

Green, D.R. (1998). Consequential aspects of the validity of achievement tests: A publisher's point of view. *Educational Measurement: Issues and Practice, 17*(2), 16-19.

Harasim, L., Hiltz, S.R., Teles, L., & Turoff, M. (1996). *Learning networks: A field guide to teaching and learning online.* Cambridge, MA: MIT Press.

Haughey, M., & Anderson, T. (1998). *Networked learning: The pedagogy of the Internet.* Montreal: Les Editions de la Chanelière.

Hiltz, S.R. (1990). Evaluating the virtual classroom. In L. Harasim (Ed.), *Online education: Perspectives on a new environment* (pp. 133-183). New York: Praeger.

Hubley, A.M., & Zumbo, B.D. (1996). A dialectic on validity: Where we have been and where we are going. *The Journal of General Psychology, 123*(3), 207-215.

Hudspeth, D. (1997). Testing learner outcomes in Web-based instruction. In B.H. Kahn (Ed.), *Web-based instruction* (pp. 353-356). Englewood Cliffs, NJ: Educational Technology Publications.

Irby, A.J. (1999). Post-baccalaureate certificates: Higher education's growth market. *Change 31*(2), 36-41.

Laffey, J.M., & Singer, J. (1997). Using Internet-based conferencing tools to support assessment. In B.H. Kahn (Ed.), *Web-based instruction* (pp. 357-360). Englewood Cliffs, NJ: Educational Technology Publications.

Maguire, T., Hattie, J., & Haig, B. (1994). Construct validity and achievement assessment. *The Alberta Journal of Educational Research, XL*(2), 109-126.

Marttunen, M. (1997). Teaching argumentation skills in an electronic mail environment. *Innovations in Education and Training International, 34*(3) 208-218.

Messick, S. (1988). The once and future issues of validity: Assessing the meaning and consequences of measurement. In H. Wainer & H.I. Braun (Eds.), *Test validity.* Hillsdale, NJ: Laurence Erlbaum.

Messick, S. (1989). Validity. In R.L. Linn (Ed.), *Educational measurement,* (3rd ed., pp. 13-103). New York: MacMillan.

Messick, S. (1992). Validity of test interpretation and use. In M.C. Alkin (Ed.), *Encyclopedia of Educational Research* (vol. 4, 6th ed., pp. 1487-1495). New York: Macmillan.

Messick, S. (1998). Test validity: A matter of consequence. *Social Indicators Research: An International and Interdisciplinary Journal for Quality-of-Life Measurement, 45,* 35-44.

Mohan, B., & Beckett, G.H. (2003). A functional approach to research on content-based language learning: Recasts in causal explanations. *The Modern Language Journal, 87*(3), 421-432.

Popham, W.J. (1997). Consequential validity: Right concern—wrong concept. *Educational Measurement: Issues and Practice, 16*(2), 9-13.

Ruhe, V. (2002a). Applying Messick's framework to the evaluation data of distance/distributed instructional programs. (Doctoral dissertation, University of British Columbia, 2002). *Dissertation Abstracts International.*

Ruhe, V. (2002b). *A course in writing effectively for UNHCR: Evaluation report.* Vancouver, BC: Commonwealth of Learning.

Ruhe, V. (2000c). Issues in the validation of assessment in technology-based distance and distributed learning: What can we learn from Messick's framework? *International Journal of Testing, 2*(2), 143-159.

Schacter, J. (1997, March). Feasibility of a Web-based assessment of problem-solving. *Proceedings of the Annual Meeting of the American Educational Researchers Association,* Chicago, IL.

Shepard, L.A. (1993). Evaluating test validity. In L. Darling-Hammond (Ed.), *Review of research in education* (vol. 19, pp. 405-450). Washington, DC: American Educational Researchers Association.

Shepard, L.A. (1997). The centrality of test use and consequences for test validity. *Educational Measurement: Issues and Practice, 16*(2), 5-8.

Stufflebeam, D.L. (2001). *Evaluation models. New directions for evaluation* (no. 89). San Francisco: Jossey-Bass.

Tennyson, R.D. (1997). Evaluation techniques in instructional development. In S. Dijkstra, N. Seel, F. Shott, & R.D. Tennyson (Eds.). *Instructional design: International perspectives: Volume 1. Solving instructional design problems* (pp. 19-26). Mahwah, NJ: Lawrence Erlbaum.

Thorpe, M. (1998). Assessment and 'third generation' distance education. *Distance Education, 19*(2), 265-286.

Varnhagen, C.K., & Zumbo, B.D. (1990). CAI as an adjunct to teaching introductory statistics: Affect mediates learning. *Journal of Educational Computing Research, 6*(1), 29-40.

Wiley, D.E. (1991). Test validity and invalidity reconsidered. In R.E. Snow & D.E. Wiley (Eds.), *Improving inquiry in the social sciences: A volume in honor of Lee J. Cronbach.* Hillsdale, NJ: Lawrence Erlbaum.

Appendix A:Criteria for Grading Field Reports

There are two options for Assignment 3. The first is focused on collaborative writing and will result in a part report; the second is on single-author reports and will result in a complete short report. In both options, participants must demonstrate summary writing skills.

Single-Author report

Executive Summary

> is a summary of the report submitted
>
> self-contained with an introduction, body, and conclusion
>
> includes only significant content
>
> adds no new material
>
> covers purpose, findings, conclusions, and recommendations (if any)
>
> is positioned at the beginning of the report

Final Draft

> has an introduction, body, and conclusion
>
> has recommendations if the nature of the reporting task demands them
>
> has headings to at least two levels
>
> has an appropriate introduction that gives purpose and organizational plan of the report being written
>
> flows reasonably well from one section to the next and from paragraph to paragraph
>
> demonstrates some interpretive reporting skills (i.e., not just description)
>
> is written in well-constructed paragraphs
>
> is free of spelling errors, and moderately free of grammar and punctuation errors
>
> is free of slang, colloquial, and highly informal language
>
> is free of discriminatory and politically incorrect language and concepts
>
> is free of overly complex and verbose language

Appendix B: Course Evaluation Questionnaire for Course Participants: Assessment and Feedback Questions

A Course on Writing Effectively for UNHCR

Course Evaluation Questionnaire

This questionnaire has been designed to obtain feedback from you on the quality of the course [on] writing effectively for UNHCR. The feedback from you and other course participants is used as part of ongoing evaluation to further improve the course materials, the tutoring, and administration. Please take a few minutes to complete it and submit it to the course administrator.

Directions: Print out this form, fill it in, and mail it to the address at the bottom of the form or reply by e-mail. If using e-mail, remember to hit the "reply" button before filling in the form, type an "x" onto the line of your response to each question.

Assessment

16.   The assessment tasks helped me to develop knowledge and skills identified in the stated learning objectives.

- ❏   All or almost all of the time
- ❏   Most of the time
- ❏   About half of the time
- ❏   Only some of the time
- ❏   Very little or none of the time

17.   The assigned written work improved my writing and analytical skills.

- ❏   All or almost all of the time
- ❏   Most of the time
- ❏   About half of the time
- ❏   Only some of the time
- ❏   Very little or none of the time

18.   Assignment tasks were specified sufficiently for me to know what I had to do for the assignment.

- ❏   All or almost all of the time
- ❏   Most of the time

❑ About half of the time
❑ Only some of the time
❑ Very little or none of the time

Tutoring

19. The tutor was interested in helping me to learn.
❑ All or almost all of the time
❑ Most of the time
❑ About half of the time
❑ Only some of the time
❑ Very little or none of the time

20. The feedback on my work was helpful to my learning.
❑ All or almost all of the time
❑ Most of the time
❑ About half of the time
❑ Only some of the time
❑ Very little or none of the time

21. The feedback on my work was provided promptly, and normally not later than two weeks.
❑ All or almost all of the time
❑ Most of the time
❑ About half of the time
❑ Only some of the time
❑ Very little or none of the time

22. The tutor gave me individual help with my learning in this course.
❑ All or almost all of the time
❑ Most of the time
❑ About half of the time
❑ Only some of the time
❑ Very little or none of the time

23.   Marked work was returned promptly.
- ❏   All or almost all of the time
- ❏   Most of the time
- ❏   About half of the time
- ❏   Only some of the time
- ❏   Very little or none of the time

24.   The comments on my marked work indicated things I had done correctly or well.
- ❏   All or almost all of the time
- ❏   Most of the time
- ❏   About half of the time
- ❏   Only some of the time
- ❏   Very little or none of the time

25.   The comments on my marked work indicated the sorts of things that I might do to improve.
- ❏   All or almost all of the time
- ❏   Most of the time
- ❏   About half of the time
- ❏   Only some of the time
- ❏   Very little or none of the time

Thank you very much for completing this feedback form.

We would be grateful if you would provide the following information in aide of our evaluation:

P1.   Which session do you belong to? (Select one)
- ❏   2000 December session
- ❏   2001 March session
- ❏   2001 June session
- ❏   2001 September session
- ❏   2001 December session

P2.   Which module options did you take? (Select one)

   ❑ Module Two (General Office Correspondence)

   ❑ Module Three (Report Writing)

Any other comments you would like to share with us (write/type below) :

Apendix C: Sample Monthly Progress Report (MPR)

Sample Monthly Progress Report (MPR)

Tutor: Name   Student: Name of Student

Email Contact Established: Yes   Extension: January 31, 2002

Date: July, 2001

	Agreed submission date:	Date assignment received:	Date assignment returned:	If revision is necessary, please provide details: section to be reworked & attempt no.	Expected Resubmission date:	Date revised work received:	Final grade:
July							
Module 1							
Module 2							
Module 3	X						
PCA: On July 17, Name of Student sent a note saying her life has been very hectic, but she is working on her course assignments.							
August							
Module 1	mid-September						
Module 2							
Module 3	X						
PCA: On August 16, Name of Student sent a note to say she was on leave and to give a target date for Module 1.							

September							
Module 1	September 20						
Module 2							
Module 3	mid-November						
PCA: On September 15, I received a note from Name of Student with a new target date for Module 1.							

October							
Module 1	September 20	Oct. 5	Oct. 10				PASS
Module 2							
Module 3	mid-November						

PCA: Name of Student has very strong writing skills, her only weakness being a tendency towards wordiness. She did some very in-depth reflection on her own writing processes. Name of Student is doing well in the course.

November							
Module 1	September 20	Oct. 5	Oct. 10				PASS
Module 2							
Module 3	Nov. 22						

PCA: On Nov. 5, Name of Student sent a note to revise her target date. She is doing well in the course. Name of Student has requested a one-month extension from me, and I wrote that this was being allowed by the course administrator given the impact of the events of Sept. 11.

December							
Module 1	September 20	Oct. 5	Oct. 10				PASS
Module 2							
Module 3	Nov. 22	December 5	December 8				PASS

PCA: On Nov. 5, Name of Student sent a note to revise her target date. She is doing well in the course. Name of Student has requested a one-month extension from me, and I wrote that this was allowed by the course administrator given the events of Sept. 11. Name of Student has made excellent progress in the course.

Chapter XIII

Online Assessment and Instruction Using Learning Maps:
A Glimpse into the Future

Jim Lee, CTB/McGraw-Hill, USA

Sylvia Tidwell-Scheuring, CTB/McGraw-Hill, USA

Karen Barton, CTB/McGraw-Hill, USA

Abstract

Online assessment, in its infancy, is likely to facilitate a variety of innovations in both formative and summative assessment. This chapter focuses on the potential of online assessment to accelerate learning via effective links to instruction. A case is made that detailed learning maps of academic progress are especially conducive to effective skill and concept diagnosis and prescriptive learning, contributing construct validity and precision to assessment results and coherence to instructional interventions. Item adaptive testing using learning maps and the paradigm of intelligent agents is discussed in the context of a vision of a seamless integration of assessment and instruction. The chapter is primarily speculative rather than technical.

A Glimpse into the Future

In this chapter the authors invite the reader to take a step back from the pressures of educational policy and politically driven educational reform movements to consider one possible direction of development of online educational assessment and instruction in the age of the Internet and advancing technology.

Instruction and assessment are closely related, integral aspects of the learning process. Instruction is the process by which learning is facilitated and guided; assessments are opportunities for learning, as well as feedback mechanisms that inform and have the potential to positively and dynamically affect instruction. It is only when this feedback provides relevant, timely information for enhancing instruction that its full potential can be realized. Online approaches to assessment are ideal for this purpose.

Imagine a classroom where students interact with an online assessment system on a weekly or monthly basis. The assessments are formative in nature (designed to inform the instructional process), as well as diagnostic, describing the specific skills a student has mastered and has yet to master in order to meet a prescribed educational standard. Linked to these diagnostic test results are instructional references and other supports to help the teacher remediate, sustain, or advance the student. With this support, the teacher is better able to meet the specific learning needs of each student and track all students' cumulative progress toward achievement of prescribed educational standards. Now imagine the same teacher delegating the teaching of some skills and concepts in each content area to learning software. As each student interacts with the software program, his or her knowledge state is continually assessed in order to customize the instructional inputs. Imagine further (if you do not mind a wildly speculative leap) an online learning environment, available in this same classroom via subscription, in which the construction of instructional inputs suggested by the ongoing assessment of the student's knowledge state is achieved by automated searches of public domain Web sites.

The argument of this chapter will be that detailed learning maps of academic progress are likely in this and coming decades to play a role in progress toward a vision of closely integrating assessment and instruction—either in the classroom, or in software, or in cyberspace.

It should be stated from the outset that there is no necessary distinction between the data required for sound formative assessment and sound summative assessment for accountability requirements. The cumulative records of student achievement, based on ongoing, detailed formative assessment, can potentially be aggregated and expressed in periodic summative reports. This chapter focuses, however, on the use of online formative test data as immediate feedback for learning and the design of instruction.

Learning Maps

One of the foundations for online assessment advances may be the representation of academic learning sequences in detailed learning maps of a particular kind, defined here as networks of sequenced learning targets. Compared to other more general methods of ordering content (for example, by grade-level collections of knowledge indicators, by statistical results, or by the definition of emerging general stages of skill and knowledge), the detailed ordering of learning targets in learning maps is especially conducive to effective concept and skill diagnosis and prescriptive learning. Learning targets may be skills, concepts, or any discrete focus for a lesson. In addition to intentional learning targets, learning maps can include transitional knowledge states (errors or partially correct knowledge) that typically occur on the learning path.

Each learning target in a learning map may be represented graphically as a node in a network of nodes. These nodes are ordered in precursor/postcursor (learning order) relationships, as shown in Figure 1, which represents the learning path to an understanding of the causes of seasons on Earth. Figure 1 is a section of a larger learning map with links to other science strands. This section of the map focuses on the learning targets that need to be mastered in order to understand the causes of seasons on Earth. The shaded nodes are those that have been mastered by the student. This particular student appears to be making the mistake, common among students and the general population, of attributing seasons on Earth to the changing distance between Earth and the sun as Earth travels around the sun in an elliptical orbit. Before the student will have a fully correct understanding of the causes of seasons on Earth, he or she will need to master the learning targets in the unshaded nodes.

Although learning sequences traditionally have been mapped in a very general way in the scope-and-sequence charts of instructional materials and in state and district

Figure 1. Example of a learning map: Understanding the causes of seasons

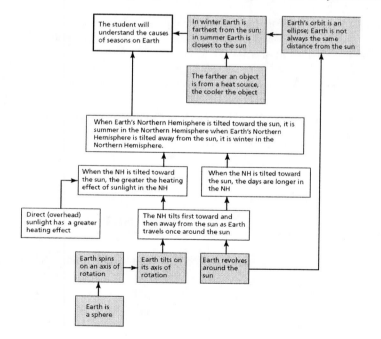

curriculum standards for kindergarten through grade 12, the detailed ordering of specific skill and concept development in learning maps is at a level of granularity that supports precise instructional intervention. It is likely—or so we argue in this chapter—that online assessments based on learning maps, currently in the experimental stage of development, will be tested more widely in classrooms throughout the United States (and probably elsewhere) in this and in coming decades.

In order to understand the power of learning maps for online assessment and for the attainment of significant academic improvement effects, the difference between a general ordering of learning objectives and the more precise ordering in a learning map should be discussed further. The ordering of learning targets in a learning map (with arrows pointing in the direction that learning proceeds) is based on the fact that skills and concepts are best taught and learned in a carefully constructed sequence. For example, a student cannot grasp the concept of seasons without a solid grounding in precursor concepts (axis of rotation, Earth's revolution, the different heating effect of direct versus indirect sunlight, etc.). The construction of this understanding must follow a path that takes into account the necessity of foundational knowledge before proceeding to the next step.

This does not mean, however, that all students follow the same path to proficiency. While some precursors of a concept or skill may be essential, others are merely facilitative and not necessary for all students. (For example, students can learn to carry in addition mechanically without understanding the concept of place value; however, understanding the concept of place value may facilitate learning how to carry in addition for some students.) For this reason, students may vary from each other in the way in which they progress through learning maps to a specified outcome; and the arrows that define the learning-order relationships in learning maps must have probabilities associated with them, based on data from thousands of students.

Precursor/postcursor relationships hypothesized by content experts and/or cognitive scientists to exist between nodes on a learning map must be continuously validated through ongoing test administrations on a variety of student populations. In this context, a node is validated as a postcursor of another node in a domain if, according to test data from an adequate student sample, there is a high probability that success on that node will not occur without success on the precursor node. Significant differences in the probability data from one subpopulation to the next may necessitate the use of different node orderings for distinct subpopulations.

Learning Maps and the Validity of Assessment

Before we outline how learning maps potentially can support integrated online assessment and instruction solutions (the future vision), it is important to stress how learning maps can enhance the construct validity of the assessment dimension of these solutions. Traditional achievement tests try to estimate a student's level of possession of a construct such as "mathematics achievement." *Construct* is the psychometric term used to refer to something to be measured (such as mathematics achievement) that can only be inferred from actual performances (such as performance on a set of mathematics test items). Developing test items for a one-time or summative test that covers all the skills that define the broad and unobservable construct of mathematics achievement is, practically speaking, impossible. Therefore, tests only sample a subset of skills from the universe of possible skills that represent "mathematics achievement" (Crocker & Algina, 1986).

In an online diagnostic environment, where many different subsets of items can be administered over time, the sample of skills covered and the number of items given is collectively much larger[1] than would be possible on a one-time, summative test. This improved sampling, in itself, increases the likelihood that a test is valid, that it accurately measures what it claims to measure.

Whatever construct each test sets out to measure must be clearly defined and accurately measured. With clear definitions and accurate measurement, the assessment is considered valid in regard to the construct, or has some level of construct validity (Messick, 1989). With the construct operationally defined (via a learning map, for example), tests and test items can be conceived and developed as evidence of the construct via observable skills.

The construct validity of the assessment can be enhanced by carefully and systematically defining many of the skills and concepts that are components of the construct being assessed. Cognitive task analyses, an inherent component of instructional design (e.g., Anderson, 1995), can be used to define constructs as collections of learning targets. For example, Deno (1997) describes the task analytic approach as a way to take a task and break it into subtasks, illustrating in linear form the requisite skills for completing the overall task successfully. Such an approach has been used in many studies, including the development of computer-based performance assessments (Mislevy, Steinberg, Breyer, Almond, & Johnson, 1999) in which items are broken down into each skill and subskill necessary to access the item, respond to the item, and provide the correct answer to the item.

In a similar way, the construction of learning order sequences in learning maps entails a precise, highly granular decomposition and definition of larger units of knowledge into specific, small steps in skills and concept development. Here the applied question is: "What skills and concepts are necessary or helpful for learning X?" This question in turn is applied to the precursors of X, proceeding backward in this way until the network of learning targets that support understanding of X has been defined. In principle, this analysis is straightforward (or straightbackward); in practice, it is messy and difficult for a number of reasons. A key point, though, is that a learning map does not have to be perfect in order to be useful. The data from test administrations over time can contribute to the improvement of the map, including alterations in the ordering and granularity of learning targets. Equally important to keep in mind is the improvement in clarity and specificity possible with learning maps (like the map in Figure 1), as contrasted with the ambiguity, incompleteness, lack of grade-to-grade articulation, and wildly fluctuating granularity that are common in the statements describing what students are supposed to know and be able to do in many state and district curriculum standards documents (the content frameworks for most current assessments).

The careful definition and precise targeting of specific skills and concepts in learning maps help to ensure that irrelevant, non-targeted skills are not necessary for success on any test item. In other words, the concept or skill intended to be assessed by each item is all that is being measured. This more detailed and precise definition of each component of the construct to be measured might be called "construct amplification." Construct amplification supports the valid assessment of the achievement of *all* students.

For example, some students demonstrate their knowledge more effectively using graphics rather than words. If visual models and modes of understanding are neglected in the definition of the construct to be assessed, the resulting tests will not accurately assess the achievement of those students. For this reason, careful attention to the definition of constructs and their components is one of the key principles of universally designed assessments, tests designed according to guidelines that will enhance their accessibility and validity for all students, including special subpopulations (Thompson, Johnstone, & Thurlow, 2002).

Learning maps represent a construct such as mathematics achievement as a collection of hundreds, even thousands, of precisely defined learning targets ordered in a learning sequence. These learning-order hypotheses have to be validated theoretically by cognitive and curriculum experts, and empirically with many populations and subpopulations of students. The validated order of the learning targets adds to the evidence of construct validity. Once the learning order relations are established, mastery of some learning targets that were not directly assessed may be inferred from the mastery of other targets. For example, mastery of addition without regrouping may be inferred from mastery of addition with regrouping. In this way the assessment of components of mathematics achievement extends via inference to include learning targets not directly assessed by items in the test.

Learning Maps and the Coherence of Instruction

The characteristics of learning maps that enhance the validity of assessments can also influence the coherence of the instruction that follows from the assessment (the instruction dimension of the integrated assessment/instruction solution). As already indicated, the statements describing what students are expected to know and be able to do in each content area at each grade level often lack precision or completeness and therefore require interpretation and elaboration before they can become the foundation for the specification of items to be used in achievement testing. Learning-order considerations are observed in the most general way in these documents, but not at the level of acquisition of specific skills and concepts. Viewed longitudinally from grades K-12, the sequencing of learning targets in each content area may have critical gaps or violate learning order considerations. Learning materials and large-scale assessments, developed by textbook and testing companies and customized for each state based on the state curriculum standards document, tend to inherit deficiencies of detail and learning-order coherence in the standards document. In this way, the decomposition and ordering of knowledge in state standards documents paradoxically tend to maintain incoherence in education while overtly attempting to reduce it.

Referring again to Figure 1, one state's curriculum standards document, for example, requires that by grade 7, all students must understand the causes of seasons. However, in the same state there is no explicit reference in the standards document to several of the precursor concepts, either in the grade 7 standards or in any of the earlier grades. The learning map fills in the sequence of detailed learning targets involved in acquisition of this concept. Assessing the student on these learning targets is necessary for precise and accurate diagnosis of the student's current knowledge state, as well as prescription of a well-ordered instructional sequence to help the student understand the causes of seasons. The results of online diagnostic assessment of a student's knowledge of the learning targets in this map provide the teacher a useful blueprint for helping the student to achieve success on this grade 7 standard. In this way, learning maps can bring increased coherence and efficiency not only to the process of assessing students, but also to the instructional intervention that follows from the use of the assessment results.

Learning Maps, Item-Adaptive Tests, and Intelligent Agents

The ability of learning maps to increase the efficiency of assessment can be exploited to its fullest potential when used to support item adaptive testing (a mode of testing in which the selection of the next test item is contingent on the student's responses to the previous test items) that utilizes the paradigm of intelligent agents.

The intelligent agent paradigm defines an agent as a system capable of undertaking *actions* in response to a series of *perceptions* (Russell & Norvig, 2002). In educational assessment, the presentation of an item to a student is one kind of action. A student's response to the presented item is one kind of perception. An intelligent assessment agent can be an online system whose actions are items and whose perceptions are student responses.

Interestingly, the perceptions of the agent, or student responses, need not be bound to a single assessment. The agent can remember the student's performance on past assessments, and begin subsequent tests or presentation of items in accordance with the agent's understanding of the student. This model can be extended even further, taking into account other perceptions (such as the student's history of interactions with instructional materials, assuming you have this data in a compatible format), producing an assessment even more precisely adapted to that particular student.

The agent's representation of the student's knowledge "state" can be based on the kind of learning maps already discussed. The knowledge state is perceived by the agent as a learning "boundary" between the mastered and unmastered targets in the learning map—the leading edge, so to speak, of the student's progressive mastery. Adaptive assessments as described herein would focus primarily on the learning targets just ahead of this boundary, where it is most likely that a student is currently progressing in understanding. The agent would tend to avoid presenting items well within the area of mastered concepts, since it already has evidence that success on these items is highly probable. The agent would also tend to avoid presenting items that assess learning targets well beyond the boundary, since it already has evidence that failure on these items is highly probable. The student's learning boundary (pattern of mastered nodes on the learning map) is in fact a collection of precise evidence for selecting each successive item to present to the student.

An intelligent item-adaptive assessment always uses the learning-order relationships in the learning map to select items with high "inferential value." (In the game of 20 questions, for example, asking whether the unknown object is "bigger than a breadbox" has high inferential value, because either a yes or a no response eliminates about half the objects in the room from consideration.) The inferential value of an item assessing a learning target in a learning map is related to the number of direct precursor and postcursor links it has to other learning targets in the map.

Whether the student responds correctly or incorrectly to the first item, the response (new evidence) results in a revised estimate of the student's knowledge state, which leads to intelligent selection of the optimal learning target to be assessed by the second item. This process continues until the student's current boundary in the map has been modified to include all the new learning targets that have been mastered.

Learning maps and the tests based on them can be designed so that wrong answers to test items provide evidence of transitional knowledge states (errors or partially correct knowledge) on the path to mastery of a learning target. For example, the map of development of understanding the causes of seasons (Figure 1) includes the misconception path taken by students who construct a naïve theory (personal misconception) regarding the cause of seasons based on the general idea that things are hotter the closer they are to a heat source. Consider the following multiple choice test item:

The temperatures in the Northern Hemisphere in winter are generally colder than in summer due to the fact that when it is winter in the Northern Hemisphere

    A.   it is more likely to snow

    B.   Earth is farther from the sun

    C.   there is more cloud cover blocking the sun's rays

    D.   the Northern Hemisphere is tilted away from the sun

Selection of answer choice B maps a student onto the misconception path in the learning map for understanding the causes of seasons.

Student misconceptions and errors are useful data in and of themselves, contributing to the accurate representation of the student's learning boundary and supporting the intelligent selection of subsequent items. The key point is that no piece of information—no perception, in agent terms—is lost to the system.

One of the interesting points about computer adaptive assessment is that by its very nature, it must continually make judgments about a student's mastery of a subject and also provide a continual update of assessment results, all while the assessment is in progress. Immediate feedback and storage of the pattern of student responses to test questions can become the basis for an ongoing calculation and prescription of the shortest instructional route to any prescribed educational goal or standard. Herein lies the potential of learning-map-based "intelligent" assessment (still perhaps decades away from realization) to support an extremely close integration of assessment and instruction in a responsive learning environment. Look again at Figure 1 describing the path to understanding the causes of seasons. The shaded learning targets on the map are nodes currently mastered by the student; the unshaded learning targets remain to be mastered before the student will have a scientific understanding of the causes of seasons.

Imagine that each of the unmastered targets in the learning map is linked electronically to a variety of appropriate online instructional activities, each teaching precisely the concept to be mastered. Once node mastery is demonstrated, a learning activity associated with the optimal next node can be tackled. The process can therefore proceed back and forth between learning activities and learning checks (assessment) until the understanding of the causes of seasons has the required depth, based on the sequence of concept development described in the learning map.

In the Meantime

Currently, in response to increased demand from state departments of education for online classroom formative assessment solutions, several assessment companies are offering online formative assessment programs in some strands of some content areas. What is motivating this investment? The increased availability of computers and online access in school systems through the United States are certainly enabling factors, but the primary motivational factor has been the apparent frustration of many educators with the traditional annual, on-demand summative assessment paradigm. Summative assessment results are intended ultimately to support gains in student learning *indirectly* via school improvement programs, identification of at-risk students, and so forth. However, a major frustration of many educators with this paradigm seems to be *the time lag between test administration and reports delivery.*

A second major frustration seems to be the *lack of diagnostic specificity in summative test reports.* Standardized norm-referenced tests report general information about student achievement, such as a percentile rating of how a student is functioning relative to peers in a given content area (e.g., mathematics), or in some general categories of instruction within the content area (e.g., measurement in mathematics). The specifics of what the student knows and does not know, at a level of detail that will support instructional intervention, are lacking in these reports. Hence, the call for online classroom formative tests that can provide a teacher with the right level of instructionally relevant information and instant turnaround time for receiving that information. Supporting the wisdom of the trend toward implementing online formative assessment solutions is a body of research suggesting that effective classroom formative assessment practices of all kinds can yield substantial academic improvement effects (Black, Harrison, Lee, Marshall, & William, 2003).

If significant achievement gains are perceived to accrue from this investment in formative assessment, testing companies will increasingly invest in the further development and elaboration of online formative assessment models and in ways to use this data for accountability purposes. The development of valid and reliable methods for aggregating classroom online formative assessment data for accountability purposes could have a watershed effect on the future of assessment. The substantial public commitment to and investment in accountability testing would then be available as a powerful support for the development of new generations of online assessment/instruction solutions.

Conclusion

Online assessment solutions with instructional links are likely to increase in popularity in coming years for the reasons cited above. Although detailed learning maps of the kind described in this chapter are difficult to construct and validate, we believe they can provide the most powerful content infrastructure for integrating assessment and instruction in the classroom, in software learning programs, and in the online environment. Compared to other more general methods of ordering content, they represent learning in a detailed way that enhances the efficiency, construct validity, and precision of the assessment as well as the coherence of the instructional intervention.

References

Anderson, J.R. (1995). *Learning and memory: An integrated approach.* New York: John Wiley & Sons.

Black, P., Harrison, C., Lee, C., Marshall, B., & William, D. (2003). *Assessment for learning.* New York: Open University Press.

Commission on Excellence in Education. (1983). *A nation at risk: The imperative for educational reform.* Washington, DC: Commission on Excellence in Education.

Crocker, L., & Algina, J. (1986). *Introduction to classical and modern test theory.* New York: Holt, Rinehart & Winston.

Deno, S.L. (1997). "'Whether' thou goest: Perspectives on progress monitoring." In E. Kameenuii, J. Lloyd, & D. Chard (Eds.), *Issues in educating students with disabilities.* Hillsdale, NJ: Lawrence Erlbaum.

Fuchs, L. (1998). Computer applications to address implementation difficulties associated with Curriculum-Based Measurement. In M. Shinn (Ed.), *Advanced applications of Curriculum-Based Measurement* (pp. 89-112). New York: Guilford Press.

Messick, S. (1989). Validity. In R.L. Linn (Ed.), *Educational measurement* (pp. 13-103). New York: American Council on Education/Macmillan.

Mislevy, R.J., Steinberg, L.S., Breyer, F.J., Almond, R.G., & Johnson, L. (1999). A cognitive task analysis with implications for designing simulation-based performance assessment. *Computers in Human Behavior, 15,* 335-374.

Phillips, S.E. (1994). High-stakes testing accommodations: Validity versus disabled rights. *Applied Measurement in Education, 7*(2), 93-120.

Russell, S.J., & Norvig, P. (2002). *Artificial intelligence: A modern approach* (2nd ed.). New York: Prentice-Hall.

Thompson, S.J., Johnstone, C.J., & Thurlow, M.L. (2002). *Universal design applied to large-scale assessments.* (Synthesis Report 44). Minneapolis, MN: University of Minnesota, National Center on Educational Outcomes. Retrieved from *http://education.umn.edu/NCEO/OnlinePubs/Synthesis44.html*

Endnote

[1] The use of learning maps as the underlying content framework for any assessment can make it possible to generate and maintain the large item pools associated with online diagnostic testing, even when the testing is customized to assess student progress toward proficiency on a given state's standards. By mapping standards and indicators in state and district curriculum frameworks to the learning targets in learning maps, the items used to assess standards in state A and the items used to assess standards in state B can be drawn from a common item repository based on the learning maps.

Chapter XIV

Authentic Assessment Online:
A Practical and Theoretical Challenge in Higher Education

Smita Mathur, University of South Florida, USA

Terry Murray, State University of New York at New Paltz, USA

Abstract

This chapter addresses the issue of authentic assessment in an online, asynchronous educational environment. Initially, a definition of "authentic" is articulated. Building on this theoretical foundation by describing authentic assessment in the face-to-face classroom, a framework for authentic assessment in the virtual classroom is developed. Next, the multiple challenges of conducting authentic assessment online are addressed. Finally, specific strategies for authentic online assessment are identified and discussed. These strategies include the use of electronic portfolios, electronic journals, assessment embedded in online discussion, and rubrics.

Introduction

This chapter addresses the thorny issue of authentic assessment in an online environment by articulating a definition of "authentic." Applying this definition, the authors describe authentic approaches to assessment in a traditional classroom. Building on this theoretical and practical foundation, frameworks for authentic assessment in an online asynchronous environment are developed. Next, the multiple challenges of conducting authentic assessment in a computer-mediated classroom are discussed. Finally, the authors identify and detail specific strategies for authentically assessing student learning online.

In designing coursework, colleges and universities are being challenged by two trends— one practical and the other theoretical. Practically speaking, academic institutions are experiencing increasing enrollments in online courses. Projections indicate that growth in enrollment is likely to continue steadily during this decade. Statistics from the U.S. Department of Education's report from the Web-based Education Commission (2000) illustrate the increase in scope and participation in online coursework on U.S. campuses. Consider these facts:

> Approximately 84% of four-year colleges were expected to offer distance learning courses in 2002, up from 62% in 1996.

> In 2000, U.S. colleges and universities offered more than 6,000 accredited courses on the Web.

> In 2002, 2.2 million students were expected to enroll in distance learning courses, up from 700,000 in 1998. (p. 77)

One of the many reasons for increased enrollment in online courses is the growing number of adult students pursuing college degrees. These students need practical, relevant, work-based knowledge and skills, and they need flexibility to accommodate work and family schedules.

Theoretically, social constructivism, as articulated by Bruner (1990), Dewey (1938), Piaget (1973), von Glaserfeld (1983), Vygotsky (1978), and others educational theorists, continues to influence the design of curriculum and instruction. This philosophy describes learning as an active process by which the teacher engages learners in inquiry and discovery, and learners apply what they have discovered by building on current and past knowledge in personally relevant ways. Constructivist approaches challenge educators to move away from decontextualized, passive, and fact-driven learning in favor of approaches to learning that are active, collaborative, reflective, and that connect learning to students' needs and life context. Social constructivism, as a widely held theory firmly grounded in research on learning and cognition, has shaped the current educational emphasis on authentic learning (Brooks & Brooks, 1993; Carpenter &

Fennema, 1992; Newman & Archbald, 1992). Authentic approaches to curriculum development, instructional design, and assessment are conscious attempts to concretely apply constructivist principles to the day-to-day practice of teachers and the concrete needs of students.

In addressing both the practical and theoretical challenges being faced by colleges and universities, an authentic approach to learning in an online, asynchronous environment seems ideally suited to supporting the goal achievement and to meeting the practical needs of this current wave of adult students. An online, asynchronous course structure offers the flexibility desired by adult learners, and authentic instruction provides the active engagement, opportunities for collaboration, and the concrete application to real-life situations that these students prefer. The combination seems an ideal solution to both the practical and theoretical challenges facing U.S. colleges and universities.

By offering authentic learning opportunities in an online, asynchronous classroom, educational institutions effectively address one set of concerns, but in doing so, create a new challenge. How does one assess authentic learning in an online environment? How can we "directly examine student performance on worthy intellectual tasks" (Wiggins, 1990, p. 1)?

What Makes Learning "Authentic"?

A Web search of the term "authentic learning" generates scores of articles on this contemporary educational innovation. Carlson (2002) describes this term succinctly: "By definition, the term 'authentic learning' means learning that uses real-life problems and projects that allow students to explore and discuss these problems in ways that are relevant to them" (p. 1). Imbedded in this definition are several generally accepted principles central to an authentic instructional approach. These principles include a focus on real-life questions and issues, an active pedagogy, collaboration, and connectedness (Carlson, 2002; Christensen, 1995; Cronin, 1993; Gordon, 2002; Newman & Welage, 1992).

Authentic learning's focus on real-world problems is a critical dimension of this approach to teaching and learning. Students see these real-world problems as relevant in their day-to-day lives. Real-world problems provide the motivation for students' to learn through their interaction with concepts, people, materials, and environments (Dewey, 1938). For Gordon (2002), this real-world quality also provides commonalities that connect students with the material by linking it to essential questions of human existence. "These questions go to the heart of our culture, history, and future as they relate to the human life cycle, command of symbols, understanding of the social web, connections to science, technology, and the natural world, and to the interdependence of the community and individuals" (Boyer, as cited in Gordon, 2004, p. 1). By emphasizing these real-world issues, authentic learning effectively engages students in the development of the practical skills of decision making and problem solving.

Drawing on its constructivist roots, authentic learning physically, emotionally, and intellectually engages learners in constructing new ideas or concepts that build on previous experiences and knowledge. It is an educational approach that challenges learners to be active participants in exploration and discovery, and instructors to be facilitators of an experiential cycle of action, reflection, generalization, and application (Luckner & Nadler, 1997). As a cognitive process (Caine & Cole, 1991), authentic discovery is both "conscious and unconscious;" it is a process through which students discover "*how* they learn as well as *what* they've learned" (p. 1).

McAlister, Lincoln, McLeod, and Maloney (as cited in Slack, Beer, Armitt, & Green, 2003) use the term "deep learning" to describe the learning gained by students who are engaged in real-life situations. They suggest that "deep approaches to learning are found in students who are affectively involved in searching for personal meaning and under-standing, seeing the whole picture, drawing in their personal experiences to make sense of new experiences, and relating evidence to conclusions" (p. 307). The reflection facilitated by teachers in an authentic learning process is essential for this deep learning.

Again, drawing on constructivist theory, authentic approaches to teaching and learning recognize the importance of collaboration. Just as Dewey (1938), Bruner, (1990) and Vygotsky (1978) emphasized that learning occurs in a social context, authentic educators emphasize that problem solving occurs when learners work together, sharing their perspectives and resources. Whether described cognitively (Vygotsky) or affectively (Noddings, as cited in Goldstein, 1999), this collaboration is understood as a partner-ship—a teaching/learning relationship. In this active partnership, the teacher engages the learner in inquiry and discovery, and the learner applies what she/he has discovered in addressing real work and life needs. This collaborative process fosters the deep thinking and substantive dialog (Newman & Wehlage, 1992) needed to support both student and teacher growth.

Newman and Wehlage (1992) observe: "As a lesson gains in authenticity, there is an increasing connection to the larger social context in which the students live" (p. 2). As students explore and understand these connections, they create personal meaning from the lessons. With this recognition of connections also comes an understanding and appreciation of the impact of this work on their immediate world.

This dynamic of connectedness extends further for students when learning is under-stood as a purposeful process where experiences build on previous experiences, and understanding evolves through systematic progressions. Knowledge, skill, and attitude learning, rather than being isolated elements taught to students, are developed progres-sively in the context of actual work. This learning can be drawn on in an integrated way for decision making and problem solving (Gordon, 2002). The lesson being experienced is more likely to be understood as what Dewey (1938) would describe as a "continuum" or what Bruner (1990) would describe as a "spiral" of evolving understanding. As learners recognize these learning connections over time, the process becomes not only active, collaborative, reflective, and relevant to learners, needs and life context. It also becomes lifelong.

Authentic Learning Deserves Authentic Assessment

If educators understand and apply the principles of authentic learning, they are subsequently challenged to assess student achievement using methods that are consistent with authentic principles. Parkany and Swan (1999) refer to assessment as the third leg of a three-legged stool of curriculum theory. They understand the other two legs to be pedagogy and learning theory. If assessment is recognized as an integral component in the teaching/learning process, as part of a central triangular structure in education, then authenticity in assessing student engagement and learning is essential to the entire process.

A significant number of theorists and practitioners have explored the implications of assessing learning authentically and developed a set of principles that effectively frame this approach. Mueller (2003) defines authentic assessment as "a form of assessment in which students are asked to perform tasks that demonstrate meaningful application of essential knowledge and skills" (p. 1). It is not a coincidence that Mueller's definition clearly incorporates the key principles of application and connectedness outlined in the previous section. In its concreteness, relevancy, and ongoing nature, authentic assessment, like authentic instruction, is concerned with practical processes and practical outcomes.

An effective way to understand authentic assessment is to contrast this approach with traditional forms of assessment. Traditional approaches to assessment are typically *curriculum-driven*. They most often elicit indirect evidence in the form of recall/recognition responses to teacher-structured questions. Traditional assessment is based in a predetermined body of knowledge and skills, and the assessments are developed and administered to determine if this set of knowledge and skills has been acquired (Mueller, 2003).

In contrast, in authentic approaches, the *assessment drives the curriculum*. Initially the teacher and students collaborate to determine the relevant knowledge and skills required to address students' problems and needs. Subsequently a curriculum is developed that will support students in acquiring this set of knowledge and skills. In this alternative model, assessment provides opportunities for students to demonstrate their acquisition of knowledge and skills, and their ability to apply them. In contrast to traditional assessment, authentic assessment seeks direct evidence in the form of concrete task performance, and these tasks are collaboratively identified, not teacher-structured (Mueller, 2003). The validity and reliability of these "authentic tasks" (Wiggins, 1990, p. 1) lies in the evaluator's ability to develop standardized criteria for scoring the products or performances. The trustworthiness of this type of assessment depends to a great degree on its effectiveness in simulating "tests'" of ability (Wiggins, 1990, p. 1).

Authentic learning focuses on process as well as content, on *how* one is learning and not just *what* is being learned. Authentic assessment can also be a productive, educational process that Wolfe refers to as an "episode of learning" for both the student and the teacher (as cited in Valencia, 1997).

Decades of research and experience have documented the field's widespread reliance on traditional forms of assessment, primarily true/false, forced-choice, multiple choice, fill-in-the-blank, and matching questions. In contrast, authentic assessment, formal and informal, formative and summative, takes on many new forms and also recognizes existing processes such as journaling and discussion as viable vehicles for assessing growth and learning. The final section of this chapter will discuss specific strategies for authentic assessment in an online teaching/learning environment, including portfolios, journaling, discussion, and self-testing, in more detail.

Authentic Assessment in an Online, Asynchronous Environment

If we accept Parkany's and Swan's (1999) assertion that assessment is part of the three-legged stool of curriculum theory, then a virtual educational stool that supports authentic learning is accordingly incomplete if the assessment of online student engagement and learning is not authentic. Fortunately, for educators who advocate authentic approaches to online learning and assessment, this theoretical and practical challenge has been met. Indeed, some theorists, researchers, and practitioners believe that this electronic medium offers unique and powerful tools and processes to support authenticity in online teaching and learning. These advocates of constructivist online teaching and learning understand the Internet as the "second major wave of the digital revolution" (Wilson & Lowry, 2000, p. 1). They also see it as "a vehicle for realizing the vision of educational thinkers like Dewey, Piaget, and Vygotsky who long ago advocated a constructivist or meaning-centered approach to learning and teaching" (p. 1).

These advocates of authentic learning and assessment are exploring the potential of using virtual coursework to support and enhance authentic approaches to teaching and learning (Baker, Hale, & Gifford, 1997; Campbell, 2004; Parkany & Swan, 1999; Slack et al., 2003; Wilson & Lowry, 2000). Their sentiments are exemplified in Greeno's call for authentic approaches in education (as cited in Wilson & Lowry, 2000). Greeno's statement is surely broad enough to encompass and capitalize on the strengths of Web-based instruction:

We need to organize learning environments and activities that include opportunities for acquiring basic skills, knowledge, and conceptual understanding, not only as isolated dimensions of intellectual activity, but as contributions to students' development of strong identities as individual learners and as more effective participants in the meaningful social practices of their learning communities in school and elsewhere in their lives. (p. 2)

Based on teaching experiences in asynchronous environments, the authors find that the Internet has the following strengths as an authentic learning environment:

1.   It supports lifelong learning.

2.   It shifts the instructional paradigm from "a teaching environment to a learning environment, with a focus on 'practice-centered learning'" (Campbell, 2004, p. 3).

3.   It provides communication tools that support dialog within and between diverse communities of learners.

4.   It fosters the collaboration needed for scaffolding, support, and shared meaning-making.

5.   Through meaningful dialog, it supports "deep learning" (Slack et al., 2003, p. 306).

6.   It provides easy access to broad, deep sources of information.

7.   It supports meaningful interaction with this information.

8.   It provides a flexibility and convenience for learners that are not feasible in the traditional face-to-face classroom (Wilson & Lowry, 2000).

Many of the same advocates of authentic educational approaches to teaching and learning have also considered online assessment methods that are consistent with a social constructivist philosophy. In exploring what happens to assessment processes when they are applied online, their writing and research provide valuable models for our work as online instructors, course designers, and instructional leaders.

In their study of student learning online, Hein and Irvine (2004) find that creative writing assignments and online discussion groups can promote deep learning for introductory physics students. Building on writing activities including journaling and creative writing assignments, voluntary online discussions were used as a vehicle for peer and faculty feedback on individual student's writing.

Of particular interest here are the multiple forms of assessment used in evaluating student performance. The processes were both formative and summative, as the instructor used rubrics; peer and instructor feedback; instructor monitoring of student understanding, as reflected in their online entries; and online portfolios. The authors' description of this discussion monitoring illustrates how this process is used in authentically assessing student learning:

> *Students' responses to the online discussion required them to use detail when discussing the principles of physics using everyday terminology. As the students' knowledge of physics expanded over the course of the semester, their responses to the online discussion topics showed greater depth and understanding. In addition, the students' use of physics vocabulary and previously studied concepts in their discussions became more commonplace.* (Hein & Irvine, 2004, p. 2)

In their emphasis on direct, relevant evidence, collaboratively identified through an ongoing assessment process, Hein and Irvine provide a solid example of authentic assessment.

In a second study focusing on the efficacy of discussion in supporting deep learning in an online classroom, Slack et al. (2003) analyze transcripts of peer-to-peer sessions of synchronous discussion. They used a well-established Structure of the Observed Learning Outcomes (SOLO) taxonomy (Briggs & Collis, as cited in Slack et al., 2003) to find evidence of the presence of deep learning.

As occupational therapy students, the participants in this study had concrete needs as they participated in this problem-based course. Through synchronous group tutorials, participation in case study-based problem solving, group discussions and investigations, and reflection and sharing, these students sought to develop the competencies required for their profession.

The SOLO taxonomy, with its ability to identify the complexity of thought in statements, proved to be an effective and authentic method for identifying deep learning using the students' statements in communication sessions. The results of this study indicate that deep learning does not occur spontaneously through online coursework, but evolves through synchronous discussion throughout the course.

It is significant here that a taxonomy has been used, not to generalize and quantify outcomes, but to "describe a particular performance at a particular time and not indicate a student's ability" (Slack et al., 2003, p. 307).

Parkany and Swan's (1999) emphasis on formative processes and authenticity in evaluating online curriculum draws heavily on a social constructivist approach to instruction and assessment. Their article, which builds on Guba and Lincoln's (1989) concepts of "fourth-generation evaluation" or social constructivist evaluations (as cited in Parkany & Swan, 1999), focuses on the use of portfolios for assessment in the online classroom. This portfolio process is intended to "provide information so that inferences can be made about student knowledge, ability, and their attitudes toward their work" (Pressley & McCormick, as cited in Parkany & Swan, p. 2). Portfolios as assessments are understood as an ongoing process as well as a product, and include work samples evaluated by rubric, peer, and instructor feedback. Consistent with authentic practices, ongoing assessment supports learning, and ongoing learning supports assessment.

Angelo and Cross (1993) explore the challenge of adjusting to student needs and accordingly adapting and improving instruction in an online teaching and learning environment. They approach this challenge by stressing the need for formative online classroom assessment of prior student knowledge and understanding.

The authors discuss key areas of focus for these formative assessments: prior knowledge and understanding, skills in synthesis and creative thinking, learner attitudes, values and self-awareness, learner reactions to the learning environment, and learner reactions to group work. It is clear in reviewing this list that the authors understand assessment as a holistic and ongoing process that needs to consider not only student learning, but the external and environmental factors that affect learning and achievement. In attending to these key areas of focus, the authors use reflective writing, invented dialogs, student opinion polls, feedback, and self- and group assessments as authentic assessment tools.

Angelo and Cross's (1993) final comments highlight the central role of assessment in the learning process and the potential of electronic technology to authentically support and enhance learning, in the face-to-face classroom, as well as online:

As you can see from these examples, assessment is integrated into the learning fabric. It is an ongoing process that is an active part of learning itself. It also can add continuous improvement to the learning environment. An online environment is not as stagnant as one might think. It is not a technology environment...it is a technology-supported learning environment. We need to bring all of our passion for good pedagogy to this challenge and we need to think creatively. The addition of new tools can expand our capacity to affect learning (p. 2).

As the chapter has evolved, it is clear that authentic approaches to assessment in online teaching and learning are not only possible, they are absolutely critical if our educational goal is to promote personally meaningful learning that addresses real-life needs and problems.

Obstacles to Authentically Assessing in an Online Classroom

As this chapter has established, principles and practices of authentic assessment are being effectively applied in the online classroom. Significantly, the obstacles to integrating authentic approaches to assessment in online coursework are more philosophical than technical. As many of the authors cited in this chapter have agreed, the electronic technology involved in teaching and learning in an online asynchronous environment *does* place limitations on participants' ability to communicate effectively. Without the use of social context cues (Sproull & Kessler, 1986), social presence and immediacy (Short, Williams, & Christie, 1976), or the ability to check perceptions and clarify understanding, effective interaction is challenging. But the most significant opposition to applying authentic educational principles comes in the form of practical and philosophical resistance to this philosophical stance.

Wiggins' (1990, 1993) writing about issues in authentic assessment addresses this resistance thoughtfully. In making a case for authentic assessment in education, he identifies three significant obstacles:

Perceptions of Authentic Assessment as Too Labor Intensive—Wiggins emphasizes two points here. First, "...it is the form, and not the content of the test that is harmful to learning" (p. 1). And second, if our aim as a society is to improve students' performance, not just monitor it, assessment must provide genuine opportunities to demonstrate not only understanding, but also the ability to concretely and relevantly apply what has been learned. If educators are committed to authentic learning, how much time are they willing to commit to supporting it through authentic assessment?

Perceptions of Authentic Assessment as Too Expensive and Time Consuming—As Wiggins also points out, many states, including California, New York, Connecticut, and Vermont, have already discovered that the time and money they have committed to judgment-based testing in the form of hands-on science testing and expository writing responses are worthwhile. This commitment to authentic forms of assessment has produced both academic improvement and teacher investment in the assessment process.

Questions of Public Faith in the Objectivity and Reliability of Judgment-Based Scores—Issues of validity and reliability are particularly contentious in educational assessment. If one is approaching assessment from an authentic perspective, it is counterproductive to establish reliability based on generalizable results. Authentic assessment is most effective when it is individualized and based on a student's specific needs. Through the process of authentic learning, a student's cognitive capacities are enhanced and a new schema is developed. Thus, the process of authentic assessment cannot be replicated and reproduced in the traditional sense. It is, however, possible to establish that the same assessment process can be modified and individualized with other students in similar learning environments.

Validity of an assessment strategy is grounded in the process of conducting the assessment itself. Ongoing communication between the students and teacher, frequent feedback, and successful completion of an authentic task all contribute to the validity of an authentic assessment. Additionally, validity of authentic assessment can be established when multiple raters independently or collaboratively come to the same conclusion about a student's performance on an authentic task. Extensive documentation of the learning experience and detailed journal entries that accurately reflect the learning process and outcome can also affirm the validity of an authentic assessment strategy. Issues of the validity and reliability in authentic assessment methods are frequent topics in articles on authentic educational approaches. Wiggins (1993) reminds us that many well-established and publicly supported state and national testing programs use human judges to evaluate portfolios, writing samples, and task performances. As Wiggins observes: "Genuine accountability does not avoid human judgment" (p. 2). We can monitor, improve, and support authentic assessment with clear exemplars, standards, and criteria. Parkany and Swan (1999) respond on a more theoretical level to this concern, emphasizing the broader understanding of the role of subjectivity and the contextual nature of validity inherent in a qualitative perspective on research and evaluation. Again citing Guba and Lincoln (1989), Parkany and Swan (1999) articulate a social constructivist paradigm of validity and reliability based on the rigorous development of authenticity.

While some of Wiggin's (1990, 1993) and Parkany and Swan's (1999) arguments in support of authentic assessment transcend the educational medium, some of them must be considered in the context of online coursework. Debates over the nature of validity and reliability demand broader philosophical discussion, but the issues of perceptions of time and labor take on increased significance in an online teaching and learning environment. Educators who have taught online are aware that though this medium is often considered as less time consuming than traditional coursework, it is often more so. In this text-based environment, adding approaches to assessment that involve additional time and effort are likely to cause instructor resistance. But if, as this chapter illustrates, assessment is understood as ongoing, and if course processes like journaling and discussion are recognized as sources of data for assessment, then assessment does not have to be an add on that demands additional time.

Additionally, online coursework is being marketed to both students and instructors as a convenient, flexible alternative to traditional coursework. Recent studies by the SUNY Learning Network (Shea, Frederickson, Pickett, Pelz, & Swan, 2000a; Shea, Frederickson,

& Pickett, 2000b) have indicated that convenience and flexibility are cited by both students and instructors when asked why they chose to take or teach online courses. In this consumer-oriented climate, there is a tendency to seek efficient means to transmit and respond to information, and to assessment learning and performance. Standardized forms of testing that can be computer processed are common in online coursework. In this context, establishing and maintaining authentic approaches to learning and assessment require a clarity of purpose and a commitment to support student improvement, not just monitor and evaluate results.

It is apparent from this brief discussion that educators who believe in and are committed to social constructivist-based approaches to instruction and assessment must be aware of these areas of resistance and be capable of responding to these concerns in an informed manner. As is frequently the case, when educational outcomes are assessed using methods that value quantifiable results, that focus on monitoring student progress not improving it, and that see objectivity in assessment as achievable and wholly desirable, voicing a compelling and well-supported alternative vision is essential.

Strategies for Authentic Assessment Online

Building on the theoretical foundations established in the first section of this chapter, this section describes strategies for authentic assessment that can be successfully executed in an online learning environment. It will identify and discuss specific approaches that can be employed to assess student growth and progress.

Table 1. Prerequisites for successful authentic assessment online

ACQUIRE RESOURCES	EMPOWER STUDENTS AND TEACHERS WITH COMPUTER LITERACY SKILLS	PLAN AND EXECUTE PRE ASSESSMENT ACTIVITIES
Networking capabilities	Analog & Digital Editing	Diagnose student competency through pre-assessment
Time	Fluency with Multi-media software	Define learning goals collaboratively with students
Financial resources	Uploading & downloading information	Determine expected outcomes
Robust computer configurations	Digital video, voice recording	Determine task for authentic learning
Efficient & reliable technical support for students & faculty	Efficiency in navigating the world wide web, creating & receiving electronic communications like email, and text messaging	Determine standard for excellence
		Determine schedule for formative assessment
		Select strategies for authentic assessment
		Collaboratively develop rubrics for assessment with students

Ready For Authentic Assessment Online

As a prerequisite to an overview of assessment strategies, it is also appropriate to acknowledge that substantial resources in terms of time, energy, and money are needed to establish any form of online authentic assessment strategy. Additionally, efficient and reliable technical support, along with appropriate networking capabilities, are essential for all students and instructors. Successful execution of authentic assessment strategies assumes that teachers and students alike have mastered computer-related skills, like using still and digital video cameras, microphones, multimedia software, uploading and downloading information, and analog and digital editing, to name a few. It also assumes that the students are made aware of issues related to plagiarism and the legal boundaries of using and posting information on the World Wide Web that are unique to the online environment. This is particularly true since the laws are rapidly evolving as new technologies become available to students and teachers. Table 1 draws attention to these prerequisites for authentic online assessment:

Before discussing specific strategies for online assessment, it is important to create a strategic framework that will support this approach. Authentic assessment must determine how effectively student performance connects thinking and doing in real-life situations. The effectiveness of an assessment strategy is determined by the extent to which the student and instructor align it with preset authentic learning goals that are collaboratively developed. Often, authentic assessment is embedded in the interactions between the student and instructor, and is reflected in the quality and depth of the instruction. Authentic assessment could also be conducted as a distinct process as the student engages in authentic learning.

Authentic assessment must occur before, during, and after the implementation of an authentic learning experience. Assessment before launching the curriculum is critical for identifying the skills, knowledge, competency, aptitude, and motivation the student brings to the learning situation. It gives an understanding of the student's strengths and weaknesses that can be used to individualize curriculum. Ongoing assessments at several points during the learning process are also important, supporting the student and instructor in understanding the evolving competencies and problem areas. Ongoing assessments permit troubleshooting as learning unfolds and provide opportunities for student-facilitator communication. They form the basis for peer feedback, serve as a motivator of learning, and contribute to the validity of authentic learning. Assessment at the end of the curriculum determines student achievement and serves as a basis for planning other learning experiences. Formative assessment strategies are often embedded in the process of planning and executing the curriculum, as opposed to a standalone activity. Embedded assessments are useful in that they take the anxiety out of the testing and grading process, save time, and keep students and teachers focused on the learning experience.

An Overview of Authentic Online Assessment Strategies

As this chapter has established, authentic assessment takes on many new forms and recognizes existing pedagogical processes as viable vehicles for assessing growth and learning. This section will briefly describe specific strategies for authentic online assessment and discuss their respective advantages. These strategies are: using e-portfolios, e-journals, e-discussion forums, and self-testing methods.

Electronic Portfolios

Portfolios, as a collection of student-produced products, provide the student opportunity to demonstrate his or her learning and progress toward achieving course objectives. As an authentic approach to assessment, portfolios give students an opportunity to display evolving proficiency in ways that are not feasible with traditional summative assessments.

Electronic portfolios take advantage of the opportunities afforded through electronic technology to digitize, organize, store, and transmit information more effectively than traditional portfolios. Electronic portfolios successfully bring together curriculum, instruction, and assessment on the World Wide Web ("Creating and Using," n.d.). They resemble the traditionally displayed portfolios in their content, goals, and process, but add the advantages of security, compact storage, and broad, quick dissemination. Currently the use of electronic portfolios is not widespread in universities and colleges, but with increased acceptance as a viable tool and advances in software that support their creation and sharing, they should become an increasingly important tool for learning and assessment. Some of the advantages of electronic portfolios are as follows:

1. Electronic portfolios can be edited, updated, retrieved, and instantly made available to several people simultaneously.

2. Electronic portfolios are user friendly. Voice recordings, digital pictures, and videos by the student, teacher, peers, and other raters can personalize electronic portfolios.

3. Electronic portfolios are designed to accept instant feedback from teachers, peers, and area experts, and provide exceptional flexibility to the process of learning and assessment.

4. Electronic portfolios make it possible to cross-reference a student's work across content areas. Different parts of the curriculum can be connected and cross-referenced easily.

5. Since it is possible to store, cross-reference, and retrieve student portfolios easily, instructors and administrators can retrieve student work from past semesters and years to display them as examples for future students.

6.   Electronic portfolios vividly describe and assess the learning processes and products.

They successfully document learning across curriculum and grade levels.

Just as the use of portfolios has gained broader recognition as a valid form of alternative assessment in the face-to-face classroom, online educators who believe in socially constructed approaches to teaching and learning will find electronic portfolios provide a powerful tool for assessing students' meaningful application of essential knowledge and skills (Mueller, 2003).

Electronic Journal Entries

Like portfolios, the process of journaling has become a broadly accepted pedagogical strategy in the traditional classroom. Educators who understand and value the role of reflection in the personal meaning-making process (Bruner, 1990; Dewey, 1938; Luckner & Nadler, 1997; Vygotsky, 1978) recognize the value of journaling as a reflective process.

Like electronic portfolios, electronic journals take advantage of electronic technology to digitize students' reflective writing. Digital information, when combined with the speed and distribution capabilities of the Internet, can be shared with an instructor and with students across time and space.

Electronic journal entries can be student-directed or instructor-directed. Student-directed entries are used to reflect on the learning process. They document change in student perceptions and attitudes, and describe problems faced and how they were overcome. Instructor-directed journal entries are goal-oriented and more formal in nature. An instructor's ongoing access to both student-directed and instructor-directed electronic journal entries provides her or him with evidence of a student's evolving thinking, learning, and application. E-journal entries can be used as a tool for learning, documenting information, and assessing. Online instructors have articulated the following advantages of using e-journaling for assessment:

1.   E-journals help in understanding changing contexts of learning and modifying expectations of tasks as needed.

2.   Peers, experts, and instructors alike may review the entries and respond to questions and problems. Since it is possible to receive frequent and immediate responses, electronic journal entries often foster relationship building.

3.   E-journals are an important way of obtaining multiple perspectives to a problem and eliciting several solutions to a problem.

4.   E-journaling is used to brainstorm and reflect on one's own work and that of others.

5.   Online journaling provides a collaborative learning environment that encourages students to question and to resolve difficulties within a social context.

6.   Sharing journal entries helps students see how others think and work.

In an asynchronous online learning environment, voice recordings, animated graphics, digital images, and videos can enhance journal entries. Additionally, in an online environment, students have access to writing aids like editing, spell and grammar checks, and appropriate software programs to enhance their written entries. For example, students can display partially created products for the instructor and others to review, assess, and comment. This iterative process provides an important vehicle for the student to obtain prompt feedback on work in progress from multiple sources. It improves the quality and depth of instruction.

E-journaling can also be used as an assessment strategy by embedding assessment into the process of journaling. Instructors can provide students with assessment rubrics that will be used to assess e-journal entries. However, using e-journals as a tool for embedded assessment can become laborious and time consuming. The following questions are necessary before deciding to use e-journals as a tool for assessment:

1. What is an appropriate frequency for journal entries?

2. Who has access to the journal entries? Is it possible to submit journal entries in password-protected spaces online?

3. How will the journal entries be used? The instructor must determine the goals for assigning e-journals. Assessment can then be based on the preset objectives.

4. How is assessment embedded in the e-journaling process? A collaboratively created grading rubric should be used to describe the assessment goals and expectations.

5. What should be included in the journal entries?

Online Discussions

If, as this chapter has asserted, learning is understood as a social process where meaning is constructed in interaction with others, then dialog with others is a critical aspect of learning. The importance of dialog in assessment has been a standard in education across centuries. The oral exam so common to secondary and college-level assessment in many countries is an attempt to ascertain what a student not only knows, but truly understands (Wiggins & McTighe, 1998).

In online coursework, structured discussion around course concepts has become a central learning activity, and students' ability to develop, state, and defend an opinion, as well as respond to other students' opinions, are common assessment criteria. Typically, an online course will be structured in modules that reflect different dimensions of the course topic. Within each module, students are challenged to productively participate in ongoing or "threaded discussions" (Shea et al., 2000a, 2000b).

Online discussions are an effective way for students to brainstorm ideas, reflect on possibilities, understand an issue from multiple perspectives, and articulate their opinions. An online discussion forum is also an important way to assess several learning competencies such as the ability to think critically, solve problems, communicate as a professional, research ideas, use technical computer skills, demonstrate articulation skills, and competently work as a team member. Assessment of the competencies can be embedded into the process of the discussion. The authors have found in their online teaching experiences that assessment embedded within an authentic task takes away the anxiety that frequently goes along with assessment. It also serves as a motivator for student learning.

Discussions that are conducted in an asynchronous online environment create some special challenges for the instructor and students alike. An effective presentation in a traditional synchronous environment includes establishing eye contact with the audience, appropriate voice modulations and tone, and body gestures. These important non-verbal tools for communication are not readily available in an online environment. Thus in online discussions, the communicators need to find alternate ways to get their point across effectively. They need to find ways to create a social presence online that facilitates communication and discussions.

The following are key considerations for embedding assessment in online discussions:

1. Consider collaboratively developing a rubric with the students that will be used to grade online discussion groups. Several rubrics are available on the World Wide Web that can be modified to fit the achievement goals.

2. Provide students with a clear understanding of expectations and what are considered acceptable postings. For example, it is important to state that postings that merely agree or disagree with another opinion do not accrue points. An appropriate posting must be a supported argument or question based on reading, research, and reflection. Students must also be aware of the expected length and frequency of postings. They should have a clear understanding of appropriate ways to cite quotations and views expressed by other authors.

3. Inform students of ways to communicate professionally and ethically in an online environment. For example, using all capital letters is considered rude and compromises reading fluency.

4. Provide students with effective and ineffective examples of postings that can serve as models. This helps students frame their initial postings, as they get comfortable with online discussion forums.

5. Provide students sufficient time to get comfortable in expressing themselves in writing in an asynchronous learning environment. Voice recordings and digital images that support the discussion can be used frequently to increase the effectiveness of an online discussion forum. It is important to recognize that in an online class, not all students have the same computer configurations. There must be a mechanism built in whereby students with better computer configurations do not emerge better than students who are working with less capable computers.

6. Provide frequent encouraging and challenging comments.

7. Ensure strong social presence (Short et al., 1976) of each member of the learning group. The authors have found that this is critical for successful online discussions. In their experience with teaching online courses, the authors have found that

with the same course, the frequency and quality of online responses is directly related to the social presence of the instructor and other members of the online learning experience. While this is also true in synchronous learning environments, it is especially meaningful in asynchronous settings.

Online Self-Testing

Traditional assessment strategies like true or false statements, multiple-choice questions, case-study analysis, and short-response questions have a place in assessment of authentic learning experiences. They guide the learning process by quickly identifying students' understanding and knowledge of content and the learning process. These traditional strategies also help pace students through online materials and serve well as reading guides. The grade emphasis on these should be minimal and should essentially be used by students as formative self-assessment in preparation for more formal summative evaluations by professional organizations.

Rubrics

The use of rubrics, like portfolios and journaling, has become a common and accepted form of assessment in education. Rubrics provide a standardized scoring guide, which includes clear criteria and standards for assessing behaviors of performance. Because rubrics clearly divide a task into distinct subtasks and assist the individual learner as well as the instructor in identifying evidence of the degree to which these tasks have been accomplished, they provide an effective, efficient tool for assessing student learning.

In assessing learning, the use of rubrics for assessment has several distinct advantages. A grading rubric affirms the student-centered approach to teaching and learning. This approach tells the student up front why they are being assessed, what the goals for assessment are, and how they can achieve the stated goals. A rubric clarifies curriculum objectives, operationally describing criteria for mastery and the range of proficiency levels. It also provides an opportunity for students to get involved with the assessment process by collaboratively developing a criterion for success. A collaboratively created rubric helps students understand the assessment process and assume responsibility for their own learning. A rubric is efficient, flexible, and adaptable, and it can be easily individualized. A rubric facilitates open communication between the instructor and the student, and can serve as a motivation enhancer for instructors and students alike. The concept of using rubrics for grading is not new to educators. The process of developing an efficient rubric has been widely discussed, and several references are available by conducting an Internet search using the keyword *rubric*. Developing and using rubrics will therefore not be discussed here.

In placing and using assessment rubrics in an online teaching and learning environment, the electronic medium provides several distinct advantages. The rubrics used for assessment can be easily shared and edited, and then stored digitally for future classes. In describing online course assessment to students, the performance standards central to rubrics clearly explain instructor expectations. In posting a course or assignment rubric, the student can download the form and use it for self-assessment and as a guide to effectively completing the assignment.

Authentic Assessment Online:
What Works and What Does Not

From this discussion, it is apparent that portfolios, journaling, discussions, and rubrics, as evidence of performance, are all effective authentic assessment tools and readily adaptable for online coursework. Used formally or informally, and as formative or summative assessment processes, they provide instructors and students with powerful tools for monitoring and assessing personally meaningful, relevant learning.

In summary, authentic assessment in the online classroom is not only feasible, it is a critical component in a socially constructed approach to teaching and learning. In developing authentic online assessment strategies, practitioners should keep the following in mind:

1.   Authentic assessment should be aligned with curriculum. It must link content with the student's authentic needs (Koelsch, Trumbull-Estrin, & Farr, 1995) and demonstrate the student's ability to solve real-life problems.

2.   Authentic assessment strategies must provide sufficient time to complete the authentic task since developing an authentic product is time-consuming.

3.   Authentic assessment strategies should be guided by student competency at the entry point of the curriculum. They should clearly acknowledge and identify the student's current level of competency and set an achievement goal based on this starting point. Success is therefore assessed based on the student's move from starting point to achievement of goal. Obviously, this is based on individual performance and not group performance.

4.   Authentic assessment strategies should include multiple raters. In addition to the instructors, learning can be assessed by parents, peers, and experts in the area under study.

5.   Competencies that require cognitive skill building are best suited for authentic assessment. However, competencies that require hands-on skills like drawing blood are best done in hybrid learning environments that combine the face-to-face instruction environment with online learning platforms (Jorgensen, 2003).

6.   Authentic assessment strategies must be fair to students of all ethnic-, language-, economic-, and gender-based groups.

The checklist in Table 2 can be used to determine if an assessment strategy can be used effectively for authentic assessment online.

Table 2. Checklist to determine the authenticity of an online assessment strategy

- Is the assessment strategy fair to students of all ethnic, language, color, and gender based groups?

- Does the assessment strategy link content with students authentic needs?

- Does the assessment strategy adequately demonstrate the student's ability to solve real life problems/situations?

- Does the assessment strategy provide sufficient time to complete the authentic task?

- Is the assessment strategy guided by student competency at entry point of the curriculum?

- Is the assessment strategy flexible and adaptable in that it can be modified if the context of learning changes?

- Does the assessment include a combination of strategies?

- Does the assessment strategy raise questions that have more than one correct solution?

- Is there provision for multiple raters?

- Does the assessment strategy provide a built-in mechanism for adequate and timely feedback?

- Are the assessment strategies described in a way that is understandable to the student and other raters?

- Is the authentic assessment strategy co-created by the instructor and the student?

- Does the authentic assessment strategy serve as a motivator for learning?

Conclusion

If colleges and universities are committed to meeting the practical needs of a growing population of adult learners, these institutions are obligated to develop and offer coursework and approaches to assessment that connect student learning to thinking and doing in real-life situations.

As this chapter illustrates, authentic approaches to instruction meet these practical needs, and this social constructivist approach to teaching and learning must be accompanied by authentic approaches to assessment. By drawing on the strengths of the Internet as an educational medium, online course developers and instructors are currently designing and effectively implementing authentic approaches to assessment. Understanding assessment as a process that *guides* instruction, instructors are challenged to adapt traditional tools such as rubrics, group discussion, journaling, and portfolios so that can be used to assess learning process and outcomes.

With a well-established and respected theoretical foundation to support it and viable models to guide its implementation, authentic assessment is a powerful and relevant tool. As this chapter illustrates, there are viable tools for authentically assessing online students' work. The greater challenge surrounding online education and authentic assessment is articulating a clear rationale for social constructivist approaches to teaching and addressing prevalent misconceptions about this approach. Our students deserve no less than an education that meets both their practical and intellectual needs. An authentic approach to teaching, learning, and assessment can provide this education, in face-to-face classrooms and online.

References

Angelo, T., & Cross, K. (1993). Classroom assessment techniques: A handbook for college teachers. Retrieved June 2, 2004, from *http://www.msu.edu/user/egidio/ Assessment.htm*

Baker, W., Hale, T., & Gifford, B. (1997). From theory to implementation: The mediated learning approach to computer-mediated instruction, learning, and assessment. *Educom Review, 32*(5). Retrieved June 18, 2004, from *http://www.educause.edu/ pub/er/review/review/Articles(/32542.html*

Brooks, G., & Brook, J. (1993). *In search of understanding: The case for constructivist classrooms.* Alexandria, VA: Association for Supervision and Curriculum Development.

Bruner, J. (1990). *Acts of meaning.* Cambridge, MA: Harvard University Press.

Caine, R., & Caine, G. (1991). *Making connections: Teaching and the human brain.* Alexandria, VA: Association for Supervision and Curriculum Development.

Campbell, K. (2004). *Text to e-text: Message design in e-effective writing for e-learning environments.* Hershey, PA: Information Science Publishing.

Carlson, A. (2001). Authentic learning: What does it mean? Retrieved July 6, 2004, from *http://pandora.cii.wwu.edu/showcase2001/authentic_learning.htm*

Carpenter, T., & Fennema, E. (1992). Cognitively guided instruction: Building on the knowledge of students and teachers. In W. Secada (Ed.), Curriculum reform: The case of mathematics in the United States. Special issue of *International Journal of Educational Research* (pp. 457-470). Elmsford, NY: Pergamon Press.

Christensen, M. (1995). Critical issues: Providing hands-on, minds-on, authentic learning experiences in the sciences. Retrieved July 6, 2004, from *http://www.ncrel.org/ sdrs/areas/issues/content(/cntareas/science/sc500.htm*

Creating and using portfolios on the alphabet superhighway. (n.d). Retrieved June 20, 2004, from *http://www.ash.udel.edu/ash/teacher/portfolio.html*

Dewey, J. (1938). *Experience in education.* New York: Collier Books.

Goldstein, L. (1999). The relational zone: The role of caring relationships in the co-construction of the mind. *American Educational Research Journal, 36*(3), 647-673.

Gordon, R. (2002). Balancing real-world problems with real-world results. Retrieved July 6, 2004, from *http://www.clearyweb.com/reform/essays/gordon.html*

Guba, E., & Lincoln, Y. (1989). *Fourth generation evaluation.* Newbury Park, CA: Sage Publications.

Hein, T., & Irvine, S. (2004). Assessment of student understanding using online discussion groups. Retrieved June 18, 2004, from *http://www.fie.engrng.pitt.edu/ fie98/papers/1375.pdf*

Jorgensen, H. (2003). Building real-life performance assessment into online courses. *Distance Education Report, 7*(12), 3-6.

Koelsch, N., Trumbull-Estrin, E., & Farr, B. (1995). *Guide to developing equitable performance assessment.* San Francisco: WestEd.

Luckner, J., & Nadler, R. (1997*). Processing the experience: Strategies to enhance and generalize learning.* Dubuque, IA: Kendall/Hunt Publishing Company.

Mueller, J. (2003). Authentic assessment toolbox. Retrieved June 18, 2004, from *http://jonathan,mueller.faculty/nocrtl.edu/toolbox/whatisi.htm*

Newman, F., & Archbald, D. (1992). The nature of authentic academic achievement. In H. Berlak, F. Newman, E. Adams, D. Archbald, T. Burgess, J. Raven, & T. Romberg (Eds.), *Toward a new science of educational testing and assessmen*t (pp. 71-84). Albany, NY: State University of New York Press.

Newman, F., & Wehlage, G. (1992). *Five standards of authentic instruction.* Washington, DC: Center on Organization and Restructuring of Schools, U.S. Department of Education, Office of Educational Research and Improvement.

Parkany, R., & Swan, K. (1999). Provaluation of an online curriculum. Retrieved June 2, 2004, from *http://www.borg.com/~rparkany/Resources/OLPA1.htm*

Shea, P., Frederickson, E., & Pickett, A. (2000b). *Factors influencing student and faculty satisfaction in the SUNY Learning Network.* Albany, NY: State University of New York.

Shea, P., Frederickson, E., Pickett, A., Pelz, W., & Swan, K. (2000a). *Measures of learning effectiveness in the SUNY Learning Network.* Albany, NY: The State University of New York.

Short, J., Williams, E., & Christie, B. (1976*). The social psychology of telecommunications.* London: John Wiley & Sons.

Slack, F., Beer, M., Armitt, G., & Green, S. (2003). Assessment and learning outcomes: The evaluation of deep learning in an online course. *Journal of Information Technology, 2*, 305-317.

Sproull, L., & Kessler, S. (1986). Reducing social context cues: Electronic mail in organizational communications. *Management Science, 32*, 1492-1512.

Valencia, S. (1997). Understanding authentic classroom-based literacy assessment. Retrieved June 18, 2004, from *http://www.eduplace.com/rdg/res/litass/*

von Glaserfeld, E. (2003). An exposition of constructivism: Why some like it radical. Retrieved June 20, 2004, from *http://www.oikos.org/vonen.htm/*

Vygotsky, L. (1978). *Mind in society: The development of higher psychological processes.* Cambridge, MA: Harvard University Press.

Wiggins, G. (1990). *The case for authentic assessment.* Washington, DC: ERIC Clearinghouse on Tests Measurement and Evaluation, American Institutes for Research.

Wiggins, G. (1993). *Assessing student performance.* San Francisco: Jossey-Bass.

Wilson, B., & Lowry, M. (2000). Constructivist learning on the Web. In L. Burge (Ed.), *Learning technologies: Reflective and strategic thinking.* San Francisco: Jossey-Bass.

Chapter XV

Performance Testing:
Validity Issues and Design Considerations for Online Testing

James B. Olsen, Alpine Media Corporation, USA

Abstract

Performance testing evaluates real-world tasks and skills with a test-display and response environment similar to, or identical with, the job environment. Performance testing offers the promise of providing more comprehensive evidence of construct and predictive validity than knowledge-based testing. This chapter presents information relevant to this promising approach to online testing. First, performance testing is defined and a historical context is presented; a series of test design questions are presented, then validity criteria, standards, and theory are recommended; and two validity-centered design approaches are reviewed. The chapter concludes with a set of implications and conclusions for further investigation.

Introduction

This chapter suggests that performance tests may offer supplemental validity evidence compared to multiple-choice tests typically used in technology-based and online testing. The principles of validity, test design, and measurement presented herein apply to both traditional, technology-based, and online assessment environments. There are test design situations when performance tests are preferable to multiple-choice testing, some situations where balance is needed between performance items and multiple-choice items, and other test design situations when the lower costs and higher efficiency (information per unit amount of time) of multiple-choice tests are preferred over performance tests. This chapter recommends a reasoned test design using the most appropriate test models and item types.

Performance Testing

Defining Performance Testing

> *Performance-based testing is a methodology for evaluating an individual by having them actually complete a real or simulated task relevant to a particular job. Performance-based testing differs from multiple-choice testing in that a performance test allows the test-taker to create a solution to solve a problem...Performance-based tests are designed to emulate what a candidate does on the job.* (Mulkey, 2001, p. 60)

Olsen and Ford (1995) and Mulkey (2001) note that job task analysis (JTA) is a key element in creating a useful performance test. Job analysis is a procedure that breaks the job down into its simpler elements. The job analysis should also include a job synthesis to integrate the job elements into meaningful, work-related, and critical tasks. The job analysis and synthesis identifies meaningful job tasks and evaluates the frequency of task occurrence, level of skill or expertise required, and criticality of successful task performance.

After the job and its components are analyzed, performance objectives can be defined to support the identified tasks and subtasks. These performance objectives can then be structured into meaningful performance situations or exercises for the candidate.

What performance testing requires are theoretical models for identifying key job-performance elements and their relationships, and structuring them into meaningful and integrated job-performance environments. These performance environments allow for assessing realistic problem-solving, troubleshooting, and diagnostic-reasoning skills.

Elements of Performance Testing

There is increasing interest in designing and developing performance assessments as supplements to conventional multiple-choice tests. These performance assessments require examinee actions demonstrating what the person "*knows* and can *do*." The performance exercises and tasks represent those required in realistic contexts and job tasks. Examples of performance tasks include installing and maintaining a software program, troubleshooting typical system problems, and predicting outcomes based on identified symptoms. Performance tasks provide information on learning and thinking processes (analysis, synthesis, problem solving, and troubleshooting), types of performance errors, and overall performance quality and competence.

Conventional test development represents the job task analysis with verbal task lists, test objectives, and selected-response knowledge tests. Unfortunately, these knowledge-based tests do not adequately measure the expert's performance competencies and skills. Real expertise is found not only in the words, but also in the fingers, in the actions, and in the gut. Effective performance tasks should be modeled to provide high fidelity rather than merely visual realism to the applied setting, job tasks, and meaningful work-like materials.

A Bakers Dozen Questions for Test Designers

This section presents a series of questions for test design consideration in determining the most appropriate combination of test and item types consistent with a given test purpose.

1. What construct(s) is the test attempting to measure?
2. What are the purposes and uses for which the test will be administered?
3. What are the most appropriate item types to meet the specified purpose of the exam?
4. How many test items of each item type can be developed to meet the planned test budget?
5. How many test items of each item type can be administered within the planned test administration budget?
6. How will the test be scored, including both automated and/or human judged elements?
7. How will security be provided for test items, test item banks, test forms, scores, and test reports?
8. What is the required type and accuracy for decisions and interpretations that will be made from test scores?
9. What are the stakes associated with scores from the exam?
10. How much time can be allocated for the assessment?
11. How close can the assessment come to meeting the purpose of the exam with less complex item and test types?
12. What kinds of validity considerations are relevant for the target exam?
13. What are the advantages and disadvantages of the chosen assessment method(s) for maintaining validity evidence to support the testing program?

Performance Test Characteristics

Performance tests and items typically share the following key characteristics:

1. Use a constructed series of actions or responses rather than multiple-choice selection from a predetermined set of answers.

2. Assess actions or behaviors of interest as directly and authentically as possible.

3. Measure individual or group performance.

4. Show evaluation of work with reference to criteria for excellence (standards) rather than by comparisons with other individuals from a norm-comparison group. Note that this characteristic is also applicable to multiple-choice items.

5. Focus as much on the process of problem solving or troubleshooting as on the end result.

6. Involve judgments of qualified performers or subject-matter experts in determining the test-scoring criteria.

7. Provide public information on the criteria, process, and products on which performers will be judged.

The 50-Year Historical Context for Performance Testing

This section presents a historical context for performance testing by drawing from sources provided by the three editions of *Educational Measurement,* a canonical reference resource. These references show that performance testing is not a new idea in educational measurement, but that for at least 50 years, measurement professionals have been interested in ways to provide more direct measurement of human knowledge, skills, and capabilities with performance tests. Performance tests measure in a public, demonstrable way what an individual knows and can do. These references also show that the professional field has made advances by building on this historical context and background. Future performance testing should not forget nor neglect its history.

1951: A pioneering reference on performance testing is David Ryans and Norman Frederiksen's chapter entitled "Performance Tests of Educational Achievement" in *Educational Measurement.* These authors note:

> *Performance tests of achievement purport to provide objective means for estimating the proficiency with which a task is performed...Performance tests must be submitted to the same empirical checks of reliability and validity as are paper-and-pencil tests of aptitude and achievement, and with the same degree of rigor.* (pp. 457, 467)

Ryans and Frederiksen (1951) recommend the following seven steps for developing a useful performance test:

1. Make a job analysis.
2. Select tasks to represent the job.
3. Develop the rating form.
4. Survey the practical limitations.
5. Develop the tentative "operating plan."
6. Try out and revise the test.
7. Prepare directions for administration and use of the test. (pp. 483-492)

1971: Educational Measurement (second edition) includes a chapter on "Performance and Product Evaluations" by Robert Fitzpatrick and Edward Morrison. These authors note:

> *Hence, it is often desirable to increase the 'realism' of the test to a degree that permits evaluation of the capability of the student to perform correctly in some class of <u>criterion situations</u>. The criterion situations are those in which the learning is to be applied...Realism may be increased both in the stimuli presented and in the responses required.* (p. 237)

This chapter discusses the use of simulations for performance-assessment. An effective simulation: (1) shows the critical elements of the performance or criterion situation in light of the test purpose, (2) specifies the minimum fidelity for each critical element of the simulation, (3) provides an adequate representation within resource constraints, and 4) adjusts comprehensiveness and fidelity to achieve an appropriate balance of the critical aspects identified (Fitzpatrick & Morrison, 1971).

1989: In *Educational Measurement* (third edition), Jason Millman and Jennifer Greene discuss "The Specification and Development of Tests of Achievement and Ability." They define an item "in the broadest sense, as any task or series of tasks presented to examinees" (p. 335).

Millman and Green (1989) suggest five substantive considerations for developing the content of tests whether in the knowledge or performance domains: (a) specifying appropriate sources for test content, (b) investigating the number of dimensions needed to adequately represent the content and scores, (c) specifying domain (referenced to a clearly specified and differentiated content domain) vs. norm-referenced (referenced to a specified normative population) interpretations of scores, (d) determining the appropriate balance between breadth of content and the accuracy or reliability of the scores representing each content component, and (e) determining the appropriate distribution of items across the individual content topics or components comprising the content domain.

For non-multiple-choice tests such as performance tests, Millman and Greene (1989) suggest consideration of partial-credit scoring or differential weighting for individual-item responses, scoring of essay performance, and simulation-item responses. For scoring performance tests, they note that "the development of scoring criteria requires clear conceptualization of proficiency, competence, or mastery in the relevant domain" (p. 344).

Validity Theory and Professional Testing Standards

Performance tests as well as knowledge tests rest on the foundation of validity theory and professional testing standards presented in this section. Lee Cronbach (1988) introduced the concept of validation as an evaluation argument:

> *Validation of a test or test use is evaluation (Guion, 1980; Messick, 1980), so I propose here to extend to all testing the lessons from program evaluation. What House (1977) has called the 'logic of evaluation argument' applies, and I invite you to think of 'validity argument' rather than 'validation research'...Validation speaks to a diverse and potentially critical audience; therefore, <u>the argument must link concepts, evidence, social and personal consequences, and values...So validation is never finished</u>.* (pp. 4-5)

Samuel Messick is a pioneering scientist in validity theory for educational and psychological testing, and his influence will be noted throughout this chapter. In his (1989b) seminal work on validity, he summarizes the key elements of validity investigations of assessment:

> *Validity is an integrated evaluative judgment of the degree to which empirical evidence and theoretical rationales support the <u>adequacy</u> and <u>appropriateness</u> of <u>inferences</u> and <u>actions</u> based on test scores or other modes of assessment. As will be delineated shortly, the term <u>test score</u> is used generically here in its broadest sense to mean any observed consistency, not just on tests as ordinarily conceived but on any means of observing or documenting consistent behavior or attributes. Broadly speaking, then, validity is an inductive summary of both the existing evidence for and the potential consequences of score interpretation and use....* (p. 13)

Messick (1989b) notes that the threats to validity can be grouped into two general classes. *Construct under representation* results from a test that is too narrow to faithfully represent the key facets of the construct. *Construct-irrelevant variance* is found when the test exhibits reliable variance that is not relevant to the tested construct(s). Messick (1994) also notes that these two classes of threats to validity are also the primary evaluation issues required for justifying the validity of performance assessments.

Table 1. Facets of validity as a progressive matrix (Messick, 1989a, p. 10)

	Test Interpretation	Test Use
Evidential Basis	Construct Validity (CV)	CV + Relevance/Utility (R/U)
Consequential Basis	CV +Value Implications (VI)	CV +R/U +VI + Social Consequences

Messick (1989a) clarifies that construct validity is the basic integrative foundation of all of the facets of validity (Table 1). "Construct validity appears in every cell, which is fitting because construct validity is the integrating force that unifies validity issues into a unitary concept" (p. 10).

In a paper specifically addressing validation of performance assessments, Messick (1994) emphasizes that performance tests should adhere to the same "general validity standards as any other test or assessment: content, substantive, structural, external, generalizability, and consequential aspects of construct validity." (Note: These six validity aspects are discussed later in this chapter.) "Performance assessments must be evaluated by the same validity criteria, both evidential and consequential, as are other assessments" (p. 13).

Messick (1994) suggests that performance assessments should be construct-driven rather than task-driven. This means that the validity investigation should focus on the relevant constructs measured by the test rather than on the specific task or item set included in the assessment.

Messick (1994) identifies three questions that must be answered by developers of either knowledge- or performance-based tests. These questions also appear in the proposed validity designs presented later in this chapter.

> *A construct-centered approach would begin by asking <u>what complex of knowledge, skills, or other attributes should be assessed</u>, presumably because they are tied to implicit or explicit objectives of instruction or are otherwise valued by society. Next <u>what behaviors or performances should reveal those constructs</u>, and <u>what tasks or situations should elicit those behaviors</u>?* (p. 16, emphasis added)

With the construct-centered approach, the investigators can examine evidence for construct-relevant variance and construct-irrelevant variance in aspects of task performance. The task-centered approach focuses on the specific tasks provided in the assessment rather than the generalizations to a larger domain of potential tasks that might have been administered. A construct-centered scoring approach leads to score criteria and rubrics across multiple tasks, rather than the specific criteria and rubric for the sampled items and tasks.

Standards for Educational and Psychological Tests

Given a validity theory, the test developer can further address specific professional standards for the validity investigation:

> *Validity refers to the degree to which evidence and theory support the interpretations of test scores entailed by purposed uses of tests. Validity is, therefore, the most fundamental consideration in developing and evaluating tests. The process of evaluation involves accumulating evidence to provide a sound scientific basis for the proposed score interpretations.* (American Educational Research Association, American Psychological Association, & National Council on Measurement in Education, 1999, p. 9)

Linn, Baker, and Dunbar (1991) provide a useful extension to the standards for educational and psychological tests by defining the following eight validation criteria for complex performance-based assessments: *(1) consequences, (2) fairness, (3) transfer and generalizability, (4) cognitive complexity, (5) content quality, (6) content coverage, (7) meaningfulness,* and *(8) cost and efficiency* (pp.16-20). These validation criteria also apply to online performance-based assessments.

Evidence-Centered Design for Validity

This section discusses the first of two recommended validity designs appropriate for both knowledge and performance-based testing.

Evidence-centered design is an approach to testing and assessment design that attempts to formalize the various types of inferences that can be derived from test scores and the types of evidence that can be marshaled in support or negation of these inferences. Evidence-centered design also attempts to build a comprehensive assessment framework and identify testing processes that support this approach. Evidence-centered design is a program with research and applications initiated at Educational Testing Service (ETS) in 1997, and continuing now at the University of Maryland, Stanford University, and other universities. The psychometric scientists using evidence-centered design include Mislevy, Steinberg, and Almond (1999, 2002, 2003a, 2003b).

Evidence-centered design involves a principle-centered validity framework concerned with all phases of educational assessment processes. It is "a principled framework for designing, producing, and delivering educational assessments," particularly assessments that include complex student models and interactive exercises and simulations (Mislevy et al., 1999, p. 1). Evidence-centered design is derived from advances in cognitive and instructional sciences, technology, and evidentiary reasoning. It includes an assessment design focused on appropriate inferences, observations to ground these inferences, situations that will evoke the observations, chains of reasoning to connect them, and a conceptual design framework with coherent assessment elements. Evidence-

Figure 1. Schematic of design and implementation (Mislevy et al., 1999, p. 3)

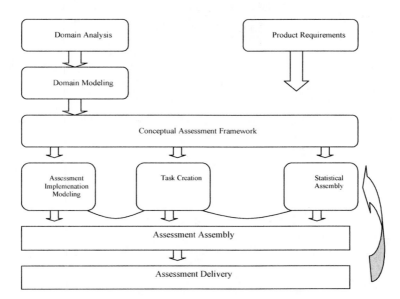

centered design provides an overall conceptual framework for assessment design, an object model for creating the specifications for particular assessment products, and software tools for creating and managing the design objects.

Figure 1 presents a schematic design for evidence-centered design. This section provides brief descriptions of key theoretical elements summarized from a recent article by Mislevy et al. (2003a). This article also includes a more elaborate schematic design.

Evidence-centered design addresses three stages of the assessment design process:

1.   Domain analysis identifies substantive elements and relations in the target domain.

2.   Domain modeling develops illustrative paradigm situations within the domain. Three types of paradigms are investigated. Proficiency paradigms model claims regarding examinees and their proficiency levels. Evidence paradigms model observable actions that examinees can say and do. Task paradigms model representative task situations where evidence of task performance can be collected. The modeling process defines relationships among the proficiency levels, what examinees say and do, and typical task situations.

3.   A conceptual assessment framework is created. The assessment framework includes student models, task models, and evidence models. The evidence models have both an evaluative or judgment component and a measurement or comparison component. The conceptual assessment framework includes an assembly model for creating appropriate assessments, and a presentation model for delivering and scoring these assessments (pp. 7-8).

Evidence-centered design uses probability-based reasoning with Bayesian inference networks from observed task and test performance to unobserved ability or proficiencies of the individual. Bayes' theorem is used for updating a prior distribution given new information to form a new posterior probability distribution. This allows for accumulation of evidence over many observations, synthesis of information from multiple lines of evidence, and use of different data sets for different students or groups of students. Other evidence linking methods can be used to define relationships between task characteristics, performances, and proficiencies.

In identifying sources of information for domain analysis, evidence-centered design investigates seven key information types:

1.   Valued work products

2.   Task features

3.   Representational forms

4.   Performance outcomes

5.   Valued knowledge

6.   Knowledge structures and relations

7.   Knowledge-task relations (Mislevy et al., 2003a, pp. 18-19)

At the present time, evidence-centered design has been applied in professional fields as diverse as language learning and information-technology training, and has proven useful for design, development, delivery, and analysis of knowledge and performance-based tasks. The use of evidential arguments and evidence and task variables allows scoring of actual performance assessment tasks and job work tasks as elements of an assessment system. Evidence-centered design uses eXtensible Markup Language (XML) data structures and records to show static and dynamic performance properties and variable states, as well as structural relationships, statistical distributions, and statistical updating procedures. The author expects to see more and varied applications of evidence-centered design.

Validity-Centered Design

This section recommends the second type of validity design for application with both knowledge-based testing or performance-based testing.

Validity-centered design (VCD) and its associated theories, methods, and realizations are centered in the work of C. Victor Bunderson and his professional colleagues and graduate students, including the author. Doctoral dissertations and papers building the elements for validity-centered design, domain theory, and learning-progress measurement include Bunderson (2000, 2003, in press); Bunderson, Martinez, and Wiley (2000); Martinez, Bunderson, and Wiley (2000); Wiley (2000); Pelton (2002); Strong-Krause (2000, 2002); and Xin (2002). The key ideas in this section are from an unpublished paper (Bunderson, 2003) provided by Victor Bunderson to the author.

Components of Validity-Centered Design

Validity-centered design is focused on designing and implementing the ideas of Samuel Messick on validity in educational and online educational and assessment environments. Messick (1988, 1989a, 1989b, 1998) has been perhaps the most influential validity theorist of the last 15 years. He developed the unified validity framework discussed above that showed that construct validity is the central, unifying concept among a variety of different views or perspectives on validity. Construct validity deals with the invisible traits or constructs that intelligent observers have formulated and "constructed" in words, diagrams, and so forth; how these invisible constructs are made visible through responses to items and performance situations; and how these responses are turned into scores. Construct validity is the link between invisible theoretical ideas about important human qualities (sometimes called "latent traits") and the scores on some instrument or measurement procedure designed to produce numbers reflecting differences in the unobservable human qualities. These numbers represent more or less of the latent trait or construct in question.

Validity-centered design is a set of methods and tools used at each of several stages of a design process to develop a learning progress system, to implement it in an online environment, and to keep improving it. The learning progress system is revised over a series of implementation improvement cycles. The learning progress system is used by teachers and students, and improved based on qualitative and quantitative results. Data are collected during each cycle of implementation and during the design process itself. Over time, data and documentation provide an increasingly strong "validity argument" for the quality of the learning progress system. The idea is that validity cannot be proven once and for all, but that evidence and argument threads can be assembled to show how well a given learning progress system, when used in certain ways, meets the multifaceted ideal of the unified validity model. Validity is much more complex and unified than usually understood. Validity-centered design identifies nine different but interrelated aspects of validity. These incorporate the six aspects of construct validity identified by Messick (1989a, 1989b):

1. Content
2. Substantive process
3. Structure
4. Generalizability
5. External
6. Consequential

Validity-centered design restructures these six aspects and then adds three new aspects: overall appeal, usability, and value and positive consequences. A comprehensive validity argument can be organized around these nine integrated aspects of validity. Table 2 shows the nine validity aspects structured into three primary classifications, each with three elements.

Table 2. Validity-centered design elements for assessment systems

I.   Design for Usability, Appeal, and Positive Expectations (User-Centered Design)

   A. Overall Appeal

   B. Usability

   C. Value and Positive Consequences (perceived)

II. Design for Inherent Construct Validity

   A. Content

   B. Substantive Thinking Processes

   C. Structural (number of dimensions)

III. Design for Criterion-Related Validity

   A. Generalizability

   B. External Validity (convergent/discriminant)

   C. Consequential (positive and negative)

Validity-centered design aspires to do more than guide and design an *assessment system*. A learning progress system also includes a *measurement system*. This system may be used for ongoing, cyclical evaluation of not only the students, but also the measurement system itself, the instructional materials delivered on the same computers as the measurement system, the adaptive research system that includes adaptation to individual differences, and the strategic implementation of learning and content management systems. The student-progress measures are a part of this comprehensive measurement system but are not all of it.

To accomplish this, validity-centered design leads to an interpretive framework with domain-spanning unidimensional scales for monitoring and measuring learning progress.

Conclusions and Recommendations for Future Investigation

It is the author's opinion that performance testing offers significant promise and value to supplement implementations of multiple-choice testing in both traditional testing and online testing environments. The author recommends analysis of the benefits, costs, and return on investment from use of performance test items, multiple-choice items, and their combinations in technology-based and online-testing environments.

There are limitations to use of performance tests in online environments. Due to the increased scope and complexity of the performance test items, fewer test items can generally be administered within a given time period and cost compared to multiple-choice test items. Multimedia computer and online environments can also display many elements of performance environments and simulations. However, specialized equipment components are often needed for adequate representation of many meaningful performance test situations.

Performance testing provides a unique opportunity and environment to create constructed-response items rather than only selected-response items. Performance testing has an extensive history as exemplified by the research references to the three editions of *Educational Measurement*. This chapter emphasizes validation issues for performance testing, and presents validity theory, standards, and issues that are crucial in performance testing as well as in selected-response testing. The chapter concludes with two validity design approaches that have high relevance for performance testing where the evidence of examinee performance includes work products; multiple-step, open-ended exercises; interpretation of streams of constructed data responses; examination of constructed diagrams; and text work products that can be judged by either human expertise or machine intelligence.

This chapter highlights the following implications for online testing. Where possible, the design and development of the online assessment should be based on a job or practice analysis. This will help to assure that the assessment is grounded in real job skills and requirements. The job analysis should include an analysis process to define the tasks and subtasks, followed by a synthesis process to create meaningful clusters or aggregates of the tasks and subtasks. These meaningful clusters of tasks and subtasks are referred to as work models or performance models. The assessment designer must then determine the most appropriate types of representation, including media, display, and response mechanisms for these work or performance models. The representation forms should ensure high fidelity to the thinking processes and content domain elements required in the work or performance models.

A test blueprint or specification should identify the content domain dimensions and elements, as well as the thinking processes or level of cognitive demand required for adequately assessing each content dimension and element. The assessment designer should also consider the appropriate balance or mix between item types needed to accurately and reliably assess the knowledge and performance skills required in each work or performance model.

The costs and benefits of using each item or task type should be investigated. The online examination should include the item and task types from this reasoned analysis and investigation. The assessment designer should then create sufficient test items of each required item type and pilot test the items with a representative sample of individuals from the target population for the online assessment. The results from the pilot test should be analyzed to determine the specific items, tasks, and scoring criteria that should be used for the operational version of the online assessment. A performance standard should be set for the online exam.

It is recommended that the results from the online operational version be analyzed on a quarterly basis to determine consistency of item and test statistics, any differential item functioning based on target demographic groups, or item and test parameter drift. There is also a need to conduct ongoing validity, reliability, fairness, and usability analyses of the operational online assessment.

The validity-centered assessment approach and validation designs discussed in this chapter should prove helpful in designing more effective and efficient assessments whether in online, computer-administered or paper-administered assessment environments. The assessment designer should develop a plan and operational procedures to ensure appropriate security for the test items, tasks, scoring criteria, and examinee results.

Research is needed to determine the unique variance or added value of performance testing when compared with traditional multiple-choice, selected-response tests.

Research is needed to determine the dimensionality and stability of curricular and training domains and sub-domains for performance tests, and for selected response tests and the development of appropriate measurement scales for these respective domains. Performance testing necessarily requires research in complex-scoring algorithms and approaches that go many steps beyond summing binary scores to create the total raw score typically used in multiple-choice, selected-response tests. Research is needed to determine the relevant validity evidence for performance tests and selected response tests, and to appropriately evaluate the validity evidence. The future will likely show the increased need for integration of knowledge- and performance-based tests This chapter has presented a few links in the journey toward more appropriate, more valid, and more useful tests of job-relevant knowledge and skills in applied contexts.

References

Almond, R.G., Steinberg, L.S., & Mislevy, R.J. (2002). Enhancing the design and delivery of assessment systems: A four-process architecture. *The Journal of Technology, Learning and Assessment, 1*(5), 3-57. Retrieved November 29, 2004, from *www.jlta.org*

American Educational Research Association, American Psychological Association, & National Council on Measurement in Education. (1999). *Standards for educational and psychological testing*. Washington, DC: American Educational Research Association.

Bunderson, C.V. (2000, April). Design experiments, design science, and the philosophy of measured realism: Philosophical foundations of design experiments. *Proceedings of the Symposium in Division D (Measurement), American Education Research Association Conference,* New Orleans, LA.

Bunderson, C.V. (2003). *On the validity-centered design and continuing validation of learning progress measurement systems*. Unpublished manuscript.

Bunderson, C.V. (in press). How to build a domain theory: On the validity-centered design of construct-linked scales of learning and growth. *Proceedings of the April 2000 International Objective Measurement Workshop*. In G. Englehard Jr., M.

Wilson, & K. Draney (Eds.), *Objective measurement: Theory into practice: Volume 6*. Norweed, NJ: Ablex.

Bunderson, C.V., Martinez, M., & Wiley, D. (2000, April). Verification in a design experiment context: Validity argument as design process. *Proceedings of the Symposium Session of the American Educational Research Association Annual Conference*, New Orleans, LA.

Cronbach, L.J. (1988). Five perspectives on validity argument. In H. Wainer & H.I. Braun (Eds.), *Test validity* (pp. 3-17). Hillsdale, NJ: Lawrence Erlbaum.

Fitzpatrick, R., & Morrison, E.J. (1971). Performance and product evaluation. In R.L. Thorndike (Ed.), *Educational measurement* (2nd ed., pp. 237-270). Washington, DC: American Council on Education.

Linn, R.L., Baker, E.L., & Dunbar, S. (1991). Complex, performance-based assessment: Expectations and validation criteria. *Educational Researcher, 20*(8), 15-21.

Martinez, M., Bunderson, C.V., & Wiley, D. (2000, April). Verification in a design experiment context: Validity argument as design process. *Proceedings of the Annual Meeting of the American Educational Research Association*, New Orleans, LA.

Messick, S. (1989a). Meaning and values in test validation: The science and ethics of assessment. *Educational Researcher, 18*(2), 5-11.

Messick, S. (1989b). Validity. In R.L. Linn (Ed.), *Educational measurement* (3rd ed., pp. 11-103). New York: American Council on Education/Macmillan Publishing.

Messick, S. (1994). The interplay of evidence and consequences in the validation of performance assessments. *Educational Researcher, 32*(2), 13-23.

Messick, S. (1998). *Consequences of test use interpretation and use: The fusion of validity and values in psychological assessment*. Princeton, NJ: Educational Testing Service, RR–98–4.

Millman, J., & Greene, J. (1989). The specification and development of tests of achievement and ability. In R.L. Linn (Ed.), *Educational measurement* (3rd ed., pp. 335-366). New York: American Council on Education/Macmillan Publishing,

Mislevy, R.J., Steinberg, L.S., & Almond, R.G. (1999). *Evidence-centered assessment design*. Princeton, NJ: Educational Testing Service. Retrieved November 29, 2004, from *www.education.umd.edu/EDMS/mislevy/papers/ECD_Overview.html*

Mislevy, R.J., Steinberg, L.S., & Almond, R.G. (2003a). On the structure of educational assessments. *Measurement: Interdisciplinary Research and Perspectives, 1*(1), 3-62.

Mislevy, R.J., Steinberg, L.S., & Almond, R.G. (2003b). Rejoinder to commentaries for "On the structure of educational assessments." *Measurement: Interdisciplinary Research and Perspectives, 1*(1), 92-101.

Mulkey, J. (2001). The anatomy of a performance test. *Certification Magazine,* (May), 58-62.

Olsen, J.B., & Ford, J.M. (1995). Performance-based testing: An advance for professional assessment. *Proceedings of the 3rd European Electronic Conference on Assess-*

ment and Evaluation, European Association for Research into Learning and Instruction, Special Interest Group on Assessment and Evaluation.

Pelton, T.W. (2002). *The accuracy of unidimensional measurement models in the presence of deviations from the underlying assumptions.* Unpublished doctoral dissertation, Brigham Young University, USA.

Ryans, D.G., & Frederiksen, N. (1951). Performance tests of educational achievement. In E.F. Lindquist (Ed.), *Educational measurement* (pp. 455-494). Mensha, WI: George Banta.

Strong-Krause, D. (2000). Developing invariant, construct-valid measurement scales in spoken English as a second language. *Proceedings of the Annual Meeting of the American Educational Research Association,* New Orleans, LA.

Strong-Krause, D. (2002). *English as a second language speaking ability: A study in domain theory development.* Unpublished doctoral dissertation, Brigham Young University, USA.

Wiley, D.A. II. (2000). *Learning object design and sequencing theory.* Unpublished doctoral dissertation, Brigham Young University, USA.

Xin, M.C. (2002). *Validity-centered design for the domain of engaged collaborative discourse in computer conferencing.* Unpublished doctoral dissertation, Brigham Young University, USA.

Chapter XVI

Assessment and College Progress:
Capacity Building Through Formative and Summative Program Evaluation

Jennifer K. Holtz, DePaul University School for New Learning, USA

Barbara Radner, DePaul University School for New Learning, USA

Abstract

This chapter clarifies opportunities that colleges have to build teaching and assessment capacity. Development of assessments measuring true student ability requires multidimensional approaches that account for performance variation over time, within and between a discipline's core principles, patterns, and relationships. Quality online assessment also actively develops a student voice, addressing the issues of passivity and academic dishonesty, by requiring students to both prepare for courses and participate differently. Building faculty capacity for assessment design is facilitated by the introduction of rubrics that are easy to use, but that are thoroughly grounded in theory and that reflect the realities of practice.

Introduction

This chapter seeks to clarify the opportunities that colleges have to build teaching and assessment capacity through systematic evaluation. Providing online education gives colleges and universities an opportunity to focus more systematically on the construction of courses and the comprehensive, consistent assessment of learners. Development of online courses with integrated, valid assessment contributes to the overall improvement of college-level teaching and learning. The chapter does not question the value of online or in-classroom courses; it instead offers recommendations for clarifying assessment of online learning in ways that are easily transferred to the classroom. It provides a basis for using assessment not only to improve learning, but also to improve instruction.

The nature of online courses demands greater attention to both construction and evaluation. A classroom instructor can see in students' expressions—visible on puzzled faces or audible in questions about a confusing assignment—whether immediate clarification is needed. An online instructor in real time also has that immediate challenge, but an asynchronous course lacks the opportunity for instant clarification. While a student in any course needs a clear map that shows the destination, landmarks, and detailed assignments, online students use the course guide more consistently than do classroom students. (There is no research to support this, but any instructor who has found that students have misplaced their syllabi has personal experience with the incomplete attention that some students pay to the course guide.)

While teachers are generally positive about distance education (Lee, 2001), assessment presents challenges that distance educators often feel unable to adequately address. Rittschof and Griffin (2003) found teacher concern about the limited types of evaluation possible online, while Robles and Braathen (2002) maintain that many online assessment methods can be simple modifications of current techniques. This chapter provides tools for assessment in online courses, based on principles that apply to any educational program. Knowing and being able to apply those principles are essential to the developer of an online course.

With the shift to standards-based education, those principles have become a preoccupation with educators at K-12 levels, but the principles are innovations in higher education. The online course can provide a model for careful linking of instruction, assessment, and integrated evaluation for all college courses. In fact, that model also has substantial potential to influence K-12 education; while standards-based curriculum and assessment are buzzwords at pre-college levels, there continues to be a large gap between principles and practice.

Colleges and universities have a similar challenge, in that accreditation is based on standards. Thus, standards-based education at the college level actually has a long history. Has it reached the classroom? Ask any instructor the basis for the content selected for a course; the response probably will reference the discipline, but not a need to meet accreditation standards. Online course syllabi make public the instruction and assessment practices of a department in a way that is quite different from the traditional course syllabus. The online course provides a blueprint with such specificity that it is possible for an accreditation organization to analyze the content thoroughly. Thus, designers of online courses need practical tools to ensure alignment between the course content and related assessments.

Background

The assessment of learning is a major field of study in itself, with a broad, specialized knowledge base and vocabulary. Three terms are of particular importance to this chapter: formative evaluation, summative evaluation, and performance-based assessment. Formative evaluation is ongoing and designed to inform the teacher and student about the status of the student in terms of the criteria for the course. Based on formative evaluation, an instructor adjusts either the course content or the methods to improve learning. Summative evaluation is a judgment; it is the grade given that is based on all the work assessed. Performance-based assessment refers to the analysis of a student's work in which the student applies the content and skills developed independently. Generally, there is an end product in performance-based assessment, and usually that product is a project, not an essay. For example, in a course on creativity and the brain, a student would not write a report on readings about the brain, but instead would create a children's book that explains how the brain works.

Assessment itself is the most important term to make clear. Only in clear curriculum with explicit standards can there be assessment. Ask students what an assessment is, and many will respond with words such as "test," "evaluation," or "grade." They may respond that assessment is "how well I'm doing." Missing from those explanations is the essential component of assessment: a standard. Assessment is determining the relative value of something; thus, the question is not how well a student is doing, it is how close that student is to the knowledge and ability required.

Issues, Challenges, and Solutions

Typically, performance-based assessment is both a more valid, more active form of assessment than a traditional exam and a solution to a problem that affects all instructors: making certain that the student whose work is graded is the student enrolled. Distance education has an even greater challenge: Is the student participating in the online discussion the student who will receive the grade? Rittschof and Griffin (2003), in both their review of distance education issues published in *The Chronicle of Higher Education* and in interviews with experienced distance educators, found that the overwhelming assessment issue of concern was accountability; specifically, who is completing the assessment task? Benson (2003), too, considers the primary challenge of online assessment to be academic dishonesty, in terms of both plagiarism and identity. However, in taking steps to prevent cheating via either a substitute for the student or plagiarism, the benefits of distance learning, typically related to flexibility, are lost (Rittschof & Griffin, 2003). Benson (2003) recommends proctoring as an alternative, and also mentions advanced identification technologies such as fingerprinting and voiceprinting, but acknowledges that these technologies are both expensive and not typically available.

However, Benson (2003) considers the benefits of online assessment to be as valuable as the challenges are detrimental. In online assessment, every learner can answer every question asked by the instructor (Robles & Braathen, 2002), as opposed to the traditional environment, where "the first student to answer is typically afforded the sole opportunity to provide an answer" (Benson, 2003, p. 72). Students who submit answers to the instructor via e-mail are most likely to experience this benefit; it is the authors' experience that online students, as with traditional classroom students, are as likely to defer to those who answer first. This is especially true when a student has already posted to a communal site the answers another would have given. Benson (2003) also considers immediate feedback a benefit of online assessment. In the case of automatic feedback, in a program that is integral to several online delivery systems (e.g., WebCT® and Blackboard®), the learner is provided with a summative grade, as well as corrective feedback on each question answered incorrectly. Alternatively, the assessments may provide feedback as the learner completes each question. For example, the feedback might provide additional information or direct the learner to related content for further study (Benson, 2003).

A solution that incorporates both formative evaluation and an emphasis on performance is to assess students on a continuing basis and on activities that are open-ended, requiring a construction of answers based on their own experience. These students are on a clearly sequenced learning journey, starting with a baseline or initial assessment, and continuing on to develop and demonstrate the knowledge provided through the course content. They are not writing essays that could be purchased online; they are developing their own ideas and responses to a dynamic dialogue as part of the course.

The hidden problem in much college curricula, a problem that the introduction of distance education reveals, is passivity. The learner has the role of receiving knowledge. The course outcome is measured not in terms of the learner's ability to transfer what is learned to another subject or topic, but through the learner's delivery of the content in a narrow context: the end-of-course final exam.

Consider, for example, an introductory economics course taught by an instructor using Samuelson's text as the basis for lectures and reading assignments, with weekly quizzes from the test bank provided to instructors using the text. Imagine students preparing for the final exam constructed exclusively from the test bank. This is an example of efficiency that increases productivity in one way: the more tests graded in less time, the more time the instructor has to research current economic trends. However, what have students learned: principles or their application? Contrast that course with one in which students respond weekly to economic news with insights based on principles developed in class, and where they complete the assessment with a comprehensive project based on the economics they have learned in which students write to advise the President. Both scenarios are possible both for in-classroom and online instruction.

Despite the substantial benefits, performance-based assessment and instruction are challenging for both the learner and the instructor. For the student, performance, activity, or application-based assessment "focus(es) on learners' abilities to apply knowledge, skills, and judgment in ill-defined realistic contexts" (Reeves, 2000, p. 105.) Reeves (2000) emphasizes the ability of appropriately designed performance assessments to engage a student's higher-order cognitive skills in tasks that are multidimensional and multi-step. In fact, MacDonald and Twining (2002) found that successful higher-order learning in an activity-based format depended on assessment tasks, but that such tasks should be integrated.

Based on constructivist theory, the active-learning model in place at Great Britain's Open University is designed to "encourage self-directed learning and metacognitive development" (MacDonald & Twining, 2002, p. 603). Courses center on virtual discussion and collaborative activity, with integrated opportunities for reflection, including course-long portfolio development. In cases where assessment tasks were not integrated into the learning activity, completion of the assessment task always took precedence over ongoing learning activities (MacDonald & Twining, 2002). However, the use of systems that do not provide integrated assessment options (e.g., WebBoard®) means that the immediate feedback benefit is dependent on instructors, a process that becomes more time consuming with each student enrolled in the course.

A Framework for Aligning Content, Instruction, and Assessment

The previous example contains issues that face every college. Which is more challenging, perhaps onerous, for the instructor—preparing and grading unique assignments or using the test bank? Yet, by developing simple, theory-based tools, instructors can see ready alternatives to the quick and simple in instruction and assessment. The theories on which DePaul University's School for New Learning (SNL) bases its assessment are Bloom's Taxonomy (Bloom, Hastings, & Madaus, 1971) and the Backward Design Process, with its related Six Facets of Understanding (Wiggins & McTighe, 1998).

Educator Benjamin Bloom influenced education internationally, particularly through his clarification of levels of understanding in a structure he identified as the Taxonomy of Educational Objectives. Bloom's work involved analyzing the kinds of thinking required to respond to different types of questions or tasks. He established a way of thinking about thinking, from the simplest level of knowing a fact, through the complex task of synthesizing knowledge and applying it in other contexts:

- **Knowledge:** recall of specifics and patterns or generalizations
- **Comprehension:** restating, interpreting, extrapolating
- **Application:** using abstractions in specific situations
- **Analysis:** identifying and interpreting relationships and principles
- **Synthesis:** creating a new and unique combination or product
- **Evaluation:** appraising with logic (Bloom et al., 1971, pp. 271-273)

His taxonomy has become a standard for analyzing the level of complexity of the cognition required by a test question, developed through an activity, and assessed through a project.

Bloom introduced the term *mastery learning*, which was his vision of how to enable all learners to succeed (Bloom et al., 1971). He emphasized developing learner capacity through formative evaluation; if a learner did not succeed on an assessment, the learner would be given additional and alternative activities to increase the learner's capacity. According to Bloom et al. (1971), course evaluation precedes course assessment. The instructor first must evaluate course content to identify essential elements. The instructor must then identify thinking processes that students must demonstrate in order for the instructor to determine how effectively students have reached course goals. Restated as objectives, those goals are the basis for course design.

Bloom et al. (1971) worked with other educators to design a system that would link instructional objectives and assessment. The *Handbook on Formative and Summative Evaluation of Student Learning* (Bloom et al., 1971) provides a general blueprint for organizing any course content via a grid used to designate levels of cognition and types of content developed. Included with the grid are blueprints for the design of courses in all major content areas, with both cognitive and affective outcomes. Table 1 is adapted from Bloom's work and is intentionally content neutral, to be adaptable to different subjects.

Using this chart, instructors can assess the content of an existing course or plan a new course. It also functions as a study tool for an exam or an assessment in itself, with essential course content in the first column and an activity for each indicated in the column corresponding to the appropriate level of cognition required of students.

Building on Bloom (1971), Wiggins and McTighe (1998) outline the three-step Backward Design Process: identify desired results, determine acceptable evidence, then plan learning experiences and instruction. Their work on authentic assessment, the Six Facets of Understanding, has been incorporated by school districts in the planning of stan-

Table 1. Chart used for course content assessment, study tool, or student assessment (adapted from Bloom et al., 1971)

	Knowledge	Comprehension	Application	Analysis	Synthesis	Evaluation
Patterns						
Ideas						
Relationships						
Principles						

dards-based curriculum, but most elements of their model are appropriate for the college-level course, and might be more easily and appropriately applied by a college than a kindergarten. Imagine a kindergarten teacher figuring out the answer for, "To what extent does the idea, topic, or process represent a 'big idea' having enduring value beyond the classroom?" Then imagine a college instructor doing the same. The question is a valuable starting point in designing course instruction and assessment.

Wiggins and McTighe (1998) quote Stephen R. Covey as they begin to explain their model:

> *To begin with the end in mind means to start with a clear understanding of your destination. It means to know where you're going so that you better understand where you are now so that the steps you take are always in the right direction.* (p. 7)

They then proceed to clarify what is important to teach and how to define the destination. It is determination of the destination, the desired outcomes, which are critical for effective assessment.

Rather than cover many topics in a survey course, Wiggins and McTighe (1998) advise that less is much more, or *uncoverage*. They recommend the instructor choose important ideas and provide experiences that enable students to grasp those ideas thoroughly. In determining what that grasp entails, they filter content by asking four questions:

1.   To what extent does the idea, topic, or process represent a 'big idea' having enduring value beyond the classroom?

2.   To what extent does the idea, topic, or process reside at the heart of the discipline?

3.   To what extent does the idea, topic, or process require uncoverage?

4.   To what extent does the idea, topic, or process offer potential for engaging students? (Wiggins & McTighe, 1998, pp. 6-7)

In performance-based, authentic assessment, students learn content issues and details that do not meet the four filter criteria as they proceed through the assessment process, gaining expertise and an expanded knowledge base. In the six facets model, the facets

Table 2. The Six Facets of Understanding rubric, with comparison to Bloom's Taxonomy level (adapted from Wiggins & McTighe, 1998, pp. 76-77)

Facet	Levels of Understanding					Bloom's Level
Explanation	Naïve	Intuitive	Developed	In-Depth	Sophisticated	Knowledge
Interpretation	Literal	Interpreted	Perceptive	Revealing	Profound	Comprehension
Application	Novice	Apprentice	Able	Skilled	Masterful	Application
Perspective	Uncritical	Aware	Considered	Thorough	Insightful	Analysis
Empathy	Egocentric	Developing	Aware	Sensitive	Mature	Synthesis
Self-Knowledge	Innocent	Unreflective	Thoughtful	Circumspect	Wise	Evaluation

themselves represent increased understanding, and students are assessed on a continuum relevant to the facet (see Table 2).

The following online assessment example from a bioethics course at DePaul University's School for New Learning (SNL) in Chicago is of a contextual, multidimensional assessment. It requires students to work through several levels of both Bloom's Taxonomy (Bloom et al., 1971) and the Six Facets of Understanding (Wiggins & McTighe, 1998). In addition, it provides the instructor with a "voice" for the student, which can help identify subsequent academic dishonesty.

The Assignment

Assignments 8 through 10 ask you to assume the role of a Tuskegee subject, a Tuskegee investigator (one designing and performing the experiments), and a Tuskegee examiner (one reviewing the study after the abuses became known). In each role, discuss whether the study was an issue of personal life, morality, public policy, and/or legality and illegality. Still in that role, describe how the principles of autonomy, beneficence/benefit, nonmaleficence/absence of harm, and justice were addressed. When you complete Assignment 10, add a few sentences about any differences in perspective you experience.

Student 1

Tuskegee Subject

I am a Tuskegee subject. The study was not based on the ethics of personal life, because the doctors who decided to not treat me were affecting people other than themselves. It was not based on the ethics of a legal decision, because there was no law that they had to avoid treating me, and I don't think that they were required to treat me either.

The study was based on the ethics of public policy and morality. When the research was done, policy accepted that it was okay to just observe what happened in some cases, especially with African-Americans. Morally, the physicians' actions were definitely interpersonal in nature—them to/against us.

The ethical principles of autonomy, benefit, absence of harm, and justice were completely ignored. I was not allowed to make my own decisions about my care, because they all lied to me and let me know very clearly what they wanted me to do. They did harm, because I suffered the effects of advanced syphilis, including becoming blind. There was no benefit to me, because even though the doctors promised care for other illnesses, they didn't really want to. There was no justice, either, but I guess they really did treat us all equally, even if it was equally unjust.

Tuskegee Investigator

I am a Tuskegee investigator. I agree that the study was not based on the ethics of personal life, because our actions affected others besides ourselves. It was definitely not based on the ethics of legality, because I was not legally required to treat or not treat anyone.

I agree that the study was one of public policy, both because it was acceptable practice to observe natural progress of a disease and because syphilis was such a widespread problem that we had to find a way to understand it for the public good. The ethics of morality applied because medical research is always interpersonal.

We observed the principles of autonomy, benefit, absence of harm, and justice, even though we did not have to because the laws making us do so did not exist. Subjects were notified that they were ill and had the option to either participate or not. They could have gone to another doctor if they wanted to. We offered them travel money, food, and treatment for other illnesses, just not the syphilis, because eventually even their people would benefit by what we learned by watching the disease. I guess we did not observe the principle of absence of harm, but we saw it as a justifiable tradeoff. The subjects were harmed, but we did not harm them directly and we learned a lot from the incidental harm they had. We treated everyone equally.

Tuskegee Examiner

I am a Tuskegee examiner. The Tuskegee study was not based on the ethics of personal life, because it definitely affected other people than the investigators. A close look at the laws in effect then will probably show that doctors were not required by law to treat anyone. The question of public policy ethics is interesting because even though policy was unfair to African-Americans, it supported the doctors' right to observe natural progress of a disease and to do what was necessary to examine a problem that affected the public. It is true that doctors treated everyone in the study equally, but the treatment was bad, even though bad treatment of African-Americans was acceptable to many people then.

The principle of autonomy was met, but only in a very basic way. Subjects were lied to when they were unable to judge truth from lies, so their choices weren't really choices. Any benefit involved was also questionable, because the benefits that the doctors said they offered to subjects were based on lies. There was a lot of harm done, although technically the doctors did not directly cause the harm because of the way that laws were written. Also, every subject was treated equally badly, so the issue of justice is also questionable.

Summary

Each one agrees on the ethical base of the question, but the principles that currently exist are different. Subjects believe that they were lied to and misled, which means autonomy was not there, they were denied real benefits and offered only benefits based on lies, definitely harmed, and treated badly, although equally badly. Investigators believe that they followed the spirit and the letter of the law, balancing benefits for everyone against harm against a few. Examiners disagree with the investigators, but say that the investigators acted the way that people then acted. By today's standards, the investigators were very wrong.

The student has actively demonstrated several levels of both Bloom's Taxonomy and various levels of the six facets. In addition, the instructor has a sense of how the student writes and the clarity with which the student presents ideas. As this is obviously not a first assignment, the student's work can be compared to previous submissions, other types of assessment, and subsequent assignments, if concerns exist about academic integrity.

Valid Assessments

Colleges that introduce online courses face the challenge of faculty transition from classroom to the online environment. While methods of instruction and assessment from the traditional college classroom can be imported into online courses, issues of passivity and authenticity of students' work make traditional assessments problematic. Yet, as demonstrated, assessments based on Bloom's Taxonomy (Bloom et al., 1971), the Backward Design Process, and the Six Facets of Understanding (Wiggins & McTighe, 1998) are readily applicable to online courses, despite being developed for the classroom. Indeed, successfully addressing the challenges of structured online instruction and assessment might lead to reform of classroom methods. Joseph Schumpeter's economic concept of "creative destruction," introduced to clarify the impact of innovations, could just as easily be applied to the potential impact of online course development, especially when those courses require students not only to prepare differently for their assessments, but also to participate differently during the course itself.

Assessment at SNL is based on the work of Bloom et al. (1971) and Wiggins and McTighe (1998), but also on the core learning competencies of college writing, critical thinking, collaborative learning, quantitative reasoning, and inquiry and research. In addition, the key concepts of self-reflection, historical consciousness, and ethical awareness are integral to each course. As complicated as that design structure might sound, implementation is simplified greatly using formal and informal rubrics, including Table 1 and Table 2, where criteria for assessing Levels of Understanding are inserted into Table 2.

Table 3 illustrates the overall construction, merging theory base, core learning competencies, and key concepts. Supporting Wiggins and McTighe's (1998) Backward Design Process, instructors plot the assignments developed in Table 1 and Table 2, then identify the core competencies and concepts represented. Instructors sometimes see the potential for incorporating another aspect; for example, one of the authors originally noted that Inquiry and Research was not represented, but was certainly applicable to the Topic Literature Review assignment, and adjusted the assignment accordingly.

Table 3. Composite SNL assessment rubric developed for the course Everyday Biomedical Ethics

Assignment Title	Bloom	Wiggins and McTighe	Core Learning Competency(ies)	Concept(s)
	(up to and including)			
Common Mistakes	Comprehension	Interpretation	• College Writing • Critical Thinking	• Self-Reflection • Ethical Awareness
Topic Literature Reviews	Analysis	Perspective	• Critical Thinking • Inquiry and Research	• Historical Consciousness • Ethical Awareness
Tuskegee Subjects	Synthesis	Empathy	• College Writing • Critical Thinking	• Historical Consciousness • Ethical Awareness
Tuskegee Investigators	Synthesis	Empathy	• College Writing • Critical Thinking	• Historical Consciousness • Ethical Awareness
Tuskegee Examiners	Synthesis	Empathy	• College Writing • Critical Thinking	• Historical Consciousness • Ethical Awareness
Autobiography and Addendum	Evaluation	Self-Knowledge	• College Writing • Critical Thinking	• Self-Reflection • Historical Consciousness • Ethical Awareness

Virtual discussion, one of 11 assessment methods described by Benson (2003), is integral to the program at SNL. While synchronous, or real-time, discussion more closely resembles a traditional classroom environment, it reduces the flexibility of distance education, especially in the case of working students, students who travel regularly, or students who span time zones. Asynchronous discussion does not limit those students, nor does it reinforce the negative aspects of an immediate-response format (Benson, 2003). Students have the opportunity to read both the assignment and other students' postings, thoughtfully prepare a response that integrates what they have read with what they believe, and only then respond to the discussion (Benson, 2003; Wade, 1999). In fact, SNL's participation guidelines clearly define the rubric to be followed, which includes evidence of personal reflection and integration of prior responses to the topic. An additional benefit to asynchronous discussion is that, especially in the case of emotional topics such as case-based ethics, students have the opportunity to modify responses that might be reactionary and detrimental to continued discussion.

"The use of threaded discussion in many distance learning classes also provides a point of evaluation through an analysis of the types of questions posed, the types of responses given, the depth of the observations between teacher and student and student and student, and the number of posted entries" (Wade, 1999, p. 95). Instructors can assess student learning over the span of a course by noting changes in the depth of a student's response, as well as the tone of the postings. However, depending on how defined the rubric and the personality of the student involved, using the actual number of postings as an assessment tool should be approached with caution.

Consider the impact of threaded discussion on the attentiveness and self-directedness of learners while reading the following exchange from a recent SNL leadership course:

Student 2

In my future professional life, I want to be a leader that provides clear direction with innovative ideas, and lead a global organization to overall success. I truly enjoy working with people, and believe that I have a good balance of a caring/requiring management style, and general management skills. With these qualities as a foundation, I want to continue to develop my visionary leadership skills, the ability to effectively assist an organization to adapt to change, and better understand global business organizations. I also want to clearly and rationally create and foster a diverse workforce and workplace. My focus area will be Business Administration with a focus on Management and Leadership.

I am currently in a leadership role, and I understand the information needed to create my professional future. By taking the appropriate business and leadership courses, I will be able to integrate and apply my knowledge from my education in my everyday work experiences. I have reviewed the SNL Course Guide and found several interesting courses, such as Social Responsibility of Leadership, The Spirit of Organizational Change, Roles and Responsibilities of Organizational Leaders, and several others that will foster my professional development. These courses should provide me with the skills and knowledge needed to attain my professional goals and create my professional future.

Student 3

Response to Student 2

I enjoyed reading your post. You seem to have clarity on your goals and the path you would like to take. I kept seeing the word "global" in your post, which is a concept I find overwhelming! I find it difficult to try to understand the variances in American culture, let alone foreign societies. You seem very aware of your goals and how to obtain them. Good luck!

Student 2

Response to Student 3

Thanks for the response, I am about 95% sure of what I want to do when I grow up, however, one of the only constants in life is change...so you just never know.

Student 3

Response to Student 2

And yet that change, in a global and national sense, is what I find threatening to career development. Do you have resources that you regularly read that you'd recommend? I know that I need to understand what you've talked about, but have no idea, really, of where to start.

Concept mapping was once limited by students' access to specialized software such as Inspiration® and MindMap®, but has become much easier to accomplish now that word processing and presentation software programs have integrated drawing tools (Benson, 2003).

Conducted periodically during a period of study, concept maps can show how student comprehension changes over time (Frederick, 2002). Concept maps provide instructors with feedback on learner understanding and identify places where instructional emphasis should be placed. As such, concept maps are good formative assessment tools. (Benson, 2003, p. 75).

For example, in SNL's "Women of Science" course, students explore the historical, societal, and technical world of a female scientist before moving on to explore the scientist's work and the ramifications of that work. A concept map diagrammed early in the course might focus on the historical and societal world, showing relationships between each. By the time students have added the remaining components, relationship lines would be expected between societal and technological, technological and ramifications, and so on.

Portfolio development is another effective method of online assessment, and one that can be formative, as well as summative (Benson, 2003; Biswalo, 2001; Brown, 2002). In its simplest form, as an accumulation of student work with periodic review and reflection, a student portfolio can easily be integrated into a course; at SNL, students often have a course-specific "personal conference," or folder, accessible only by the instructor and the student.

For example, in an ethics course students are asked to follow a clearly defined rubric to document their current opinions about the topics to be addressed in the course, and to write an ethics autobiography. Subsequent work is saved in the personal conference, as well as posted to the virtual discussion. However, the saved work includes personal reaction that the student might not feel comfortable making available to the class. Instructor-student conversation occurs within the personal conference. Finally, students revisit their initial opinions, reflect on them in light of what they learned in the course, and write an addendum to their autobiographies. Such a portfolio integrates higher-level cognitive skills, complex learning, and multistage tasks. In fact, every instructor who uses multiple techniques can create a summative portfolio system, especially those who teach online, where student work can be archived.

Problem-solving simulations engage students' higher-level cognitive skills through guided, real-world learning experiences (Benson, 2003). For example, at *www.dnai.org,* Cold Spring Harbor Laboratories maintains a Web site that addresses the pseudoscience of eugenics, including the laboratory's role in its promulgation. Associated with the site is a series of excellent learning modules about the very real applications of genetics, including problem-solving simulations about the role of genetics in solving crimes, determining the identity of bodies (focusing on the last royal family of tsarist Russia), and the biochemistry behind DNA molecules. Each module is interactive, most modules incorporate immediate feedback, and some include assessment tools that can be printed or downloaded for submission to an instructor.

The use of *individual and group projects* is highly recommended, especially group projects (Benson, 2003; McLoughlin & Luca, 2002). Project work employs higher-order cognitive skills in professional-level tasks that are multidimensional and collaborative, and that involve project management skills (Benson, 2003; McLoughlin & Luca, 2002; Reeves, 2000). The product can be Web-based, such as videotape, presentation software, or posted written product, and is limited only by the resources available to the students and teacher (Benson, 2003).

Group projects at SNL incorporate both *peer feedback* and *informal student feedback*, two more of Benson's options and methods routinely used by the authors in both classroom and online courses. Peer assessment results in "increased student responsibility and autonomy" (Zhi-Feng Liu & Yuan, 2003, p. 350). Students find "peer assessment challenging, beneficial, making them think more and learn more. In another study, Gatfield (10) indicated a positive acceptance by the students in the method of peer assessment. Students in Gatfield's study pointed out they have understood the assessment process, peers can assess fairly and so on" (Zhi-Feng Liu & Yuan, 2003, p. 350). Moreover, peer and informal student feedback are easily arranged in the online environment, employing "rich and easy methods of obtaining informal feedback on individual student progress" (Benson, 2003, p. 77). One-minute papers, peer and group assessment tools based on clearly defined rubrics established prior to commencement of the project, and open-ended student conversation are simple options (Benson, 2003; McLoughlin & Luca, 2002).

The dialogue also provides students a perspective on their own work, as well as the work of others. The following exchange by SNL students in a research methods course demonstrates the integrative and evaluative thinking that develops.

Student 4

The Effectiveness of an Age-Restricted Community in Reducing Suicidal Thoughts Among the Elderly

Hi (Student 5). I read your proposal and thought it was very interesting. Your literature review makes sense to me, especially since you included adult development as a topic. I don't know whether the discussion of suicide needs to include teen suicide, though, because it sounds as if the reasons are very different. I wonder whether the reasons for older-person suicide will change as the Baby Boomers get older? Should that be included, or do you think that's even been looked at yet? Your methods both are asking for the same information, so you have a true mixed method design. I can't tell whether your informed consent arrangement is okay. It seems as if this would be a tricky thing. Do you think people will be honest during interviews? Surveys make sense since their names aren't on them, but there has to be a way for the survey to be tied to the interview, so I wonder whether they'll feel comfortable talking about it. Just a thought.

Student 6

Cloning: Changes in Perspectives Over 10 Years

I agree with you that cloning isn't a good idea. But remember when we talked about how you have to put your personal opinion aside as much as possible if you do a research project on something you have an opinion about? I don't think you've done that enough. A lot of your resources are from anti-cloning groups or have an anti-cloning message, but you have to talk about both sides. It sounds kind of like you're working on a debate topic, where you talk about just one side. I like your methods, though! You have a quantitative way to track publications and a way to evaluate how they change. Just be sure that you count both sides. And I think the reason you're having trouble designing a consent form is because you aren't going to talk to people. I think this is one of those projects that is exempted. You should ask Jennifer whether you need to do this.

Self-assessment is consistently incorporated into SNL courses, particularly in conjunction with portfolio development, peer feedback, and concept mapping, as described. During 2004, SNL introduced a framework for self-assessment in both online and classroom courses, based on recent developments in historical consciousness. Called "then-now-next," this simple assessment structure asks students to report at the beginning of the course their understanding of the major elements of the course. Then at midpoint and at the completion of the course, they update that explanation and project how they will apply their new knowledge "next"—in their work, in their life, in their studies.

Incorporating peer review and self-assessment into online courses is not only cited as pedagogically sound, but it also eases the work required from faculty who use diversified, performance-based assessment methods. In addition, activities which require a student voice are inherently active and, to a larger degree, identify and address concerns about both passivity and academic dishonesty. Diversified, sequential assessment reveals depth of understanding, while accounting for individual learning styles and normal student variation, whether during a term or an entire program of study.

Conclusion

Quality assessment leads to excellence in instruction through quality evaluation. The development of assessments that truly measure student ability require multidimensional approaches that account for performance variation over time, within and between a disciplines' core principles, patterns, and relationships. Quality online assessment also actively develops a student voice, addressing the issues of passivity and academic dishonesty, by requiring students to both prepare for and participate differently during courses.

SNL faculty have successfully developed assessments based on Bloom's Taxonomy (Bloom et al., 1971), the Backward Design Process, and the Six Facets of Understanding (Wiggins & McTighe, 1998) for both online and classroom courses. Developing assessments that are multidimensional in terms of the type of activity, the theory on which each is based, and the level of sophistication expected from the student implies a level of faculty sophistication as well. Building faculty capacity is facilitated by the introduction of rubrics that are easy to use, but that are thoroughly grounded in theory and that reflect the realities of practice. Incorporating rubrics, theory and reflective practice, every college can build teaching and assessment capacity through systematic evaluation.

References

Benson, A.D. (2003). Assessing participant learning in online environments. *New Directions for Adult and Continuing Education, Winter*(100), 69-78.

Biswalo, P. (2001). The systems approach as a catalyst for creating an effective learning environment for adults in part-time and distance learning. *Convergence, 34*(1), 53-66.

Bloom, B., Hastings, J., & Madaus, G. (1971). *Handbook on formative and summative evaluation of student learning.* New York: McGraw-Hill.

Brown, J.O. (2002). Know thyself: The impact of portfolio development on adult learning. *Adult Education Quarterly, 52*(3), 228-245.

Lee, J. (2001). Instructional support for distance education and faculty motivation, commitment, satisfaction. *British Journal of Educational Technology, 32*(2), 153-160.

Macdonald, J., & Twining, P. (2002). Assessing activity-based learning for a networked course. *British Journal of Educational Technology, 33*(5), 603-618.

McLoughlin, C., & Luca, J. (2002). A learner-centred approach to developing team skills through Web-based learning and assessment. *British Journal of Educational Technology, 33*(5), 571-582.

Reeves, T.C. (2000). Alternative assessment approaches for online learning environments in higher education. *Journal of Educational Computing Research, 23*(1), 101-111.

Rittschof, K.A., & Griffin, B.W. (2003). Confronting limitations of cyberspace college courses: Part I: Identifying and describing issues. *International Journal of Instructional Media, 30*(2), 127-141.

Robles, M., & Braathen, S. (2002). Online assessment techniques. *The Delta Pi Epsilon Journal, XLIV*(1), 39-49.

Wade, W. (1999). Assessment in distance learning: What do students know and how do we know that they know it? *T.H.E. Journal, 27*(3), 94-96.

Wiggins, G., & McTighe, J. (1998). *Understanding by design.* Alexandria, VA: Association for Supervision and Curriculum Development.

Zhi-Feng Liu, E., & Yuan, S. (2003). A study of students' attitudes toward and desired system requirement of networked peer assessment system. *International Journal of Instructional Media, 30*(4), 349-354.

Chapter XVII

Evaluating Content-Management Systems for Online Learning Programs

Deborah L. Schnipke, Virtual Psychometrics, LLC, USA

Kirk Becker, University of Illinois and Promissor, USA

James S. Masters, University of North Carolina at Greensboro and Promissor, USA

Abstract

Creating quality assessments typically requires the involvement of many people who require access to the item and test information, which is stored in repositories called item banks or, more appropriately, content-management systems, since they store many kinds of content used in the test development process. This chapter discusses the types of options that are available in content-management systems and provides guidance about how to evaluate whether different content-management systems will meet an organization's test development and delivery needs. This chapter focuses on online, fully Internet-enabled applications, since those applications have the most features.

Introduction

Everyone is assessed and evaluated throughout his or her entire life, both formally and informally. Some of these assessments are in the form of tests—either written (e.g., multiple-choice or essay tests) or performance-based (e.g., the driving portion of a driver's license exam). Because everyone has been assessed many times, it sometimes seems that creating a test is routine and simple—write some items, package them into a test, administer the test, and give a score based on the performance. When tests are used to make important decisions about the test takers' future (e.g., whether they can work in the field they have trained for), it is imperative that the test be psychometrically sound.

That is, the scores must be meaningful: the scores should be accurate (i.e., be reliable) and their interpretations should be backed by evidence and theory that supports the proposed uses of the test (i.e., be valid; AERA, APA, & NCME, 1999). Ensuring the psychometrics integrity of a test is much more complex than the simple steps mentioned above. Following the general approach of major test publishers (such as Educational Testing Service or ACT, Inc.), the steps for developing a psychometrically sound test might be:

1.   Carefully determine the content domain of the test (e.g., focus groups with subject matter experts, job task analysis, etc.).
2.   Develop a detailed test blueprint to map the test to the domain of interest.
3.   Write items to match the test blueprint (e.g., in terms of specific content areas, item types, conventions).
4.   Review the items for technical and editorial accuracy.
5.   Field test the items to gather statistical evidence about the items.
6.   If a pass/fail or similar decision will be made with the scores, determine those cutscores using psychometrically accepted methods.
7.   Build the operational test forms using the field-tested items such that the test scores will be reliable, valid, and fair.
8.   Publish the test for delivery.
9.   Administer the test and score the test takers.
10.   Monitor the test results.
11.   Field test new items for future forms.
12.   Refresh or replace operational test forms periodically to prevent items from being used for too long; these forms must be statistically comparable to previous forms.

Before desktop computers and the Internet were widely available, the test development process used by major test publishers was rather tedious by today's standards. For example, one method of keeping track of item revisions and statistics was to keep every item on a 4x6" index card with statistics placed on labels on the back. As the item was revised, new versions of the item were stapled to the front, and as the item was administered multiple times, new versions of the statistics were added to more cards.

To assemble items into test forms, test developers sorted through the cards, grouped them into test forms while balancing content and statistical properties. All of this was done manually. After the forms were approved, the items had to be retyped to create test booklets, which were then printed, copied, and distributed. Examinees took the test, and then waited several months to get their results while the tests were mailed back, answer sheets were scanned on mainframe computers, and results were compiled and analyzed.

Computers revolutionized how item and test data were stored and how tests were produced (Baker, 1986; Bergstrom & Gershon, 1995; Wright & Bell, 1984). Item banking software has been developed to manage the items, item statistics, classification codes, and other information about the items, alleviating the need to manually track this information. Item banking systems usually store information about the test and summary statistics about the items as well.

The Internet also brought about major changes. Test developers, psychometricians, subject matter experts, and committee members began sending files through e-mail, rather than the mail. This greatly reduced turnaround time on reviewing items, comments, and so forth, but had the potential for significantly reducing security if files were sent unencrypted.

Another advance came with the advent of laptop computers that could be taken to remote committee meetings. To maintain the security of the item banks, normally a subset of the banks was exported, and all changes from the meetings were painstakingly entered into the item bank and carefully checked.

The desire to share information over the Internet and to review items and tests at remote committee meetings has led to fully Internet-enabled item banking applications that allow multiple authorized users to access the item bank from anywhere that has access to the Internet. These systems provide much greater security than sending files via e-mail, and are far more efficient than exporting the item bank for offline review, then re-importing the changes.

Today's advanced Internet-enabled systems are also far more than a repository for storing items and their statistics. They store all kinds of content and are now often being called content-management systems, a general term used to describe a system used to organize and facilitate collaborative content creation. A high-quality content-management system facilitates the entire test development and delivery process. The present chapter discusses the types of options that are available in content-management systems specialized for assessment and provides guidance about how to evaluate whether different content-management systems will meet an organization's test development and delivery needs. This chapter focuses on online, fully Internet-enabled applications, since those applications have the most features. The chapter first covers the general issues faced by organizations when implementing an assessment program, using a psychometric perspective. It provides a series of questions that an organization must answer to determine its assessment needs. When evaluating various content-management systems, the organization can compare its answers for each content-management system to determine which best meets its needs. The information provided in this chapter is intended to help organizations create a disciplined approach for evaluating their own test development requirements, and make informed decisions on how to select and implement a content-management system best suited to their needs.[1]

Online Content-Management Systems

Ideally, content-management systems specialized for assessment data provide secure, widespread access to items, item data, and tests. The time and effort required to produce quality assessments frequently requires the participation of dozens of individuals, including item writers and other subject matter experts, psychometricians, program managers, data entry technicians, and multimedia developers. Aside from the communication challenges facing these collaborators due to their different job goals and workplace competencies, there can be technical challenges of time and proximity that make it much more difficult to produce assessment instruments that meet rigorous standards of reliability, validity, and fairness under tight production constraints and rapid development cycles of the modern online learning environment. Online content-management systems can enable these disparate collaborators to review and revise item and test data in real time, even if they are geographically spread out.

Storing assessment content in a database does little to help team members create a quality assessment if they do not know how to access or use it or, worse, if they do not understand its relevance. Experienced test developers know that content management for assessment includes an array of features necessary for easy item-data management (Bergstrom & Gershon, 1995). Items need to be stored accurately and be easily retrieved based on numerous criteria. Test developers must be able to associate cross-references with their content and define a variety of item attributes such as item content codes, text references, and item statistics. When evaluating content-management systems, it is important to recognize the importance of features like these that make the processes of inputting, storing, and retrieving test data as efficient as possible. A quality content-management system, then, puts people in touch with assessment data in meaningful ways and aids test development teams to build assessments efficiently within an environment that minimizes human error.

To allow for rapid development of assessments for online learning programs, the item-banking system should integrate directly with the organization's content delivery system (Schroeder, 1993). The content-management system may be thought of as the overarching system for storing and managing test content, and providing test development and delivery tools. By integrating the various aspects into a single technology application, a quality content-management application can not only help facilitate rapid content deployment, but help reduce the likelihood of errors developing because all operations are housed under a single, integrated application.

No evaluation of a content-management system can be complete without considering security (Schroeder & Houghton, 1996; Way, 1998; Way & Steffan, 1997). The item pool is the most valuable asset of any assessment program. As such, content-management systems must be secured for online transactions by guaranteeing very high levels of both physical and authentication security. The extent to which physical security can be enforced depends on how these systems are designed to send and receive online transactions. Ideally, no direct access to the database should be granted to any user, and all transactions should pass through either a proprietary application or, if the system is Web-enabled, an application server. With regard to access security, user ID and password authentication should be enforced at all levels. Different users will need access to different functions and features, and a quality content-management system will make it easy to assign varying access rights. While a high-quality content-management system must permit access and participation from remote subject matter experts, item writers, and other test developers, it must do so in a way that does not compromise the security of the content.

It is not enough to create an assessment in a secure manner. The assessment also needs to be delivered to examinees in a secure and reliable manner. Results need to be returned to the sponsor organization in the form of data and reports. The data need to be accurately and securely stored. The data must also be easy to retrieve and summarize, but only by authorized users of the system.

One potential issue with item banking systems, content-management systems, and learning management systems in general is that each system may have its own proprietary data structure, and transferring information between systems is not trivial. If an online learning program wishes to use multiple systems or change systems, considerable effort may be required to move the data between systems. To address this issue, standards for learning and test content have been developed, such as the Shareable Content Object Reference Model (SCORM) used by the U.S. Department of Defense (for an example, see *www.adlnet.org*). By using standard data formats and structures, data can be passed between compliant systems, which may be a large benefit to a program that wishes to have the option to use multiple systems.

Understanding the sometimes dizzying array of requirements associated with content-management systems demands a disciplined and thorough understanding of how the assessment will be used and how the results will be interpreted. The questions in the following sections are intended to help organizations consider what aspects of a content-management system are most important for their particular needs. This information will help the organization evaluate the various content-management systems to determine which will best meet their needs.

Laying the Groundwork

As an organization evaluates content-management systems, there are several questions that need to be considered to make sure that the various needs of different users will be met. These questions include: Who will require access to the data and information? What information will they need access to? How and where will they access the information?

Who Will Require Access to the Data and Information?

There are a minimum of three categories of users who will require access to item and test data and information. The first group consists of the measurement professionals who work on the tests. Test developers and editors work primarily with the items and the forms. They need to enter, edit, and classify new items in the system; develop and publish new forms; and manage the pool of items (e.g., taking inventories and performing periodic reviews). Psychometricians are generally most interested in analyzing the item and test statistics. Working with committees of subject matter experts or using equating procedures, they use the information to set the passing standards for new forms. Psychometricians may also assist the test developers by developing scoring routines.

The second group consists of the clients and subject matter experts who work with the test developers and psychometricians. Subject matter experts are often asked to review, revise, and approve items and forms. Clients may want to monitor their item pools. They may also want access to retired items to publish sample tests or practice items. Clients also need access to examinee information and results.

The third group of people who will likely need access to the data and information are the program directors or account managers. Program directors and account managers need access to information about all aspects of the program including examinee results, testing volume, and financial reports.

What Information/Tools Will They Need Access to?

There are several types of information and tools that different users will need to access. Information includes item data, other test content, and examinee results. Tools include test-building tools, querying tools, and summarizing tools. Access to the raw data is required for anyone who needs to check a result, confirm a response, or analyze the data in any way. In general, data within the system must be organized in a logical way. Data must be available for export in a format that can be readily imported into a variety of external systems. Ideally, the exports should be customizable if required by a client.

Item data. Item data include the items themselves, plus any information that is specific to the items. The associated information may include item ID, content codes, item statistics, cases/exhibits, item-specific help screens, item feedback, enemy associations, item author, item status (e.g., pretest or operational; scored or unscored), references, keywords, comments, description, version number, item-timing information, and user-defined attributes. The system must be flexible to allow users to adapt the system to their needs, rather than adapting their needs to the system capabilities. The item bank and test administration engine must know what each of these elements is and how to use the information. For example, indicating whether an item is scored or unscored is not useful unless the administration engine carries out the scoring according to the codes.

Test data. At a minimum, test data includes the list of items to be administered (or a pool from which to select the items) and information about how to select the items (e.g., fixed sequence or an adaptive algorithm). Test data may also include test name, test version, comments, time limits, time limit warnings, whether a response is allowed on a timeout, test scoring algorithm, interpretations for scoring ranges (e.g., fail/pass/pass with distinction), test level feedback, permissible navigation tools for the test takers (e.g., specifying whether examinees can review previous items), an indication of whether examinees must answer the items before moving to the next item, message screens, and score reports.

Examinee data. Examinee data includes the responses they gave to each item, ideally not only their final response, but also the history of all responses they selected for each item. In addition, examinee data includes time spent on each item (ideally time spent on each visit to the item), test score, test interpretation (e.g., pass/fail), and comments. There should be a complete record about each examinee's testing experience, indicating all the screens they viewed, for how long, and every response they gave. This type of record summarizes the entire testing experience, which is invaluable for research purposes, investigating examinee complaints, and for confirming test results.

Test-building/summarizing tools. Test-building tools include tools for specifying what elements are incorporated in the test and in what order, and specifying how the test is scored. Automated test assembly is another possible test-building tool. Other test-building/summarizing tools include calculating word count, overlap between test forms, test level statistics, the number of items with each key position (i.e., the number of items with "A" as the correct answer, "B" as the correct answer, etc.), and the number of items by content code, status, author, or other code. Other tools include summarizing questions with missing codes or statistics, summarizing which codes are used on the test, summarizing user-defined codes, and listing the text of any custom scripts used on the test. Users also need a tool for updating fields in multiple items at once.

Querying tools. Users need to be able to search for specific information in the item banks, thus the system must have extensive querying capabilities. Users need to be able to query on content codes, status codes, user-defined codes, statistics, item types, text strings, and enemies (items that cannot be administered to the same examinee). Users must be able to combine queries using logical operators (and, or, and not). After users generate a query, they need to be able to do things with the result, such as insert the items into a test, update the items simultaneously, and export data for the items.

Examinee-summarizing tools. Examinee-summarizing tools include calculating examinee test results for both individual examinees and groups of examinees (e.g., item-level data, scores, and pass/fail status), summarizing registration and testing volume, creating accounting reports, item usage reports, and so forth.

How and Where Will the Different Users Access the Data and Information?

Users will find the system most useful if they can access it from a variety of locations, including from work, home, and while traveling. One of the obvious benefits of an online content-management system is that it can be made available anywhere the Internet is available. For those occasions when Internet access is not available, users must be able to export the data in a format that is accessible (i.e., rich text files or spreadsheets), make their changes, and import the data back into the system. It is critical that access be limited to authorized users and that data access be secure.

Determining the Features of an Online System

The appropriateness of an online environment for a particular program depends very much on the requirements of the program and the resources available to that program (Choppin, 1985). For example if assessments are provided in a location with slow Internet connectivity, an online delivery system is inappropriate for media-intensive items. Issues of content, item type, item and test scoring, delivery model, delivery location, and stakes all need to be considered when deciding whether an online environment is appropriate for an assessment program.

Where Will the Assessment be Offered?

Probably the most important question relating to the delivery of online content is whether the assessment will be predominantly server-side or client-side. The answer to this question will be impacted by the program requirements for where the assessment is offered. A server-side assessment is appropriate when maximum flexibility is required for the assessment environment. Self-administered assessments, or assessments occurring in highly variable locations, are prime candidates for server-side delivery. In environments where physical security can be maximized, or where processor-intensive algorithms are needed, a client-side model is more appropriate for administration. Client-side administration may offer a more standardized environment.

What Type of Content Will be Assessed?

The content of the test and the types of items featured on the test may make online assessment infeasible. Assessments featuring video and sound stimuli may be flexible in terms of delivery platform while requiring fast and reliable Internet connectivity. Tests that require precise graphics or colors (e.g., color-vision assessment or medical slides) require a standardized platform for the delivery of content as well as fast Internet connections. Any items involving precise stimulus or response timing (e.g., reaction time tests) require standardized delivery platforms. Interactive items may not be graphics-intensive, but may require additional software or processor time to run. Because of the built-in features of browsers, programs requiring multi-language presentation or software plug-ins may be more cost effective in a browser-based environment.

How is the Assessment Administered and Scored?

The algorithms used to score items and tests, and the frequency with which those algorithms are run, will also influence the choice of administration environment. Highly iterative or otherwise processor-intensive scoring models could slow down the administration of an assessment, often to unacceptable levels. Although simple item response theory (IRT) algorithms no longer take an enormous amount of time to process, there are still other procedures that cannot feasibly be executed during test administration. It is possible to administer complex and innovative assessments online without regard to complexities of scoring if results are not reported immediately. Written assessments (e.g., essays) on online assessments are almost exclusively scored after the assessment is completed.[2]

Closely related to the scoring of the test is the delivery model. Adaptive tests require ongoing scoring and item selection, as well as relatively large banks of items, while fixed-form tests require little by way of continuous processing and are relatively small. Recently introduced adaptive testlets require large banks of content, but relatively little computation during administration.

How Often is the Assessment Updated?

The updating of an assessment covers both the introduction of new forms as well as the development of new items. The capability of assessment locations for receiving electronic files will impact the frequency with which updates are made to content in a client-side administration (Luecht & Nungester, 1998). Expectations for changes to active and experimental items will therefore need to be taken into account when implementing an online assessment program.

What are the Stakes of the Assessment?

The stakes of the assessment include the importance of assessment results to examinees and the public. Flexible assessment locations are less important when security of content and authentication of examinee identity is critical. Experimental, research-based assessments, on the other hand, may be less concerned with who is taking an assessment than with the widespread use of the instrument.

Testing programs will generally have features important to both client-side and server-side, online and offline, and complex vs. traditional formats. The intention of this section is to highlight the issues that interact and influence decisions for the structure of an online assessment.

What Student Learning Outcomes Will be Measured?

The particular student learning outcomes that will be measured will also play a role in determining what features are important in the item-banking or content-management system. Once a program has articulated student learning goals, it can design ways to assess whether students have met them, and the test development and delivery systems must support the desired types of assessments.

Will Multiple Systems be Used?

If multiple systems (e.g., learning management systems, item-banking systems, delivery systems) will be used, how well do they share data? One way to promote ease of data sharing is to use systems that conform to the same standards, such as SCORM. When evaluating a system, things to consider include: which standards are supported, how many of the standards have been implemented, can the system be customized to work with another particular system, and exactly what data is stored. Even systems that are SCORM compliant may have implemented the standards slightly differently, so asking these questions is important.

Prioritization of Features

Choosing or developing an online item-banking, assessment delivery, and reporting system requires prioritization of features according to the needs of an assessment program. The checklist in Table 1 offers one method for making decisions on the structure of a program and whether the system fits with the program needs. The table lists common features of assessment programs relevant to content-management, delivery, and data services (Bergstrom & Gershon, 1995; Schroeder, 1993). For each feature, the relative needs of the assessment program and the importance of those needs can be indicated. Assessing the importance of the program features will allow for prioritization when mutually exclusive features are selected (e.g., low-speed connections and graphics-intensive stimuli) or when budgeting the program.

Conclusion

Early item-banking systems were essentially a repository for storing items and their statistics. They have evolved over time into powerful content-management systems that combine item banking, test building, and test delivery. Each content-management system has different features, and each program has a different set of requirements. It is important to have a disciplined and thorough understanding of how the assessment will be used

Table 1. Summary of sample prioritization features

Consideration	Program Characteristic		Importance	Comments
Item Banking				
Where are item reviewers located?	Geographically diverse	Central location	1 2 3 4 5	If geographic diversity for item writers or reviewers is an important aspect of the program, online access to item banks will be a key feature of the item banking software.
Where are item writers located?	Geographically diverse	Central location	1 2 3 4 5	
Test Assembly				
How often is the assessment updated?	Frequent need for updates	Static test/few updates	1 2 3 4 5	Situations in which content is frequently (or continuously) updated are prime candidates for server-side administration.
What are the stakes of the assessment?	High stakes	Low stakes	1 2 3 4 5	The ability to tailor access privileges for content is vital for high-stakes assessment programs.
Test Delivery				
Where will the assessment be offered?	Controlled environment	Flexible/uncontrolled environment	1 2 3 4 5	A flexible or uncontrolled environment will generally require online administration using a server-side delivery model.
Connectivity of assessment locations	High speed	Low speed	1 2 3 4 5	The need to accommodate low-speed connectivity will require either offline administration or minimal graphics and interactivity.
What type of content will be assessed?	Graphics intensive	Text/low graphics	1 2 3 4 5	Complex and graphics-intensive items present a risk for online server-side administration.
	Complex/interactive	Simple/traditional	1 2 3 4 5	
Integrity of the stimulus	High precision needed	Stimulus variability acceptable	1 2 3 4 5	The need for precise standardization of stimulus presentation requires quality control at all computers used for the assessment.
How is the assessment administered?	Processor intensive	Low processor demand	1 2 3 4 5	If item scoring is not integral to administration processor-intensive scoring, algorithms can be ameliorated through delayed reporting of assessment results. A client-side model should be considered when both scoring and administration require advanced algorithms.
How is the assessment scored?	Processor intensive	Low processor demand	1 2 3 4 5	

and results will be interpreted so that a systematic approach can be followed in evaluating the various systems to determine which best suits an organization's needs. The best approach is to consider in advance who needs access, the types of information that will be required, how the users will access the system, where the tests will be administered, what type of content will be on the test, how the test is administered and scored, how often the tests are updated, and the stakes of the test. After answering these questions, evaluating the different content-management systems becomes much more systematic,

Table 1. (cont.)

Consideration	Program Characteristic		Importance	Comments
How often is the assessment updated?	Frequent need for updates	Static test/few updates	1 2 3 4 5	From the perspective of administration, a server-side model is best when an assessment is frequently changed or updated.
What are the stakes of the assessment?	High stakes	Low stakes	1 2 3 4 5	Authentication of results is critical in a high-stakes situation, however an online system may still be used to deliver assessments to a secure location.
Security				
Where will the item bank be hosted?	Local server/network	Hosted server	1 2 3 4 5	With a local server, security is limited to the operating environment on the user's network or system.
How is the assessment delivered?	LAN/local server	Online delivery	1 2 3 4 5	Restricting access to the assessment through the use of a LAN or local server will provide a more secure delivery.
How is data accessed?	Direct access to database	Layers of security and authentication between database and user	1 2 3 4 5	The risk of providing direct access to content or results cannot be understated. Even small programs should carefully consider the security of the database.

allowing an organization to most efficiently and effectively determine which system will best meet their needs.

References

AERA, APA, & NCME (American Educational Research Association, American Psychological Association, & National Council on Measurement in Education). (1999). *Standards for educational and psychological testing.* Washington, DC: American Educational Research Association.

Baker, F.B. (1986). Item banking in computer-based instructional systems. *Applied Psychological Measurement, 10*(4), 405-414.

Bergstrom, B.A., & Gershon, R.C. (1995). Item banking. In J.C. Impara (Ed.), *Licensure testing* (pp. 187-204). Lincoln, NE: Buros Institute of Mental Measurements.

Choppin, B. (1985). Principles of item banking. *Evaluation in Education, 9*, 87-90.

Luecht, R.M. & Nungester, R.J. (1998). Some practical examples of computer-adaptive sequential testing. *Journal of Educational Measurement, 35*(3), 229-249.

Masters, G.N., & Evans, J. (1986). Banking non-dichotomously scored items. *Applied Psychological Measurement, 10*(4), 355-367.

Schroeder, L.L. (1993). Criteria for an item banking system. *CLEAR Exam Review,* 16-18.

Schroeder, L.L., & Houghton, P.D. (1996). Software review. *Clear Exam Review,* 13-14.

Way, W.D. (1998). Protecting the integrity of computerized testing item pools. *Educational Measurement: Issues and Practice,* 17-27.

Way, W.D., & Steffen, M. (1997, April). Strategies for managing item pools to maximize item security. *Proceedings of the Annual Meeting of the National Council on Measurement in Education,* San Diego, CA.

Wright, B.D., & Bell, S.R. (1984). Item banks: What, why, how. *Journal of Educational Measurement, 21*(4), 331-345.

Endnotes

[1]   Although it is possible for a program to create its own item-banking or content-management system, most programs have found that it is more cost effective to hire a company that provides such services or purchase an off-the-shelf product, unless the company's needs are extremely simple.

[2]   Several companies, including Vantage, Educational Testing Service (ETS), and Pearson/Knowledge Analysis Technologies, have text-analysis/essay-scoring methods, which may soon allow for immediate scoring of complex constructed-response data.

Section V

Combinations

Chapter XVIII

Learning by Doing:
Four Years of Online Assessment in Engineering Education Research

John C. Wise, The Pennsylvania State University, USA

Sang Ha Lee, The Pennsylvania State University, USA

Sarah E. Rzasa Zappe, The Pennsylvania State University, USA

Abstract

This chapter describes the experiences of a team of researchers in the College of Engineering at Penn State who have spent the past several years using the Internet to collect student data. From surveys that were created and posted with little regard for their utility, the authors have reached the point in which they routinely use the Internet to gather quality data from alumni, graduating students, and other populations beyond the college. This chapter will acquaint the reader with these experiences and expose him or her to practical applications of online social science instruments in a higher education environment.

Introduction

There is worldwide interest in the improvement of education in the science, technology, engineering, and mathematics (STEM) disciplines. Evaluating and assessing the effects of various innovations is critical to the sharing of effective techniques. This chapter will describe the experiences of a team of researchers in the college of engineering at The Pennsylvania State University (Penn State) who have spent the past several years gathering student data through use of the Internet. Beginning from a naïve approach in which surveys were created and posted with little regard for their utility, the authors now routinely use the Internet to gather quality data from alumni, graduating students, and other populations beyond the college.

The objectives of this chapter are to acquaint the reader with these experiences and to expose him or her to practical applications of online social science instruments in a higher education environment. Four different projects relating to assessment are briefly described, emphasizing how online data collection was used for each. Further details on each project, if desired, can be found through the references.

Background

The world of engineering education changed with the advent of the Engineering Criteria 2000 (EC2000), instituted by the Accreditation Board for Engineering and Technology (ABET). EC2000 redefined accreditation criteria for engineering programs, launching an increased emphasis on the assessment of student learning and the effects of the educational experience. When the authors began to look at educational research and assessment needs within the college, they immediately saw a need to use respected instruments with sufficient reliability and validity. Two possible approaches for assessment were: (a) to continue to pay on a per-use basis for commercial instruments with established credentials, or (b) to develop instruments that were tailor made to meet needs. Initially, the authors looked beyond the established instruments and tried to bring some newer ones into play. Eventually, a combination of the two approaches was adopted.

This chapter reports on an attempt to measure intellectual development using an online version of a newer and objectively scored instrument, the evaluation of a new minor within the College of Engineering using both online data collection and supporting qualitative measures ("mixed-methods"), a classroom-level study to measure the effect of a new instructional method on students' self-directed learning, and an effort to establish validity and reliability using online data collection. The format will be to describe the purpose of each project, summarize the experience, and list the "lessons learned."

Main Thrust of the Chapter: Four Examples

First Steps: Measuring Intellectual Development

Description. In 2001, there was a study underway at Penn State (since completed) related to the intellectual development of undergraduates (Wise, Lee, Litzinger, Marra, & Palmer, 2004). This study made extensive use of student one-on-one interviews to gather evidence of intellectual development according to the Perry Scheme (cf. Perry, 1999). Speaking generally, the Perry Scheme identifies several epistemological positions adopted by students as they develop their worldview through college. Students tend to begin their undergraduate years with a dualistic right/wrong view of knowledge, and progress from dualism through recognition of multiple viable points of view to acceptance of relativism. Although the findings were intriguing, indicating that "intellectual development" may be a common outcome that could be used to compare traditional and innovative courses, the cost of data collection was prohibitive. What was needed was an objectively scored instrument that could be used to rapidly place a student within the Perry Scheme and that was sensitive enough to detect subtle differences in ways of thinking. A search of the literature identified the Zhang Cognitive Development Inventory (ZCDI; Zhang, 1995) as the latest instrument of this type. Originally designed as a Chinese-language instrument, the reliability of the English version was adequate to the authors' needs, who obtained Zhang's permission to convert the instrument to an online format and to conduct tests.

Why an online format? With any new psychometric instrument, it is necessary to collect data from a large sample of respondents in order to conduct various statistical tests—specifically, tests for reliability and validity. Using a paper test requires room rental, travel time for the proctor and respondents, time taking the test, and time for grading. Selecting an online approach gave us the following significant advantages:

1. **Convenience:** Respondents could log on and complete the instrument whenever they had the time. There was minimal impact on their schedules. There was no need for a proctor or a room in which to administer the instrument. (This type of data collection is most appropriate for low-stakes types of testing and assessment in which verification of the identity of the respondents is not a requirement.)

2. **Scoring:** Responses were written to a data table on a secure server at the College of Engineering. All of them were available *in real time* for scoring and analysis.

3. **Networking Benefits:** Respondents from within the College of Engineering could be linked, with their permission, to other databases within the college. This means that there was no need to ask for demographic information, which was already available via linked database tables. For example, semester standing, GPA, SAT scores, ethnicity, and gender could all be determined in this way.

4. **Validity/Feedback:** Additional questions could be asked related to the instrument itself, and the response automatically forwarded to the researcher. In this way,

insight could be gained into how the test-takers are interpreting both questions and answers. Otherwise, researchers are forced to make assumptions as to how respondents understand the questions they are answering, and test-takers have no outlet to express concern that their responses will be properly understood.

The online version of the instrument went through two rounds of formative assessment in which a small group of students was asked to complete it and then participate in focus groups in order to collect feedback to improve the instrument. These focus groups were conducted in person, as all participants were enrolled at Penn State. However, it would have been relatively easy to conduct online focus groups for geographically dispersed populations. The results of the focus groups were found to be quite important to instrument development, as the group identified numerous ambiguous statements that needed to be corrected before the instrument was unleashed on the larger population. Their perspectives, which may be seen as representing the typical respondent, resulted in other changes made to the instrument. For example, students suggested style changes such as color-coding for separate sections.

E-mail invitations were sent to 6,000 students in three colleges: Engineering, Liberal Arts, and Education. More than 1,300 responses were obtained, which proved ample to conduct reliability tests, factor analysis, and cluster analysis. Demographic data was obtained by linking to the college database as described above. The data was available for analysis immediately upon submission by the respondents. The reliability of the online version of the instrument, calculated using Feldt's W statistic, was statistically similar to the previously reported values for Zhang's paper version (Feldt, 1969; Wise, 2002). Unfortunately, the instrument turned out not to be appropriate for our needs, as it was unable to measure the fine changes in intellectual development that occur between semesters for undergraduates.

Lessons learned. The utilization of online data collection provided us with many advantages over the traditional pencil-and-paper test administration. First, the authors learned that online versions of psychological instruments can provide important additional data by simply asking students to comment on the quality of the instrument. This can be a critical benefit for instrument development, as it provides validity evidence based on the thinking processes of the participants. Instead of inferring a respondent's meaning on each item, it is possible to ask for clarification or explanation from each respondent while the test is being taken. While this technique is not new, asking for this type of feedback from over 1,000 respondents is certainly not common.

Another advantage of online data collection is that *time* is no longer a hindrance, as, depending on the purpose of the administration, respondents may complete the instrument at their own convenience. Further, use of an online instrument removes the barrier of *place*. People can respond from any location that is equipped with an Internet connection. Samples can be drawn from geographically dispersed populations with an ease that could only have been dreamt of by previous generations of test developers.

This was also the authors' first experience with the ability to analyze data in "real time." While it was interesting, the authors were not able to take full advantage of this feature. A Web interface that generates live reports of the results (e.g., frequency distributions and statistical tests) being submitted may prove to be preferable in the future.

Assessing Engineering Entrepreneurship: Mixed Methods

Description. The authors' next major project was the assessment of a newly created minor in Engineering Entrepreneurship, funded by a grant from General Electric. Students who enroll in the minor are required to take four core courses, which connect business principles, creativity, and engineering (for details of this program see *http://e-ship.ecsel.psu.edu*). As part of the requirements of the funding agency, an extensive assessment plan was created to measure the potential effects of the minor on the development of the knowledge, skills, and attributes thought to be necessary for effective entrepreneurship. A mixed methods approach to assessment was utilized, incorporating qualitative information as well as quantitative information. The quantitative data was primarily collected over the Internet. The research question explored the effects of the entrepreneurship program: Are students more likely to display the skills and attributes necessary to become an entrepreneur?

Three different, existing scales were identified and converted to online form. They were General Enterprising Tendency (Caird, 1991), Entrepreneurial Self-Efficacy (Chen, Greene, & Crick, 1998), and a leadership scale (Wielkiewicz, 2000). Students were invited to complete the combined form when they took their first entrepreneurship course and again when they were about to graduate from the university. The online format was chosen to have the minimum impact on the course instructors. Unlike the ZCDI, the sample obtained was not large enough to gain statistical significance in the findings, although the longitudinal trends were all in the expected direction. Qualitative methods in the form of focus groups and interviews supplemented the quantitative findings. The combination of the two methods proved critical to the success of the assessment effort.

Lessons learned. As with the ZCDI, tests of reliability showed that the online version of these instruments were as statistically reliable as their source versions. The authors gained confidence in the conversion of instruments, as well as the use of the Web as the primary source for data collection. However, we did learn a valuable lesson from this project regarding the possibility of a reduced response rate using online methods. Online data collection cannot provide the same large response rate obtained by physically entering a classroom and administering a pencil-and-paper instrument to a captive audience. When the population is small, as in this case of a cohort of students trying out new entrepreneurship courses, the response rate is critical. If participation cannot be guaranteed, the online approach should be abandoned and pencil-and-paper versions administered during class time. If other factors such as time and budget call for the use of online data collection, incentives such as extra credit may help to improve the response rate. Another potential concern with online data collection in this instance is that the sample obtained may not be representative of the population, having somewhat different characteristics. Therefore, if only a small sample of individuals respond to a survey, generalization to the larger population may be questionable.

An additional problem was a lack of strict controls on the timeframe during which students were able to enter information. After receiving e-mail invitations, students were able to complete the survey at any point in time during the academic year. While some students completed the survey immediately, others waited several months to do so. This resulted in difficulty understanding the results of the analyses, as students completed the instruments at various times after entering the entrepreneurship minor. Therefore, stricter controls need to be in place to manage data entry times in the online environment. While not a problem in a reliability study such as the ZCDI, this was a serious error in this assessment effort as the time at which the students completed the survey threatened to confound our understanding of potential effects.

Although much more time-consuming, the use of qualitative methods in the assessment was found to provide valuable and rich information about the minor. However, the use of qualitative data limits the generalizability of the results to the sample of participants. Only a small sample of students could participate in the focus groups and interviews. Therefore, utilizing a mixed methods approach of both qualitative and quantitative methods provided the most comprehensive information about the effects of the minor. With the expense and time-consuming nature of qualitative methods, online qualitative tools should also be explored, in order to develop improved methods for organizing and analyzing this type of data.

Conducting Classroom Research: Self-Directed Learning Readiness Scale (SDLRS)

Description. The previously mentioned changes in the accreditation requirements for engineering and engineering technology programs have increased the emphasis on lifelong learning as a skill to be included in the undergraduate curriculum (Accreditation Board for Engineering and Technology, 2004). Lifelong learning includes both the skills required to participate and the motivation for doing so (Candy, 1991). This construct can be measured using the Self-Directed Learning Readiness Scale (Litzinger, Lee, & Wise, 2004; cf. Guglielmino, 1977). A series of studies were conducted at Penn State using this instrument (Litzinger, Wise, Lee, Simpson, & Joshi, 2001; Litzinger, Wise, Lee, & Bjorklund, 2003; Litzinger et al., 2004). For one portion of this project, an online version of the SDLRS was developed and tested.

In this implementation of online assessment, the authors asked students in single courses to respond voluntarily to the online form of the SDLRS. Several students participated, but the response rate overall was less than 10%. Due to this low response rate, the online version of the SDLRS was abandoned in favor of in-class administration of paper forms.

Lessons learned. The difficulties in this project were similar to those encountered in the assessment of the Entrepreneurship minor. Primarily, when dealing with intact classes, students seemed to find it more convenient to complete the form during class rather than doing so outside of class time. Whereas the ZCDI was extracurricular by nature, the online SDLRS was connected to the course and therefore seen as an added (and unexpected) burden. Given the optional status, many students chose not to participate in the survey. As in the case with the entrepreneurship project, participation rates may have been improved if: a) there was an added incentive (i.e. participation points), and b) the instructor announced at the beginning of the semester that the online assessment would take place.

Instrument Development: Index of Learning Styles (ILS)

Description. This final project is currently underway. Richard Felder and associates at North Carolina State University have designed and developed an online instrument that purports to measure the respondent's learning style. The Felder-Solomon Index of Learning Styles (ILS) is available for use without charge, and is accessed over 100,000 times per year by users worldwide (cf. *http://www.ncsu.edu/felder-public/ILSpage.html*). Reliability studies have been performed, yet it has not been extensively tested for validity (Zywno, 2003).

The ILS uses a dichotomous scale, which forces the respondent to choose between two responses, which in some cases could be equally incorrect in describing the participant. In order to get higher reliability coefficients without changing items, the authors developed a version using essentially the same items, but with a five-point Likert-type scale instead of the dichotomous options. Both versions were posted on the Internet. Students at three different colleges within Penn State were identified randomly and invited to complete the instrument. When they logged in, they were randomly assigned to either the two-point or the five-point version. Exactly two weeks after their first submission, they were contacted again via e-mail and asked to fill out the other version. This interval was programmed automatically, and increased the likelihood that the interval between the first and second administrations would be consistent for all respondents. The reader should note that this would be logistically impractical in a traditional context, but was nearly effortless in the online environment.

As with the other online instruments, data was available in "real time," so analysis could begin as soon as enough responses had been obtained.

Lessons learned. This was the first time that the authors used an automated follow-up message for longitudinal data collection, and it worked very well. The initial respondents could complete the instrument at their convenience, perhaps several days after receiving the invitation, and the system could still follow up exactly a week after their submissions.

Within one month of receiving approval to begin research, 1,133 respondents provided data for this study and data analysis was complete In other words, use of the Web for data collection makes it possible for a major comparison of psychometric instruments to be conducted in as little as one month!

Future Trends

While the authors have been encouraged to expand their online assessment efforts, it is also important to note some disadvantages that have been encountered. Specifically, it is difficult to obtain a representative sample. The population under consideration must be limited to those who have both an e-mail account and access to the Internet, so results cannot be generalized to larger groups unless Internet users and non-users can be shown to have similar characteristics. A newer limitation is the increasing ability of e-mail clients to filter mass mailings, treating them as "SPAM" messages. This potentially limits the contact sample to those who do not have active SPAM filters.

Several advantages, however, are apparent when using online data-collection techniques in social science research, and indicate possible directions for future development.

1.   It is much easier to address large populations. With minor variations, the authors' reliability and validity studies could be conducted using worldwide samples without the need for trained proctors.

2.   If institutional data is available, demographic information can be excluded from the online form and filled in automatically (with permission from the respondents). This shortens any instrument under consideration, thus improving its efficiency.

3.   Data collected through online instruments can be "cleaned" automatically through filters and programming to reduce the need for the researcher, for example, to convert text to numbers before analysis. Future trends may include automating analyses in order to present data to the researcher in real time through graphs and tables. This ability may encourage the use of psychometric measures in classroom situations where a teacher may not have access to a skilled statistician.

4.   It is much easier to carry out longitudinal data collection. Follow-up contacts can be programmed to relate to the reception time of initial data. With the increased availability of the World Wide Web, participants may be contacted years after they have participated in a study and asked to contribute additional data.

5.   There is a significant savings in time, effort, money, and convenience when using online data-collection techniques. Once the system has been tested, a study could essentially run itself. One example that comes to mind is a senior exit survey that checks the school calendar to find out when classes will end in a particular semester, queries the student database to identify the students who should be graduating, sends an automated message to them (addressed from the dean) asking them to complete an online survey regarding their thoughts on the undergraduate experience, then analyzes the results and reports them to different departments through graphs and charts, all within moments of data entry by the students.

Conclusion

As outlined in this chapter, online data collection provides several advantages for researchers either developing or using social science instruments. The authors have used online instruments in various forms for different projects over the past several years. The most successful use in the projects has been in the design, development, and testing of the instruments themselves. For instrument development, large numbers of participants were obtained, thus reducing concerns about sample size and generalization to a larger population. The authors have had less success when using online instruments to assess the effects of learning in smaller (class-size) populations.

Some recommendations to consider when using online assessment tools include:

1. Provide incentives for respondents such that the benefits of participating (convenience, participation credit, etc.) outweigh the costs.

2. Test the instrument before implementing it on a large scale. Gather formative feedback from a select group that represents the intended audience. Check the data on the "back end" to be sure that it will be usable.

3. Use the online environment to maximize the data. When practical, link to existing databases at your institution to obtain reliable demographic data. If the data need not be collected in one sitting, allow for the respondent to return to where he or she left off at any time (contrast this to a pencil-and-paper administration). Make the questions dynamic, so that the user does not, for example, have to skip questions that do not apply—these questions can be programmed not to appear at all.

4. Add text areas where appropriate to allow respondents to expand upon their answers. Forced-choice instruments can be frustrating for people who fall between extremes, and respondents often want to explain why they answered in a certain way. This data can be examined in all cases, or only considered when unusual responses are noted. Again, this is something that would be very difficult in a pencil-and-paper environment, but not in an online administration.

The authors have only scratched the surface of the possibilities with the projects mentioned in this chapter. As techniques are refined and shared among practitioners, the use of the online environment for the design, development, and testing of psychometric instruments will only increase, resulting in more effective instruments for assessment and evaluation.

References

Accreditation Board for Engineering and Technology. (2004). Criteria for accrediting engineering technology programs. Retrieved May 15, 2004, from *www.abet.org/ images/Criteria/T001 04-05 TAC Criteria 1-19-04.pdf*

Caird, S. (1991). The enterprising tendency of occupational groups. *International Small Business Journal, 9,* 75-81.

Candy, P.C. (1991). *Self-direction for lifelong learning: A comprehensive guide to theory and practice.* San Francisco: Jossey-Bass.

Chen, C.C., Greene, P.G., & Crick, A. (1998). Does entrepreneurial self-efficacy distinguish entrepreneurs from managers? *Journal of Business Venturing, 13*, 295-316.

Feldt, L.S. (1969). A test of the hypothesis that Cronbach's alpha or Kuder-Richardson coefficient twenty is the same for two tests. *Psychometrika, 34*(3), 363-373.

Guglielmino, L. (1977). Development of the self-directed learning readiness scale. *Dissertation Abstracts International, 38*, 6467A.

Litzinger, T.A., Lee, S.H., & Wise, J. (2004, June). Readiness for self-directed learning of engineering students. *Proceedings of the 2004 American Society of Engineering Education Annual Conference*, Salt Lake City, UT.

Litzinger, T.A., Wise, J.C., Lee, S.H., & Bjorklund, S. (2003, June). Assessing readiness for self-directed learning. *Proceedings of the 2003 American Society of Engineering Education Annual Conference*, Nashville, TN.

Litzinger, T.A., Wise, J.C., Lee, S.H., Simpson, T., & Joshi, S. (2001, June). Assessing readiness for lifelong learning. *Proceedings of the 2001 American Society of Engineering Education Annual Conference*, Albuquerque, NM.

Perry, W. (1999). *Forms of intellectual and ethical development in the college years: A scheme* (2nd ed.). San Francisco: Jossey-Bass.

Rzasa, S.E., Wise, J., & Kisenwether, L. (2004, March). Evaluation of entrepreneurial endeavors in the classroom: The student perspective. *Proceedings of the Annual Meeting of the National Collegiate Inventors and Innovators Alliance,* San Jose, CA.

Wielkiewicz, R.M. (2000). The leadership attitudes and beliefs scale: An instrument for evaluating college students' thinking about leadership and organizations. *Journal of College Student Development, 41*(3), 335-347.

Wise, J., Kisenwether, L., & Rzasa, S. (2003, June). Assessing engineering entrepreneurship. *Proceedings of the 2003 American Society of Engineering Education (ASEE) Annual Conference and Exposition*, Nashville, TN.

Wise, J.C. (2002). *Assessing intellectual development: Assessing the validity of an online instrument.* Doctoral Dissertation, The Pennsylvania State University, USA. *Dissertation Abstracts International*-A 63/09, 3166.

Wise, J.C., Lee, S.H., Litzinger, T.A., Marra, R.M., & Palmer, B.A. (2004). A report on a longitudinal study of intellectual development in engineering undergraduates. *Journal of Adult Development, 11*(2), 103-110.

Zhang, L.-F. (1995). *The construction of a Chinese language cognitive development inventory and its use in a cross-cultural study of the Perry scheme.* Unpublished Doctoral Dissertation, University of Iowa, USA.

Zywno, M.S. (2003, June). A contribution to validation of score meaning for Felder-Solomon's index of learning styles. *Proceedings of the 2003 American Society of Engineering Education (ASEE) Annual Conference and Exposition*, Nashville, TN.

Chapter XIX

The Role of Assessment and Evaluation in Context:
Pedagogical Alignment, Constraints, and Affordances in Online Courses

Julia M. Matuga, Bowling Green State University, USA

Abstract

The purpose of this chapter is to facilitate discussion regarding the contextualization of assessment and evaluation within online educational environments. Three case studies will be used to frame questions, issues, and challenges regarding online assessment and evaluation that were influenced by pedagogical alignment and environmental affordances and constraints. These reflective case studies, highlighting the author's experiences as a teacher, researcher, and instructional design team leader, will be used to illustrate assessment and evaluation within three very different educational contexts: an online K-12 public school, an undergraduate online course, and a learning community designing online graduate courses.

Introduction

The assessment and evaluation of students, teachers, or courses is often discussed in conjunction with predetermined learning, course, or program objectives and is most frequently focused upon the summative evaluation of students. Assessment and evaluation of students, teachers, or courses is rarely discussed in relation to other instructional features such as the perception of students, instructor expectations, instructional strategies, or educational contexts. Isolating assessment and evaluation from the context in which those actions take place has been relatively commonplace, that is, until the prevalence of online teaching and learning has, albeit slowly, moved the issue of context to the forefront of pedagogical discussions (Gibson, 1998).

Assessment and evaluation can be interpreted as social activities that are carried out within complex pedagogical contexts. The view that assessment and evaluation are situated within sociocultural contexts owes its theoretical foundation to Vygotskian theory (Kirshner & Whitson, 1997). From Vygotsky's sociocultural perspective, all learning is, in essence, social (Vygotsky, 1978, 1986). Situating assessment and evaluation as essentially social activities, influenced by unique affordances and constraints of a particular educational context, is a critical pedagogical component when designing and teaching online courses.

The primary purpose of this chapter is to foster discussion regarding the contextualization of assessment and evaluation within online educational environments in which they are designed and utilized. To facilitate this discussion, the author will focus on two themes relating to the contextualization of assessment and evaluation. First, this chapter will discuss the potential of situating summative assessment within the pedagogical alignment of online courses. In this chapter the author will also discuss how the context of an online environment may constrain and afford the assessment and evaluation of students, teachers, and courses.

Three brief case studies will be presented to illustrate questions, issues, and challenges that arose while using assessment and evaluation within the context of online learning. The cases that the author presents in this chapter describe three different online teaching and learning projects in which she has been involved in various capacities as teacher, instructional design team leader, and researcher. While these case studies do not present an exhaustive list of assessment and evaluation issues, individual case studies presented here highlight several critical issues and challenges that arose within three very different educational contexts: an online K-12 public school, an undergraduate teacher education course, and a learning community designing online graduate courses.

Summative Assessment and Pedagogical Alignment

Before discussing the role summative assessment plays in the alignment of pedagogical variables, it may be beneficial to define key terms used throughout this chapter. First, assessment refers to the information collected to document student progress towards a learning objective or what a student has learned (Banks, 2005). Assessments may be standardized or created by teachers, vary in degree of formality, or be used for summative or formative purposes (Banks, 2005). The primary goal of summative assessment is to document or measure student performance regarding predetermined learning standards or outcomes (Banks, 2005; McMillan, 2004). While formative assessment refers to "information that is provided to students during instruction to help them learn" (McMillan, 2004, p. 106), summative assessments are typically formal assessments that are used at the end of a lesson, instructional unit, or course (Banks, 2005). Evaluation refers to the activity of making judgments about student learning based on information garnered from assessments (summative and formative) and from observation that may or may not be quantifiable (Banks, 2005; Hanna & Dettmer, 2004).

Summative assessment is one of many instructional variables that must align with other pedagogical variables to support effective teaching and learning (Hanna & Dettmer, 2004). Summative assessments are also used by educators and instructional designers to gauge the quality of the alignment of pedagogical variables. Instructional alignment, also called systematic instructional design, is often discussed in relation to aligning instructional goals, curriculum, and activities to educational standards or outcomes (Gagne, Briggs, & Wagner, 1992).

The effectiveness of any course, whether a traditional, face-to-face course or an online course, depends upon the alignment of a wide variety of personal, instructional, and environmental factors, some mentioned above.

The primary idea grounding instructional alignment is that the alignment of instructional (i.e., subject matter, learning theories, instructional objectives, assessments, etc.) and individual (individual difference, transfer of learning, etc.) elements is not hodgepodge; some elements of instruction and summative assessment fit better with others. There is a "goodness of fit" between the instructional and assessment elements used for teaching and learning within particular contexts. It is important to remember that teaching is not a prescriptive science. While selecting and utilizing the most effective instructional and individual elements to maximize teaching and learning may be informed by what is known about both processes from a variety of sources (i.e., research, theory, experience, observation), the alignment of instructional and individual elements is also something of an art (see Matuga, 2001). Pedagogical alignment refers to the alignment of these variables—the science and art of teaching.

Situating summative assessment within the context of online courses challenges traditional views of student, teacher, and course assessment and evaluation. However, pedagogical alignment also includes more elusive characteristics such as the expectations, motivation, and communication skills of faculty and students. The context of the electronic environment, perhaps more than a traditional face-to-face environment, requires an elevated level of transparency about the design of instruction and assessment and evaluation practices (Sheingold & Frederiksen, 2000). Assessment and evaluation should be situated within the larger community of stakeholders investing in teaching and learning within the context of online environments. The emphasis on the summative evaluation of students, like forced-choice quizzes and tests, is prevalent in the distance learning literature. While the summative evaluation of students is critically important, formative assessment is often an overlooked element that is critical for successful teaching and effective student learning, regardless of whether the course is offered face-to-face or online.

Constraints and Affordances of Formative Assessment and Evaluation

Formative assessments are typically informal, flexible tools that are used to regulate and maximize instruction and learning, evaluate student-teacher interactions, and assist individual students while instruction is ongoing (Banks, 2005; Holmberg, 1989; McMillan, 2004). Formative assessment of student learning within online learning environments may require using multiple resources that may not be identified a priori. In addition to the information garnered from course objectives, performance standards, and student achievement, Holmberg suggested that experts, stakeholders, online educators, and students may all be important resources used to evaluate the effectiveness of online courses. The unique affordances and constraints on formative assessment of students, teachers, and courses within the context of online classes raise several important issues and challenges facing teachers and students. As stated earlier, there are two resources used to inform formative evaluation: formative and summative assessments and observations that may or may not be quantifiable. Teacher and student observations of teaching and learning are routinely used by teachers and students as a resource for formative assessment, but are not routinely quantified.

For example, many of the informal cues that students and teachers rely upon for formative assessment within traditional face-to-face environments are constrained within online settings. Notably, nonverbal behaviors like facial expressions, body language, gestures, and voice-related cues (McMillan, 2004), which provide both students and teachers with informal information about student learning in classroom contexts, are typically not available within online environments. Mehrabian (1981) estimated that 93% "of a message is communicated by nonverbal factors" (as cited in McMillan, 2004, p. 107). In the author's experience, this loss of nonverbal cues frequently contributes to misunderstandings and/or miscommunication within online environments, or online communication about what was originally thought of as a clear message by the sender (a teacher or learner). For teachers and students, finding themselves within an online environment without the nonverbal and visual cues that guide their understanding of informal, formative evaluation of teaching and learning presents a profound loss of a relied-upon source of information.

The lack of nonverbal and visual cues, however, may also be viewed as an affordance within an online learning environment. Requiring that teachers and students come to an understanding of shared expectations and communicate thoughts effectively, for example, is essential for effective teaching and learning in face-to-face and online environments. As an online teacher, it only takes one awkward experience of miscommunication with students before learning to pause and ask oneself, "Is what I am saying clear? Am I making sense?" "Can my students understand what I am trying to say?" "How can this be misinterpreted by someone else?" before sending the next message to students. This is, hopefully, also a lesson learned by students within online teaching and learning environments. These self-guiding questions have the potential of becoming a method of formative assessment emerging from the context of online teaching and learning. Within face-to-face environments, these questions (if even asked) are negotiated within the context of the classroom largely by utilizing nonverbal and visual cues that are exchanged between teacher-student and student-student.

An increasingly complicated view regarding the role of formative assessment and evaluation in online teaching and learning is emerging, one in which the traditional environmental boundaries, affordances, and constraints are more elusive. While nonverbal and visual cues represent just one example and do not encompass all sources informing formative assessment and evaluation, they do illustrate one important challenge regarding formative evaluation within online learning environments. To illustrate issues, questions, and challenges regarding assessment and evaluation, three different online teaching and learning projects from the author's personal experience will be used.

Case Studies

The three case studies presented in this chapter emerged from the author's own personal online teaching and learning experiences as a teacher, instructional design team leader, and researcher. Each case study presented here offers a different perspective on several key issues regarding summative and formative assessment and evaluation. These self-reflective case studies also facilitate an ongoing discussion about assessment and evaluation of online learning and teaching.

On a practical level, the author struggled with the arrangement of the case studies. Should they be arranged in some conceptual manner? Should they be arranged by the roles that the author played (researcher, instructional design team leader, and teacher) in these projects? In the end, the author decided to arrange the three case studies in chronological order to illustrate a more autobiographical perspective of the role that assessment and evaluation played in transforming the author's own understanding of teaching and learning within online environments.

Case Study #1: Teaching Teachers to Teach Online

Several years ago while the author was a graduate student at a large Midwestern university, she was asked to teach an online undergraduate course in educational psychology. Educational psychology is a course that covers a variety of topics, including student development (cognitive, emotional, and moral), learning theories, instructional strategies, motivation, classroom management, and student assessment and evaluation. While the author had been a K-12 classroom teacher and had taught educational psychology face-to-face before, she had never taught an online course and was unsure about what to expect from herself and her students. She was able to design the course according to her own pedagogical preferences and was not provided guidelines or requirements regarding online assessment and evaluation.

Assessment and evaluation. Before the course started, the author recognized that it would be important not to alter the course or course assignments too much throughout the duration of the course. Perhaps this recognition came from the knowledge that if the author were taking an online course for the first time, she would prefer to know what the entire course "looked" like before starting the semester. Therefore, she maintained many of the traditional methods to assess student learning that she incorporated in her face-to-face educational psychology course, such as quizzes, tests, papers, projects, and performance measures. The author simply translated many of the assessments that she used in her face-to-face course to her online one. In teaching her first online class, however, the author was faced with one important summative assessment and evaluation challenge.

In her face-to-face class, the author often facilitated regular course discussions in which students would apply what they had read in the educational psychology textbook to case studies. The case studies that were used in class highlighted the application of theory and concepts to a small vignette that was usually situated within a K-12 classroom. Since the author's undergraduate students were preservice teachers, this activity allowed them multiple opportunities to apply theory to classroom practice, albeit in a simplified, simulated manner. When utilizing case-based discussions during a face-to-face class-room session, students interacted with each other, presented their own views and perspectives, and negotiated their understanding of the case study.

The author was faced with two related instruction and assessment problems. First, she had to figure out a way to structure an online discussion in such a way that ensured student participation and discussion, promoting interaction rather than parallel partici-pation. The author also struggled with how to effectively assess student participation in these online discussions. These two problems, one dealing with instructional design and the other assessment, were intimately linked together in practice.

The author first began by organizing small, semester-long groups of four to five students as the cornerstones for the instructional design of the course. To promote a sense of ownership and maybe to engineer some social structure to support student participation, the author saw that these groups were provided with their own discussion board, were able to give their group a name (hopefully to promote a group identity), and had a group discussion board to discuss private, nonacademic issues not directly related to class issues. Each week, in addition to reading the assigned textbook chapter, each group also was assigned a case study to read. Required discussion questions to which each student had to respond were posted weekly, but to ensure student-to-student interaction, students were also required to respond to other student postings within the same week time period. To assess their level of participation in this weekly online discussion activity, the author awarded students a "discussion grade" for posting a response to the original question that she had posed. This, however, would not in and of itself foster the goal of promoting student-to-student interaction. Therefore, students were also re-quired, on a weekly basis, to direct a comment, question, or constructive feedback to a peer's original posting within their group. Students were assessed, in large part, on the quality of their responses.

While the author had contemplated and attempted to work out the potential "kinks" in summative assessment within the course while designing it and before she started to teach it, unforeseen issues related to formative assessment and evaluation arose while the author was teaching the online undergraduate educational psychology course. One unique feature of this online course, however, was the opportunity to utilize the subject matter being taught to explore the ways in which students' views of teaching and learning were influenced by their own learning experiences within an online environment. When students were learning about motivation, for example, the author would have them discuss motivational theories and strategies as they related to the assigned case study. but would also ask them how their own motivation was being influenced by the online learning environment. Engaging in repeated episodes of reflection about teaching and learning in a course about teaching and learning with these students became an incredibly powerful formative assessment and evaluation tool.

In addition to missing information garnered through observation, such as visual and nonverbal cues mentioned earlier, for example, students raised the issue social comparison plays in teaching and learning, and how the online environment disrupts the methods used by students to evaluate their own progress within a course. For example, one student commented:

> *I think that the only hard part was that we did not know how well we [were] doing as individuals compared to other students in the class. I do like being able to see what I get on certain assignments and talk about them with other students.*

However, while this lack of social referencing information apparently interfered with this student's ability to gauge how he was doing in class compared to his peers, other environmental constraints were perceived to be an advantage in relation to assessment and evaluation of student learning in this online course.

According to quantitative measures obtained from the final course evaluation, students felt that assessment practices used to evaluate student learning in this course were fair and equitable (see Matuga, 2001, for details). When asked to reflect upon the assessment and evaluation practices in this online course, one student reasoned: "One good thing about the Web course is that there is hardly any teacher bias." This student perceived a degree of anonymity within online environments that afforded him protection against teacher bias in the assessment and evaluation process. The student comments presented here and those made throughout the semester illustrate underlying student views, expectations, and assumptions that influenced the perception of teaching, learning, and assessment within the context of this course.

Issues and challenges. The author's first experience teaching online was truly a learning experience. She learned a great deal about the importance of the pedagogical alignment of instructional variables and encountered unexpected sources to inform the summative and formative assessment and evaluation of teaching and learning (Matuga, 2001). As stated earlier, one unique feature of teaching educational psychology is that the content of the course focuses upon teaching and learning processes. Within the author's traditional face-to-face courses, she relies upon modeling to illustrate learning theories and instructional strategies. The greatest challenge that the author faced as a first-time online teacher, however, was not an instructional design dilemma or a summative assessment problem, but more of an ethical dilemma regarding summative evaluation.

Was teaching this particular course online the most effective method to teach these students?

After the author had completed teaching the online educational psychology course, she found herself uneasy with the final summative evaluation of student learning in that course. Within the online course, the author relied upon case studies to present opportunities for students to connect theory to practice, but what bothered her throughout the semester was that she was not able to witness the direct application of educational psychology to classroom practice. This direct application was something the author routinely asked her face-to-face students to do through a variety of assignments and classroom activities. The author was somewhat comforted by the fact that all students, whether they were in a traditional or online environment, were required to tutor a child while they were enrolled in educational psychology.

The author was also confident that she developed assessments that would evaluate the degree to which students learned the content of educational psychology in her face-to-face or online class. Examining those underlying expectations and comments made by students in relation to her own interpretation and expectations of student learning became a critically important informal assessment tool within the online course. The lessons that the author learned as a result of reflecting upon those experiences, as will be seen in the other case studies presented in this chapter, were ones that the author was able to apply to future experiences.

However, evaluating preservice teachers within the online course without the benefit of what might be called contextually valid assessments troubled her a great deal. In essence, she was discomfited by the fact that while her students may have known about teaching and learning processes and may have been able to apply them to case studies, the author was not afforded the opportunity to witness their ability to apply this knowledge within the context of a "real" classroom. The author's students were preparing to be classroom teachers within traditional face-to-face contexts, not teachers within online learning environments.

Case Study #2: EFFECT

In 2002, the Ohio Learning Network (*www.oln.org*) developed the Learning Community Initiative to provide fiscal support to learning communities in higher education to utilize technology in ways that explored the potential of improvement of teaching and learning processes. The Ohio Learning Network (OLN) funded 21 learning communities and five colleges/universities to host learning community institutes throughout the state of Ohio. A grant was awarded to the EFFECT (Educational Foundations for Every Classroom Teacher) learning community, a small group of faculty and administrators at Bowling Green State University (BGSU). The author was the EFFECT learning community team leader, and she designed and taught one of the proposed EFFECT courses slated for online development.

The primary goal of the EFFECT project was to create four online graduate courses in educational foundations: Philosophy of Education, History of Education, Research in Education, and Contemporary Theory and Research in Classroom Learning. These courses were identified at BGSU by university and college administrators as being in "high demand." First, students enrolled in all post-secondary teacher education programs at BGSU were required to take courses in educational foundations. Additionally, there was and continues to be a general shortage of qualified faculty to teach these graduate courses, especially at remote sites across northwest Ohio.

While the EFFECT learning community contained administrators and faculty, the administrators were primarily involved in larger learning community discussions regarding policy, logistics regarding the piloting of the EFFECT courses, and the evaluation of the project. For example, the administrative members of the learning community were very interested in piloting the EFFECT courses, with groups of BGSU students completing course work at regional sites off campus (i.e., high schools, community centers, etc.). To meet the needs of these BGSU students, university faculty (most often part-time adjunct faculty) travel to various off-campus cohort sites, like area secondary schools, to teach BGSU graduate courses. Providing off-campus cohorts with qualified faculty to teach educational foundations has been an ongoing struggle and has contributed to the identification of EFFECT courses as being in "high demand." While piloting online graduate courses with off-campus cohorts was in some ways beneficial (e.g., easy access), there were also a number of difficulties with utilizing a cohort to pilot the EFFECT program (e.g., the cohort mentality, expectations, etc.). These will be presented in greater detail later in this chapter.

Assessment and evaluation. It became apparent through community discussions that faculty members wanted to have a common foundation to anchor the online graduate courses. The learning community members chose to emphasize three common goals in each of the online graduate courses, establishing a shared vision across all EFFECT courses. First, all EFFECT courses would emphasize the development and application of technological skills in teacher education at the post-secondary level. After completing an EFFECT course, graduate students (i.e., classroom teachers seeking master's degrees) should be able to apply and utilize technological tools for effective communication and research. The EFFECT team members felt that as classroom teachers, students enrolled in EFFECT courses should develop a modicum of technological skills (i.e., posting in a discussion board, utilizing e-mail and chat functions, downloading and printing Adobe documents, using electronic resources and search engines for research purposes, etc.) while enrolled in an EFFECT course. As BGSU had just acquired user-friendly Blackboard as a portal and course management tool, the team felt that these minimal technological skills would not be overly taxing on its students (many of whom were first-time online students), but might also prompt more technological integration in their teaching within K-12 classrooms.

By the end of the project, classroom teachers enrolled in the EFFECT courses did acquire basic technological skills to send files as attachments, utilize discussion boards and chat rooms, and read Acrobat documents. While this may not seem to be very technologically sophisticated, for first-time online students the utilization of these skills was a great accomplishment. Therefore, at the conclusion of the pilot phase, the EFFECT faculty felt that its goal for increasing the technical competence of K-12 classroom teachers was fulfilled.

Second, courses would promote self-regulatory awareness to help facilitate student completion of online courses. It was a goal of the EFFECT learning community that students enrolled in EFFECT courses should be able to identify their own needs as online learners in order to participate as active members of an online learning community. Due to the collective concern regarding the retention of students in online courses, faculty generated several strategies to promote self-regulation within an electronic environment in which normal regulating cues are absent. For example, students were required to complete several formative online self-assessments pertaining to the planning, monitoring, and evaluating of their own learning. EFFECT instructors also discussed and adopted two elements of course design that they believed would foster self-regulation: keeping changes in requirements/activities to a minimum once a course was launched, and establishing and maintaining weekly patterns of learning activities (e.g., posting a discussion response every Wednesday by noon).

The EFFECT faculty also concluded that the structure of weekly sessions within the courses helped students regulate their own learning. With very few exceptions, students participated in the established pattern of weekly behavior in each of the EFFECT courses. In other words, students rarely missed or forgot to participate in the required online activities. Additional features of the EFFECT courses also may have helped meet this goal. For example, at the beginning of the semester in the Contemporary Theory and Research in Classroom Learning course, student groups were assigned the task of coming up with a group name and expectations for group participation. This group identity and commonly constructed expectations for group interactions may have contributed to the regularity with which individual members participated in weekly activities.

Third, each EFFECT course would emphasize the acquisition and application of content-area knowledge, educational theory, and research to the classroom teacher's educational practice. By emphasizing the connection between theory, research, and classroom practice, the EFFECT team hoped that students would acquire a strong knowledge base within each of the educational foundation areas. Students who completed an EFFECT course would be able to identify, analyze, synthesize, and evaluate major theories and research associated with a particular content area within educational foundations and apply them to their own classroom practice.

Final projects and research papers best illustrated the impact that the educational theories and research discussed in EFFECT courses had on K-12 classroom practice. While no data was collected to provide additional evidence of this insight, the scope and nature of the final projects produced by students in EFFECT courses did illustrate the influence that online discussions and activities had on classroom practice. For example, two EFFECT students from different school districts collaborated to construct a new kindergarten grade card in accordance with research on learning and assessment in the early grades. This grade card was then distributed to other kindergarten teachers, parents, and administrators within those school districts and will be adopted the year after this writing as a common assessment and diagnostic tool in all kindergarten classes within both districts.

To evaluate the larger EFFECT project goals, learning community members discussed the possibility of commonly shared assessments among EFFECT courses. Due to diverse models of pedagogical alignment based upon the disparity of course content, however, it was decided by each faculty course designer to utilize course-specific assessments within individual courses to evaluate student performance. With the exception of a common semester-end course evaluation and the fact that each graduate course required a culminating research paper/project, the three online EFFECT courses did not share a common assessment.

Issues and challenges. Faculty members participating in the EFFECT project had to address the question of how to design an online graduate course that was pedagogically sound within the context of the academic rigor of their own content area or discipline, while still meeting the larger EFFECT project goals established by the learning community. One of the most pressing and overarching challenges was presented to the EFFECT faculty by university and college administrators. During initial discussions regarding the EFFECT project, university and college administrators requested that off-campus cohorts be utilized to pilot the EFFECT online graduate courses.

Utilizing off-campus student cohorts presented several unforeseen challenges for full-time faculty teaching EFFECT courses. For most of the students participating in this pilot, for example, the EFFECT course was the last course they needed to complete their degree program. Compounding this problem was the fact that students were mandated to complete the educational foundation courses online and were not provided an option to take these courses face-to-face by program administrators. Second, in all likelihood the online EFFECT course was the first course taken by these off-campus students that was taught by a full-time faculty member. It became readily apparent to faculty team members that there was a disparity in academic expectations for graduate student performance between EFFECT faculty and off-campus cohort students. These two issues were common points of discussion for the EFFECT faculty throughout the project. While clarifying EFFECT faculty expectations for student performance was emphasized at the start and throughout the duration of the EFFECT courses, a few students remained somewhat resentful about workload issues and the fact that they had to take their last required course online.

Case Study #3: TRECA Digital Academy (TDA)

The author first became involved with TRECA Digital Academy (*www.treca.org*) in 2002 when asked by the dean to investigate potential partnerships between the university, online K-12 public schools, and other stakeholders in online education in northwest Ohio. TRECA's Digital Academy (TDA) is one of the largest K-12 online, non-profit public schools in the state of Ohio. TDA students work independently and in collaboration with others through a series of curriculum blocks for each course in which they are enrolled. As an online K-12 school, TDA has to adhere to the same state regulations that govern other K-12 schools in Ohio.

TDA's primary goal, according to its mission statement, is "to prepare students for lifelong learning and intelligent decision making" (TRECA Digital Academy, 2004). Administrators and teachers felt that most students entering TDA were doing so with the performance goal orientation, focusing too much on their performance within courses rather than learning and mastering curriculum material and skills needed to "prepare students for lifelong learning and intelligent decision making."

The TDA faculty and administration sought to challenge what they perceived as preoccupation with grades by students and parents entering TDA, a preoccupation that was not aligned to their mission statement to promote lifelong learning. TDA adopted a new evaluation system which they called the Continuous Progress Model (see TDA, 2004). According to the Continuous Progress Model, student work would be evaluated according to the degree to which it exhibited understanding of concepts taught in the lesson. For example, TRECA teachers evaluated student performance based upon whether or not students exhibited a deep (Qualification Level 3), adequate (Qualification Level 2), or minimal (Qualification Level 1) understanding of material. If an assignment indicated that students did not understand a lesson or information that they were supposed to learn, teachers could ask them to "rethink and redo," or give them an "X," which would indicate that the students turned in the assignment, but it would not be evaluated. Students could resubmit assignments for evaluation to earn a higher "qualification level."

Assessment and evaluation. The Continuous Progress Model, adopted by TDA, shares some similarities with a mastery model of learning. Decisions regarding the assessments utilized in courses to evaluate student learning were left to the individual instructor. For example, a teacher may use an examination, project, paper, performance measure, or, more likely, a combination of these tools to evaluate student understanding of curricular content and demonstration of skills needed for learning and decision making.

One of the affordances that is available to TDA, that is not common to more traditional face-to-face schools due to the bureaucracies of other school "systems," is the flexibility of implementing novel evaluation strategies and systems used for evaluation without going through multiple levels of administrative red tape. While assessment tools remained relatively unchanged at the classroom level (i.e., use of exams, projects, papers, etc.), the evaluation of student learning throughout the system was changed to meet larger institutional goals. This innovation was driven by a shared vision of TDA faculty and administration concerning the possibilities of evaluating online learning. While in theory the adoption of TDA's Continuous Progress Model as an evaluation tool should bring about the increased development of student orientation toward learning rather than performance, it is still too early to tell whether or not the reformed evaluation system is successful.

Issues and challenges. Two issues have arisen that are relevant to the topics discussed in this chapter. The Continuous Progress Model used by TDA and its influence on stakeholder expectations, primarily parents' and students' expectations, regarding evaluation systems within online teaching and learning environments continues to pose a challenge. For example, TDA teachers and administrators recount that parents and students had a difficult time adjusting to understanding what the levels of continuous progress meant. Parents and students have requested TDA teachers and administrators to translate the various continuous progress levels into grade-level equivalents. This raises some very interesting questions regarding the underlying assumptions about the meaning and purpose of summative student evaluation and how they relate to expectations of student success. As Courtney (2001) stated, it may seem that online environments would support the transformation of pedagogical innovations, like novel evaluation structures. However, as this case study illustrates, pedagogical innovations, like the evaluation system mentioned here, may be constrained by general understandings of how corresponding pedagogical features in face-to-face environments are framed, discussed, and understood.

The second issue that emerges from this case is the idea that new evaluation systems may have the ability to transform student learning goals. In essence, this is related to the notion that assessment and evaluation of student learning have the potential to transform educational values. What do evaluation assessment systems mean within particular educational environments? What kinds of educational values do these evaluation systems promote? What are some of the challenges facing teaching, learning, and assessment when evaluation systems change?

Insights and Conclusions

The case studies and related themes are discussed throughout this chapter to contextualize assessment and evaluation within three different online teaching and learning environments. The case can be made that as researchers, instructional design team leaders, and teachers, we must reflect upon our own views on summative and formative assessment and evaluation. Understanding personally held views of summative and formative assessment is a critical component to understanding how these beliefs fit together within a system of pedagogical variables. Due to unique affordances and constraints of technological environments, this understanding becomes critical when designing and evaluating online instruction (see Fuller, Norby, Pearce, & Strand, 2000).

Through her various experiences with online teaching and learning, including those experiences presented here, the author has come to four general understandings regarding formative and summative assessment and evaluation. First, selection and utilization of appropriate summative assessment tools must be pedagogically aligned with other instructional variables for an online course to effectively support teaching and learning. The potential power of reflection in assessment cannot be understated. As Courtney (2001) remarked, "This kind of experience [reflecting] may lead some faculty to question what about their teaching is critical to the success of learning and what was simply conventional and convenient in the traditional face-to-face format" (p. 233).

Second, the summative evaluation systems used by teachers and administrators may have the potential to influence how teachers, administrators, parents, and students view online teaching —and learning. Furthermore, this potential may be fully realized within online educational contexts, which may have more administrative flexibility, structure, or a faculty with a willingness to examine teaching and learning in different ways from traditional face-to-face education. As seen with the TDA case study, an online educational organization may have the potential to change and shape itself by adopting novel evaluation systems. Research in this area is needed to investigate the potential new evaluation systems have on changing the values of community members and influencing the ways in which teaching and learning, both online and face to face, are perceived.

Formative assessment and evaluation also have great potential to change perceptions of teaching and learning within and between educational contexts. For example, the

EFFECT case study illuminated a larger institutional problem. During the EFFECT project, the issue was raised by faculty regarding the inconsistency of academic expectations and requirements between on-campus, off-campus, or online educational foundation courses. One of the main outcomes of the EFFECT project was faculty discussions about the academic expectations and requirements of graduate students, and how those related to quality control and program evaluation of the EFFECT project. These frequent discussions, raised by EFFECT faculty then brought to the larger educational foundations faculty, helped institute a general statement of what is expected of *all* students enrolled in educational foundation courses, regardless of whether they are on campus, off campus, online, undergraduate, or graduate. The EFFECT project provided faculty with an opportunity to reflect on online educational practice as members teaching in two different learning communities, online and face to face, that resulted in new programmatic requirements and standards in different educational contexts (online, face to face, and off campus).

Lastly, while summative assessment and evaluation may be determined and driven by learning, course, and program objectives, formative assessment and evaluation in online courses may owe more to shared understanding and expectations between stakeholders, teachers, and students that comes from their reflections. As stated, the role of reflection to establish understanding and examine expectations of those participating in online teaching and learning processes is important. Teacher reflection and self-assessment, as formative assessments tools, are powerful methods used to evaluate effective online teaching and learning while students are engaged in the learning process (McMillan, 2004).

The case studies presented here offer a personal perspective on the issues and challenges that the author has faced assessing and evaluating online students, courses, and programs. As an online teacher, the author has learned much about using summative and formative assessment and evaluation within her courses. As a researcher, the author is beginning to understand some of the potential of viewing online environments as parts of contextualized, educational systems. As Gibson (1998) stated, "Our challenge as researchers is to begin to better understand learners in context and the impact of their learning, both positively and negatively, on those who share their lives in the multiple interacting contexts that contain them" (p. 121). However, it would be more accurate to say that as teachers and researchers, we also need to understand ourselves and our views on teaching and learning to better understand assessment and evaluation within the context of online teaching and learning.

Being cognizant of one's own philosophy of teaching and learning, and how that influences curriculum, instruction, and student learning, is important in teaching any class. At the time the author designed and taught the online educational psychology course outlined in the first case study, she had never taken an online course and did not, honestly, have any desire to do so. But the lessons she learned about assessment and evaluation from teaching her first online class contributed to her participation as an instructional designer and researcher within other teaching and learning communities, notably the EFFECT learning community and TDA project mentioned. As Sheingold and Frederiksen (2000) suggested, the process of contextualization within teaching and learning in online educational environments has tremendous potential to reform assessment and evaluation beliefs and practices. If one of the goals of reflective practice is to make the assessment and evaluation of students transparent, then faculty and stakeholders in online education need to incorporate reflective practice as a critical pedagogical component, capable of shaping evolving educational systems.

References

Banks, S.R. (2005). *Classroom assessment: Issues and practices.* Boston: Allyn & Bacon.

Courtney, S. (2001). Technology and the culture of teaching and learning. In D. Lieberman & C. Wehlberg (Eds.), *To improve the academy: Volume 19* (pp. 232-249). Boston: Anker.

Fuller, D., Norby, R.F., Pearce, K., & Strand, S. (2000). Internet teaching by style: Profiling the online professor. *Educational Technology and Society, 3*(2). Retrieved June 20, 2004, from *http://ifets.ieee.org/periodical/vol_2_2000/pearce.html*

Gagne, R.M., Briggs, L.J., & Wagner, W.W. (1992). *Principles of instructional design* (4th ed.). Fort Worth, TX: Harcourt Brace.

Gibson, C.C. (1998). The distance learner in context. In C.C. Gibson (Ed.), *Distance learners in higher education: Institutional responses for quality outcomes* (pp. 113-126). Madison, WI: Atwood.

Hanna, G.S., & Dettmer, P.A. (2004). *Assessment for effective teaching: Using context-adaptive planning.* Boston: Allyn & Bacon.

Holmberg, B. (1989). *Theory and practice of distance education.* New York: Routledge.

Kirshner, D., & Whitson, J.A. (1997). Editors' introduction. In D. Kirshner & J.A. Whitson (Eds.), *Situated cognition: Social, semiotic, and psychological perspectives* (pp. 1-16). Mahwah, NJ: Lawrence Erlbaum.

Matuga, J.M. (2001). Electronic pedagogical practice: The art and science of teaching and learning online. *Educational Technology & Society, 4*(3). Retrieved May 14, 2004 from *http://ifets.ieee.org/periodical/vol_3_2001/matuga.html*

McMillan, J.H. (2004). *Classroom assessment: Principles and practice for effective instruction* (3rd ed.). Boston: Allyn & Bacon.

Sheingold, K., & Frederiksen, J. (2000). Using technology to support innovative assessment. *The Jossey-Bass Reader on Technology and Learning* (pp. 320-337). San Francisco: Jossey-Bass.

TRECA's Digital Academy. (2004). TRECA Digital Academy: Grading system. Retrieved August 24, 2004, from *www.treca.org/curriculum_folder/assessment.html*

Vygotsky, L.S. (1978). *Mind in society: The development of higher psychological processes.* Cambridge, MA: Harvard University Press.

Vygotsky, L.S. (1986). *Thought and language.* Cambridge, MA: Massachusetts Institute of Technology.

About the Authors

David D. Williams is a full professor in the Department of Instructional Psychology and Technology, David O. McKay School of Education, Brigham Young University, USA. His research interests include cross-cultural evaluation issues, evaluation in schools and universities, evaluation of technology-based teaching and learning, and philosophical, cultural, and moral foundations of evaluation.

Scott L. Howell is the assistant to the dean for the Division of Continuing Education at Brigham Young University (BYU). He assisted BYU in launching its online learning and assessment initiative (1999-2003) as the director of a new Center of Instructional Design (CID). Dr. Howell is widely published and respected for his work in distance education and online assessment. He received his PhD in instructional science, specializing in assessment and measurement, an MS in community education, and a BS in business management.

Mary Hricko is an associate professor of libraries and information services at Kent State University. She serves as the library director of the KSU Geauga Campus Library. She has published and presented numerous articles and papers on academic support services in distance education, information literary, and web accessibility.

*   *   *

Karen Barton is a research scientist at CTB/McGraw-Hill (USA). She has direct experience in education as a teacher, researcher, and psychometrician. Her work and research deals mostly with large-scale testing at the state level, and includes calibrating and equating within and across years, score investigations, Bayesian performance indices, online assessments, distracter analyses, and reliability and validity studies, as well as research on accommodations for students with disabilities and English Language Learners, and universal design of assessments. She has a BS in psychology, an MS in special education, and a PhD in educational research and measurement.

Kirk Becker is a psychometrician with Promissor and a graduate student at the University of Illinois at Chicago. He has researched psychometric issues on his own and with researchers including Dr. Benjamin D. Wright at the University of Chicago, Dr. Larry Nucci at the University of Illinois at Chicago, and Dr. George Karabatsos at the University of Illinois at Chicago. Kirk specializes in the analysis of complex test data and the fundamentals of measurement. He holds a BA in psychology from the University of Chicago and is currently ABD in educational psychology at the University of Illinois at Chicago.

John T. Behrens is senior manager of assessment development and innovation at Cisco Systems, Inc. (USA). He oversees the strategic direction and implementation of assessment-related activities in the Cisco Networking Academy Program and the Cisco Certification Programs. In this role, John has overseen the deployment of 38 million classroom assessments and hundreds of thousands of certification exams. Prior to joining Cisco, he was an associate professor of psychology in education at Arizona State University. John has published chapters in a number of widely used psychology reference books, along with articles in a range of educational, psychological, and statistical journals.

Krista Breithaupt is a senior psychometrician at the American Institute of Certified Public Accountants, and holds a PhD in educational measurement from the University of Ottawa, Ontario, Canada. Previously, she worked on development, scoring, and operational maintenance, and for a variety of assessments in health, psychology, and education. These included professional licensing examinations, advanced specialty certification examinations, and measures developed for national and international registries of health information and distance learning programs. Her interests include modern measurement techniques applied to education and health disciplines, and Internet-based learning assessment.

Ni Chang is associate professor of education at Indiana University - South Bend (USA). She has been incorporating computer technology into curriculum and instruction at the university level during the past eight years. Her areas of research interest include, but are not limited to: (1) integration of computer technology into curriculum and in a process of teaching and learning, (2) effective instruction and curriculum design, and (3) effective assessment.

Susan J. Clark is a graduate research assistant and a PhD candidate in instructional psychology and technology at Brigham Young University, Provo, Utah (USA). Her responsibilities as assistant to Trav Johnson, the faculty development coordinator over instructional evaluation, include design and development of the OnSET (Online Student Evaluation of Teaching) Web site at *http://OnSET.byu.edu* as well as an item bank and faculty resource pages for BYU's online student ratings.

Paula B. Doherty is vice president of institutional effectiveness at Peninsula College (USA), where she has administrative responsibilities for institutional research and assessment. She earned a BA in political science from Gonzaga University, an MLS in library and information science from the University of California at Los Angeles, and a PhD in computing technologies in education from Nova Southeastern University.

Jennifer K. Holtz joined DePaul University's School for New Learning (USA) as assistant professor in 2003; she designs and facilitates science and health science learning experiences, and mentors adult learners. Before joining DePaul, she conducted clinical and educational research, and designed and implemented problem-based and experiential learning experiences in research for resident physicians affiliated with the University of Kansas School of Medicine - Wichita.

Tracy A. Irani is assistant professor in the Department of Agricultural Education and Communications at the University of Florida (USA). She received a BA in journalism and communications from Point Park College, an MA in corporate communications from Duquesne University, and a PhD in mass communications from the University of Florida. Dr. Irani joined the University of Florida in 1999, and holds a teaching and research appointment in the area of agricultural communications.

Trav D. Johnson is assistant director of the Brigham Young University Faculty Center (USA), where he oversees TA development and the assessment of teaching. Before accepting his current position at Brigham Young University, Trav worked in the Office of Instructional Resources at the University of Illinois where he coordinated faculty and course evaluation programs. His research interests focus on the use of faculty and course evaluation in instructional improvement.

Patricia Ann Kenney has a PhD in mathematics education from the University of Texas at Austin. She teaches research design in the university's School of Education and works closely with Charles Peters in the MAC Program. Prior to this, she spent 10 years as a research associate at the University of Pittsburgh's Learning Research and Development Center. Her research interests include mathematics assessment, and assessment more generally.

Jim Lee is a senior content application specialist at CTB/McGraw-Hill (USA). His background includes work as a learning disabilities specialist in a child therapy clinic, and several years teaching in the field of New York public school special education classes and California private schools. In his work in the area of science assessment at

CTB/McGraw-Hill, he has focused on the development of learning maps describing the sequence of concept acquisition in core strands of science learning. In recent years he has extended that effort to include the development and application of learning maps in all content areas. He has a BA in creative writing, an MS in special education, and has completed his coursework for a PhD in the diagnosis and remediation of learning disabilities.

Sang Ha Lee is a doctoral candidate in educational psychology at The Pennsylvania State University (USA) and has completed the Master's of Applied Statistics as a concurrent degree. He earned his BS and MEd in mathematics education from the Korea National University of Education. He taught mathematics in South Korea for eight years. He is currently completing his dissertation research on a goodness of fit index in hierarchical linear modeling.

Faye L. Lesht is head of the Division of Academic Outreach in the Office of Continuing Education, University of Illinois at Urbana-Champaign (UIUC) (USA). She also holds an adjunct faculty appointment in the College of Education at UIUC. Faye serves as co-chair of the Graduate College Committee on Extended Education and External Degrees (CEEED). Her research interests include student retention in distance programs, services for distance learners and faculty, program development, and academic leadership.

Roy Levy is a doctoral candidate in measurement, statistics, and evaluation at the University of Maryland (USA). His work has focused on applications of Bayesian inference methodologies to assessment and psychometric model calibration, and on model fit assessment and model comparisons procedures.

Colla J. MacDonald is a professor of curriculum design and evaluation in the Faculty of Education at the University of Ottawa, Canada. Her research focuses on e-learners and e-learning environments. She has published several articles and book chapters on e-learning, has designed and delivered several online courses and learning objects, and was a winner of the 2004 WebCt Exemplary Course Award. She also supervises several graduate students working in the area of e-learning, and together they developed and published the demand-driven learning model (DDLM), a model for designing superior e-learning, as well as a companion online survey to evaluate e-learning courses and programs.

Bruce L. Mann is a professor of education at Memorial University, Canada. His empirical studies of Web course behavior are cited in journals and textbooks. His first book, *Perspectives in Web Course Management,* initiated guest speaking engagements and visiting appointments at Edith Cowan University in Australia, McGill University in Canada, and Scuola Superiore G. Reiss Romoli, the largest post-secondary distance education facility in Italy. His new book, *Selected Styles in Web-Based Educational Research,* is due for release this year.

Before joining Promissor in 2000, **James S. Masters** was a senior test developer working on several major certification programs. He managed all aspects of the test development—from job analyses, to exam blueprint development, to item writing, to exam development and review, to establishing the passing standard. Since joining Promissor, he has worked on account management, test development, and psychometrics for several certification programs on a variety of platforms including computer-based delivery, Internet-based delivery, and paper-and-pencil delivery. James is currently working on a PhD in educational measurement from the University of North Carolina at Greensboro (USA).

Smita Mathur is an assistant professor of education at the University of South Florida in Lakeland, Florida. Her research interests relate to acculturation among recent immigrants, authentic assessment, and creating social presence in asynchronous teaching environments.

Julia M. Matuga earned a PhD in educational psychology with an emphasis on learning, cognition, and instruction from Indiana University, Bloomington. A former K-12 art teacher, she is currently assistant professor of educational psychology within the Division of Educational Foundations and Inquiry at Bowling Green State University (USA). Her research interests include the development and use of self-regulation strategies (i.e., private speech) by children, online teaching and learning, and design-based research. She has also designed and taught undergraduate and graduate online courses in educational psychology.

Robert J. Mislevy is a professor of measurement, statistics, and evaluation at the University of Maryland (USA), and before that was distinguished research scientist at ETS. His research applies developments in statistical methodology and cognitive research to practical problems in educational measurement. His work includes a multiple-imputation approach for integrating sampling and psychometric models in the National Assessment of Educational Progress, and with Linda Steinberg and Russell Almond, an "evidence-centered" assessment design framework. He received AERA's Raymond B. Cattell Early Career Award and the National Council of Measurement's Award for Career Contributions, and has been president of the Psychometric Society.

Rae-Anne Montague is LEEP coordinator and a doctoral candidate at the Graduate School of Library and Information Science, University of Illinois at Urbana-Champaign (UIUC) (USA). Her research interests include online education, learning technologies, diversity, and information literacy. Recent activities include works focusing on effective practices in online education and development of an online consortium. Rae-Anne holds an MS in library and information science, completed online (UIUC, 2000) and an MEd in curriculum and instruction from St. Mary's University in Halifax, Nova Scotia, Canada (1994).

Terry Murray is a lecturer in the Humanistic/Multicultural Education Program in the School of Education at the State University of New York at New Paltz (USA). He is currently a doctoral candidate at the University at Albany. His dissertation work focuses on the nature of relationship in online, asynchronous course work.

James B. Olsen, Vice President and Chief Scientist at Alpine Media Corporation (USA), has 28 years of assessment technology expertise. He is recognized for pioneering innovations in computerized, adaptive, and performance testing. Jim is a primary contributor for the Association of Test Publishers (ATP) *Guidelines for Computer-Based Testing.* He is an annual speaker for the ATP Conference on Computer-Based Testing. He is a principal investigator for National Science Foundation and U.S. Department of Education computerized assessment grants. He has authored foundational publications on computerized testing, technology assessment, and measurement. His PhD in instructional psychology (1978) is from Brigham Young University.

Vaughn J. Page is a doctoral candidate in human resource education at the University of Illinois at Urbana-Champaign (USA). He also serves as an adjunct instructor in career & organizational studies at Eastern Illinois University in Charleston, Illinois, and the Professional Adult Comprehensive Education (PACE) program at Millikin University, Decatur, Illinois. His current research interests center on communities of practice and knowledge management. Page earned a BS in career & organizational studies and an MS in training & development from Eastern Illinois University.

Charles W. Peters earned his PhD in curriculum and instruction from the University of Wisconsin, Madison. He coordinates and teaches in the Secondary MAC (Master of Arts with Certification) Program at the University of Michigan's School of Education (USA). Prior to this, he served as secondary English language arts consultant for Oakland Intermediate School District in Waterford, Michigan, for 26 years. His research interests include the design and implementation of K-12 English Language Arts Curriculum and the alignment of curriculum, instruction, and assessment.

Naomi Jeffery Petersen is assistant professor of education at Indiana University - South Bend (USA). Her scholarly interests center on assessment literacy, positive psychology, and systems theory in communities of learners, including these four strands: (a) adjunct faculty involvement in schools of education, (b) strategic planning by preservice teachers to develop classroom cultures of community, (c) the use and effect of field trips on student learning and the community resources that serve as destinations, and (d) the combined effects of multiple community resources serving refugee families and how their agents are prepared to do so.

Barbara Radner directs the Assessment Center of the School for New Learning, DePaul University (USA), which coordinates the development of assessments of student learning through courses and independent projects. She has taught courses in assessment and curriculum design, and has worked on initiatives in assessment and educational design with museums, schools, and educational publishers. She currently directs a federally funded initiative in the analysis of effective ways to increase student learning of mathematics through the professional development of educators.

Christian M. Reiner works as an assessment and evaluation specialist in the Center for Instructional Excellence at Purdue University in West Lafayette (USA). He is involved in the assessment and evaluation of teaching and learning in various ways including consulting, teaching workshops, and designing and implementing assessment and evaluation tools for individual faculty and programs.

T. Grady Roberts is assistant professor of agricultural education at Texas A&M University (USA). He earned his PhD from the University of Florida in 2003, where as a graduate assistant he conducted research related to evaluating distance education. Currently, he teaches and conducts research related to agricultural science teacher preparation and experiential learning.

Valerie Ruhe holds a PhD in educational measurement from UBC. In her dissertation, she demonstrated with authentic data that Messick's framework provides a comprehensive assessment of the merit and worth of distance instructional programs. She is the state program evaluator for reading recovery at the University of Maine (USA). She is currently conducting a series of statewide longitudinal research projects on how at-risk first-graders perform on standardized measures of fourth-grade literacy. Her Web page is at *www.umaine.edu/edhd/faculty/ruhe.htm.*

Sarah E. Rzasa Zappe is the teaching and learning assessment specialist at the Schreyer Institute for Teaching Excellence at The Pennsylvania State University (USA). In this position, she provides assistance to faculty in assessing innovative methods and techniques in the classroom. She received her BA in psychology from the University of Connecticut and her MS in educational psychology at Penn State, where she specialized in testing and measurement. She is currently a doctoral candidate in the same program.

Deborah L. Schnipke provides psychometric consulting for all aspects of testing programs to clients in a variety of fields. She conducts psychometric analyses and evaluations of exams and programs, performs psychometric research to support clients' current and future needs, and introduces testing innovations including Rasch measurement, 3 PL item response theory, response-time analyses, and adaptive testing. In addition, she conducts psychometric training workshops, gathers and analyzes psychometric requirements, writes technical documentation, and provides other services as needed. Deborah earned her PhD in quantitative psychology from Johns Hopkins University. She is a frequent speaker, reviewer, discussant, and author for major psychometric journals and conferences.

Christopher D. Sessums currently serves as director for distance learning in the Office for Distance, Continuing, and Executive Education at the University of Florida (USA). Christopher collaborates with college faculty and administrators across campus to leverage university resources to create and support distance learning courses and programs. Since June 2000, he has directed the Office of Correspondence Study, which enrolls more than 3,500 students annually. Christopher received both his BA and MEd from the University of Florida. He is currently working on a PhD in the College of Education's School of Teaching and Learning focusing on online teaching styles.

Najmuddin Shaik is research programmer of the Division of Academic Outreach in the Office of Continuing Education, University of Illinois at Urbana-Champaign (UIUC) (USA). His PhD is in human resource education from UIUC, and his MS in computer science is from Northern Illinois University. He has been active in the areas of designing e-learning systems, program evaluation, and psychometrics of scale development. His recent publications focus on the areas of scale development, program evaluation, and computer-mediated communication. He has presented his work at national and international conferences, including online conferences.

Linda C. Smith is professor and associate dean at the Graduate School of Library and Information Science, University of Illinois at Urbana-Champaign (USA). She has provided administrative oversight of LEEP, the online option of the GSLIS MS degree, since January 1997, as well as teaching LEEP courses on a regular basis. Her research interests include models of online pedagogy, and the impact of new technologies on reference and information services.

Ricky Telg, Associate Professor in the University of Florida's Department of Agricultural Education and Communication (USA), teaches courses in agricultural communication and instructional technologies—such as Web design and nonlinear video editing—as well as courses in news writing and distance education. He has received UF's College of Agricultural and Life Sciences' Undergraduate Advisor of the Year and Undergraduate Teacher of the Year awards. He has numerous paper presentations at regional, national, and international meetings, and article publications on distance education- and agricultural communication-related topics.

Sylvia Tidwell-Scheuring is director of publishing systems at CTB/McGraw-Hill. With a BS in physics, and as a co-inventor on a number of pending patents involving the application of artificial intelligence, Sylvia applies modern software techniques (including artificial intelligence and expert systems) to the task of improving the measurement of student achievement. She also uses these techniques to create mechanisms that improve efficiency and accuracy in the development of assessments for learning. As a former teacher, and as a parent who is currently home schooling her three children, Sylvia has a special interest in the day-to-day needs of instructors in the classroom. Having taught science and math for preschool, grade school, high school, junior college, and medical school, she understands the value of having the proper tools for instruction and assessment at all grade levels. She is dedicated to empowering instructors of all kinds with a new generation of assessment tools.

John C. Wise is director of engineering instructional services at Penn State's College of Engineering (USA). In this capacity, he provides assistance to faculty members and teaching assistants in the areas of teaching, learning, and instructional technology. He also provides educational assessment support for the College of Engineering. He earned his BA in liberal arts from the University of the State of New York, and his MS and PhD in instructional systems from Penn State.

Bruno D. Zumbo is professor of measurement, evaluation, and research methodology, and of statistics at the University of British Columbia in Vancouver, Canada. His research interests include statistical theory, quantitative research methods, testing, evaluation, and mathematical and statistical methods. He has 150 publications, including three books, 91 refereed journal articles, 15 chapters, and eight edited volumes. He is also the principal investigator on several large research grants for the Canadian federal and provincial governments. His Web page is at *www.educ.ubc.ca/faculty/zumbo/zumbo.html*.

Index